More praise for

FOR ADAM'S SAKE

A *Wall Street Journal* Best Book of the Year

"Others have written about slavery's tentacular reach. But Ms. di Bonaventura goes further. The book is brilliantly served by the author's legal training, as she chases the Winthrops' and Livingstons' fluctuating fortunes from provincial colonial courts to the Privy Council in London and wades through the epic inheritance battles and property disputes of her highborn cast. . . . [A]n incomparably vivid panorama of colonial New England society and as enthralling a portrait of family life there as we are likely to have."
—Kirk Davis Swinehart, *Wall Street Journal*

"A work of astonishing ingenuity, intellectual and emotional depth, and (most of all) brilliant writing." —John Demos, author of *The Unredeemed Captive: A Family Story from Early America*

"An impressively researched and fine-grained account of the intimately intertwined lives of several families and their slaves. . . . Di Bonaventura's lucid prose sometimes reaches something close to poetry. . . . In telling the Jacksons' story, she has recovered from centuries of oblivion people of colonial America's lowest order, restoring them not just to history, but also to their individuality and humanity. It is a mighty achievement."   —Fergus M. Bordewich, *American Scholar*

"A fascinating view into the little-known world of slavery in the North, *For Adam's Sake* is well-researched and cogently written. Allegra di Bonaventura's rich account complicates the traditional narrative of slavery and race in early America, showing the ways in which the peculiar institution was woven into the fabric of life in parts of New England."   —Annette Gordon-Reed, author of *The Hemingses of Monticello*

"Readers will walk away with a fascinating double portrait of a slave family and their owners in 18th-century Connecticut. . . . Di Bonaventura's achievement is to make the familiar seem strange, turning a topic we thought we knew so much about into something that feels new."
—Eric Herschthal, *Daily Beast*

"This is an extraordinary story about ordinary people in a pre-Revolutionary New England family. Among the people are a master and his slave, the only account of such psychological depth I have seen in all the family histories of New England. Impeccably researched, elegantly written, *For Adam's Sake* is a model of its kind."
—Joseph Ellis, author of
Founding Brothers: The Revolutionary Generation

"Di Bonaventura . . . masterfully weaves together the trajectories of several local families. . . . [She] is able to recover many of the surprising alliances, intimacies, and betrayals that played out in the crucible of this small, interconnected community. . . . Readers will find a beautifully written and engrossing family drama. Essential."
—S. Condon, *Choice*

"*For Adam's Sake* achieves an amazing, seemingly impossible conjunction—the best book ever on New England family life and the best book ever on the family context of American slavery, neither pretty—a riveting story and great history based on astounding research."
—Jon Butler, author of
Becoming America: The Revolution Before 1776

"Thorough and imaginative. . . . The scholarship is stellar."
—*Kirkus Reviews*

"Engrossing. . . . This is an important examination of an often neglected aspect of our colonial heritage."
—*Booklist*

"The murders, attacks against churches, suicides, and illicit sex in *For Adam's Sake* kept me turning pages, but Allegra di Bonaventura's

best stories are of black New Englander John Jackson (whose strategies for recovering his scattered family included a daring midnight raid across Long Island Sound, a legal challenge that took six years to partially succeed, and even a gut-wrenching decision to become his wife's master's servant) and his son Adam, who for half a century knew slavery at its most intimate."   —Woody Holton, author of
Abigail Adams

"When the subject of slavery arises, colonial New England rarely comes to mind, but di Bonaventura . . . shows in this gripping dual biography that the institution has a rich history in the region."
                                                                                —*Publishers Weekly*

"In *For Adam's Sake*, Allegra di Bonaventura has painted a rich canvas of the eighteenth-century town of New London, Connecticut. In the foreground are Adam Jackson, a slave, and Joshua Hempstead, his owner. For the title, the author pays tribute to Adam and to all the other bondsmen of early New England. The book is a great story; great history."   —William S. McFeely, author of
Sapelo's People: A Long Walk into Freedom

"Allegra di Bonaventura's dazzling debut illuminates the social landscape of colonial New England in all of its fascinating complexity. Centering her study on the port town of New London, Connecticut, and building on the diary of shipwright, yeoman farmer, and community leader Joshua Hempstead, *For Adams's Sake* traces the entangled histories of New Englanders—prominent and marginal, free and enslaved—across the generations. With deep research and scrupulous fidelity to her sources, di Bonaventura enables us to hear the voices of her subjects and glimpse the rhythms and ruptures that defined a world we thought we had lost."   —Peter Onuf, Senior
Research Fellow, Robert H. Smith
International Center for Jefferson Studies

FOR ADAM'S SAKE

A Family Saga in Colonial New England

Allegra di Bonaventura

LIVERIGHT PUBLISHING CORPORATION

A DIVISION OF W. W. NORTON & COMPANY

NEW YORK / LONDON

For information about permission to reproduce selections from this
book, write to Permissions, Liveright Publishing Corporation,
a division of W. W. Norton & Company, Inc.,
500 Fifth Avenue, New York, NY 10110

For information about special discounts for bulk purchases,
please contact W. W. Norton Special Sales at
specialsales@wwnorton.com or 800-233-4830

Manufacturing by RR Donnelley, Harrisonburg
Book design by Brooke Koven
Production manager: Anna Oler

Excerpts from *The Diary of Joshua Hempstead: A Daily Record of
Life in Colonial New London, Connecticut, 1711–1758* (New London,
CT: New London County Historical Society, 1999) reprinted with
permission of the publisher.

Maps by William Keegan

Library of Congress Cataloging-in-Publication Data

Di Bonaventura, Allegra.
For Adam's sake : a family saga in colonial New England / Allegra di
Bonaventura Liveright Publishing Corporation. — First Edition.
pages cm
Includes bibliographical references and index.
ISBN 978-0-87140-430-5 (hardcover)
1. Hempstead, Joshua, 1678–1758. 2. Jackson, Adam, 1700–1764.
3. Slavery—Connecticut—New London—History—18th century.
4. Slaves—Family relationships—Connecticut—New London—
History—18th century. 5. Slaveholders—Connecticut—New London—
Biography. 6. Slaves—Connecticut—New London—Biography.
7. New London (Conn.)—History—18th century. 8. Connecticut—
Church history—18th century. 9. Connecticut—History—Colonial
period, ca. 1600–1775. I. Title.
F104.N7D5 2013
974.6'020922—dc23
[B]
2012045996

ISBN 978-0-87140-776-4 pbk.

Liveright Publishing Corporation
500 Fifth Avenue, New York, N.Y. 10110
www.wwnorton.com

W. W. Norton & Company Ltd.
Castle House, 75/76 Wells Street, London W1T 3QT

1 2 3 4 5 6 7 8 9 0

For John Demos

CONTENTS

Upon a Fit of Sickness

All men must die, and so must I;
this cannot be revoked.
For Adam's sake this word God spake
when he so high provoked.
Yet live I shall, this life's but small,
in place of highest bliss,
Where I shall have all I can crave,
no life is like to this.

ANNE BRADSTREET

Sketches of New London in the Late Seventeenth and Early Eighteenth Centuries

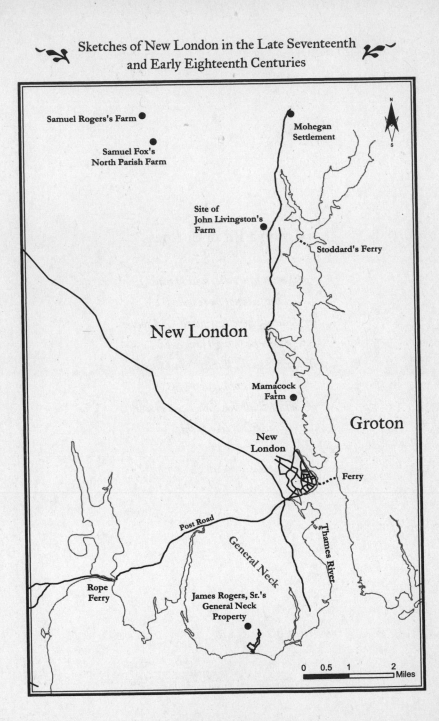

Samuel Rogers's Farm

Samuel Fox's
North Parish Farm

Mohegan
Settlement

Site of
John Livingston's
Farm

Stoddard's Ferry

New London

Mamacock
Farm

Groton

New
London

Ferry

Post Road

General Neck

Thames River

Rope
Ferry

James Rogers, Sr.'s
General Neck
Property

0   0.5   1   2
                    Miles

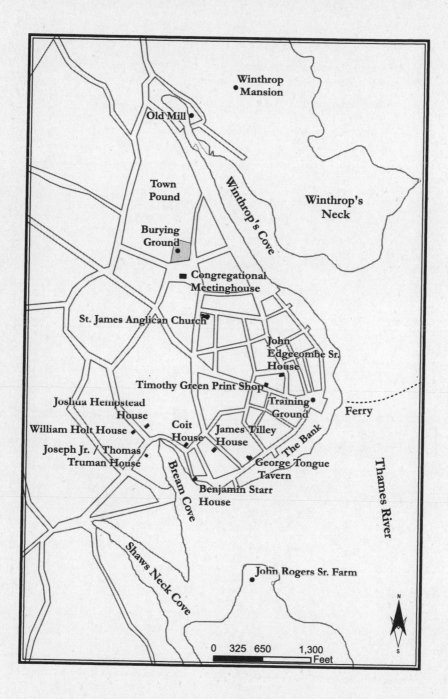

Winthrop
Mansion

Old Mill

Town
Pound

Winthrop's Cove

Winthrop's
Neck

Burying
Ground

Congregational
Meetinghouse

St. James Anglican Church

John
Edgecombe Sr.
House

Timothy Green Print Shop

Joshua Hempstead
House

Training
Ground

Ferry

William Holt House

Coit
House

James Tilley
House

Joseph Jr. / Thomas
Truman House

The Bank

George Tongue
Tavern

Thames River

Bream Cove

Benjamin Starr
House

Shaws Neck Cove

John Rogers Sr. Farm

0   325 650   1,300
                          Feet

N
S

INTRODUCTION

THIS BOOK began as a study of Joshua Hempstead of New London, Connecticut, and the diary he kept for nearly forty-seven years. Adam Jackson—a little-known New Englander who inhabited Joshua's household for most of his adult life—changed all that.

Joshua's diary is one of the great private documents of early New England, but it is especially rare for the modest background and dogged constancy of its writer—a far cry from the celebrated diaries of elite educated New Englanders like the Boston judge Samuel Sewall or the Westborough, Massachusetts, clergyman Ebenezer Parkman. Born in 1678, Joshua was the son of a wheelwright from the colonial provinces. His only formal education was a shipwright's apprenticeship, and yet from the age of thirty-three onward, this devoted father of nine sat down nearly every day of his life to fill a diary that documented his work, his family, and his town. And the diary is not all that has survived the centuries: Joshua wrote and left behind reams of other documents, now in state and local archives, and even his house still stands—having become a historic-house museum after the last Hempstead descendant to occupy it died in 1937. In spite of this remarkable collection of sources, however, historians did not rush to engage directly with Joshua and his diary.[1]

When Joshua died in 1758, the diary stayed in private hands, parceled out in sections among different branches of his family. Several remained in the house he had occupied, which is in part why the diary continued largely unknown outside the New London area. That changed in the late nineteenth century, when the New London County Historical Society came into possession of three sections and subsequently published them in 1901; it has since published a new edition and a companion guide. Although publication made the diary accessible to a broader audience, it did not dramatically change its reception: Joshua's journal remained a tool principally for antiquarians, genealogists, and local historians. Professional historians came to know the Hempstead diary and its usefulness in documenting important events such as the Boston fire of 1711 or the Great Awakening of the 1740s, but none were drawn to tackle it as a whole—deterred, perhaps, by its repetitive almanac style and emphasis on farming and weather.[2]

When I opened Joshua's diary for the first time, I was immediately captivated by its cryptic prose and elusive portrait of the life of one man. Most intriguing, however, was the extraordinary view it offered of the home and family of an ordinary New England tradesman. Wanting to know Joshua the husband and father, I began to wade slowly through thousands of entries filled with words like "corn," "rain," "died," and "son" in seemingly endless rounds—quite unsure of what these everyday recurring lines might eventually reveal.

At the outset I hoped that Joshua's diary would permit me to place men firmly in the domestic life of the family—research that would complement the work of historians who have drawn attention to colonial women's contributions beyond the realm of the household, and to economic life in particular. Joshua's diary portrayed a man who embodied a treasured archetype of New England manhood—the hardworking, principled patriarch with a profound devotion to family and community. It even revealed him as a compassionate, hands-on father who was deeply engaged in the lives of his children and grandchildren. But the Connecticut shipwright and his diary had more to offer than his example. Beyond the diary's drumbeat of dates and crops, birth and death, lay a much richer vision of colonial New England.[3]

I set to work trying to recapture life inside the Hempstead house, spending months indexing its countless entries to identify patterns and changes—it was detailed and fascinating work. As I did, however, I kept bumping up against one particular member of the Hempstead household, a man called Adam. At first glance he might easily be mistaken for a relative, neighbor, or simply one of the many hired workers Joshua employed during his lifetime. But Adam was none of these. In 1727 Joshua had purchased Adam Jackson, a fellow New Londoner, as his slave. Adam subsequently spent nearly three decades in the Hempstead household, living and working in close proximity to his master.

At first I saw Adam largely through the prism of Joshua's life, as I would any other figure appearing in the pages of the Hempstead diary. But the more I read, the more I could not gloss over the other man—and the other family he represented—standing just across the room from the shipwright and father I had come to admire. Having set out to write a book about a great New England diary, I was confronted with a much larger and unexpected story—one that resonates perhaps more deeply in our own time. It would not be enough to write a history of the Hempstead diary. For Adam's sake, I needed to read between the lines of Joshua's entries and look beyond the clapboards of his house to find out more about Adam Jackson and others like him.

It is no secret that even New England households of modest means held servants. Less recognized is that many also held slaves in small numbers, especially along the region's coastline and in its urban centers. When most Americans think of American slavery, they generally conjure up images of plantation slavery in the nineteenth-century South. But there had been other slaveries—even in the North—and the "forgetting" had been purposeful. New Englanders in the nineteenth century had studiously erased and omitted inconvenient and unsavory aspects of their region's collective past in favor of a more heroic and wholesome narrative of their own history.[4]

Joshua and Adam's story asks us to confront some of the uncomfortable truths about the history of the North—but it is a portrait with many dimensions, not so easily labeled or understood. The cramped houses of early New England forced a kind of intimacy on families of every class that could sometimes blur distinctions and even create unexpected opportunities for those at the bottom of the pecking order. Colonial New England remained a deeply hierarchical society with slaves, but its rules and customs in the early decades of English settlement were still in flux. Life on the fringes of the English empire was not so well ordered that the borders of class, gender, and even race could always be easily patrolled.[5]

MY SEARCH for Adam Jackson began with Joshua's diary, with its entry upon entry about this enigmatic New Englander. Inherently problematic as the creation of the man who owned Adam, the diary still provides an unparalleled window into the daily life of an early eighteenth-century American bondsman. While most of the English New Englanders who appear in the diary are identifiable through probate, church, land, or town records, African New Englanders like Adam are much harder to find, commonly deprived of leaving their own definitive marks on the written record, in the form of a will or a purchase of property. Most are discernible only through the chance bill of sale, advertisement about a runaway, or brief remark in local records. Given the evidentiary realities, I knew there was little likelihood that I could learn much more about this man who had been a key member of the Hempstead household for so many years. Then again, maybe I would get lucky.[6]

As it turned out, the Foxes, who originally owned Adam, belonged to the extended Rogers family, a wealthy and unconventional merchant clan with a propensity for religious fanaticism and public spectacle. The Rogerses spent many days in court, embroiled in protracted internal and external conflicts. By a stroke of implausible good fortune for a historian, one of these strands of litigation involved not just Adam Jackson but his entire family. There would be much more to discover about Adam, and my search would lead me further still—to other families like the Jacksons, who lived on the edge and at the heart of New England society during this earliest period of American history. What I found defied easy stereotypes and forced me to look with new eyes at the New England family.[7]

The book that resulted is not about slavery as such but about families deeply affected by the practice. Servitude was almost unavoidable in early New England, although its form and impact varied dramatically across individuals and bloodlines. Men and women like Adam Jackson, however, who lived out most or all of their lives in servitude, were once excluded from standard histories of New England. *For Adam's Sake* embraces their lives and experiences, but it does not set them apart. Instead it places the Adam Jacksons of colonial America alongside its free yeomen and rarefied elites at the center of a broad historical narrative—where of course they were at the time.

New England families were an Atlantic world writ small. Neither simple nor one-dimensional, they are not easily categorized as a series of "types." These dynamic early households held men and women of every background, thrown together in the forced intimacy of everyday life. Slavery, a domestic institution in New England, was just one aspect of these quotidian arrangements. Deep interconnections of work, faith, law, and kinship related every family to those around them and linked them up and down the social scale. Within a generation or two of English arrival, these ties were already elaborate and complex, decipherable only to those with lived, local knowledge.

The small world of the early New England town was an interwoven and knotted mesh of individuals and families that implicated every inhabitant. This social fabric held deeply ingrained patterns, but it also contained surprising patches of ambiguity and opportunity. Every family endured shocking reversals—wounds and strivings powerful enough to destroy. A slave might free himself from bondage, while his master, a son of privilege, crumbled and broke under the weight of his own pedigree. A "mulatto" servant might imagine and even make himself "English," as his slaveholding neighbors signed their own sons over to years of servitude. A kindhearted widower could devote himself to motherless children but still enslave another man's boy without a whiff of remorse.

An early New Englander, navigating the contours of his social world on instinct, saw no paradox in these circumstances. Changes of fortune were around each corner, and every New Englander knew he might be next—struck down or lifted up through a change of faith, a turn in the law, or simply by breathing in the wrong air at the wrong sickbed. Such unpredictable upheavals were common to every family history, an American history that no one—from the lowliest slave to the colonial governor—could entirely escape.

FOR ADAM'S SAKE

Chapter One

"AS IN THE BEGINNING OF THE WORLD"

S TANDING IN his front yard in Connecticut in the spring of 1648, Robert Hempstead could picture an apple tree rising above him, offering shade and fine English fruit for generations. He had chosen a planting spot just east of the small house he had fashioned two years earlier, a makeshift shelter for himself and his wife. Since his house had gone up, Robert had become a father, a fact that became a matter of family distinction. Hempsteads would long speak of this daughter, Mary, as the first child born of English parents in the town of New London. One day Mary would stand under the sapling her father planted that spring, bite into its fruit: yellow apples that smacked of English forebears. In the growing tree Robert may have envisioned a promising future for his family—a comfortable subsistence, even property passed down for generations—here along the banks of a new river Thames.[1]

Like most of his neighbors Robert was a yeoman farmer; he also probably practiced a trade, although town records never mentioned what sort. He may have tried his hand at blacksmithing, given the store of iron, bellows, and hanging scales he kept at home. Trained blacksmiths were in short supply across early New England, and the new hamlet would have welcomed even mediocre work. But Robert spent most of his time clearing his fields and tending livestock, when he was not helping other men to do the same.[2]

When Robert and his fellow planters first landed on Connecticut's southeastern shore in 1645, they christened their settlement "Pequot" after its Algonquin inhabitants, but the name would not stick; within a few years they began to call their town New London and later generations would call its river, the Thames. Naming a collection of simple huts and dirt pathways with less than forty male inhabitants and their dependents after the great English metropolis—then the largest city on earth—was an audacious choice, but Robert and the other planters had high hopes for their far-flung outpost of empire. The harbor was the deepest in New England, and there was no reason to think in those early days that the fledgling port could not one day rival Boston or New York. Even in the first months the planters welcomed trading ships from other shores: one from New Netherland, another from Virginia. Looking onto the harbor, they could imagine it proliferating with sails, brimming with cargo.[3]

For Robert and the other planters, New London had not been their first stop in New England. After crossing the Atlantic and arriving in Massachusetts Bay Colony, they chose to follow the governor's son, John Winthrop, Jr., and establish a new settlement in Connecticut under his able leadership. Robert wanted this new home to last, his family to prosper. The dampened sapling whose roots he covered with dirt toward the end of the 1640s was just one small feature of the plans he had for the modest plot of rough sloping land that was now his. All around him other migrant fathers—husbandmen and tradesmen of the "middling sort" who also traced their roots to English villages—set similar dreams in motion, building homes and planting trees for their children and grandchildren.[4]

Grand aspirations aside, New London during the 1640s and 1650s offered few immediate comforts. Houses like Robert's were small, wooden, and slapdash, freezing in winter and sickly hot in summer. Roads, where they existed, were glorified dirt paths, rutted by wheels and riddled with stones. Lacking the necessary fencing to hold them in, cattle, pigs, and sheep roamed the settlement. Supplies of food and clothing were limited, and the principal sources of public "entertainment" were weekly Sabbath meetings and sporadic court sessions. Every moment of every day—except Sunday—hard physical work loomed. Death, too, was never far away.

Despite the hardships, Robert and the other planters could look beyond the trials of those first years, finding hope for the future in the faces of their children and in the farms and homesteads that rose around them. Slowly their town took shape during the 1640s and 1650s, converging in a humble cluster of landmarks on "meetinghouse hill." Although they had first gathered to worship in homes or outbuildings, in 1655 the planters could look with pride at the town's first Congregational meetinghouse, modest and unheated though it was. Having no bell, they used a drum to call to assembly. Next to the meetinghouse they began a burying ground, digging and marking graves on land that slanted down pleasingly toward the river and Long Island Sound. They would need this cemetery more than anyone would care to think. Just across the road the planters set out a municipal pound to hold stray livestock, retrievable for a charge. This modest hub atop the hill formed the social and political heart of a young New London, the place where congregants worshipped, freemen gathered, and lawbreakers faced punishments—stocks, whipping, and even death—in the open air.[5]

To cross town from meetinghouse hill, Robert Hempstead could have taken the town street toward the harbor, a dirt road that served as a main thoroughfare, dotted with some of New London's more desirable residences. Following it toward the water, he could see Mill Cove to his left, site of a gristmill after 1650. Ahead to the right stretched the Bank, a rim of waterfront land, most of it open commons. After doing business at the harbor, Robert might have stopped at a tavern for news and refreshment. With a pint of cider or a dram of rum in his belly, Robert had only a short walk to Bream Cove and his own lot.

As one of thirty-four original planters, Robert received initial allotments of land that included outlying meadow and uplands, along with an in-town house-lot of around thirteen acres. He and his heirs were also entitled to share in future divisions of community land. Robert's lot was not the most prestigious in town; nonetheless the unassuming location did offer certain advantages, particularly for trade. Bream Cove was a landing place with a clear view of waterfront traffic. From there Robert could trade beyond his neighborhood of farmers and craftsmen and gain easy access to the town's first shipyards, which were hungry for hardware, anchors, and wood. Exchanges of goods and labor were probably brisk between Robert and John Coit, a Massachusetts shipbuilder who constructed a house and shipyard on the cove beginning in 1650, within sight of Robert's lot.[6]

LIKE THE apple sapling he planted so expectantly, Robert, too, had come by ship from England, a strand from the Old World hoping to take root in the New. When he packed for America, however, Robert was fully grown. Born in the first decade of the seventeenth century in the north Essex village of Steeple Bumpstead, he joined a great wave of English migration that included numbers of other men, women, and children from Essex and its neighboring county of Suffolk. Many of these migrants were religious reformers who hoped to purify the Church of England by reviving church discipline and purging it of rites and ceremony not found in scripture—for this reason they were sometimes called Puritans. Although he shared their southeastern roots and middling status, Robert left no evidence that he considered himself one of them. He did not even own a Bible.[7]

During Robert's youth there had been a strong drive to restore purity to the Church of England—a reaction in part to the church's increasing rigidity and hostility to reform. In the 1630s under Catholic-leaning Charles I, Archbishop William Laud had reasserted traditional ceremony and liturgy, and his actions had radicalized reformers. Some, like the Pilgrims, became separatists who created new, reformed churches outside the Anglican establishment—first in Holland and then in Plymouth Colony in Massachusetts. Others, like John Winthrop and the founders of Massachusetts Bay Colony, hoped to achieve purification from within by establishing a reformed branch of the Church of England in the New World, following early Christian models. Although he was one of the many Essex and Suffolk men drawn to Winthrop's vision of a "City upon a Hill," Robert Hempstead may not have shared the intense religious sentiments of some of his neighbors. Perhaps instead the lure of profit had stirred him from his native village to make what the Massachusetts minister Samuel Danforth once called this "errand into the wilderness."[8]

Robert belonged to the reformist religious mainstream in New England. Like most early colonists in Connecticut and Massachusetts Bay, Robert adhered to, or at least acquiesced in, a strict Calvinist Protestantism inspired by the Puritan reform movement and embodied in Congregationalism. In both colonies Congregationalism was a state-authorized religion in which observance was mandatory, enforced through criminal sanctions. Repeated absence from Sabbath meetings, for example, was a misdemeanor punishable by a small fine. A progressive tax or rate, levied on all men of property, supported the local minister and meetinghouse while also promoting conformity. Failure to pay led to arrest, fines, and property seizures. Like most of his neighbors, Robert became an observant if unremarkable member of his congregation, which was the first to be established in New London.[9]

Religious observance during this period in New England, however, was far from uniform. The Congregational orthodoxy familiar to men like Robert Hempstead in the colonies of Massachusetts and Connecticut evaporated quickly beyond their borders. The Massachusetts exile Roger Williams had founded Providence Plantation along Narragansett Bay in the late 1630s, only a short sail from Robert's New London. A refuge for tolerance, Rhode Island became a wellspring of dissenting Protestant sects and even a shelter for Old World Catholicism and Judaism. Neighboring New Haven Colony, established in 1638, remained most strictly Congregational, but it bordered New Netherland, a culturally diverse commercial colony run by the Dutch West India Company in what became New York. There the official religion was the moderate Dutch Reformed Church, although the real creed was trade and profit. As he established his family in a low-lying, working quarter of New London, however, Robert Hempstead showed little interest in religious controversies at home or abroad. Instead his principal purpose lay in building a foundation of economic prosperity for future Hempsteads. Robert believed that his sons and grandsons, slated for lives in labor and trade, might also become men of property and standing.[10]

THE SAPLING Robert Hempstead planted in the 1640s could have come from his own store of seeds and cuttings, brought gingerly from England in the hold of a ship. Another possible source was New London's formidable leader, John Winthrop, Jr., who regularly collected and distributed precious English stock within the colonies. Winthrop had followed his father, the founder and governor of Massachusetts Bay, to New England in 1631. Then in his mid-twenties, the younger Winthrop had already studied at Trinity College, Dublin, read law at London's Inner Temple, and traveled through Europe and the Ottoman Empire before he arrived on American shores. A polyglot intellectual, he combined his impeccable Puritan lineage with a roving mind and a forward-looking inclination toward religious toleration. New England would not alter his nature.[11]

Outwardly Congregationalist, Winthrop was also a leading proponent and practitioner of Christian alchemy, a chemistry that embraced the study of medicine, mineralogy, husbandry, and botany, and imbued them with spiritual meaning. These intellectual interests defined his colonial hopes and aspirations. In New England he saw opportunities everywhere to apply the principles of godly science—whether building saltworks, digging mines, or improving agriculture. The New England of Winthrop's vision was an example of reform, a laboratory for alchemical experimentation, and a place of innovative enterprise where individuals could organize nature and society to a degree unimaginable in the Old World. Winthrop's alchemical dreams were radical and idealistic, but they were grounded in the same fundamental optimism that lay at the foundation of nearly every European venture in America.[12]

When Winthrop first arrived in New England, he had not necessarily planned to go to Connecticut. In fact he continued to travel back and forth between New and Old England for some time, establishing himself in public life while maintaining and cultivating his far-flung alchemical interests and connections. In Massachusetts he founded the town of Ipswich and served as a governing assistant. In the 1630s, however, trouble was brewing in southeastern Connecticut. A long-standing rivalry between the Pequot and Mohegan, with their Narragansett allies, had intensified with the arrival of Europeans— and then erupted into armed conflict. Algonquian-speaking peoples in the area were already pursuing different strategies to cope with English encroachment and the physical and psychological disloca- tion that came in its wake. While the Pequot chose to resist English settlement militarily, Mohegan under the leadership of their sachem, Uncas, chose to align with the colonists, even waging a brutal cam- paign against their Pequot rivals in what would be called the Pequot War. The Western Niantic, who were Pequot tributaries, fought with the Pequot and were almost entirely destroyed—their remnants subsequently subsumed by the Mohegan. The nearby Narragansett, along with their Eastern Niantic allies, followed a third path and declared themselves neutral (although the degree of that neutrality can be debated, given that some did participate in attacks against the Pequot). Within a few years, the Narragansett would reject submis- sion to any colonial authority and instead seek royal protection by direct petition to Charles I.[13]

In the midst of the conflict, Winthrop received a temporary com- mission as governor of Connecticut Plantation, a collection of four fragile settlements—a small garrison at Saybrook and the "river" towns of Windsor, Wethersfield, and Hartford, which all together consisted of only a few hundred male inhabitants and their depen- dents. (New Haven, which would merge with Connecticut Colony in 1665, was still a separate colony under separate government, with fewer than one hundred male inhabitants.) In the heart of the vola- tile Connecticut River valley, Saybrook was particularly vulner- able. During his short tenure, Winthrop substantially fortified the garrison settlement, thereby enabling it to withstand a protracted Pequot siege.[14]

The Pequot War became a doomed fight for the very survival of the Pequot as a viable tribal unit. Although they were able to inflict considerable damage on, and spread fear among, the English, the Pequot were repelled and ultimately decimated by a coalition of Massachusetts, Connecticut, and their Native American allies. The defeat of the Pequot meant opportunity for John Winthrop, Jr., however. After the war ended, Massachusetts Bay expressed its gratitude to him for his defense of Saybrook with a large grant of territory in southeastern Connecticut, including the rich grasslands of Fisher's Island. The grant comprised desirable agricultural land with plentiful fishing waters and superior access to Long Island Sound at the deepest harbor in New England, but it also carried weighty symbolic importance as the heart of territory associated with the now-defeated Pequot.[15]

With this new proprietorship, Winthrop set his sights on establishing a Connecticut plantation. The Pequot War had exacted a terrible toll on Algonquin in the area, yet it would remain well populated with native people, including Mohegan, Niantic, Narragansett, and even Pequot, a small number of whom managed to survive the war and its aftermath. English authorities divided some survivors among the Narragansett and granted the Pawcatuck, or Eastern Pequot, a reservation in North Stonington; a second group, later known as the Mashantucket Pequot, were conferred a reservation in 1666 and placed under Mohegan control. Winthrop's broad vision for southeastern Connecticut left little room for Algonquin life as it once was, however. He saw the new plantation as a center of the alchemical colonial enterprise—a place where cutting-edge economic development projects, like the saltworks he had already established at Salem, Massachusetts, or the ironworks he founded at Saugus, would foster the betterment of a Christian New England.[16]

AND THIS was how, in 1645, Winthrop came to set out with a small party of colonists, including Robert Hempstead, to begin a new Connecticut plantation at what would become New London. The first years of settlement, as he later wrote, required a tremendous amount of sheer physical labor, "there being buildings, fencings, clearing and breaking up of ground, lands to be attended, orchards to be planted, highways and bridges and fortifications to be made, & all things to do, as in the beginning of the world."[17]

Creating a world anew also meant establishing the rudimentary structures of government. For these, Winthrop's planters followed models based recognizably on the English parish, adapting them to New England's particular circumstances. Like most New England towns, the settlement at New London was both a corporate entity and political unit. Winthrop, Robert Hempstead, and the other founding male planters were proprietors of the corporation of New London, entitled to share in decisions about the distribution of collectively owned land. The planters were also freemen; having attained minumum property requirements and sworn an oath of loyalty, they could vote and were obliged to pay taxes. At annual town meetings freemen passed ordinances, levied taxes, and elected one another to town offices. All able-bodied men were required to enroll in local militias and attend regular training.

Each town also participated in colony-wide governance, sending representatives to a legislative assembly and joining Connecticut's nascent legal system. At the top, the Court of Assistants, made up of the governor and his council, served as a high court in Hartford, with a right of appeal to the king's Privy Council in London. At the bottom, magistrate's courts with a local assistant or justice of the peace presiding, offered petty civil jurisdiction. Inferior or county courts served as intermediate trial courts.

Coming to southeastern Connecticut, John Winthrop, Jr., stayed first on Fisher's Island, but eventually New London's principal inhabitant made his home on the mainland at Winthrop's Neck, a craggy, marshy spur of land on the eastern bank of the Thames between the river and the town center. Here Winthrop built a substantial mansion house with adjoining orchards and gardens. And when New London completed its gristmill not far from the mansion around 1651, it granted Winthrop and his heirs a monopoly on its operation in return for its maintenance.[18]

A draw to outsiders, the Winthrop mansion was often a full house. When they were not in Hartford or Boston, John junior, Elizabeth, and their four young children, including sons Fitz-John and Wait Still, all called the mansion home. At any given time the household played host to visitors, agents, and servants of various sorts. One such agent was Samuel Beebe, a Northhamptonshire husbandman who came to work for Winthrop in the 1650s, eventually becoming a large local landholder in his own right. The Winthrops were also one of New London's first families to own a few African-origin slaves. Local Algonquin rounded out the household, providing farm and domestic labor whether as indentured servants or hired day workers.[19]

The Winthrop house was a focal point in New London, not simply as its leading residence or one of the few stone structures in town. Among his many accomplishments, Winthrop was revered for his skills as a medical practitioner and his treatment of English and Algonquin patients alike without charge. A progressive alchemical physician, he largely abandoned the medieval humoral model of the body in favor of chemical and herbal remedies. Using antimony and niter or saltpeter as principal ingredients, Winthrop created a variety of medicines. Alchemists considered these dangerous purgatives divinely blessed, their medicinal and spiritual effectiveness dependent on the skill of the practicioner. The medicine that became most associated with Winthrop after his death was an all-purpose remedy he developed called rubila, a reddish, powdery mix of antimony and saltpeter that induced intense "purifying" diarrhea and vomiting. His mansion house in New London became a destination for New Englanders seeking his ministrations, with up to ten staying to receive treatment at any given time.[20]

To inform his medical work Winthrop consulted a range of imported books. Some of these New England rarities adorned his New London chambers, although the bulk of his library, a collection that grew to more than one thousand volumes, remained with his family in Boston rather than be risked to the wilds of Connecticut. During Winthrop's chemical experimentation and medicine making, smoke emanated from the mansion's rooms, giving the house the appearance of a kind of mystical laboratory on the edge of the Thames. Such visions contributed to Winthrop's already powerful aura and the reverence New Londoners felt for him. Within the Winthrop family and their Boston circle, however, grumbling had already begun: Its promise notwithstanding, New London was simply too remote and crude—its people too coarse and unfit—for the extraordinary gifts of John Winthrop, Jr., and his line.[21]

* * *

LIKE JOHN WINTHROP, JR., Robert Livingston, too, belonged to a family of religious exiles from the British Isles, though in their case orthodoxy first led the Livingstons to the European continent. A Livingston son also would end up in New London, but it would take another generation and several more relocations before that happened. Robert's mother and father were Scottish Presbyterians who, like the English Puritans before them, had left their island home when confronted by Anglican domination. Robert was born in a tiny Scottish border village, the fourteenth child of a staunch, fourth-generation Presbyterian minister and prominent disciple of John Calvin. When Robert's clerical father, John Livingstone (Robert later dropped the *e*), refused to swear an oath of loyalty to the newly restored Charles II, he was banished in punishment and fled to the tolerance of the Netherlands in 1663 with his wife and two youngest children.[22]

John Livingstone was already in his sixties when the family arrived in Rotterdam and joined a small community of Scottish exiles. There the cleric retreated into a contemplative old age, writing his memoirs and occasionally preaching for the Scottish congregation. As John gradually retreated from public life, his nine-year-old son, Robert, who had probably never shown much interest in the old man's sermons, found himself captivated by his new surroundings—the Netherlands of the Golden Age was a world glistening with possibilities.[23]

Robert Livingston encountered the Netherlands at the peak of its influence. All around him a flowering of science and culture beckoned: Extraordinary advances were being made in mathematics, medicine, engineering, law, and philosophy, all disseminated by a thriving book trade. It was the age of Rembrandt and Vermeer, but feats of artistic expression apparently made less impression on the young Scot than the country's dominance in trade—evident in the teeming shipyards, warehouses, and stores that crowded the unapologetically commercial port city that had become his second home. By his own admission, Robert's father was able to support his family only with the help of his wife's small inheritance. The experience of his parents' constrained finances left Robert with a determination to better himself: If the father felt contentment in a notable lack of "covetousness," the son would make up the difference.[24]

Robert grew up fluent in Dutch and English, but especially conversant in Dutch business practice and accounting, which allowed him to take his place among the Anglo-Dutch merchant elite; by the time he was fifteen he was keeping an account book in Dutch. At nineteen he set his ambitions on Puritan Massachusetts, where his father's reputation as a leading Presbyterian exile who had stood up to Charles II carried considerable weight. He landed in Massachusetts Bay in June 1673, a year after his father died, but soon abandoned the rigid piety of Boston for the secular commerciality of Anglo-Dutch New York. Having come under English rule in the 1660s and again in 1674, New York was a place where the bilingual and bicultural young Scot was uniquely positioned to succeed. By January 1674, Robert Livingston had found a promising situation in the garrison town of Albany and was ready to make a name for himself. A gateway to trade between Native America and Manhattan, Albany was soon to return once more to English control.[25]

It did not take the young Scot long: Robert purchased a town lot, began to participate in local government, and established himself in trade, beginning by supplying New York beaver pelts to his New England contacts. He also took a position as secretary at the vast Manor of Rensselaerswyck near Albany. He secured his position in society, and, as one of the richest men in the colony, when his employer died, Robert married the man's wealthy widow, Alida Schuyler van Rensselaer, in 1683, himself becoming the manorial patroon and proprietor. Robert rechristened the property Livingston Manor and pursued life there on a grand scale, using tenant farmers and slaves to run large operations that included grain farming, beer brewing, and timber production. At some point he adopted the Dutch Reformed faith, although religion to Robert was little more than a social convention. He also undertook a considerable public career, occupying a range of high positions, including assemblyman and secretary to New York's Board of Indian Commissioners, and paving the way for a Livingston political dynasty among his many descendants. For the immediate future, however, and for the six surviving children he would have with Alida, Robert Livingston's legacy was more basic: Turning his back on his family's long clerical heritage, the hard-nosed Scot would focus on earthly pursuits and even achieve a certain notoriety for ambition and greed.[26]

WHILE ROBERT LIVINGSTON was still walking the cobblestones of Rotterdam, the English colonist James Rogers trudged back and forth along the dirt path between his New London mansion and his bakehouse, the smell of burning wood and biscuit wafting through the air. Rogers's prinicipal product was hardtack, a useful and durable food source handy for the work of war and seafaring. Once cooled and packed in barrels, Rogers's hardtack left for distant ports in the Chesapeake and the West Indies. The baker had moved to New London from Milford in 1660, looking for a more active port for trade. Milford had been sorry to see him go. Born perhaps in Shakespeare's hometown of Stratford-upon-Avon in 1615, James Rogers had arrived in Connecticut in the 1630s, served in the Pequot War, joined the Milford congregation, and risen to local prominence there. Developing his commercial baking business into a small trading empire, Rogers was already one of the richest men in Connecticut Colony by the time he moved to New London. There only his neighbor, John Winthrop, Jr., exceeded him in wealth.[27]

In fact Winthrop himself had helped to lure Rogers to town, offering him land on Winthrop's Neck for a house and bakery—a location convenient to the mill Rogers would lease, and next door to Winthrop's own home. Like Winthrop, Rogers built his house and bakery of costly stone, but the two neighbors saw each other only intermittently after the move. A few years earlier, in 1657, Winthrop had become governor of Connecticut, by then a growing colony of twelve settlements and five thousand inhabitants—about one-quarter the population of Massachusetts Bay. His new position meant that he was often away from New London, engaged in the demands of public life in Hartford and elsewhere. In the meantime Rogers established himself firmly in the social and political fabric of his adopted town, joining New London's First Congregation with his wife, Elizabeth, and earning repeated election and appointment to public office, even to the colonial legislature.[28]

Rogers was New London's wealthiest new resident, but the budding settlement was attracting a roster of other new men as well. Many, like Rogers, were involved in trade, while others pursued farming and artisanal work. The brothers Jeffrey and Christopher Christophers settled near the harbor and became merchants to the West Indies. John Prentice came to blacksmith but then abandoned his craft to sail ships. Next door to Robert Hempstead's lot on Bream Cove, Joseph Truman built a farm and tannery, his vats adding new business—and a foul smell—to the neighborhood.[29]

Even Winthrop's Neck greeted new residents: Both Fitz-John and Wait Still Winthrop returned to their childhood home in 1663, after some years away in Boston, Hartford, and London. Despite the advantages in wealth and opportunity that their Winthrop ancestry provided them, neither possessed their father's intellect or vision. After failing the Harvard entrance exams in his teens, the elder, Fitz, had traveled to England looking for adventure and found it serving as an officer in the army of General George Monck, who had fought for Oliver Cromwell but ultimately ushered in the Restoration of Charles II. After 1660, when Fitz's regiment disbanded, he spent several dissolute years in London—amusements that came to a crashing halt when his father and younger brother, Wait, came to collect him in 1663. Refusing his father's charge to marry in the mother country, Fitz had had little choice but to return to humdrum New England.[30]

Visiting his brother in London just three years before it would be destroyed by the Great Fire, nineteen-year-old Wait must have been amazed by this sprawling medieval city of wooden houses and half a million inhabitants—although the youth from the colonies seemed to regard admittance to its high society as a Winthrop birthright. Unlike Fitz, the more bookish Wait did attend Harvard before dropping out in 1660, his studies providing enough of a foundation to allow him to pursue a medical sideline for the remainder of his life, like his father.

After a glamorous sojourn of many months in England, the Winthrop brothers' return to New London in 1663 was a bitter pill. Even though their father's Connecticut landholdings, which totaled well over twenty thousand acres, would make them rich on paper, the properties generated little income, were loaded with debt, and might be sold only at discounted prices, if at all. Only the livestock farm at Fisher's Island was profitable. Reluctantly both Fitz and Wait settled into the management of the holdings, their frustration expressing itself in frequent litigation with neighbors, tenants, creditors, and the town of New London itself. Wait in particular appeared to see the courts as the channel to exact reprisals for his dissatisfactions. Their father's dream of New England as the apex of alchemical achievement would never be realized in the hands of his petulant and superior sons.[31]

As the town expanded and the Winthrops' neighbor, James Rogers, grew older, he too began to sour on life at Winthrop's Neck, retreating from active business life and gradually transferring his affairs to his grown sons. Perhaps it was simply old age that led him to leave the "best address" in New London by the end of the 1660s for a sprawling property along Robin's Hood Bay about five miles away; certainly a long and nasty legal fight over property boundaries initiated by Wait Winthrop must have made moving all the more agreeable. The two men did eventually come to terms, but the niggling Wait never lost an opportunity to nurse a grudge. James Rogers's new home by the bay must have been a salve for any lingering grievances. An expanse of old field and meadow, the property led down to a sandy beach that offered magnificent views of Long Island Sound and, on clear days, even of Long Island itself. In the warmest months Mohegan wigwams speckled the waterfront, which was a time-honored summer fishing site. The General Neck, as this part of New London was called, was terrain sparsely settled by the English. For those colonists who made homes there, life on the neck felt removed and slightly wild. That remoteness in miles, and in spirit, made it a ready haven for religious dissenters, especially Baptists, who could practice their faith away from the disapproving eyes of Congregational and civil authorities.[32]

On the General Neck the James Rogers household remained large, containing at various times as many as six of James and Elizabeth's seven children. With an affluent and well-connected merchant father, the Rogers children grew up in relative privilege. By colonial standards the household was quite cultivated, accustomed to entertaining men of power and sophistication in the colony. Wealth and respectability made the Rogers children desirable marriage partners, able to join with New London's "better" families. Still, Rogers did not push his five boys to join the ranks of a true colonial elite. He did not send any of them to Harvard or to Old England, as his neighbor John Winthrop, Jr., had done. Instead Rogers prepared his boys to take their places as prosperous local men, engaged in trade and landholding. Samuel Rogers, his eldest, assumed control of his father's bakery operations. His four younger sons were in and out of their father's home during the 1660s and 1670s, as they prepared to establish households of their own. Two became comfortable landowners and one, James junior, was an enterprising shipmaster who also ran a tannery and cooperage. Their sisters settled locally as well. The eldest, Bathshua, married in 1670, while her younger sister, Elizabeth, was still a child living at home.[33]

Of all the Rogers children, the third son, John, stood out. As a young man he already showed a cerebral bent, even as he took part in his father's mercantile affairs. John often served as his father's scribe, writing deeds and other legal and commercial documents that hinted at other underlying proficiencies. With his sharp intellect and family advantages, John seemed to have a charmed life among New London's prosperous set well within his grasp. This happy fate appeared even more secure in 1670 when the twenty-one-year-old married Elizabeth Griswold, a daughter of Matthew Griswold, one of Saybrook's wealthiest inhabitants and a descendant of Sir Humphrey Griswold of Malvern Hall, Warwickshire. Elizabeth was also a child of privilege. She had grown up on a vast tract of many thousand acres in a mansion house called Black Hall, and in a family known for its beautiful women.[34]

At the time when James Rogers, Sr., moved his family to the General Neck, the Rogerses were firmly established near the top of New London's small social world. James's boys had only to follow a modest course of learning, trade, and work to be assured reputable positions in local politics, commerce, and church affairs. Because James plowed his wealth into land and livestock, the furnishings of his new home were relatively modest. James and Elizabeth Rogers's marital bedstead was the best piece in the house, in keeping with contemporary custom. It probably took pride of place in the principal first-floor room, or hall. Dining at the Rogerses was simple, requiring at most three small pewter platters, three bowls, three plates, and one large platter for the entire household. The family shared two Bibles.[35]

In one respect, however, James Rogers's wealth and rank were apparent: Among his three beds, husbandry tools, basic wooden chest and chairs were four unique belongings. Toward the end of the century—probably in the 1670s—this patriarch had acquired property interests in several human beings. Two men and two women had joined the household as "servants," as his will would later describe them—a term then used to describe both indentured servants (who served for a set period of years) and perpetual slaves.[36]

Four was a large number of servants for New London and for New England generally—especially during the seventeenth century. Without a cash crop like rice or tobacco, there was no economic justification for large-scale slaveholding in New England, a region where householders prized heat conservation over spaciousness. All but the finest seventeenth-century New England houses required masters and servants to share close quarters and limited space. Most masters in New England held only one or two servants at any given time; owning an interest in the labor of four made Rogers stand out.

The Rogers servants were typical of men and women living at the margins of colonial New England society: William Wright was a free Algonquin who served Rogers under an indenture, an agreement whereby Wright provided labor in exchange for room, board, and perhaps basic occupational training. Wright spent years in the Rogers household, during which time he may have adopted his English name. Most days Wright likely worked in husbandry, farming land and tending livestock alongside members of the Rogers family. As the eighteenth century approached, Algonquin like Wright increasingly sought work as servants or even day laborers in English households. Wright's indenture appeared to have been voluntary, although he joined numbers of other Native people already living and working in English households in the aftermath of the Pequot War. Still other Algonquin found themselves in forced indentures when they faced criminal or civil damages in court that they could not pay.[37]

Wright's decision probably reflected the limited economic options available to him as a propertyless Algonquin man. He may also have had a very specific reason to indenture himself to James Rogers, however. Wright wanted to marry Hagar, a "Negro" woman and Rogers slave who had come from the West Indies, the source of most New England slaves in this earliest period. Wright made a deal with Rogers: He would buy his wife in return for six years' service. Apparently James Rogers had readily agreed to Wright's proposal, having already promised Hagar freedom once she turned thirty-six. Reportedly Rogers even gave the pair a wedding dinner to celebrate the marriage and their agreement.[38]

As Wright labored in the soil, Hagar did the work of women—cleaning, preparing food, and caring for children. Her biblical name—after the Egyptian bondswoman who became Abraham's second wife—probably came from a New England slave trader or master, perhaps from James Rogers himself. Each week the Wrights might have trekked with the Rogerses to town, or to a house on the neck, to attend Sabbath meetings. At a minimum their master exposed them to Bible readings at home. Hagar was not unusual in receiving her master's approval to wed. It was common for New England slaveholders to encourage marriage, as both a check on sexual misbehavior and a way to increase their property holdings. The law in New England deviated from the English custom of using paternal descent to determine status. Instead it drew on the Roman doctrine of *partus sequitur ventrem*, or "offspring follow the womb." A child born to Hagar Wright while she was still a bondswoman would be a Rogers slave, even if her husband, Wright, were free.[39]

"Mulatto" Adam, as he was referred to in James Rogers's will, was a third Rogers servant. Like William Wright, he was a freeman indentured for a period of years. English and African, Adam had probably been born in New England, perhaps even in his master's house. Men of mixed heritage like Adam Rogers were a familiar part of life in early New England and an inevitable result of colonization. Only in the colonies of Virginia and North Carolina did legislators attempt to distinguish between mulattos and other people of African origin. Although the English who came to America professed to disdain miscegenation with Native Americans or Africans, they nevertheless did mix with other ethnic groups, whether by force or consent. Native Americans and Africans also chose one another as partners, in part due to the dearth of Algonquin men and African women. Later, historians would largely ignore New Englanders like Adam Rogers who did not fit neatly into fixed racial categories or into English New England's account of its own homogeneity and autonomy.[40]

The offspring of multiethnic unions were nevertheless a clear presence in early towns like New London. These men and women had multiple identities, although when they formed families themelves they usually chose partners of combined Algonquin or African origins. "Mulatto" Adam Rogers served alongside the Rogerses' fourth servant, Maria, a young woman who faced her own particular difficulties. "Deaf and dumb," as James Rogers described her in his will, Maria could not hear or speak. Whether she had felt rage or resignation when she was sold to a New England shipmaster in the West Indies and put on a sloop bound for oblivion, she could never speak of her ordeal.[41]

New England mariners worked the triangular slave trade between the North Atlantic coast, the West Indies, and Africa, but they sold most of their human cargo in English plantation colonies in the islands and the American South, where prices were comparatively high. Part of the "dregs" of the trade, Maria was worth little in the West Indies, where she had received her "Spanish" name, as New Englanders would describe it, and she would have likely been unsalable in demanding Southern markets. It was not unusual for "faulty" stock like Maria to turn up in New England, where buyers could be less exacting. A servant deemed deficient might find herself in Boston or Newport or even in a gritty outpost like New London.[42]

Getting Maria would have been simple. With his extensive trading contacts, James Rogers could have placed a "special order" for a female slave with a New London or Newport shipmaster. Rogers might have been initially unaware of Maria's deafness, a condition that could have gone unnoticed during the vicissitudes of passage or been willfully concealed at the point of sale. Rogers might have also purchased Maria on a trip to a port city in Massachusetts, Rhode Island, or even New York, where slaves were sold in greater numbers. Alone and unable to hear or speak, Maria must have found her adjustment to her New World particularly wrenching. Once at the Rogerses', Hagar Wright could have given the foreign-born girl comfort and guidance, although the more experienced woman might also have resented a newcomer—especially one with a burdensome handicap.

From a historical perspective Maria's wordless arrival in New England underscored the collective silence that was to come. She could not speak, but even if she could have, Maria would have left little mark on local records. At best the enslaved appeared as bit players in the dramas of their masters' lives, mentioned in passing in a diary, letter, or account book. Often, bondspeople like Maria only came to light in writing at a master's death: a bequest in a will or an entry in an estate inventory. Time also took an inevitable toll, erasing people and experience not easily captured in documents. Once-meaningful objects were cast aside or mislaid; families were dispersed and vanished from a place; vital stories were forgotten and lost. At more than three hundred years' distance, piecing together a life like Maria's is capricious work, grasping at shadows. Against these odds the faint outlines of her story survive nonetheless. This lone slave girl would become the unlikely matriarch of another large New England family: the Jacksons of New London.

ALTHOUGH HAVING more than a few servants was unusual in New England, the general practice of household service was widespread. Families from all but the lowest rungs of the socioeconomic ladder routinely employed indentured servants or hired day laborers to help with household, farm, and craft work. Slaveholding, albeit much less common, also began early in New England's history. When Robert Hempstead and John Winthrop, Jr., first settled New London in 1646, a few African-origin slaves were already living nearby in New Haven Colony. By the 1670s the practice of slavery had gained a secure foothold in Connecticut through a combination of legislation, everyday practice, and small consignments of bondsmen tucked into West Indian cargoes or carted over from nearby colonies. Unadorned advertisements announced the unhappy arrivals: "A Parcel of Negro Boys and Girls"; "Just Arrived a Likely Negro Man, and Five Sturdy Negro Boys."[43]

New England colonists did not routinely enslave local Algonquin, except in the aftermath of military conflicts. A wave of enslavement took place after the Pequot War, but most dramatically one generation later as a consequence of King Philip's War in the 1670s, so-called after the English name of the Wampanoag leader, Metacomet. This latter conflict shook a fragile New England to its foundations. The war had one of the highest percentages of loss of any in American history—1.5 percent mortality among the English population, and up to 15 percent among some Algonquin groups. It also left scores of refugees in its wake, many of them widowed Algonquin women and orphaned children. As the colonists gained dominance in the fight, they enslaved Algonquin captives, particularly able-bodied men, sometimes even sending them to abject bondage in the sugar plantations of the Indies or farther still. A number even ended up as galley slaves in the service of Charles II of Spain, such as the shipment of ten—including a father and son—that landed in Tangier or another that was sent to Cádiz. To deal with the problem of non-violent Algonquin captives and refugees in their midst, however, Connecticut authorities distributed these casualties of war among the colony's settlements, where selectmen placed them in households as servants. To the English the arrangement was to have the dual benefit of providing needed forced labor and necessary assimilation, eradicating "dangerous" Algonquin culture. Captive service was to be temporary, however—not more than ten years and until the age of sixteen—but some colonists conveniently "forgot" when a captive's term lapsed, leaving refugees to continue as slaves, even after they were legally free. Few were more egregious in profiteering from King Philip's captives than Governor Winthrop's son Fitz, who served in the conflict and then used captives to work Fisher's Island. Unsatisfied with his allotment for Fisher's around the time of his father's death in 1676, Fitz bought ten more captives on "spec"—not to employ them in productive labor but simply to ship them off to Barbados and sell them for a quick profit.[44]

These overlooked remnants of past Indian wars were in the minority, however. Most slaves like Hagar and Maria could trace their origins to the African continent. In New London they found themselves near the heart of New England slave country. Many of the region's bondsmen and -women were concentrated along a swath of coastal terrain stretching between the ports of Newport, Rhode Island, and Boston—New England's principal city. Only a quick boat ride from New London, Newport was the capital of the region's slave trade. In between lay the rich agricultural lands of the Narragansett, where colonial planters practiced slaveholding on the largest scale in New England. Narragansett landholders used slaves to operate commercial dairy farms, producing one of the finest regional cheeses, a Cheshire reserved primarily for export. Although New London County's inferior land could never support large-scale agriculture of any kind, Rhode Island's nearby slave culture spilled over easily into its less prosperous neighbor in the form of widespread small-scale slave ownership. As a result more New London families like James Rogers's held slaves than in any other part of Connecticut. For Hagar Wright, Adam Rogers, and Maria, New London County's slaveholding culture meant that they would never be too far from another African New Englander—whether that was two farms away or even in the same house.[45]

BY THE 1650s Robert Hempstead had created a foothold in New London for a young, growing family. His small dwelling on Bream Cove now held three children, including his second child and only son, Joshua, born in 1649. Robert had aspired to create a groundwork of prosperity for his descendants, but he would not be there to implement his plan. His time with his children proved tragically brief: In 1655 he died suddenly, eight years before the Livingstones fled to welcoming Rotterdam and around the time that Maria arrived in an unwelcoming New England. Robert Hempstead was only in his mid-forties, and his legacy could easily have ended there, with the seventy-seven pounds of iron in his inventory and the usual dispersal of his widow and three children—including the ten-year-old Joshua—into a new marriage and new households.

But this ordinary Essex husbandman was no haphazard smithy, at least when it came to crafting his last will and testament. In his last act Robert harnessed the authority of law and language to shape the fates of generations to come. This was something that New Englanders like Maria, a woman and a slave, were entirely powerless to accomplish. But Robert saw his opportunity and took it; in his will he invoked an already anachronistic form of property tenure—entail—hoping to ensure that his New London house-lot would pass from eldest Hempstead son to eldest Hempstead son for all time. This unusual provision set Robert apart from the majority of New England fathers: Entailment was a practice more readily associated with English aristocrats disposing of grand landed estates than with a Connecticut yeoman leaving behind thirteen acres. In land-rich New England, only a dwindling minority of colonists followed the English custom of primogeniture, which entitled an eldest surviving son to inherit his father's entire nonmovable estate. Fewer still deployed entail to compel future generations to preserve real property along a male line. Robert's will therefore gave his first-born male descendants an uncommon birthright. With that simple stroke of a pen the Essex yeoman laid a foundation for Hempsteads on Bream Cove for more than three centuries.

Chapter Two

THE ROGERENES

FROM THE earliest days, religious radicalism was at the heart of the colonial venture in New England. Settlers in Massachusetts, Connecticut, and Rhode Island could trace themselves to religious reform movements in Old and New England, whether Pilgrim separatists in Plymouth or nonseparating Congregationalists in Boston. Tolerating opposition did not necessarily go hand in hand with reform, however: Each religious movement saw itself as having the potential to become the new enforceable standard. During the seventeenth century, while the profit-seeking Chesapeake struck a path of relative tolerance—Virginia maintaining the Church of England and Lord Baltimore creating a haven for Roman Catholics in Maryland—the New England Congregational colonies of Massachusetts Bay and Connecticut kept a tight grip on orthodoxy.

When faced with dissent, Massachusetts Bay chose to quash it from the outset. As early as 1635, authorities exiled Roger Williams from Boston for his errant beliefs, then banished Anne Hutchinson three years later for heresy, citing her transgressive views on predestination. (To Hutchinson, God's chosen "elect" could sin freely without endangering their salvation; moreover, "good works" in life were not a necessary affirmation. To the dominant Massachusetts clergy who insisted on good works in life as evidence of salvation, such beliefs were against God's law and an implicit encouragement of dissolution and disobedience.) Subsequent dissent, after Williams and Hutchinson, met with a similarly hard response in Massachusetts during the seventeenth century. Connecticut followed its neighbor's lead in demanding conformity, while the Rhode Island of Roger Williams pursued its own course of tolerance, attracting a remarkable array of religious reformers and outcasts of every sort.

For more than twenty years after settlement, the planters of New London remained pleasantly unmindful of the religious stew that simmered next door and how it might spoil their own tranquility. But porous borders and a vibrant coastal trade fostered strong family and business ties between New London County and adjacent Rhode Island. It was only a matter of time before that colony's religious radicalism, like its slaveholding culture, infected its Congregational neighbor. When radicalism did arrive, however, no New Londoner would have expected it to come by way of a principal family, one that had been a source of leadership and pride. From the outset many in town felt a sense of betrayal that was both theological and personal. Passions proved strongest, in fact, among New London's upper crust, who seemed to regard the change in conscience as a kind of class treason.

Nothing about the commercial baker James Rogers or his family during their first twenty years in New London gave any clue that they would become a source of spiritual conflict. In the questioning mind of James's third son, John, however, the early seeds of discontent were planted. This transformation probably began innocuously enough—perhaps with a friendly invitation for a thoughtful young man to join in a day's worship. Something about his encounters with a handful of impassioned Newport believers spoke to him as nothing ever had—rousing old personal demons and new inner purpose. Whatever the reason, this golden son of New London turned his back on the religion of his youth forever. There would be a heavy price to pay.[1]

IN THE fall of 1670, John Rogers had much to be thankful for as he wed his young bride, Elizabeth. His father, James, had provided for the couple in spectacular style. Not long before the marriage the baker had given his third son one of the finest properties in New London. About two miles north of town, Mamacock—an Algonquian word meaning "great hook"—was a large jut of rocky land, with abundant salt hay and easy river access. The road to Norwich, entrepot for the fertile farmlands of the Connecticut River valley, ran right through the farm, bringing a steady flow of visitors and information. On Mamacock, John Rogers built himself a great house with spacious rooms, each equipped with the rare luxury of a fireplace. The main hall alone was twenty feet square, enormous by contemporary standards. Deeply enamored of his new bride, John took the extraordinary step of signing over the entire property—house and all—to Elizabeth, at a time when most married women owned no property at all. There the young couple could live quietly at some remove and yet still be able to reach town easily by boat, horse, or foot.[2]

Married life appeared to begin contentedly for John and Elizabeth Rogers. While Elizabeth occupied herself with a household that no doubt included at least one or two servants, John was busy with his father's commercial affairs and the management of his own lands. Before long the pair welcomed two children, a son and daughter named after their parents. They must have attended meetings at New London's First Congregation, where Mr. Simon Bradstreet (a Harvard graduate and son of Massachusetts governor Simon Bradstreet, Sr., and the poet Anne Dudley Bradstreet) had taken over the pulpit. With Elizabeth and the children installed comfortably at Mamacock, John often traveled to Newport at his father's behest. New England's second port after Boston, Newport was an excellent place to do business. Its impact on John, however, went far beyond any practical experience in commerce.[3]

Coming to Newport in the 1660s and 1670s, John Rogers found a cosmopolitan little city by New England standards, dominated by the shipping trades. In many ways Newport was a far cry from staid and dingy New London. The city positively bristled with activity—much of it commercial and religious. Its merchants led the pack in New England slave traffic. Piracy or privateering—capturing foreign ships and their cargoes on commission—was a Newport growth industry. Walking the waterfront, one could hear the din of its wharves and shipyards. The smell of molasses hung thick in the air, as men turned it to rum that they would trade for slaves. Some Newport traders sold their human cargo straight off the ships' decks. And at certain corners—Mill and Spring Streets, perhaps, or North Baptist and Thames—one might also chance upon a little slave market: the children of Africa on improvised stands against the backdrop of Rhode Island liberties.[4]

Most New Englanders visiting Newport would have been less troubled by the city's slave markets than by the hodgepodge of religious faiths everywhere on display. Apart from trade, religion was Rhode Island's other great enterprise: a "colluvies" or cesspool of religious enthusiasms, as the Boston Congregational minister and theologian Cotton Mather unflatteringly put it. To John Rogers, whose frame of reference had been the unembellished walls of New London's Congregational meetinghouse and the sermons of Mr. Bradstreet, Newport's colorful assortment of Quakers, Huguenots, Presbyterians, Catholics, Baptists, and Seventh-Day Baptists was no less than astonishing. One wonders what the boy from Winthrop's Neck thought encountering Spanish-Portuguese Jews who had taken refuge in the small Rhode Island city from Brazil and the Portuguese Inquisition during the 1650s. For many visitors the religious panorama might have remained a wild curiosity, worthy of long conversations back home at the supper table, but nothing more. John, however, chose to enter the maelstrom.[5]

THE BAPTIST movement began toward the end of the sixteenth century with English exiles in Amsterdam; it made its way to New England by the 1630s. In Rhode Island, Baptists found a true home. Roger Williams established North America's first Baptist church in Providence in 1639, and Newport Baptists followed with their own congregation in 1644. Predictably, Massachusetts Bay and Connecticut Congregationalists were much less hospitable, doling out persecution by varying degrees. Although the two sects had much in common, including descent from the theologian John Calvin, most New England Congregationalists in the seventeenth century found a Baptist movement in their midst difficult to abide.[6]

Although superficially minor, the theological differences between Congregationalists and Baptists had profound implications for both the afterlife and the here and now. Each group adhered broadly to a concept of the "elect"—men and women chosen by God to enjoy grace and salvation. Congregationalists believed that God alone determined election before the beginning of the world, while Baptists regarded atonement as general—Christ had died for all, so anyone might achieve salvation through the exercise of free will (just as he or she could fall from grace through bad personal conduct). To embrace grace a Baptist convert underwent a conscious believer's baptism as an adult, often accompanied by the laying on of hands. The Baptist interpretation of grace was a direct assault on Congregationalist ideas about God's sovereignty—that he alone chose who would be saved. It also invited judgments about how individual Congregationalists lived their lives. Baptists' fierce support of religious liberty and the complete autonomy of individual congregations also ran headlong into Congregationalist ideals of conformity. At a more visceral level, many ordinary Congregationalists simply found Baptist practice strange and even disturbing, whether it was the disordered prayer and preaching at Baptist gatherings or the bizarre spectacle of grown men and women dunked in the public drink.[7]

The Baptist idea of general atonement also had practical implications that threatened the prevailing social order in New England. As early as the mid-seventeenth century, American Baptists, especially those in Rhode Island, began to treat believers equally, embracing men and women of any origin or status as full congregants, able to possess all the rights and obligations of membership. The First Baptist Church of Newport, in fact, could claim the first African-American Baptist as a member: "Jack, a colored man," baptized along with four English brethren one cold morning in November 1652. The first recorded Algonquin Baptist, a man called Japheth, was also one of the Newport flock. English colonial Congregationalists, too, had made efforts to christianize New Englanders of African and Algonquin origins, but they did so from a distinct posture of superiority. The relative equality of Baptist believers clashed with a Congregationalist hierarchy that organized the meetinghouse by rank—the best pews allotted to the "best" families—and that granted deference to a leadership of educated divines.[8]

The independence of Baptist congregations made them especially vulnerable to splintering. One early offshoot was the Seventh-Day Baptists, who emerged in England during the 1650s and 1660s. These "Seventh-Day" Sabbatarians, or simply Sabbatarians, interpreted the seventh day—Saturday—as the true biblical Sabbath. One such English Sabbatarian was Steven Mumford, a wealthy merchant who emigrated to Newport in 1664. Mumford joined the First Baptist Church and soon drew others from the flock to his Sabbatarian way of thinking. After some agonized soul-searching, he led a breakaway group of six followers, including his wife, in a split from the non-Sabbatarian Baptists. The break was amicable, however, and Mumford's faction kept a loose affiliation with their mother church. His tiny Seventh-Day or Sabbatarian Baptist Church, where members spoke in tongues, preached, and prophesized, was the first of its denomination in North America.[9]

Though John Rogers was an out-of-towner, he had begun to take part in First Baptist meetings during his trips to Newport. Naturally prone to self-examination and renovation, he felt the draw of reformist, purist Seventh-Day theology after Mumford's arrival. He began to attend Mumford's meetings and by 1675 had undergone a conversion experience, surrendering himself wholeheartedly to Sabbatarianism. From the first, John Rogers was eager to share his "good news" with family, friends, and neighbors back home in New London. The heady love he felt for his newfound faith was blinding, overpowering. It awakened in him many new ideas and sensations—the call to lead not least among them.[10]

Within the Rogers family, John's conversion created a major domestic crisis. As news of it spread across New London, family members faced a choice. Most decided to follow the lead of their patriarch, James Rogers. Despite the fact that James had lived a life of success and conformity, he seemed to bathe in the bright light of his son's emergence as a spiritual force and leader. The elder Rogers avidly embraced his son's convictions and encouraged the rest of his family to unite and follow. Siblings joined—including the baker

Samuel, the yeoman Joseph, the sailor-cooper James junior, the yeoman Jonathan, and the youngest, Elizabeth. None among them, however, was more committed to John and his beliefs than his sister Bathshua. Just two years apart, she and John seemed to share the kind of unwavering bond forged in close childhood.[11]

By 1678 the Sabbatarians had grown to some thirty-seven members: twenty in Newport; seven in Westerly, Rhode Island, and at least ten in New London under John's leadership. But once awakened, the spirit of reform burned white hot in John Rogers, and he soon felt the need to form his own, more orthodox wing. Rogers and his followers—who emerged as a motley assortment of well-heeled proprietors and working servants, devout religionists and just plain cranks—would bear the inimitable name of Rogerenes. They would also hold the unique distinction of being the first homegrown sect to emerge among the English in America. Religious belief would set this first American sect apart from the start, but other attributes would define them as true outliers.[12]

The Rogerenes were not a chance group of dissenters, easily silenced or relegated. Theirs was a kind of "domestic" or family religion that drew members almost exclusively from established local families like the Bolleses and Waterouses, connected to the Rogerses by blood, marriage, or servitude. True to these domestic origins, adherence to the radical faith correlated almost entirely with family relationship well into the nineteenth century. Kinship fostered fierce tribal loyalties. Their leader was not only forceful and charismatic, he was also rich, giving the movement a protective cover of wealth. John Rogers could meet any legal challenge and, though sorely tempted, authorities were hard put to crush him when they needed the Rogers family's tax payments to support public coffers. For New London the Rogerenes' uncommon mix of family, wealth, and zeal—in the midst of bruising official intolerance—would prove a bitter recipe.

THE ROGERENES fitted squarely within the Rhode Island traditions of extreme liberty of conscience and Baptist perpetual self-reform from which they had sprung. At home in "the land of steady habits" of Connecticut, however, "John Rogers and his crew," as one New Londoner described them, seemed at best dangerous fanatics, at worst unvarnished outlaws. Rogerenes advocated toleration and a separation between church and state, while Connecticut law required conformity to a state-sanctioned religion. When Rogerenes refused to pay a minister's rate or tax in support of a "corrupt" ministry, authorities satisfied the rate through criminal prosecutions, fines, and confiscations.[13]

What rankled Connecticut Congregationalists most, however, was the Rogerenes' confrontational Sabbatarian stance. Not satisfied to practice their faith quietly, the Rogerenes wanted to correct the errors of their Congregational neighbors, citing God—who "spoke" directly through the body of their leader—as their ultimate authority. The group worshiped any day of the week and at any location, but on Sundays, while the colony gathered in meetinghouses all day, Rogerenes openly flouted the law by putting themselves to work, often at menial labor. In keeping with the concept of general atonement, the Rogerenes welcomed men and women of every origin as full congregants. In fact Japheth, the first known Algonquin Baptist, who was originally part of the Newport Baptists, later joined the Rogerenes. And it was probably John Rogers himself who immersed the first woman of African origin in New London's Thames to become a Rogerene in 1687—a woman who was very likely a Rogers family slave, perhaps even Maria.[14]

Doctrinal conflicts aside, Congregationalists regarded Rogerene ways as an attack on their core values and as a constant, nagging reproach. Adopting plain dark dress, for example, Rogerenes made women in even modest frippery appear vain, and men in full-bottomed wigs ostentatious. Rogerene spontaneous praying and speaking in tongues—professing direct communion with the Holy Spirit—were a challenge to Mr. Bradstreet's erudite sermons, casting these in a stilted, even antiquated, light. When the Rogerenes rejected the best medical understanding of the day in favor of faith healing, they also called into question the moral and intellectual authority of the educated elite—most notably the Winthrops. For some New Londoners the sight of Rogerenes blatantly baptizing each other in the Thames might have been the final straw. For others it was Rogerene-Baptist egalitarianism that grated most. Many English colonists could not stomach seeing women, Algonquin, and even Africans speaking their minds and offering discourse as equal communicants. To them the display must have appeared unseemly, even frightening—and there was no mistaking its dangerous frontal swipe at English patriarchy and society.[15]

Congregationalist neighbors were not the only ones deeply affected by Rogerene social leveling. For the Rogers family itself, parity in religion had weighty domestic implications. The Rogerses were religious radicals, but they were also wealthy slaveholders. In their colonial surroundings, slavery was widely accepted and even endorsed by law, church, and government. Congregational ministers set the tone. As town leaders and moral arbiters, these clergymen led in slaveholding as a group, owning bondsmen in greater numbers than did their parishioners. Members of a professional class, ministers had greater need to use outside labor, and they recognized no moral directive against purchasing that labor by trading and owning other human beings, even citing Old Testament slavery as a model and justification. Ironically, clerical training prepared ministers especially well to trade slaves, giving them the creditworthiness and far-flung social connections that facilitated exchange across colonies. Parishioners were less likely to challenge slaveholding, even in their own minds, when their ministers were conspicuous practitioners. In this atmosphere, Rogerene egalitarianism posed a sharp contrast. Rogerene masters and servants—even slaves—who prayed together as equals would find it increasingly difficult to go home and resume their respective places in the social pecking order. For the Rogers family in particular, Rogerene egalitarianism was on a collision course with their slaveholding lifestyle.

John Rogers's own atttitude toward slavery was deeply ambiguous. He did not articulate a clear ideological position against slavery, but there were signs—in spite of his own slave ownership—of emergent antislavery sympathies. Decades later, after John's death, the Rogerenes would openly oppose slavery. During his lifetime, however, a seeming paradox hung over the Rogers family and its Rogerene members. They were willing to defy the law and suffer for their religious beliefs, yet despite treating servants and slaves as spiritual equals, they remained slaveholders, never willing to rebel completely against the convention of enslavement.[16]

Some in the Rogers family appeared to arrive at a compromise position, releasing certain slaves after a period of service. At the same time, in personal and affecting ways, John and other members of his family would challenge the very exploitation in which they participated. Their equivocal posture toward slavery played out openly in one place, with one particular family, and over several generations. Maria—the lone slave girl in James Rogers's house on Robin's Hood Bay—and her Jackson family descendants would compel the Rogerses to look face-to-face at the conflict within.

ON A Saturday in May 1675, William Edmundson, along with two companions, stepped cautiously toward a General Neck house. A Quaker from Old England on a mission to spread the faith, Edmundson had time for only a short stopover. Known for bringing the Society of Friends to Ireland, Edmundson had heard of this small party of Baptists five miles outside New London who kept the seventh day. He relished the chance to look in on these remote dissenters who dared to differ "from the generality of the people," and hoped to share his own Quaker message.[17]

Inside the house, absolute silence reigned as the believers sat in contemplation. When Edmundson first entered, the Sabbatarians were afraid. Once assured he meant no harm, however, the believers invited the three visitors to sit and stay "a pretty while in silence." After a time Edmundson engaged the group in a gentle debate about scripture, taking exception to their observance of the seventh day and of baptism by water. The English Quaker later described them in his journal as "very moderate," "tender and loving." Then he went on his way.[18]

The group Edmundson observed that day were John Rogers's steadfast band of Rogerenes, though their leader himself was absent.

Looking back on the encounter, Edmundson would recall another detail. Among the pensive and earnest Baptists assembled in the house, he remarked, were a number of "servants and negroes." Members of assorted Rogerene households, these men and women had been among the earliest converts to John Rogers's brand of Baptist theology. Like the Rogerene family itself, "servants and negroes" had provided a captive audience and fertile ground for recruitment. The indentured Algonquin William Wright and his enslaved wife, Hagar, were probably among the first to join. Wright would become one of John Rogers's most loyal followers.[19]

There is no proof that Maria converted with the Wrights, or that John Rogers dunked her in the Thames along with sisters and brothers, "servants and negroes." But there is also no evidence that she did not follow her master's son in his new faith along with other members of the household. Rogers family servants and slaves could not leave any record of how they experienced the swirl of new ideas and dramatic conversions around them. Presumably a slave like Maria had little choice but to follow—to whatever degree necessary—the religion of her master. Just as servants accompanied masters to the Congregational meetinghouse, Maria likely would have had to engage, to some degree, with the Rogerene movement. For some servants, Baptist egalitarianism—the chance for spiritual fellowship as equals—might have had a distinct appeal in its own right, even if they inwardly harbored different beliefs. Others were surely convinced of the truth of John Rogers's teachings and could give themselves over unreservedly.[20]

For Maria the stakes soon became even higher. As the Rogers family was swept into a religious tumult during the 1670s, Maria's own life also changed irrevocably. Toward the end of the decade she became a mother. She probably felt the ordinary joys and fears of motherhood from the moment of her daughter's birth, but those ups and downs were always shadowed by the knowledge that her precious girl belonged to James Rogers. It was Rogers who likely gave the child her name, Joan—from the Hebrew for "God is merciful"— and it was Rogers who would determine what would ultimately happen to her after she left her mother's arms. At some point, sooner or later, he might also take Joan from her. Even as Maria swaddled the infant girl, however, another fact appeared undeniable to anyone who looked at her: Joan's father was English.[21]

At the time when Joan was born, New Englanders had yet to sharpen the words they used to describe race. The false dichotomy of black and white—or even red—was a thing of the future. When it came to Europeans, including English colonists, New Englanders typically identified them by their countries of origin. A man from England was an "old England man," an Irishman was an "old Country man," and a native-born English colonist, a "New England man." A visitor from France or even French Canada was "french [*sic*]" and Native Americans also often received the distinction of being Mohegan or Narragansett or Niantic—rather than simply "Indians"—in early colonial records. Occasionally, colonists also loosely distinguished Africans by native region in writing, particularly in advertisements for sale or for runaways. For people less easily classified, however, New Englanders used labels and categories that remained blurry and malleable, with the same person sometimes portrayed differently on separate occasions or at different times over the life course. Generally speaking a "Negro" referred to someone with a dark complexion and thereby ostensibly African origins. The term "mustee" usually described an ethnic combination of African and Indian, while "mulatto" implied a mix of European and African ancestry. These distinctions were often clumsy judgments about appearance: skin color, hair texture, facial features. Frequently they were also ambiguous, one master writing in 1722 how his "man" Sandy had "long wool on his Head for a Negro, and looks something like a Mulatto." Uncertainties could stem from genuine doubt about a person's origins, but they could also convey differences or changes in how an individual was perceived. A man in early New England could go from being "Negro" to "mulatto," for instance. Once in a great while, he might even travel the distance from "Negro" or "mulatto" to "New England man."[22]

Contemporaries judged that Maria's infant, Joan, had an English father, the kind of assessment New Englanders made routinely. In Joan's case fortune provided an extraordinary, highly discerning informant. Long after her death the Boston gentlewoman Sarah Kemble Knight became one the best-known women in colonial America. Widowed relatively young, Madam Knight was active in commercial affairs and even ran a small school, but she achieved posthumous celebrity for her writing. A colorful, often humorous journal she kept during a round-trip journey between Boston and New York in 1704 and 1705 has become a pillar of early American travel literature. As it happened, the savvy and perceptive Madam Knight spent the latter part of her life in the New London area, where her only child married. Living there, she would become well acquainted with Maria's daughter, Joan—well enough to identify her confidently as a "mulatto woman." And Knight was not the only one to make this judgment. Others, too, even John Rogers himself, described her as "mulatto." Indeed, the consensus in and around New London was that Joan's father was an Englishman, but if anyone other than Maria and the man himself knew his identity, they appeared to have kept it to themselves.[23]

Although sex with a woman outside marriage was a crime, contemporary authorities turned a blind eye when Englishmen had sex with, or even raped, enslaved women. It is impossible to know the degree to which English masters (or other men) preyed on their servants, but the presence of "mulatto" men and women, even in small numbers, attests to its occurrence. At several centuries' distance, the Rogers men look like leading contenders to be Joan's father. They, above all others, had ample means and opportunity to exploit Maria "deaf and dumb." As Maria's owner, with physical and legal power over her, James Rogers, Sr., could have fathered Joan, but every one of his six sons—including the maverick, John—had also been old enough to coerce or to rape. Perhaps Joan's paternity had been an open secret in the Rogers family, or an unspoken but fiercely guarded truth.[24]

However Joan's birth affected the Rogerses, though, that impact was small compared with the hard reality Maria faced. Whatever she had already endured, she confronted motherhood alone, surrounded by daily reminders that her dear Joan—her one child and the only thing in the world that was truly hers—was the property of another. She embraced or did not embrace the Rogerene faith that spun around her, she attended meetings quietly and obediently, and she did her work, for there was little else she could do. All the time Maria watched her baby grow—perhaps even saw hints in the child of the father never named—and waited for the day she must have known would come, the day when Joan would be taken from her.

AROUND THE same time that Maria bore a baby she was certain to lose, John Rogers confronted a family trial of his own. New Englanders enjoyed attending court sessions. They provided diversion not only as ritual spectacles, but also as morality plays in which all the characters were thoroughly known to an audience hungry for gossip and retribution. One such sitting of the General Court, the colony's high court, attracted its share of observers on a spring day in Hartford in May 1675. There had never been a session quite like it in Connecticut's short history, nor would there be a similar one anytime soon. The issue before the court involved a prelude to divorce, but this was no ordinary divorce, and the couple in question no ordinary couple.

A crowd of spectators had filed into the courtroom, ready to see a dangerous new radical get his comeuppance. The onlookers were hoping for salacious details, and they were not disappointed; one of them, New London's minister, Mr. Bradstreet, even took notes. John Rogers had been away from the General Neck when Edmundson, the English Quaker, had visited his flock, because Rogers had been in Hartford, ready to answer grave charges against him. Appearing in court that May day must have been strain and humilation enough for Rogers, but he was also reeling with pain and heartbreak over the source of the allegations to be aired against him: It was his cherished bride, Elizabeth, who now stood before him, pointing a finger in blame.[25]

Although she had initially joined her husband in exploring Baptist beliefs, Elizabeth Rogers had then balked at his growing extremism. Urged by her conservative and concerned Congregational parents, she had left John in 1674 and returned to her natal home in Saybrook with their children. Her parents encouraged her to take the next step a year later and petition for divorce. In her complaint to the court, Elizabeth and her father originally cited "breach of covenant and neglect of duty," legal language for her assertion that Rogers's new beliefs represented a violation of their marriage contract.[26]

Although Elizabeth's case was unusual, the idea of divorce was not. Early Connecticut divorce laws were remarkably liberal, in fact. One reason for this liberality was that Puritan New Englanders regarded marriage as a civil contract rather than a religious sacrament. Divorce was simply breach of contract to be decided by a civil court. In Old England, by contrast, church courts had jurisdiction over the sacrament of marriage, and divorce was largely unattainable. In the colonies, New York and Virginia followed English models, while South Carolina disallowed divorce under any circumstances. As early as the 1630s, however, wives in colonial Connecticut and Massachusetts (and it was usually a wife) could petition for divorce on a number of grounds, principally desertion or adultery, and most female petitioners were successful during the seventeenth century. Over time, Massachusetts courts increasingly declined to grant divorces on grounds other than adultery, but there was no such shift in Connecticut, making it the most "divorce-friendly" common-law jurisdiction before 1800. When Elizabeth Rogers came before the court in 1675, however, her accusations were anything but typical. Beyond the charge of religious heterodoxy, she offered a string of monstrous allegations against John, many of them capital crimes.[27]

Mr. Bradstreet watched the proceedings he would later depict in writing, as Elizabeth asserted her claims against the young husband she now called "vile" before a grand jury. Only twenty-six and the father of two, John Rogers already showed a single-minded willingness to pay any price for his beliefs, a trait that became the hallmark of the man. In his account, Bradstreet registered disapproval of Rogers's recent embrace of "Anabaptism," or rebaptism, regarded by Congregationalists as the beginning of a consequential fall into heterodoxy. But the minister's theological disagreements with Rogers did not prepare him for what came next. John Rogers, Elizabeth claimed, had committed "fornication with a Negro, an English maid and Indian squaws"; he had even attempted murder by "giving ratsbane [arsenic] to the Negro woman by whom he has a bastard yet living."[28]

But these were not all. Elizabeth's charges then began to enter the realm of the bizarre. Next came "sodomy with a man called Sherwood." This alleged victim (or willing accomplice?) was the New Londoner George Sharswood, who had died a year earlier from the "flux," or dysentery. The accusation of sodomy must have taken place after Sharswood's death, given that minister Bradstreet himself had attended the parishioner's deathbed, commenting approvingly on his spiritual state: "I doubt not but he is at rest in glory." As if sodomy were not enough, however, the most explosive charges came last: Elizabeth declared that her husband had committed "bestiality with mares, cows, goats, sheep, sows, bitches, and a tame moose that Major [Fitz] Winthrop" kept as a kind of pet, wandering perhaps around Winthrop's Neck. She added that John had confessed his previous crimes to her privately before marriage, and she had forgiven him. The combined allegations were so outrageous that they became legendary in New London, providing proof of degeneracy for his detractors and proof of conspiracy for his supporters. More than two hundred years later, scandalized historical writers even omitted them from the retelling of events, prudishness trumping general disapproval of Rogers during the Victorian period.[29]

Elizabeth, a "prudent sober young woman" according to Bradstreet, made a compelling witness. Under the circumstances her divorce from Rogers was assured, but her criminal accusations against John seem far-fetched nonetheless. Further information comes from an unexpected source. After his visit to the Rogerenes on the General Neck, the Quaker missionary William Edmundson had continued along his way to Hartford. During meetings and encounters in the capital city, he roomed at a house with another man he called "the Baptist." He engaged the stranger in a theological discussion, and afterward "the Baptist"—none other than the fiery John Rogers himself—shared his troubles with Edmundson. Rogers complained how civil authorities, working in concert with Elizabeth's parents, were using "some ill fact he had committed before he was

her husband" to take her away from him. In his appeal to Edmundson for sympathy, however, Rogers did not assert his innocence.[30]

Rogers also offered no denials in court—a defiant stance he often
assumed during subsequent public conflicts. Nevertheless the grand
jury declined to indict on technical, procedural grounds. Some on
the jury might have thought that an indictment, and nearly certain
conviction, simply went too far—no matter how disagreeable they
found Rogers and his ideas. The general opinion among colonists,
however, was that the accusations were true. "The whole bench, and
all sober persons, judge him guilty," Bradstreet observed. A few centuries' distance makes it easier perhaps to be skeptical of Elizabeth's
outlandish accusations. True or false, they do invite speculation
about Maria and her daughter, Joan. Was Maria the "Negro woman"
John had tried to poison? Was Joan the "bastard" child yet living?
Intriguingly, there was another mixed-race and likely "bastard"
child in the James Rogers household along with Joan: the indentured
"mulatto" servant Adam Rogers. About him, James senior's will
offered this tantalizing piece of evidence: In its last line he exhorted
his children to "remember Adam." Did he refer enigmatically to a
mix-raced "bastard" son (or grandson) he would not acknowledge
openly in writing? Once free of his indenture, Adam did use the
Rogers surname, but a freed African might do so simply as a matter
of convenience. In Adam's case, however, a blood connection appears
to have existed. His modern descendants report to have identified
a genetic link between the James Rogers family and their ancestor.
While Adam's heritage is no proof of Joan's, of course, it might signal
a pattern of behavior among the Rogers clan.[31]

After Elizabeth was granted a divorce in October 1676, giving
her permission to reside with her father, John agonized over the loss
of his wife, refusing to acknowledge the result as legally or morally
binding. Within a year, however, she had taken the next step, seeking legal custody and child support for their two young children,
and expressing her desire to protect them from their father's errant
ways. Again her request was highly unusual, for fathers' claims to
their children were considered virtually unassailable. Elizabeth won
her case nevertheless, becoming in all likelihood the first divorced

mother in American history to win custody of her children. (John did secure the return of his beloved Mamacock in their settlement, however.) Some felt that Rogers had lost custody because he "went raging and raving to that degree, that no sober Person could have thought him to have been fit a minute out of Bedlam." It was a measure of the court's contempt for him that John Rogers would embody this formidable legal precedent. But for Rogers the man, the result was an unspeakable, shattering loss from which he would never recover. His new convictions had cost John Rogers his family, and the cumulative ordeal exposed a raw fearlessness in him. Elizabeth's leaving had been a hard teacher, and he now had nothing to lose.[32]

With Elizabeth and the children gone, Rogers became increasingly radicalized. He would remain vehemently unattached for the next two decades and more, insisting that Elizabeth was still his wife in the eyes of God. Elizabeth, meanwhile, remarried in 1679 (although her son John junior later claimed that she fell into a terrible guilt-ridden depression thereafter). Rogers's solitary state added complexity to the sexual politics of his egalitariansim and his slaveholding. To his followers he appeared an example of rigor and purity, but doubtless he was also a strange, tormented, and passionate man. He may have exploited Maria or other Rogers servants sexually, but he would later also go to unusual lengths to protect family slaves, especially Maria's own descendants, who may or may not have been his relatives. Even if Maria's descendants were Rogers kin, moreover, such protection was exceedingly rare: Having a child with a slave certainly did not mean a master would embrace that child. Not even John Rogers would do that.[33]

Even putting domestic politics aside, to most of his Congregational neighbors John Rogers was political poison. After he lost his family he threw himself entirely into leading his flock of Rogerenes, and his confrontations with the authorities became increasingly antagonistic. They began with his failure to pay taxes in support of the Congregational ministry. As early as 1677 the county court imposed an unprecedented penalty on Rogers: continuous monthly fines of five pounds (at a time when the average young Connecticut father at the subsistence level owned some forty to sixty pounds in real property). Refusing to pay, Rogers claimed he was "laid in iron chains, cruelly scourged, endured long imprisonments, set in the stocks many hours together, out of the bounds of all human law, and in a cruel manner." They were the first steps on a long, uncompromising road.[34]

As JOHN ROGERS grappled with the disintegration of his family and the persecution of his faith, another New London man coped with his own adjustment to this cold and distant place. Of African origin, the newcomer had been born in the West Indies, or perhaps even Africa, and ended up in the islands where plantation owners had raised sugar and worked Africans pitilessly since the 1640s. By his late teens he may already have endured more than a decade laboring in the hot sun, speaking an African, French, or Creole tongue. His life changed abruptly when a stranger came, looked him over, made his purchase, and took him away. Put on a sloop headed north, perhaps in irons, the young "Negro" was probably the only man aboard who was neither English nor free. The stranger who had taken him, he would learn, was a foreign shipmaster called Jonathan Parker, who brought him to a place that might as well have been at the end of the earth—a place called New London. The arrival could not have been more different than that of a man like Robert Livingston, coming from Holland to make his fortune. This stranger came against his will and with no idea what awaited him—his very life in the hands of men who thought nothing of buying and selling him.[35]

Arriving in New England, the young African could leave no record of his name. If Parker knew it, he did not write it down. The youth first appeared in colonial records in 1686, having spent a summer or more as Parker's slave. The Connecticut shipmaster lived on Mill Cove near the Winthrop mansion and the former Rogers homestead, putting the young African near New London's harbor and town center. There the African might have worked as a stevedore in a warehouse adjacent to the house, loading and unloading goods from nearby ships. In the shipmaster's household, he accustomed himself to the disagreeable climate and improved his English, for he mastered "the English tongue plainly," according to a subsequent bill of sale. He probably heard nothing of the deal Parker struck with a fellow merchant that August—a deal that would alter the course of his life. The shipmaster owed money, and he decided to settle the debt by handing over his unnamed "Negro" bondsman of eighteen, whom he depicted in the exchange as "fit for service that is to say neither blind, deaf, nor lame, nor having any sore about him or other disease."[36]

In October 1686, Parker delivered the youth to his new quarters. The bondsman pleased this new owner, who after a short trial, paid the additional four pounds they had agreed he was worth. The young man had never encountered anyone quite like this new master—an odd, lonely character without a wife or child—and he had no inkling what belonging to this man might mean. For now it was all the youth could do to gain his bearings, improve his English, and try to make sense of these new surroundings. It was enough, even, to stumble over the unfamiliar Algonquian word: *Mamacock*. Against these and other hurdles he would struggle and persist, tackling each new and unfamiliar challenge. Within a few years there would even be another name to say—one of his own choosing. The "Negro" bondsman who came from the Indies would soon be calling himself John Jackson and seizing a future—a life of his own.[37]

JOHN JACKSON knew the West Indian and the internal New England slave trade from the cruel side of the transaction, having experienced both firsthand before his twentieth birthday. By contrast, most New England slaveholders like John Rogers could view the North Atlantic slave trade from some distance, shielded from its extremes. The trade familiar to most in the region was a small-scale, local affair, just as dark and brutal in the purchase transaction but haphazard and familiar compared with the wholesale buying and selling of quantities of slaves in the South, the Caribbean, or even the urban North. A ship used exclusively to transport slaves to market was an unusual appearance in a minor New England port like New London. The region's local market was neither large nor profitable

enough to justify the frequent assumption of that kind of investment risk. Of course a Connecticut colonist could always travel to
Newport or Boston, where the market and selection of slaves were
considerably larger, but slave owners often preferred to make such a
costly purchase from people they knew and trusted at home, just as
Rogers purchased Jackson from Parker and even negotiated a "trial
period" to make sure the bondsman lived up to his expectations. By
the time Jackson would have children of his own, natural increase
among African-origin slaves in New London County could also satisfy a portion of local demand.[38]

The most common way for bondsmen to arrive in New England
was on consignment through the West Indian trade, as John Jackson
had, with local shipmasters like Parker purchasing the occasional
slave during the course of a voyage. Vessels embarking from New
London routinely traveled to and from the Indies in a matter of
weeks; less frequently, ships followed longer, more circuitous routes,
exchanging one cargo for another in a series of ports and transactions
intended to maximize profits. Few records for voyages before 1700
have survived, but evidence from the eighteenth century provides a
window into the trade. A local brigantine, the *London*, for example,
sailed on an ambitious twelve-month voyage in 1733 bound for Ireland, Madeira, Cape Verde, Surinam, and Boston, before returning
home. With space and inclination, the master of the *London*, just like
seamen on the small sloops that hopped to and from the Indies, could
take on a slave or two in the islands to trade upon his return. Often
shipmasters purchased a slave at the special request of an acquaintance or customer. When he lived in New London in the 1720s, for
example, Fitz Winthrop's nephew, John IV, asked a captain to "pro-
cure a likely healthy Negro boy of about twelve or fourteen years old
from Barbados." In similar fashion the master of the sloop the *Mary*
picked up a "Negro boy" valued at fifty pounds from Montserrat at
the behest of another New Londoner.[39]

Subjected to the hardships of travel, the dramatic change in climate, and the ordeals of passage and enslavement, human cargo could
be fragile. At times, imported slaves never made it to New London,
as when a local diary recorded how "3 Negroes died in . . . passage"

aboard the brig *Hartford*. Alternatively, "new" men and women sometimes succumbed shortly after they arrived, sick, cold, and traumatized. Such was the fate of an unnamed "Negro Woman" in 1735, "come Lately from ye West Indies," who was soon dead. By surviving the voyage to Connecticut, John Jackson overcame his first major ordeal as a New England slave.[40]

Alongside the importation of slaves, New Englanders who often knew each other personally, like Parker and Rogers, also traded Africans internally in a "plain and open market." For most of the individual men, women, and children bought and sold, the cursory records of these momentary transactions offer the only remaining clues to their existence. Sales might be advertised in regional newspapers or posted near the meetinghouse, but many simply took place through word of mouth. Most slaves were sold individually, like "Thomas aged about thirty-nine years" and "Quamino [an Ashanti name meaning "born on Saturday"] aged about forty years"—both sold in New London during the 1730s. Occasionally a slaveholder bought in bulk. When the New Londoner John Merritt sold one-half of his four-hundred-acre farm in the 1720s, he included one-half of the eleven slaves associated with the property—although just how he divided "Negro man Cesar, boy Joe, alias Joseph, woman Rose, man Sampson, man Buscoe, [man] Sharper, woman Sevilia & her child . . . boy Harry, boy Billy, boy Andrew" in half was left unsaid. Mothers and infants were often sold as a unit, like the "Negro woman named Sylvia aged about eighteen years and a Negro child . . . aged about eight months."[41]

When the bondsman John Jackson arrived in New London in the 1680s, conflicts between the Rogerenes and local authorities had begun to heat up. John Rogers toughened his tactics, while the cast of public characters also changed, bringing men to power with feelings hardened toward Rogers and his activities. Simon Bradstreet died in 1684, and the town hired Gurdon Saltonstall—another son of an illustrious Massachusetts family that traced its American roots to Saltonstall's grandfather Sir Richard—to replace him as New Lon-

don's minister. He was ordained in 1691, taking charge of a congregation of sixty-eight members and presiding over the town's brand-new
meetinghouse, which had been built at great expense (in particular to
members of the Rogers family, who were large taxpayers). The new
minister erected a grand house on meetinghouse hill and laid out a
wide gravel path to the meetinghouse, allowing the Saltonstalls to
proceed smartly each Sabbath on their way to worship.[42]

One of a handful of colonists (like John Rogers's ex-wife Elizabeth) descended from a knighted ancestor, Saltonstall had an M.A.
from Harvard with an equally lofty attitude. A man of intellect
and accomplishment, he could also be pompous and arrogant. He
naturally gravitated to the only family in New London he deemed
worthy of his association and one he knew from Massachusetts—
the Winthrops—and to a close relationship with the family patriarch
and his parishioner, Fitz. The two families had a history: Saltonstall's grandfather Sir Richard had been friendly with Fitz's father,
John junior.[43]

Like minister Saltonstall, the Winthrop scion, Fitz, was also
rising in stature, serving as Connecticut's only member on the
Massachusetts-based Council of the Dominion of New England—
James II's doomed and unpopular attempt in the late 1680s to con-
solidate colonial governance from New York and New Jersey to
present-day Maine by usurping now-established colonial liberties
in religion, taxation, and law. (The Dominion was one of a series
of attempts by the Crown to enhance and unify imperial control
over the colonies, efforts that colonists generally found unjust and
oppressive.) When the council disbanded, Fitz continued to serve
Connecticut Colony in various public roles from his home base in
New London. He probably had little use for the Rogerene leader,
John Rogers, but it was the traditionalist Saltonstall, Fitz's good
friend and minister, who would emerge as the Baptist renegade's
chief adversary.[44]

As sides were taken in the public arena, the Rogers family faced
the loss of their patriarch in 1687. James senior had been a bulwark of
strength since his son's conversion, and his death produced a chasm
within the family. From among his children, James had chosen his
son John and daughter Bathshua to administer his estate, picking

John, perhaps, because of his intellect and spiritual leadership. His choice of Bathshua made sense for different reasons: This dutiful daughter had already been caring for her mother, Elizabeth, who had been a sick, "bedridden woman" (probably afflicted with a stroke) for some years, as a grandson later recalled. Widowed and a mother of five herself when her father died, Bathshua had occupied a room in her parents' house with some or all of her children perhaps as early as 1682, allowing her to attend to her aging father and sick mother (although she and John were not named their mother's legal guardians until a decade later). As a female caregiver, the widowed Bathshua had been an obvious choice over her younger sister, Elizabeth, who had moved to Plum Island off the northern tip of Long Island after her 1680 marriage to Samuel Beebe, the son of the old Winthrop retainer of the same name. Although the ailing matriarch, Elizabeth Rogers, kept mostly to her chamber, "incapable of managing any business and not able to take care of herself," she would survive her husband, James, by many years.[45]

In her parents' home, Bathshua had taken on the duties her mother was unable to perform, supervised both parents' care before her father's death, and acted—as one of her sons would later explain—the "mistress" of the house in every way. She certainly could not have managed as well without the labor of enslaved Maria and Hagar Wright, who would have helped her run the household and attend to the needs of elderly parents and young children. Recognizing her filial devotion, James senior directed in his will that Bathshua should always have a room in his house. Maria and Hagar, of course, received no such acknowledgment, appearing instead in James's inventory as chattel alongside one ox, six cows, and two sows. Three years after her father's death and at age thirty-nine, however, Bathshua remarried and moved into the nearby house of her second husband, Samuel Fox, combining his six children with at least two of her own. Attending now to two households, Bathshua relied on another person who was able to accompany and help her. Maria's enslaved daughter, Joan, though just an adolescent girl around the same age as Bathshua's youngest daughter, Bathshua, had likely become invaluable. Joan had also, in the intervening years since her birth, become Bathshua's property.[46]

Joan's early years are largely hidden from view. Born to Maria in the James Rogers, Sr., household and raised there, she must have come under Bathshua's authority while still a young child. She grew up working and living around Bathshua's children, who were roughly her contemporaries. The younger Bathshua, in particular, might have been a childhood companion. Not every moment of every day, even for an enslaved child, was spent in hard labor. Joan and the child would have had opportunities for ordinary, everyday exchanges—perhaps even learning to sew, cook, and spin together—watching Hagar, Maria, or Bathshua. Growing up in a devoutly Rogerene household, Joan was almost certainly a Rogerene herself.[47]

As a child slave, Joan would have performed work typical of all but the most privileged young girls beginning around the age of five or six—spinning yarn, preparing food, and washing and making clothes. After Bathshua Rogers Fox's remarriage in 1690, Joan must have also helped her mistress watch the youngest Fox stepchildren and care for the son Samuel ("the Younger," so called to distinguish him from his elder half brother, Samuel "the Elder") Bathshua soon had with her new husband. Bathshua would always maintain that Joan had been a gift from her parents—a credible claim, given that Bathshua lived with and cared for them during their old age. She might have reasonably made a special request to keep Joan—the bonded servant she had known since the girl's birth. Whatever the content of the two women's relationship, the legal and emotional ties between Bathshua and Joan were sealed during this period in the 1680s and 1690s, as mistress and slave traveled back and forth between the Rogers and Fox households on the General Neck, Joan working as Bathshua required.[48]

A native of Massachusetts, Bathshua's second husband, Samuel Fox, was a prosperous, well-established freeman by the time they married in 1690. Born in 1651, Fox had moved to Connecticut during his twenties and served as a militiaman in King Philip's War, even participating in the infamous Great Swamp Fight of December 1675, when English forces slaughtered hundreds of Narragansett, including many women and children, who were taking cover in a swamp encampment at Kingston, Rhode Island. Although he had suffered personal losses of his own (his first wife died young and his second, town records tell, had "bled to death," perhaps from smallpox), the twice-widowed Fox had become a well-to-do landholder and a member in good standing of the First Congregation. As a sideline, Fox was a fellmonger, or pelt dealer. Although the heyday of the fur trade had already passed, the market for fur could still provide a good supplemental living, particularly in a place like the General Neck.[49]

Despite having been an Indian fighter as a young man, Bathshua's husband spent the rest of his life in regular contact and commerce with Algonquin. Indigenous people were important suppliers of beaver, deer, and other wild-animal skins, moving easily to and from Indian country to places on the fringe of English settlement like the General Neck. The Fox household was often filled with the sights and sounds of buyers and sellers, Algonquin and English, coming to trade.[50]

Marrying Bathshua Rogers derailed any plans Samuel Fox might have had for a life of contented respectability, however. He quickly adopted her Rogerene ways and a brotherly relationship with John Rogers along with them. Fox's conversion earned him formal excommunication from the Congregational Church, not to mention several personal run-ins with the law. These paled, however, in comparison to the confrontational stance taken by his redoubtable bride, Bathshua, whom he could not or did not try to restrain. Within a few years of their wedding day, both husband and wife became embroiled in the Rogerene struggle. Fox faced his own stand-off with the authorities in February 1694 when he was caught eel fishing on the Sabbath with his brother-in-law John. (Fishing was apparently an illegal Sunday ritual for some Sabbatarians, especially on the General Neck.) Convicted of Sabbath breaking, Fox paid his fine and went home. John Rogers was not so compliant. He refused to pay and was imprisoned in the makeshift New London jail.[51]

The Sunday after her brother's incarceration, Bathshua staged a protest. Coming the several miles to town, she entered the meeting-house in the midst of Mr. Saltonstall's morning service and loudly announced before the assembled congregation that she had performed menial labor in violation of the law. Authorities seized her immediately and put her in stocks. The commotion of her outburst and apprehension, however, allowed her brother to escape. When Saltonstall later began the afternoon service, John Rogers appeared back in action—thrusting open the meetinghouse doors pushing a wheelbarrow. It must have been quite a sight when the Rogerene leader rolled up toward the pulpit, shrilly calling out his wares (the wheelbarrow almost certainly contained shoes of his own making; the wealthy merchant had taken up the humble craft of cobbling as biblically sanctioned manual labor). Once they got over their initial shock and disbelief, members of the congregation pounced on Rogers. Apparently frustrated and unsure of what to do, town authorities took the extraordinary measure of simply forcing the Rogerene leader to stand fifteen minutes on a ladder with a rope around his neck, while leaning up against the town gallows. It was meant to be a spontaneous punishment and public reproach, but the exercise made little impression on Rogers and they flung him back in jail.[52]

From his crude confinement, John Rogers hung a handwritten "Proclamation" out a window, declaring his opposition to "the Doctrines of Devils"—later published in *A Mid-Night-Cry from the Temple of God to the Ten Virgins*. For this last gesture the authorities charged him with blasphemy, an accusation that led to his transfer to a more secure imprisonment in Hartford, where he awaited trial and certain conviction before the General Court. There, Rogers later wrote, he endured whips and chains. At his sentencing the court required Rogers to submit a bond to secure his good behavior. Rogers deemed the order a sacrilege and refused to comply, so he remained in prison.[53]

The strength of his determination proved greater than the court had bargained for. John Rogers ended up serving more than three years in prison at a time when long-term incarceration was extremely rare and highly impractical, given inadequate facilities, personnel, and resources. Lengthy imprisonment was seldom a criminal punishment, in fact, but could arise in the highly unusual circumstance of a defendant like Rogers relentlessly failing to comply with court orders, fines, and bond submissions. Once Rogers finally did finish out his term, Saltonstall, whose delicate pride had been wounded in the attacks on his sermonizing, brought a civil suit against him for defamation. Saltonstall also served on the bench of the court that determined the outcome—a conflict of interest which the colonial court blithely tolerated—so it was no surprise when the plaintiff-judge won a spectacular and highly retaliatory damage award of six hundred pounds.[54]

During John Rogers's incarceration in Hartford, two dramatic events took place that became linked in the minds of many New Londoners. The town's newly built meetinghouse burned to the ground, and the meetinghouse in nearby Stonington suffered a most vile "abuse." Thinking back, some townspeople recalled hearing John Rogers's sister Bathshua Fox and other Rogerenes in heated conversation, perhaps even plotting the meetinghouse fire. An indictment came down, and she and William Wright, her father's onetime Algonquin servant, were accused of both crimes. Facing a Connecticut judiciary packed with Winthrops, Saltonstalls, and their assorted allies, Rogerenes could count on being convicted. The county court found Wright guilty of "abusing the Stonington meeting house and daubing it with his own dung," ordering him "severely whipped" and returned to prison until he could post bond. A jury found Bathshua triply guilty: of the meetinghouse burning, "fouling" the Stonington meetinghouse, and "wicked contrivances of poppets."[55]

According to the verdict, Joan's mistress had made dolls and placed them in the New London meetinghouse before it burned. To contemporary eyes the dolls must have been a threatening symbol, an implicit, conscious evocation of Old World magic and superstition that Congregational New Englanders had worked hard to purge from within, but that ran deeper than their leaders cared to admit. Weak and credulous minds, authorities would have feared, might wonder if Bathshua's dolls could work real, "wicked" power over them. For her involvement in these crimes, Bathshua was fined and ordered to submit a large bond of two hundred pounds to pledge her good behavior. She returned to her family, but Bathshua Rogers Fox would not give up her tenacious defense of her brother or her faith. The example of her loyalty was not likely lost on her young slave, Joan.[56]

Bathshua's codefendant, William Wright, did not fare as well. Although he, too, received a fine for his involvement in the meeting-house case, he was later accused of helping a fellow prisoner escape detention and further of continuing to refuse to submit to the law against Sabbath breaking. His defiance kept him in the Hartford jail, along with John Rogers, longer than anyone could have expected.[57]

With Bathshua returned safely home, however, she and her husband, Samuel Fox, transplanted their dissident household around 1698 from the General Neck to the North Parish (now Montville), to a spot that came to be called Fox's Mills after the saw- and gristmills that Samuel constructed and operated there. Home to Mohegan and Pequot, the North Parish was a newer section of the colonial town around eight miles distant from meetinghouse hill.[58]

For enslaved Joan, who was then probably around twenty, the move came after years of upheaval and turmoil. Outwardly father-less, during the 1690s she had likely lost her mother, although no record of Maria's death survives. The Rogerene troubles also probably weighed deeply on her—both as a matter of religion and as a frightening, destructive force in the households and families she knew best. Leaving the General Neck was a change and an adjustment, but the move held possibilities of a better future. Their new surroundings also placed Bathshua Fox and Joan much closer to John Rogers and his household. Traveling to town, the women could use the Norwich Road, which passed right through Mamacock.[59]

Chapter Three

"FORE-RUNNERS OF EVIL"

T HE WANING decades of the seventeenth century brought dark times to New England. A palpable sense of decline enveloped the region as it grappled with a series of disasters, a debilitating war, and a pervading spiritual malaise. Events in Old England seemed to confirm colonists' apprehensions, even calling into question the very survival of the New England undertaking. The fall of Oliver Cromwell's Protectorate marked the end of Puritan ascendency in the mother country; colonial Congregationalists perceived the Restoration of Charles II in 1660 as a disheartening defeat of their cause. This defeat was made worse by the subsequent passage of the repressive Clarendon Code—a series of parliamentary statutes that reestablished the supremacy of the Anglican Church. Although the code's effect in New England was largely symbolic and psychological, it seemed to many that the Puritan "moment" had passed.

At home, New England Congregationalists faced their own internal crisis of faith, which was manifested in the declining number and caliber of their church members. From the first the Congregational Church was a closed society to which only "saints" could belong. "Saints" had to experience personally God's saving grace and convincingly depict this experience to the members of their church—

literally telling the story of their conversion—to attain election to membership. Many of the founders' children, however, never experienced conversion, and so never sought membership. This troubling state of affairs led the ruling synod in 1662 to offer a compromise in the form of a "half" membership, which some derisively called the halfway covenant. By "owning the covenant" with a verbal assertion of commitment to Christ and congregation, halfway members would receive all the privileges of membership, except receiving communion, and they could have their children baptized in the church.[1]

The compromise of the halfway covenant kept many second- and third-generation colonists within the Congregational fold, but New Englanders recognized within it the symptoms of waning orthodoxy and devotion to faith. Over the next decades, that perception became an undeniable fact. New London's First Congregation was fairly typical. Between 1670 and 1690, the number of full members dropped by 50 percent, even as the overall population grew. Colonists who joined congregations as full members—once the backbone of New England settlements—became a permanent minority after 1700. The growing ranks of "dissenters" from the Congregational norm—whether Baptists, Rogerenes, or even Anglicans reasserting themselves, a trend that began in the 1680s—only sealed colonists' apprehensions about a moribund New England.[2]

If the slow crumbling of Congregationalists' religious ideals were not enough to make the colonies deeply uneasy, a series of calamitous events seemed to push New England civilization to the very brink of destruction. In 1675, under increasing land pressure and incensed by the recent executions of three tribal members for the murder of an Algonquin Christian convert and English informant, the Wampanoag leader Metacomet (or King Philip) led allied Indian forces in a series of raids that soon escalated into a full-fledged war with the English. After two terrible years of fighting, the English prevailed, but King Philip's War had devastated the region, and the fatalities on both sides would have profound implications for survivors in the years to come. Then, in November 1676, only months after hostilities ended, Boston endured a great fire that destroyed much of its north end, an eerie repeat of the Great Fire of London just over ten years earlier. During the winter that followed the Boston fire, a ship infected with smallpox arrived on nearby Nantucket, triggering a mainland epidemic and reminders of the recent Great Plague of London along with it.[3]

Only a year later New Londoners were haunted by an evil portent of a different sort. Shots were fired to send out an alarm on a night in June after three Mohegan—Keweebhunt, with Nucquitatty and his wife—discovered a grisly domestic scene in the North Parish. Approaching a dark house where they had traded venison earlier the same day, the three saw the front door hanging open and heard gurgling sounds coming from just inside. The unearthly noise proved to be five-year-old Mary Bolles gasping her last breaths, her head split open with an ax. Stoking the fire for light, they searched the room and soon found the body of Mary's three-year-old brother, Joseph, his head and face hacked apart. At the foot of a bed lay the children's dead mother, Zipporah, next to the slab of venison the Mohegan had sold her earlier that day. By her side they discovered baby John, the lone survivor, soaked in his mother's blood. The Bolles husband and father had been away from home that day, unable to protect his family from destruction.[4]

The Mohegan who had reported the massacre cast suspicions on two Indians who had been in the area, Resuekquinek and Sucquaunch, and the authorities indicted the unlucky pair. The real culprit emerged soon after: a sixteen-year-old English youth named John Stoddard, "a most terrible wicked boy" who had given his parents no end of troubles, according to Simon Bradstreet. Stoddard's culpability became clear within two months of the Bolles murders, when the boy's baby half brother was found dead from a hatchet blow to the head and Stoddard blamed "Indians." As it turned out, the slaughter of the Bolles family took place after Mistress Zipporah had rebuffed Stoddard's request to board there for the night and he grabbed the family's ax to retaliate for her rejection. He eventually confessed to the murders and was hanged, but the gruesome massacre was deeply disquieting to Stoddard's New London neighbors— in particular, perhaps, because it had been committed not by enemies or outsiders but by one of their own.[5]

Colonial New Englanders experienced their world as an unpredictable and frightening place, not the pious idyll nostalgically conjured by later American generations. And if they were inclined to see impending doom in the waning century, they could find it aplenty. Two years after the Bolles murders, inhabitants in New London looked aloft to behold a comet in the night sky. A comet visible to the naked eye is a rare event, occurring once or maybe twice in a lifetime, but to New Englanders the hoary sphere bursting across the heavens was an unwelcome, unsettling vision. The Boston merchant and magistrate Samuel Sewall observed in his long diary, "leaving the world in a fearful expectation of what may follow . . . [Comets] are by most thought to be the fore-runners of evil coming upon this world."[6]

In 1679, New London was still a small encampment of around one hundred householders whose future was by no means secure. Most of those in town, like other Connecticut colonists, lived in relative poverty, eking out a bare subsistence and ever conscious that death and catastrophe could strike without warning, signaling God's disapproval or censure. New London's families handled the pervasive disorder and disenchantment in a variety of ways. The Rogerses, led by the peerless John, rejected the comfortable conventions of wealth and Congregationalism and forged a new relationship with God. Their course would be a hard and costly one, but they would remain fortified by solidarity and righteousness. The Hempsteads continued along the path laid out for them by the immigrant Robert, working tirelessly toward a future of economic prosperity and stability, though they grappled with a succession of grievous personal losses. Even that simple goal, however, was beyond the reach of the African bondsman John Jackson and the family he created over the next decades. Jackson's aims for his family would be plain and grave. To be and own oneself, to be together, and to be free—these would be everything and more than any Jackson might dream of.[7]

ON THE same Bream Cove lot Robert Hempstead had settled in the 1640s, his son, Joshua, laid the foundation for a new house in

1678, drawing the stones that would support it from the surrounding yards and fields. When the foundation was done, neighbors would come and help raise the frame. It was a scant two years since King Philip's War had ended, yet Joshua already had his sights set on larger, sturdier accommodations than the glorified shack his father had built more than thirty years before. It was time to expand, time to improve, and Joshua, a wheelwright and veteran woodworker, envisioned a house for the ages. The new two-story, two-chamber structure would eventually have a back kitchen and small room above, along with a lean-to workshop off to one side. As Joshua set stones into place, his fine, old apple tree might have caught his attention, a herald of the dead father whose face he could not quite remember. The yellow fruit of England had resided here longer than the native son who now admired it. The tree would outlast him, too—so close to this new house that children could watch its fruit ripen from the upstairs windows and fancy themselves able to reach out and pick it.

More than twenty years had passed since Robert's death in 1655. Difficult years: Joshua had been just five when his father had died. His mother had remarried, but her own death soon afterward quickly shattered that re-formed family. The boy must have ended up in the care and service of a local wheelwright, where he could have been placed by relatives or town authorities. (The choice of an allied trade might have pleased his father, Robert, the dabbling smith; blacksmiths and wheelwrights were a team, the smithy attaching rims and "shoes" to the wheelwright's carts, wagons, and sleds.) Joshua would come of age all but alone in the world, sobered by violence, loss, and privation. At least two sisters remained local, marrying and settling around New London. Finishing his training as a wheelwright, he married a girl from Saybrook, Elizabeth Larrabee, and took possession of his father's home at Bream Cove. Already Robert's entail of the property had done its work, assuring his orphaned son a place among the landed, artisanal men of the town.[8]

Coming to Bream Cove as an independent man and householder, Joshua Hempstead began to take on a modest role in town government, filling posts as fence viewer, collector of taxes, and grand juror—this last position a frequent stepping stone to higher office.

By the 1680s, New London's second Hempstead appeared poised to emerge as a respected town leader, just as his father, Robert—a frequent selectman—had been. He and Elizabeth, like most of their generation, had also become halfway members in the First Congregation, allowing them to baptize their six children (two of whom died in infancy), including an only son born within months of the raising of Joshua's new house. These children, Robert Hempstead's grandchildren, joined New England's third generation of colonists, "sinner[s] into an evil world," to use their minister's turn of phrase.[9]

JUST FIVE years after he built his new house at Bream Cove, Joshua Hempstead lay inside ailing, the faces of friends and family, wife and four surviving children surrounding his bedside. He was in a fight for his life, delirious with fever and exhaustion. The anxious assembly watched his spiritual demeanor, alert for lapses into hysteria, despair, or faithlessness. But the wheelwright kept his composure even as death appeared certain. One thought troubled him, however. Though he knew the hardships and disappointments of orphaned children only too well, he had never written a will. With all the work of houses and wheels, carts and fields, he had not put into words everything he had intended. The lives of three daughters and one son now hung in the balance and visions of their fatherless future filled Joshua Hempstead with dread.[10]

Joshua called over a neighbor, Charles Hill. A girdler, or belt-maker, who was also New London's town clerk, Hill listened and wrote as Joshua spoke. Elizabeth would have her "widow's thirds" as was her legal due, including one-third of his nonmovable estate, housing, and lands until her remarriage. Their movable goods—furnishings, linens, and kitchen goods—should remain hers always. To each of his girls, Joshua promised a parcel of land.[11]

He then came to his only son and namesake. Joshua junior was only five years old, yet to him would fall the bulk of the estate, and in him rested his father's greatest hopes. The Bream Cove property would be his through entail, of course, when he married or reached twenty-one. Until then, Elizabeth should sell off livestock to pay for his upbringing. But to this inheritance his father added another provision, a very unusual one: This boy—who like his father and grandfather would work the land the rest of his life—must also be "well educated and brought up in learning."[12]

The day Joshua Hempstead, Sr., wrote his will, no one at his bedside thought that the wheelwright would survive his illness. But Providence had other ideas. Some time after, Joshua senior rose from his sickbed and resumed his place as a householder, neighbor, husband, and father; he even added three more daughters to the family. Five years later, however, this second Hempstead patriarch died suddenly, just as the first Hempstead, Robert, had done. Joshua senior was only thirty-nine, and his cause of death was not recorded, but 1689 was the hottest summer any colonist could remember, and it gave shelter to a virulent smallpox epidemic that devastated New London and many other towns; this father of seven may have been among the many casualties that July and August. The half-decade's reprieve he had enjoyed since the first writing of his will had given the wheelwright time to implement some of his aspirations for his only son. Nevertheless, it was the special provision in that testament—like Robert's entail a generation earlier—that would set the child apart.[13]

Education distinguished Joshua Hempstead, Jr., from the other neighborhood boys. For an artisanal family like the Hempsteads, an education did not mean attending college or engaging a private tutor as a Winthrop, Livingston, or Saltonstall would do. Education was instead part-time schooling in a nearby home combined with apprenticeship training. It was learning enough, however, for this third Hempstead to cultivate a life in writing. Even as a child, Joshua junior took quickly to the pen, drawing apparent pleasure from refining a well-formed, deliberate hand. While other local boys remained satisfied to write like the provincial artisans and yeomen they would become, making crude signatures and scratching out basic accounts, Joshua junior aspired to dominion over the written word. Perhaps writing also filled a void, connecting him to a father who had wanted him to learn but had left him too soon. His early affinity for lettering would grow into a devotion that would last a lifetime.

*   *   *

AS THE fatherless Joshua Hempstead, Jr., learned to master the
written word, the African bondsman John Jackson accustomed
himself gamely to life at Mamacock farm with his new master, the
Rogerene leader John Rogers. In only a few years, Jackson began
to feel some sense of belonging that went well beyond the bare fact
of being owned. There was a place for him here in this world apart,
this uncommon community of Rogers family, servants, and coreli-
gionists that baptized its members in the nearby Thames and buried
its dead in a small graveyard on the property. Living here and in
John Rogers's household, Jackson became his master's servant and
his disciple.

Already within four years of arriving from the West Indies, Jackson was even enough of a Rogerene to be prosecuted for following their dissenting ways. At twenty-two, he was charged with the
crime of "doing servile work on the Lord's day" along with Rogers himself, the servant William Wright, and Thomas Jones, a fellow Rogerene and Mamacock neighbor. Convicted, Jackson and the
other Rogerenes defied an order to pay a token statutory fine of ten
shillings, enduring imprisonment and property seizures instead. As
Jackson's master, John Rogers was liable for his servant's share. Perhaps this was the only occasion when the law caught up with Jackson
for Rogerene beliefs, but the episode revealed him to be, at least to
some degree, a Rogerene.[14]

When not defying the law and the dominant religion, John Jackson would have spent most of his days during the late 1680s and
1690s working in John Rogers's fields, yards, and woodlots. Jackson learned the art of husbandry, for he identified himself in legal
records as a "husbandman"—the same agricultural work plied by the
vast majority of New England men, whether English or African. He
had come to New England by force as an article of trade, but he did
not remain one. Within a few years of his purchase, John Rogers
simply freed Jackson. The gesture acknowledged loyal service, but it
also may have reflected Rogers's growing unease with slaveholding.[15]

John Rogers's treatment of the William Wrights, former servants
to his father, James senior, also suggests this possibility. After his

father's death, John Rogers took on the remaining three years of William's indenture, along with the ownership of his enslaved wife, Hagar. When the indenture was up, John Rogers honored his father's agreement by giving the Wrights their freedom. Years later, when Hagar found her free status challenged, Rogers would also defend that freedom in court by testifying in her favor.[16]

Although John Rogers was highly unusual in taking these first steps in opposition to slavery, he was not entirely alone. His perhaps unlikely ally was the diarist and Massachusetts jurist and merchant Samuel Sewall, who wrote New England's first antislavery tract around the same time that Rogers freed Jackson. Along with Wait Winthrop, Sewall was a member of the Puritan old guard, and he had access to the burgeoning antislavery literature emanating from England and a wider Atlantic world. Sewall was also a man of conscience—the only magistrate who participated in the Salem witch trials ever to apologize for his actions. (His fellow magistrate Wait Winthrop, for example, never did recant.) As did many early critics, Sewall focused on the safer political territory of the slave trade in his *The Selling of Joseph: A Memorial*, rather than on slaveholding itself, though his words were an inherent attack on slave ownership.[17]

Sewall's contribution to the discussion had come on the heels of a 1693 antislavery publication by Philadelphia Quakers and directed at other members of their sect: *An Exhortation & Caution to Friends Concerning Buying or Keeping of Negroes*. As the century progressed, Quakers would advance the cause, but in 1700 it was Sewall who went further, advocating the abolishment of the trade entirely. Nonetheless Sewall's position, like John Rogers's, remained ambivalent. Evidence from his diary shows that the Boston magistrate continued to hire slaves and, if he was not a slave owner himself, members of his own family certainly were. Few New Englanders were ready to fight slavery in a concerted way in 1700.[18]

Securing liberty at the end of the seventeenth century, John Jackson and Hagar Wright joined the very small but undeniable ranks of free people of African origin who then inhabited southern New England, particularly along its well-traveled coastline, and also aboard its trade ships, as seafaring "Black Jacks." Once free, former bondsmen like Jackson and Hagar inhabited the fringes and nether

regions of colonial English society in the company of other Africans, Algonquin, and even Scots and Irish—who, although technically free, were never full participants in the worlds and minds of
their colonial English neighbors.[19]

No record survives to pinpoint the moment when John Jackson
gained his liberty, but it may have coincided with his taking of a
surname—a rarity among African New Englanders before 1700.
Jackson did not adopt his master's name, as was common, but
instead took a name with no obvious New London connection, one
that would become popular decades later among other Northern
freedmen. It was a vital assertion, not to mention a practical need,
for a newly freed man to take a second name, a family name. With it,
Jackson quite literally became his own. A surname allowed him to
assume an identity distinct not just from his master but also from his
past as an object of ownership. This new name could not erase Jackson's history, the one implied by the color of his skin and the cadence
of his voice, but it did permit a transformation. The barely indistinguishable "Negro man about the age of eighteen years" of 1686
could become John Jackson, freedman of New London, by 1700.
The former slave of unknown origins would always be an African
to his English neighbors, but Jackson could still be a free inhabitant, appearing as his own man in tax rolls, church records, trade,
and litigation. Becoming John Jackson would also allow him to share
his name with a wife, as well as with any children they might have
together.[20]

However, for John Jackson, becoming free did not mean severing
ties with his master, or even leaving servitude behind. As a freedman, Jackson continued to live at Mamacock, occupying a house
near the Rogers mansion and continuing to work as his former owner's servant. Jackson was legally free, but practical everyday distinctions between freedom and servitude, slaves and servants, could be
subtle in early New England. The word "servant" itself was ambiguous and could mean indentured servant, wage laborer, or perpetual
slave, depending on its usage. Within these categories were even
finer shades of difference that men and women understood almost
instinctively, having received an unwitting instruction in social
ordering from their earliest days. By adolescence, New Englanders

would have mastered the local social taxonomy, even practiced the art of maneuvering at its more malleable edges.[21]

Although John Jackson was no longer chattel, and could even own property himself, an ex-slave in colonial New England was not necessarily "free" enough to strike out entirely on his own. Even if someone had been willing to sell him a parcel of land and the town permitted the transfer, a husbandman like Jackson would still need additional capital for land, tools, and livestock, which most free Africans—and the poor in general—sorely lacked. As with any poor man, Jackson's best option was to sell his labor by indenturing himself for a period of time. An indenture to John Rogers, the man who had owned him from the age of eighteen and who later freed him, was probably a logical and easy progression for Jackson—not a confounding paradox as later generations might suppose.[22]

Working for John Rogers had its benefits. Jackson had probably developed a familiar camaraderie with his former owner. Slaveholding in New England households had a strong paternal quality, the roles of master and father having certain attributes in common. A master like Rogers was by definition a fatherly figure to Jackson, an older man to whom he owed obedience and with whom Jackson had long planted and plowed, chopped and carted, prayed and worshipped. They had probably traveled together to Newport, Boston, and other towns where Rogers went on mercantile and spiritual business. Together they had suffered for their convictions. But the relationship between Rogers and Jackson seemed to transcend the obligations of master and servant, even the bonds of faith. At his master's suggestion, Jackson had built himself a house at Mamacock by the Rogers homestead. He stayed there many years. A master was bound by custom and morality to support a freed slave in times of economic and physical duress, but John Rogers went far beyond any such duty when it came to John Jackson. Death alone would sever the connection between them. In his own right, Jackson would also prove a formidable patriarch with a distinct legacy—not in grand ideas or accumulated wealth, but in dogged, splendid determination. John Jackson would make the most of what little life had offered him.[23]

Chapter Four

"BROUGHT UP IN LEARNING"

SOMETIME IN the year 1692, Joshua Hempstead, Jr., must have found himself in the hall of the Edgecombe house on New London's main road, flanked by his six sisters and five new stepsiblings, looking on as his mother married a local tanner. It was probably a comforting sight. Joshua had watched his mother struggle to care for him and his sisters in the years since his father's death, yet he had been powerless to protect her. Growing up without the support of a father or paternal grandfather, Joshua surely knew that his own economic and political prospects were diminished. For his mother and younger sisters, the tanner John Edgecombe might now fill in some of the gaps left by their father's absence, but the remarriage had come too late to make much of a difference in Joshua's life. By the day of the wedding Joshua already stood on the cusp of manhood, well into an apprenticeship in the shipwright's trade. His time and labor were spoken for—a future on the wharves of New London already evident. For the third in this ill-fated line of Hempsteads, it would have been hard not to think of all this—of everything that had been and that would come—as the teen took in the otherwise happy proceedings at his mother's second wedding.

Like his father before him, Joshua Hempstead, Jr., had grown up knowing the hardships of fatherlessness. After Joshua senior's death, the family might have stayed on in the Bream Cove house for a time, relying on servants, family, or neighbors to do the dead master's labor. Overburdened with housework and the care of her four youngest children, Elizabeth had needed to sell property out of the estate to provide for the family. On her own, she could prepare her daughters to be wives and mothers, but she was in no position to teach her only son even the basic skills he needed. Certainly she was ill-equipped to fulfill her dead husband's wish that the boy be "brought up in learning." Like most New England girls of her generation, Elizabeth Hempstead had a limited education; she probably had some ability to read, but she could barely write and could therefore offer him no valuable instruction in letters. Elizabeth also coped with an added challenge: her third daughter, Phoebe, was mentally disabled from birth and required considerable extra attention. Contemporaries regarded Phoebe as "a Poor Idiot," as her brother, Joshua, later wrote in the unapologetic idiom of the day. (Idiots, as opposed to lunatics, were "natural fools," born with a condition that rendered them legally insane.) Caring for Phoebe must have taken a toll on the Hempstead family, but especially on her mother.[1]

Scanning the surroundings the day of the wedding, however, a hopeful son might have approved of his mother's choice. Father Edgecombe's house was one of the better ones in town, a fortified stone structure that had been used as a safe house and arms store during King Philip's War. It stood at a key intersection along the main street, between the harbor and the meetinghouse. In Edgecombe, a widower and father of five, Joshua encountered a patriarch who embodied English roots and traditions. Town records gave this distinctive description, conspicuous for a settlement filled with its share of English migrants: "John Edgecombe, son of Nicholas Edgecombe of Plymouth in Old England," implying that Edgecombe asserted those roots pointedly to his neighbors. Joshua's new stepfather had emigrated to New England from Plymouth in his twenties, bringing with him not just tools and supplies but also the old ways of England.[2]

For Joshua, Edgecombe's ostentatious Englishness contrasted with his own experience. Death's toll on the Hempstead line had meant that Joshua could only imagine such an immediate, flesh-and-blood connection to English origins. Visiting with his mother and siblings, he may have regarded the Edgecombe coat of arms hanging in the hall, or examined the gold signet ring with an ancestral crest that his stepfather used to seal documents. At the Edgecombes', "old-fashioned" furniture reminiscent of Tudor England—a bed, a chest of drawers, a table—might stir his nascent historical awareness. Aside from the old apple tree in the yard at Bream Cove, the family possession that harked back most meaningfully to English forebears for Joshua was the ancient musket his grandfather Robert had brought from the Old World for Hempstead men to use in the New. By contrast, Father Edgecombe's attitudes and his impressive array of possessions loudly announced his English provenance.[3]

With twelve children between them, Joshua's mother, Elizabeth, and John Edgecombe created a large family, to which they added a son of their own, Thomas, in 1694. Joshua's eldest sister, Elizabeth, who had married the innkeeper John Plumb, Sr., a few years before the Edgecombe wedding, was a neighbor. Between these two households, Joshua could piece together a renewed sense of family and kinship that would carry him forward. Another constant stood nearby, reassuringly tangible in its wooden boards and stone foundation. The house at Bream Cove would always embody family for him, representing not only the father who had lived there all too briefly but also the grandfather he had never known. Both had left their mark on the land, even as the place stood empty or leased out until its inheritor came of age. Silently, the house bore witness to Joshua's years of loss and dislocation. Walking alongside it to and from the shipyards, the teenage apprentice was inevitably reminded of his past. At the same time, more than anything else he knew, the house represented his future.[4]

WHEN HIS mother married John Edgecombe, Joshua Hempstead had already begun an apprenticeship with the shipwright Thomas Mitchell. Joshua probably began his training early—perhaps even at ten after his father died. No indenture contract with Mitchell survives, but a still-extant indenture agreement for his stepbrother Samuel Edgecombe gives a parallel account. Samuel, too, was a ship-wright's apprentice. In the indenture, Samuel's master agreed to teach the "art and mystery" of his craft in exchange for the boy's labor and obedience until the age of twenty-one, when a man reached major-ity and assumed an independent legal status. Until then, Samuel lived under his master's roof and authority, where he was to receive food, clothing, and basic maintenance like laundry and medical care. At the end of his term, Samuel was entitled to receive two suits of apparel (an ordinary one for work and a better one for the Sabbath) and a broadax: an essential tool and potent emblem of their trade. The agreement omitted one typical obligation: teaching the appren-tice to read and write. Sixteen when the contract took effect, Samuel, who signed the contract himself, probably arrived proficient at both.[5]

Joshua Hempstead entered into a similar arrangement with his own master, Thomas Mitchell, who ran a shipyard near the town fort at New London Harbor, supplying sailing vessels for the West Indian trade. Around the time Joshua began his apprenticeship in the early 1690s, Mitchell lived in a rented house with his wife and children on New London's main road. The spot was convenient to the wharves; it also put Joshua close to his extended family of Edgecombes and Plumbs. Living with Mitchell, Joshua would have been included in his master's broad concept of family. The youth would eat, sleep, and work there, taking direction and discipline from his master and mistress. All the while the third New England Hempstead would also hold on tightly to the remains of his first family, scattered in and around the Edgecombe house near the center of town.[6]

SINCE MEDIEVAL times, the practice of apprenticing or "putting out" had been commonplace in the English world, and colonial par-ents transferred it easily to the New England setting. Parents who "put out" their children were not lacking in love or attachment, but regarded apprenticeships as an important aspect of child rear-ing. Good seventeenth-century parenting for boys meant preparing them to practice a trade and become productive, responsible men.

Although a boy might learn a trade while living at home, either from his father or through day labor, formal apprenticeships provided wider options, and many colonists regarded them as the best over-all method to train and discipline beloved children. A master and mistress, some believed, could assert authority over a spirited youth more effectively than could a father or mother. An important phase of child rearing, apprenticeships also constituted a form of service.[7]

Servitude was part of the common experience of most New Englanders and an essential part of family life. Boys from middling artisanal families like the Hempsteads were accustomed to spend-ing a period of time as servants in other people's homes, just as they could expect one day to preside over servants and apprentices in their own. For most boys like Joshua Hempstead, that period of service took place during late childhood and was temporary. Service meant something quite different to poor or enslaved children, who endured even longer indentures or permanent bondage without the prospect of ever emerging from servitude. Nevertheless, there were obvi-ous parallels between forms of service whatever their duration and content—a quality of shared experience, however limited.[8]

Among servants, artisanal apprentices like Joshua Hempstead were fortunate. For them, service was a means to acquire a trade and "calling," even to assemble a set of vital skills in literacy, mathemat-ics, and commerce. Upon completing his term, a young artisan could begin to fulfill the colonial ideal of manhood—he could pursue his calling, accumulate property, and support a household and family as its head. Once established, he imparted his skills and experience in turn to a new generation of boys through sons, servants, and wards.[9]

Apprenticeships provided work training, but they also taught experiential lessons in family living. In New England, it was a gen-eral custom for an apprentice to reside with his master under his paternal authority. In another man's house, men-in-training learned to master a trade, but they also observed a man's dominion over his domestic realm. When they began to oversee households of their own, newly minted artisans could draw on their own experiences as sons and stepsons, but also as servants.

The shipwright's trade was a natural choice for a New London boy in the 1680s and 1690s. A seafaring town, New London had attracted shipbuilders to its shores from the first decade of settlement. In the 1690s, the West Indian trade continued to expand, changing the face of New London and its shoreline. Wharves and shipyards lined the harbor, and the demand from the shipping industry naturally fueled growth in the allied maritime trades. These associated trades, including shipwrighting, coopering, sailmaking, blacksmithing, and ropemaking, could sustain an unusually high proportion of local boys. For Joshua Hempstead, who had grown up watching sturdy sloops materialize in Coit's yard next door, training to be a shipwright was second nature.[10]

Shipwrights like Mitchell sometimes received a commission to build an entire vessel from start to finish in their own yards, but they also took on piecework in other yards, completing one portion of a ship to satisfy an order or to fill in lag time between larger projects. Daily life for an apprentice like Joshua meant dividing his time between various yards, including Mitchell's; working alongside masters, midlevel journeymen, and other apprentices; and carrying his tools on his back as he moved from job to job. As part of his training, Joshua also learned elementary account keeping and the closely guarded lore of ship design. A novice in the yard, Joshua performed basic ship carpentry—sawing planks, drilling tunnels, squaring and shaping timber with his adze—the archetypal shipwright's tool that was difficult and treacherous to master.[11]

Shipbuilding could be exciting and dramatic work. Among all the wood arts, it reigned supreme. Men turned long flat planks and crooked irregulars into wondrous, floating crafts that bore great weight—things of beauty and compact engines of commerce. In England, the shipwright was unquestionably a first among equals in woodcraft, the holder of unmatched technical and design capability and acknowledged as such. But in provincial New England, shipwrights were less able to distinguish themselves from other woodworkers, lacking sufficient numbers and the protective barriers of guilds. Still, shipbuilding on both sides of the Atlantic was the most industrial premodern enterprise, its "mechanics" among the most technologically advanced of the day. Once a master shipwright, Joshua would be able to do the extraordinary—fashion ships from board—but he could also apply that training to a wide range of ordinary woodwork like erecting fences, framing houses, making furniture, and building coffins.[12]

Entering the company of shipwrights, a boy like Joshua Hempstead stood in the forefront of the technical use of wood, but he also drew on the broader, all-pervading wood culture of New England. Immigrants like his grandfather Robert had arrived in the colonies accustomed to a small, deforested island where wood was scarce. They greeted New England's enormous stands of native trees and sheer mass of "unimproved" land with astonished wonder. Wood and its abundance suffused the New England experience, surrounding everyday life with not just trees and timber but wooden buildings, furniture, and tools. That abundance permitted a profusion of woodcrafts and ingrained local knowledge of trees and timber. To become a shipwright, a boy needed to acquire this subtle understanding of the wooden world around him. For Joshua, a lifetime in woodcraft began at the side of a wheelwright father. By the time his father died, ten-year-old Joshua would already have been intimately familiar with his work, having watched and helped Joshua senior make the wheels, carts, and carriages that constituted the wheelwright's trade.[13]

There were special advantages to learning from a wheelwright, for his trade was not just any woodcraft. Fixed on function rather than style, wheelwrighting conveyed ancient understandings of wood and method, knowledge not easily calibrated. A wheelwright's son learned early to recognize wood's properties by simply viewing trees where they grew—the soil, site, and slant speaking volumes about what lay underneath the bark. In the trunks of trees, Joshua would have begun to see the wood within, and even the nascent beams, joints, posts, shingles, forks, and axles that wood could become. In the shop, a wheelwright's son also studied the lessons of an exacting trade that required wood to curve, bear weight, and endure stress at the same time. From generation to generation, the careful traditions were passed down—how to angle a spoke, how to profile an axle— methods based on intuitive perception gleaned through experience rather than numerical principles. All this Joshua Hempstead brought with him to Mitchell's yard, even as a boy.[14]

MASTER THOMAS MITCHELL'S tutelage in wood proved a worthy education, but it was not the only one Joshua Hempstead received. Although most New Englanders were not cultured or learned by the standards of a European capital, they were a highly literate population in the early modern world. During Joshua's generation, New England colonists achieved adult male literacy of around 90 percent—a rate that would be sharply reduced, however, if it included women. New Englanders cultivated a traditional form of literacy that emphasized reading over writing and relied on the memorization of certain texts—often scriptural or religious passages—to learn to read. Literacy encompassed a range of skill sets from only being able to read some print to signing one's name, or perhaps even to writing sophisticated prose.[15]

Above all, learning to read began with listening. Joshua's first lessons were likely his father reading from the Bible and his minister preaching from the pulpit. He would have continued to learn by memorizing and presenting short texts and catechisms within the family. Beyond home-taught literacy and "reckoning," his mother and father likely supplemented his education with part-time schooling, as did other New England parents. Such school would have consisted of regular visits to, or even a short-term residence at, the home of a local schoolmaster or female schoolteacher, where a boy could increase his proficiency at reading, writing, and mathematical "ciphering." By the time he arrived at Mitchell's, Joshua would have been well on his way to attaining a credible mastery over basic words and numbers.

If middling boys like Joshua could expect to learn to read and write, and even attend school, their experience contrasted with that of their African peers. An enslaved youth like John Jackson was unlikely to acquire foundational skills in reading and writing, although a non-English indentured servant might achieve some competence. Most people who could not write at all "signed" documents simply with an *X* as their "mark." Jackson himself probably could not write, but when he entered agreements he sometimes signed with a more distinctive symbol, a circle or letter *O*, displaying perhaps a greater awareness of the written word. A New London woman called Sarah, an indentured "mustee" servant, showed a lesser degree of English literacy when she signed with an arrow-shaped mark: >—a distinctive riff on English lettering that she may or may not have intended to evoke her Algonquin heritage. In their proficiencies, Jackson and Sarah did not fall outside the mainstream of servile and female New Englanders. Joshua Hempstead's mother, Elizabeth, appeared only slightly more adept at writing than John Jackson, for example, with her *H* demonstrating some grasp of letters. By contrast, the "mulatto" Adam Rogers (servant to James Rogers, Sr.) easily outshone Elizabeth Hempstead Edgecombe with his ability to write and even embellish a well-formed signature with a certain calligraphic flourish. For "mulatto" Adam, both his status as a male indentured servant and his mixed background (or covert Rogers lineage) had given him the opportunity to learn to read and write well.[16]

Receiving a basic foundation in literacy at home and at Mitchell's, Joshua Hempstead quickly moved past the norm. From an early age he showed a penchant for writing and even a desire to preserve what he penned—for his words to matter. His first surviving writings are pages of a notebook from his seventeenth year at the tail end of his apprenticeship. The notebook itself provides a remarkable peek into the life of a teenage apprentice, but its very existence—at a time when Joshua had no father to preserve his work and no natal home of his own—affirms a strong desire to serve as a historical eyewitness. Glimpsed through the lens of these pages, the novice shipwright emerges, head in his papers, quill in hand, taking notes, and working out knotty questions of arithmetic and commerce—eager to become an able craftsman and trader.

On their face, the pages of Joshua's notebook reveal little about his inner life. A good deal of the book is taken up with exercises in the typical mathematical fare of a junior tradesman. Mitchell assigned Joshua quantitative riddles that reflected real-world application over abstract principles: "Four men . . . sent a venture to sea of 60 hogsheads: ye one [had] a 3th, other a 4th, ye other a 5th, ye other a 6th. I desire to know each man's proportion." On other pages, Joshua charted with words the tools that filled his shipyard hours: broadaxes, gimlets, gouges, chisels, and planes.[17]

In between, however, there was time for distractions, leisure enough to indulge in the characteristic contemplations of youth. When he was not engrossed in his work, Joshua doodled from nature or imagination in his notebook; he copied poems from friends or periodicals circulating around town. The names peopling Joshua's world appeared in its pages like unexpected guests: "John," "Benjamin," "Christopher," "Jonathan." The apprentice wrote them again and again, even flirted with other signatures next to his own. (The "John" was likely his friend, fellow shipwright, and lifelong neighbor, John Coit.) All together the notebook gives an amiable, if sparse, account of apprentice life.[18]

To be a craftsman "brought up in learning" was a solid, useful foundation, but it was also a limited kind of education. Joshua would be invaluable in the shop and yard, but he would never enter a professional class. He would not attend college, would not be a clergyman, and would never join the other occupations that were just beginning to professionalize. Many physicians and most members of the bar still received their training through apprenticeships rather than formal education, but these elevated professions were nonetheless beyond the reach of the orphaned, wheelwright's son.

A shipwright "brought up in learning" could nevertheless become scholar enough to develop a love and command of words, apart from his mastery of wood. Joshua's apprentice notebook was probably the first small channel for his impulse to write. Before long, no notebook or accounting would satisfy him, and Joshua Hempstead would begin the first entries of a full-fledged chronicle.

As Joshua Hempstead embarked on his apprenticeship in shipwrighting, a boy of about the same age named John Livingston was being groomed for a different kind of future. For him, there would be no period of service. John was the eldest son of the Scotsman Robert Livingston, the patroon and proprietor of Livingston Manor, who had grown up in Rotterdam and come to New York to make his fortune. John was destined to know only one side of servitude, as an owner and master. Childhood training was designed to prepare Livingston not for a life in the shop or yard, but for leadership and nearly limitless prospects in colonial trade, politics, and possessions.[19]

John Livingston—"Johannes" to his mother, Alida—had been born with a silver spoon in his mouth. Or, more pertinently, a fork. As early as the 1690s, at a time when most children in the colonies took their food from the end of a spearing knife or perhaps a spoon, and eating forks were a rare luxury, young Livingstons were accustomed to using a full set of silver cutlery. John and his seven siblings inhabited the highest reaches of Anglo-Dutch colonial society. He grew up fluent in both Dutch and English, donning ruffles and lace, closing his jackets with silver buttons, and combing his hair with ivory. As a youth, he received instruction in merchant accounting and law. He also had the run of the manor library, a collection of classical and contemporary texts that emphasized histories, including works by Plutarch, Livy, and Tacitus, though his meager academic accomplishments suggest that he made little use of it.[20]

Like Joshua Hempstead, John was ready to begin a period of independent instruction as he approached his tenth year. At that time, however, his Albany surroundings were in turmoil, caught in the wake of the Glorious Revolution of 1688, when the Catholic James II was deposed and the Protestants William and Mary ascended to the English throne in his place. King James had been deeply unpopular with religious nonconformists on both sides of the Atlantic, but for New Yorkers and New Englanders his colonial policy and aggressive reassertion of imperial power was nearly as offensive as his Catholic faith. James's consolidation of colonial adminstration from Maine to New Jersey under the much-resented Dominion of New England outraged many colonists. The Dominion trampled on treasured colonial laws and custom in its promotion of the Church of England and its dismantling of legal codes, colonial assemblies, and other institutions of representative government.

Some New England leaders, including the brothers Wait and Fitz Winthrop, had stomached service on the Dominion's governing council, despite their deep reservations. Other, more opportunistic politicians, including Massachusetts' Joseph Dudley, followed their individual self-interest by allowing themselves to blow with the prevailing political winds, a perceived betrayal that was duly noted by many of their fellow colonists.

The subsequent regime change in London created a dangerous power vacuum on the American side of the Atlantic. Even after James II was gone, most of his officeholders remained in place in the colonies, given the inevitable communication, administrative, and manpower delays—some would eventually even secure reappointment by William III. These officials provided irresistible sitting targets for colonists' pent-up anger. By April 1689, for example, the inhabitants of Boston took to the streets in open revolt against Sir Edmund Andros, the royal governor who presided over the reviled dominion and was its most visible symbol in the colonies. Boston's predominion political elite, with Wait Winthrop in prominence, seized the opportunity to take the reins of power, holding Andros captive until he managed to flee to England (though not before he reportedly made a failed and ignominious attempt to escape disguised in women's clothes). Wait's political rival Joseph Dudley, who had briefly and enthusiastically served as the Dominion's governor, followed Andros into self-imposed exile in England.[21]

Repercussions in John Livingston's home colony of New York were even more dramatic than the overthrow in Massachusetts. While most New Yorkers favored William and Mary's ascension, two factions emerged with different ideas about how and when the transfer of administration should take place. The first, made up largely of lower- and middle-class artisans, shopkeepers, farmers, and workers, favored the immediate ouster of James II's officials, including Andros's lieutenant governor, Francis Nicholson. A second powerful faction, concentrated in the Hudson Valley around Albany, drew support from the moneyed and titled patroon and mercantile class (many of whom held official positions). This patrician party—in which Robert Livingston and his wife's brother Peter Schuyler played leading roles—feared a popular uprising and favored a regular transfer of power through new appointments from London or simply the retention of old ones, a process that would certainly take many months.

When news of the Boston revolt spread through New York, a grassroots movement to remove the previous royal administration took hold among the colony's populist faction. When the resistance reached Manhattan, it escalated into armed rebellion by the militia, with Capt. Jacob Leisler at its head. By June 1689, Nicholson, like Andros, had fled to England, and Leisler had seized control of most of the colony, assuming Nicholson's title of lieutenant governor for himself in the belief that his authority was sanctioned by the new monarchs. Bolstered by its alliance with the Iroquois, however, the garrison town of Albany remained firmly in the patrician camp and refused to submit to Leislerian rule.[22]

As New York grappled with Leisler's rebellion, the Nine Years' War—"King William's War" in the American theater—erupted in Europe. In New York, this imperial war began as a series of menacing raids and counterraids in the northern reaches of the colony between the French and English, along with their respective Native American allies. The war increased Albany's isolation and sense of vulnerability, and a massacre at the English frontier settlement of Schenectady in February 1690, in which most inhabitants were killed or captured, brought the city to the brink. The following month Robert Livingston left Alida and their children for Hartford and Boston, commissioned by Albany (still a renegade city in the now-Leislerian colony of New York) to seek New England financial and military support for a unilateral assault against the French. Both colonies rejected his appeals, however, and as he anticipated his empty-handed return, he learned that Albany had finally submitted to Leisler's rule and joined a unified defense against French Canada. Having finally gained control of Albany, Leislerian officials sought retribution against its leaders: A charge of treason against Robert soon followed.[23]

Facing a capital charge, Robert decided to remain exiled in Connecticut, spending time in both Hartford and New London, where he stayed in the home of his old acquaintance Fitz Winthrop—then general of the Connecticut militia. When New York and New England finally agreed on a major joint offensive against Canada, Robert used his channels of influence to have Fitz named commander of a ground force to assault Montreal. Fitz repaid the favor by bringing Robert back to Albany under his military protection to be reunited with his family. When Fitz led his troops north from Albany in July 1690, Robert returned to Connecticut, this time arranging for Alida and the children to join him.[24]

Like the concurrent naval assault on Quebec, Fitz's ground expedition on Montreal ended in failure—in Fitz's case in a humilating retreat brought on by widespread disease and supply shortages. (The war dragged on after that, to reach only a short-lived peace between the French and English in 1697.) In the meantime, Robert Livingston bided his time with his family in Hartford, awaiting the arrival of New York's newly appointed royal governor, Henry Sloughter, and Leisler's certain downfall. Before March 1691 was out, Robert's hopes were realized: Sloughter arrived and Leisler surrendered. Robert and Alida immediately returned home to greet the new governor, so they were back in New York when Leisler was executed for treason that May.[25]

WHEN ROBERT and Alida traveled home in the spring of 1691, they left one member of the Livingston family behind in Connecticut. Their eldest son, John, would stay to follow a period of training during which he would not work with his hands or use tools, but would instead pursue a patrician version of the apprenticeship Joshua Hempstead was experiencing with shipwright Mitchell at the same time. The Livingston scion would live in the homes of other men to glean a bit of book learning and an even more important education in making social and political connections.

Robert asked Fitz Winthrop, who had returned home from his Canadian withdrawal, to watch over John and supervise his education. From his own time in Hartford, Robert may have chosen a tutor there for John himself, or perhaps he left that decision up to Winthrop. Though Fitz would not be John's guardian in any legal sense, formal and informal guardianships were common in early New England in the event of a father's death or absence. Such guardians, like masters, were substitute fathers who were expected to take their responsibilities seriously.

In setting up the arrangement for his son, Robert drew on a long family connection. The Presbyterian John Livingstone, Robert's clerical father, had corresponded with Fitz's grandfather, Massachusetts Bay founder John Winthrop, Sr., and contemplated a move to the Bay Colony. Nor would it have escaped the shrewd Robert that Fitz was a man with whom it was useful to foster bonds of friendship and reciprocity. Fitz had risen in stature in the years since he had returned from his English adventures of the 1660s. He was wealthy and powerful in both Connecticut and Massachusetts, despite his losses in Canada. As a Winthrop, too, Fitz traveled in New England's highest social circles, a milieu to which Robert wanted his son to become accustomed.[26]

John's time in Hartford did not go as his father had hoped, however. The tutor's lessons did not captivate the Livingston heir, and Hartford, though a colonial capital, was still a dull, distinctly provincial inland settlement—hardly the sort of place that would inspire a Livingston scion used to the relatively metropolitan streets of an Anglo-Dutch port like New York City. John's tutor may have simply given up, for the boy made little progress in his studies. By winter, John was expected back home, so Fitz brought the boy to New London to secure the child's passage.

Having been entrusted with the education and well-being of Robert Livingston's eldest son, Fitz was embarrassed when he found himself face-to-face with the boy's lack of advancement. Writing to Robert, Fitz admitted reluctantly, "I have also to tell you, to my sorrow, that [John's] improvement in his learning is not so much as I expected." Fitz blamed a careless teacher, but that was only part of the truth. In spite of his opportunities, the Livingston heir had little taste for study, and Fitz had unwisely left the boy and his tutor to their own devices—a neglect of his duty as guardian, however informal the arrangement. Once in New London, John lingered for months waiting for safe passage home with little more to do than read from the library, wander the dirt roads of the shabby town, and amuse himself amid the abundant fields and livestock. Young John cut quite a figure in 1690s New London in his flowered waistcoat, lace cravats, laced sleeves, blue velvet knee breeches, gold buttons, gloves, and fine red stockings. The contrast with local boys like Joshua Hempstead, walking the wharves in coarse homespun shirts and leather breeches, was striking.[27]

One bright spot in John's stay may have been Fitz's daughter, Mary, a pleasing child around his own age. Mary had little experience beyond New London, Hartford, and Boston, and she had lived a quiet life. She must have been slightly in awe of the exotic Dutch New Yorker who entered her world with talk of Manhattan and Livingston Manor. For his part, John was probably blithely unaware of the shadow hanging over Mary's lineage as the product of an irregular—even scandalous—union.

There was a serious blemish on Fitz Winthrop's good name that would have ruined most men. Irregular sexual relationships might be tolerated among the European aristocracy, but colonial New London was a long way from Paris or London. Fitz had reconciled himself to a provincial existence and his role as a dutiful civil servant, yet the outdoorsman and soldier had stopped short at complying with New England's parochial social conventions. Having refused his father's attempts to marry him off in England, Fitz eventually took up with a local girl, Elizabeth Tongue, the daughter of George Tongue, the proprietor of a popular New London tavern along the Bank. Fitz and Elizabeth lived together openly and out of wedlock for years, and although they may have married at some point after the death of Fitz's father, John Winthrop, Jr., Elizabeth's continued use of her maiden name suggests otherwise.[28]

Their relationship was unconventional, to say the least, but in deference to Fitz's father and family, most New Englanders kept their comments and disapproval to themselves. Few would have cared to undergo the collective existential ordeal of a Winthrop fornication trial. Given the persistence with which he tried to secure a shipmaster to bring John back to his parents, Mary's father, Fitz, probably felt more than a little relieved to send the boy on his way.

The episode in guardianship and education had been a dismal failure, and the best thing Fitz could say about it was that it was over. With the boy at long last out of sight, Winthrop could put the whole unfortunate episode out of his mind.

ALTHOUGH JOHN'S mother, Alida, was culturally Dutch and his father Robert a Scot, these Livingston parents aspired to have their sons become English gentlemen who could comport themselves according to the latest standards of civility. Among members of the extended Livingston family, England was even called "home." Not surprisingly, when John was fourteen and Robert needed to travel to London, he took the opportunity to bring his gentleman-in-training with him. The trip did not go as planned.[29]

Their London-bound ship, the *Charity*, lost its rudder in a mid-crossing storm and floated for four harrowing months in the Atlantic. On board, they made do with only "20 gallons [of water] for 25 souls," drinking daily rations of a pint of sour beer and a small pint of water until rain replenished their supplies. Food dwindled to "one half biscuit a day" along with a bit of salt meat, bacon, oatmeal, and peas, and whatever private stash individuals had managed to hide. After a big storm during which the ship took on water, the survivors frantically pumped and worked "to throw over board the fine beavers and peltries, . . . bear skins, elk skins, chamois skins, indigo, and cocoa, until at last they came to the ginger," six or seven thousand pounds of which rested in the gunner's cabin. Passengers and crew succumbed to the bitter cold and lack of sustenance only to "be thrown over board without being mourned." Near the end of four months John was sick, weak, and probably near death, when the ship landed miraculously on the Portuguese coast.[30]

Father and son took the overland route to Britain through Spain, riding mules, dining with dignitaries, and viewing Catholic sites while reviling the locals as "wicked, superstitious, poor, proud, beggarly people." This string of near-death experiences, followed by intense culture shock, might have driven other men to religion — but not the Livingstons. In his shipboard journal, Robert earnestly wrote how "I prayed for His grace to make me persevere therein and promised that I would pray three times a day and would try to lead a godly life." But the vows of future piety Robert made aboard the *Charity* fizzled quickly when he reached firm ground and resumed a life notable for its venality. (Even his own son-in-law, a fellow Scot with whom he had a good relationship, would one day lament that Robert's "exorbitant love of money should rob [him] of natural affection, reason, and religion.") Once the Livingstons finally arrived in the English capital, John had a brief interlude at "William Bridgeman's boarding school in Wood Street for 10 shillings a week," while his father appeared in gold lace before the Lords Justices, the Plantation Office, and New York's soon-to-be governor, Richard Coote, the Earl of Bellomont. Robert even found the time to take a walk in the countryside with his old friend Fitz Winthrop, who was visiting England at the same time.[31]

PRIVATE TUTORS and European tours formed the core of John's education, but a Livingston scion was sure to receive another kind of training, an "apprenticeship" in the art of mastery itself. From both his father and his mother, Alida, John learned the management of servants and slaves on a grand scale. Among the many objects, associations, and experiences that defined John as a member of a rarefied colonial elite was his family's relationship to its workforce at Livingston Manor, near Albany. With more than 160,000 acres, Robert and Alida Livingston relied on tenant farmers and a few African-orgin slaves (whom the Dutch had employed since the beginnings of New Netherland) to populate and develop the property.[32]

Livingston Manor was just one of a number of enormous land grants that New York bestowed on its entrepreneurial elite during the seventeenth and eighteenth centuries to encourage the settlement of vast hinterlands and prevent encroachment by land-hungry neighboring colonies. Included in these grants were forfeiture clauses designed to enforce settlement targets, and large proprietors or patroons like Robert Livingston seized on a tenancy model as the fastest way to populate the land—often with mixed results. But even among the major grantholders, the Livingstons managed to distinguish themselves through the ruthlessness of their tenancies. Robert and Alida first carved out farms that were too small to be profitable, then charged excessive rents so that tenants were sure to fall behind. If a failing tenant wanted to sell, the Livingstons were entitled to extract one-quarter of the tenant's improvements as well as the accumulated arrears. These coercive terms kept some tenants in a state of quasi serfdom on the manor. They also provided Robert's eldest son with a persuasive lesson in exploiting labor for personal gain.[33]

John and his siblings were also accustomed to seeing their parents buy, sell, and work bondsmen and -women on the manor. As a merchant, Robert had easy access to Manhattan shipments of enslaved people arriving from the West Indies and, occasionally, Africa. He could also make purchases around Albany from other slaveholding colonists. John grew up around his parents' slaves: the Jamaican-born bondsman who spoke English and had trained as a shepherd, whom Alida described as large and one of the most beautiful "Negroes" she had ever seen; the small, unseasoned boy from Africa who spoke "mostly Negro." John saw some sold away, probably even watched parents separated from children. In spite of their track record in unforgiving tenancies, however, the Livingstons did not have a local reputation for being especially harsh slave owners. Still, John's younger brother Gilbert, the family "black sheep" who later became an undistinguished New York assemblyman known for his lassitude and good looks, once beat a family slave to death—a "punishment" for running away. At the time of the assault, Alida Livingston tellingly expressed considerable regret at the financial loss of her chattel but appeared unperturbed that her son had committed a vicious murder.[34]

With at least eleven tenant families in residence in the mid-1690s, the number of tenants at Livingston Manor exceeded the number of bondsmen. Nevertheless the manor was still a relatively large slave enterprise by New England standards, with the number of bonded workers ranging from around nine to seventeen in the late seventeenth century. Like bondspeople throughout the Northeast, Livingston slaves performed agricultural labor, did important errands, and carried out much of their work without constant direct supervision. While small numbers of enslaved men in the northern colonies did become skilled artisans, they remained the exception. An estate like Livingston Manor, however, was large enough to deviate from regional patterns and allow for the use of slave labor in production beyond the ambit of farm and household, if only to a limited degree. For example, manor slaves ran and even supervised the operation of a gristmill, where they turned wheat into flour ready for export. Living arrangements also differed. Given their numbers, Livingston slaves lived mostly in outbuildings rather than at home with their owner's family, as was the norm in New England. Occasionally, the Livingstons even boarded their slaves with manor tenants, crediting the tenant family for related expenses.[35]

On the verge of manhood, John Livingston emerged from his "apprenticeship" in privilege a well-traveled, multilingual sophisticate. John's academic education had been spotty at best: a few rounds with various tutors, some time in a Manhattan mercantile house, but nothing in the way of higher learning. John nevertheless had all the superficial trappings of his station. He spoke and dressed well and could mingle easily with the cream of colonial society. To justify a sense of his own exalted place in the world, the eldest son of Robert Livingston needed only to survey the broad expanse of acreage, tenants, and slaves at Livingston Manor to find ready confirmation. When far from the manor, John could draw on his apparent inclination toward shallowness to nourish a lofty self-assessment. Still, he was not without ambition. With the patroonship in his back pocket, John hoped first to achieve some distinction in his own right before settling into a life of refined rusticity.[36]

Chapter Five

"FORNICATION AMONG YOU"

ALTHOUGH EARLY New England has become synonymous with upright behavior and sexual repression, in fact out-of-wedlock sex in the eighteenth century was not rare. Even though unwed sex was an undeniable transgression, New England law and culture provided a variety of opportunities for redemption, including marriage, punishment, and public confession before one's congregation. In practical terms, fornication usually became a matter of real public concern only after a woman became pregnant. For many couples a quick marriage solved the problem; those unwilling to marry, however, faced the possibility of criminal prosecution. Over the course of the eighteenth century, fornication became the most frequently prosecuted criminal offense in New England, although the trend may have had less to do with a desire to enforce morals than to provide child support for illegitimate children through court-ordered judgments. Unmarried sex took place in every echelon of society, as Fitz Winthrop's example makes clear, but its repercussions varied considerably depending on where one stood on the social scale or in the local political scheme.[1]

The yeoman shipwright Joshua Hempstead was never formally accused of fornication, but he may have indulged in the pleasures of the flesh before he wed his future bride, Abigail Bailey. Hers had been one of the names Joshua scrawled dreamily in his apprentice notebook: "Abigail; Abigail Bayley; Bayley; Abigail Bailey."[2]

Abigail came from Southold, Long Island, in the colony of New York, the eldest of five daughters of Stephen and Abigail Cooper Bailey. A maritime and shipbuilding community founded in the 1640s by New Haven Congregationalists, Southold had strong cultural and economic bonds to Connecticut Colony across the Sound, making it a natural place for a New London boy to look for a wife. Several families owned property in both towns, most notably the Beebe in-laws of John Rogers's sister Elizabeth. Long Islanders were a mix of English, Dutch, and Algonquin peoples—including the Montauk and Shinnecock native to the Hamptons, who suffered increasing displacement by Europeans. At the time of European settlement, much of colonial Long Island had come under Dutch authority. After England conquered New Netherland in 1664 and assumed control of the island a year later, the north end retained certain elements of Dutch culture, as was evidenced by the windmills scattered throughout the landscape. The three English towns of Southold, Southampton, and East Hampton were adamant in their cultural Englishness, however. Even when the Dutch reasserted their rule over New York for fifteen months in 1673, they chose instead to submit to Connecticut and British authority. An English daughter of Southold like Abigail was nevertheless accustomed to Dutch language, neighbors, and traditions, a familiarity she brought with her to her New London home—perhaps along with the Dutch Bible later found in the house.[3]

Abigail's father, Stephen, was a well-respected freeman and property-holder who held the post of overseer ("selectman" in Connecticut parlance) and served as Southold's town clerk for more than a decade. The Bailey house stood where the "town street" met the "road to the shipyards"; during Abigail's childhood it was filled with the sound of wheels spinning yarn, the stock-in-trade of unmarried girls. As the eldest of five sisters, Abigail would have been the first to learn to milk her mother's cow; the first to mend her father's shirts; the first to cook the family dinner: she was probably well prepared for marriage when a teenage shipwright's apprentice from across the

Sound came "a visiting" with an interest in courting her. Joshua may have known the Baileys through social or commercial connections; perhaps he had even met Abigail when they were children. As with most young couples, even across the Sound, visiting and courting provided ample opportunity to get to know each other better.[4]

Around her twentieth year, Abigail married Joshua Hempstead—probably in the hall of the Bailey house in Southold. With her father's blessing and provisioning, she would have embarked on a sailboat bound for Connecticut. On board with her might have been a first-rate milk cow, needed to establish her own dairy, and the rest of her marriage portion—an assortment of movable goods, as was the customary entitlement of a daughter of an upright family. That portion consisted of items necessary for a wife to establish her own household; at a minimum Abigail's had to include a bed, kitchenware, and a chest laden with clothes and linens, many of her own making. What she lacked Joshua might have provided, or they would work together to acquire over time. Abigail left behind four younger sisters: Temperance, Mary, Hannah, and Christian, each of whom married and established her own family on Long Island. As Abigail made her way across the water, the excitement of beginning her married life undoubtedly mingled with the usual concerns about assuming the roles and responsibilities of a wife and mother. She would always be a Bailey, but her approaching commitments would have loomed large as the New London shipyards—familiar to nearly any Southold girl—gradually emerged in the distance and the dark frame of the twenty-year-old house at Bream Cove came into view. Anticipating her transformation into a Hempstead wife, Abigail could not have imagined how old Bailey ties would remain vital to the very survival of the new family she was about to create.[5]

Joshua was around eighteen when he married Abigail. It was unusual for a man to marry before reaching his late twenties, when he was more apt to have sufficient means to support a family and household. Even less common was a man marrying before twenty-one, the age of majority. As his dead father's minor heir, however, Joshua could come into his inheritance—and with it, his autonomy—by marrying, prospects that would have been strong incentives to wed. The scribbling in his notebook, however, suggests that the union was not merely practical, and that Joshua hoped to find in Abigail his "partner soul," as another eighteenth-century New Londoner put it. Certainly the quick appearance of a first child—a boy called Joshua junior—after their unusually early marriage indicates that sexual attraction and even fornication between the young couple were not out of the question.[6]

If they did not engage in fornication themselves, Abigail and Joshua were surrounded by couples who had. Within a few years of their marriage, two of their close neighbors were charged with the crime. The newlyweds Susanna and Samuel Fosdick presented a typical case, easily convicted on the heels of Susanna's early pregnancy. Paying a modest fine, they left the court duly humbled, but able to rejoin the community without any lasting stigma. When a couple did not marry as the Fosdicks had, however, fornication and bastardy charges provided a social safety net for illegitimate children. Typically, courts first charged the mother, requiring her to name a father. Once she identified a father, courts could charge and convict him, holding him financially responsible for half of the child's maintenance until the youngster was old enough to be "put out" to service.[7]

Sometimes, however, accusations exposed marital dynamics in unpredictable ways. The tanner Thomas Truman and his wife, Susanna, were newlyweds who shared the old Truman house on Bream Cove, which Thomas's father, Joseph, had built after he settled in New London, within view of Joshua's front door. With Susanna already pregnant, the whole town suspected the Trumans of fornication, but Thomas felt wrongly judged. When a grand jury "presented" him for the crime, he met the charge with outraged denial. Susanna, he told the court, had been "with child by fornication [with another] at the time of his marriage to her." He was certain of this, never having had "carnal knowledge of her" before becoming her husband. In an unusual act of public retaliation, Thomas took matters into his own hands and lodged a formal complaint against his wife, perhaps hoping to avoid supporting the child himself. Fornication charges typically arose through local grand jury presentments that tinged criminal accusation with community reproach. A distressed groom prosecuting his wife for having sex with another man before marriage was quite a novelty.[8]

In court, two Truman sisters-in-law testified to having heard Thomas confront Susanna about her pregnancy, reportedly declaring, "I pity you with all my soul and am sorry that you are no more sensible of ye condition you have under yourself and me too."[9]

Susanna made no reply, so Thomas persisted: "Tell me; I shall not like you a bit the better for the denying of it . . . I am as likely to believe you as another."[10]

The admission one sister-in-law finally heard Susanna give was as brazen as it was dubious. The father, she claimed, was "a man at New Haven." She had forgotten his name and, not inconveniently, he "was dead now."[11]

Like many such cases, the Trumans' predicament drew in family members and neighbors. Just across the highway lived William Holt, whom both the Hempsteads and the Trumans considered an immediate or near neighbor. When Holt first heard that Thomas intended to marry Susanna, he felt obliged to question her himself, believing she was already pregnant. The emboldened Holt challenged "whether it was Thomas Truman's." He was dismayed by Susanna's audacious response: She would never reveal the father's identity and would probably marry Thomas anyway. The well-intentioned neighbor admonished her: "If [Thomas] was not the father of it, she could not expect much comfort with him." Susanna's matter-of-fact retort was that "she must do as well as she could." Making use of her unsuspecting bridegroom, Susanna had made a calculation that at once attempted to preserve her reputation and cover her sin, while securing a good home for herself and her child.[12]

Because families in early New England shared close and crowded quarters, couples like the Trumans and Hempsteads knew little real privacy. The fact that Thomas and Susanna Truman were in the company of others when they had their devastating conversation about the child's paternity was not surprising. One sister-in-law lived with them, and Thomas's sister visited regularly and freely, just as the Hempstead sisters did next door. A variety of family combinations, including widows and grown children, fathers and sons, and adult siblings like the Trumans often shared homes that received regular visits from still more relatives. Neighbors—especially those close by or hired as help—enjoyed largely unfettered access to a house and its occupants. New Englanders actually expected close neighbors to be conversant with the goings-on in the homes around them, a familiarity that led William Holt to comment directly and knowledgably on the Trumans, even to sit in judgment over them.[13]

As in any early modern Western society, men in New England held formal legal, political, and economic dominion over women. Colonial women like Susanna Truman and Abigail Hempstead could not vote or hold office, and they were more likely to be illiterate than men. Unless widowed, women could own personal property only through fathers, husbands, brothers, or guardians. In prescriptive literature and the law, colonial men like Thomas Truman and Joshua Hempstead were indeed the masters of the family and the household. By contrast, a lone woman, widowed or unmarried, was an inherently suspect figure—particularly vulnerable to charges of immorality, or even witchcraft. Despite such hard-cast images of a male-dominated society, however, a lack of civic power did not prevent women from exerting considerable influence over homes and families, even across the interconnected worlds of neighborhood, local exchange, and church. Husbands like Thomas and Joshua ostensibly dominated, but in reality wives could hold considerable sway, as Susanna's defiant stance—in combination with her certain guilt—suggests.[14]

The Trumans' fornication case exposed cracks in the veneer of men's supremacy. By seeking redress in court, Thomas subjected Susanna to public scrutiny and reprimand. Even in the male domain of court, however, she refused to play the contrite reprobate and instead proved her real mettle by challenging the legal underpinning of his accusation on its own terms. In a document inscribed "wife against husband," written on her behalf by an unidentified counselor, Susanna defended herself by arguing that Thomas lacked legal standing to prosecute her. Man and wife were one entity under the common law, she explained, and a complainant could not bring an action against himself. The argument was as clever as it was compelling. Using the very restrictions the law imposed on women to construct her defense, Susanna, with unseen help, turned the patriarchal legal scheme on its head. She dodged prosecution and then, perhaps most tellingly, went on to have a long and uneventful marriage to Thomas Truman in spite of this initial betrayal. Indeed, early charges of fornication, even under the worst of circumstances, were not necessarily an obstacle to a peaceful and prosperous family life.[15]

SUSANNA'S GROWING belly had prevented the Trumans from avoiding a fornication charge, but other New Londoners, including perhaps Joshua and Abigail Hempstead, had better luck or were simply quicker to take action. John Livingston, the heir to New York's Livingston Manor, was also never formally accused of fornication. But while Joshua Hempstead might have slept with his future wife on the road to an early marriage, Livingston pursued dubious relationships as a matter of course. By the time he returned to New London at the turn of the eighteenth century, Livingston already had at least one sexual exploit under his belt—a first rehearsal in playing the rake. At just seventeen, he had caused his parents considerable hand-wringing when, according to his mother, he pursued a woman "who is 28 years old and has a mouth as if she followed the army all her life." Even though John insisted to his parents that "he would not be so crazy as to throw himself away"—not exactly a refutation— Albany gossips seemed convinced that the rumors were true. Robert and Alida acted quickly and managed to reel in their teenage son enough to keep the scandal under wraps. At the same time, John Livingston had already proved himself willing to take risks for love, and even to lie about it.[16]

After this amorous encounter, it did not take long for the Livingston heir to become embroiled in another, far riskier sexual intrigue. By the late 1690s, John had returned from his trip to England and begun to work for his merchant father in the Port of New York. Around this time he again visited New London—the site of his failed venture in schooling as a boy—as a guest of the Winthrop family. At this point, the town seemed a most unlikely locale for the Livingston heir. Beguiled by the drawing rooms of New York, Boston, and London, and destined for a manorial seat, he would never have considered staying in this mean, provincial backwater, had it not been for a girl. Since John's last visit, his former guardian, Fitz Winthrop, had become governor (in 1698) and was engrossed in public affairs, traveling frequently between Hartford, New Haven, and New London. He was so preoccupied with his work, in fact, that during Livingston's stay he failed to notice that his former ward and his daughter, Mary, were falling hopelessly in love under his very nose.[17]

Only when John presented his plan to wed Mary Winthrop as a fait accompli to Fitz and his own parents did their full-blown romance come finally to light. The liaison was not simply bad form, it was also a crime. Suitors who courted girls toward marriage without informing her parents could face criminal sanctions and a fine of five pounds. Nonetheless, many fathers, once they recovered from the shock, might have been thrilled at the pairing—Livingston was expected to become a very wealthy man, and his family, if not always well liked, was certainly well connected and powerful. By most accounts, Mary Winthrop, the illegitimate granddaughter of a Connecticut innkeeper (her Tongue grandfather) could have anticipated a much lesser match—even with a gubernatorial father and the Winthrop name. The long-standing political friendship between Fitz and Robert Livingston only appeared to affirm the alliance. But Fitz was taken aback when he discovered John Livingston's designs on his only child, and he immediately opposed the union—a reaction that implied misgivings about Livingston's character. What may have disturbed Fitz most was that John Livingston had secretly taken the liaison with Mary to a point of no return—perhaps even to bed. As a result Fitz was boxed in, stripped of his paternal prerogative and authority. In Livingston's clandestine liberties the governor probably felt the sharp sting of personal betrayal.[18]

Fitz was not the only one to harbor serious reservations about the marriage. John's parents were also aghast, though for quite different reasons: Robert and Alida's alarm centered around Mary Winthrop's legitimacy. The "bastard" daughter of a common-law marriage, even that of a colonial governor, was not the sort of partner they had envisioned for the future owner of Livingston Manor. Mary may have been sweet and even lovely, but she was surely no match for the style and refinement of New York or Boston girls, given her obscure provincial upbringing. When Robert and Alida grilled their son about the Winthrops' marital status, he responded with an earnest, if comically inaccurate, report that he had made inquiries and found the governor and his concubine to be duly married, assuring Mary's legitimacy. His account was either ignorant or intentionally specious.[19]

If Livingston is to be believed, the false information came directly from Fitz's friend and minister, Gurdon Saltonstall, who had attested "that [the Winthrops] were as certainly married as God was in heaven and that all ye People here knows it as well as he so that there was no scruple of any such thing here among ye people for they know better." Saltonstall's exaggerated protestations were curious in the face of common knowledge that Fitz Winthrop and Elizabeth Tongue were most certainly not married at the time of Mary's birth. (They may have married when Mary was six, after the death of her grandfather, John Winthrop, Jr.—or perhaps her parents simply maintained a common-law union.) But the town minister had his own reasons for corroborating the moral credentials of his most prominent parishioner. By the time of John Livingston's amorous sojourn in New London, Saltonstall had come to rely on Fitz's support against his enemies in town, John Rogers chief among them. On the eve of Fitz's return from a trip to England in 1697, for instance, the town clerk had written excitedly that his coming would "dispel and scatter those clouds of darkness which some persons of evil principles and mortal enemies to our worthy Minister, have late been endeavoring and contriving . . . your happy arrival will rejoice him and make him twenty years younger." (Soon after Fitz returned, Rogers continued his harassment of Saltonstall nonetheless, spreading rumors around New London that the minister was afraid to debate him publicly.)[20]

In any case, third- and fourth-hand versions of the truth were not enough for Robert Livingston. His son had already pursued a relationship with Mary Winthrop to an unseemly degree by the time Robert sent an emissary to New London to parley directly with Fitz. The man he chose was a fellow Scot and Boston postmaster-bookseller named Duncan Campbell, who traveled to New London to make inquiries around town about Mary's legitimacy. New Londoners appeared willing to vouch for the Winthrop marriage to Campbell, although some admitted that the nuptials had not been public. Satisfied, Campbell visited with Fitz at his mansion on the neck and discussed the marriage prospects, treading softly but unmistakably around the governor's plans for his estate. Even the possibility of Mary's illegitimacy might be smoothed over by a fine settlement in her favor. The Livingstons' concerns were eased when Campbell cheerfully confirmed Fitz's intentions to provide well for his only child.[21]

In the meantime, John Livingston cast the situation in the best possible light to his parents. His was simply a tale of true love, young and pure, and he wrote to them, pressing his desire to marry: "I would rather choose to die than to leave her, for she is ye only one in all the world to me." Breathlessly he pleaded, "It can hardly be recalled without trouble and vexation and sorrow on both sides which we should think very hard for to be parted asunder, for it would certainly break both our hearts."[22]

They were pretty words, but behind them Livingston had shown a careless, even destructive streak. Beyond questions of personal happiness the choice of a wife was a key decision for any man, and one that would significantly impact his ability to fill the important roles of husband, father, and head of household. For a man of Livingston's status, marriage also represented a critical social and economic alliance that few men could afford to squander. John Livingston's approach to this pivotal decision had been impulsive and ill considered at best, and it had serious implications for his future.

Secret courtship had given John and Mary a bumpy start, but both sets of parents soon relented, their initial reservations eased by mutual assurances of a sizable inheritance. With their families' blessings, John and Mary Livingston wed in 1701, and the future for the worldly son of the New York patroon and the agreeable daughter of the Connecticut governor still looked bright. In spite of the irregularities, observers regarded the union "a happy match"—a colonial power couple who united two leading families.[23]

Although John and Mary Livingston had different upbringings

and backgrounds, the pair still had much in common. Raised in privilege, they shared a vision of a joint domestic future that included a
large house, property, servants, and children. Neither identified with
a conservative religious camp. John was raised Dutch Reformed, but
religion played only a perfunctory role in his life. Many in Mary's
Winthrop clan, once the keepers of Puritan Congregational ideals,
were moving toward an embrace of the Anglican Church—the very
faith their forebears had left behind. Livingston himself appeared
to give religion little thought, but he was joining a distinctly anti-
Rogerene faction in New London when he married Mary Winthrop.
Even though he personally had no bone to pick with John Rogers, he
would be no friend to him.[24]

Among those who celebrated the Livingston marriage were
John's sister Margaret and her husband, Samuel Vetch. A newlywed
herself who had settled in Boston, Margaret took a keen interest in
her brother and his domestic affairs. John Livingston and Samuel
Vetch got along well—both were men who preferred action to words.
Vetch was an unusual character by New England standards, and one
Livingston must have found compelling. A buccaneering Scot with
an uncanny ability to reinvent himself, Vetch in his early thirties
had already experienced a lifetime of adventure, much of it grueling.
Born to an itinerant and persecuted Scottish clergyman who lived
under a penalty of banishment during the reign of Charles II, Vetch
spent much of his childhood as a fugitive in Scotland and the north
of England. He took refuge in Holland at fifteen with his father and
his brother William. In 1688, James II granted toleration to Scottish
Presbyterians, and the senior Vetch returned to his pastoral career in
Scotland. With their father gone, the Vetch boys abandoned university studies at Utrecht for the martial life, electing to fight with William of Orange's Protestant army in Scotland and the Netherlands.[25]

In 1698 Samuel embarked on a new adventure as an officer in the
disastrous Darien expedition, a patriotic attempt by the Company of
Scotland to establish the trading colony of Caledonia on the isthmus
between North and South America. After leaving Edinburgh with
the overwhelming support of the Scottish people, the Darien settlers, including two of Robert Livingston's own brothers, quickly

collapsed under the weight of internal dissension, disease, and lack of provisions. Most of the enterprisers died of sickness and starvation in the colony, but a few managed to escape by boarding ships for North America.[26]

Vetch arrived in New York on a ship also called *Caledonia* in August 1699, nearly dead with hunger and fever. By the spring of 1700, however, he was apparently healthy and financially on his feet again, probably having helped himself to proceeds from the *Caledonia*'s cargo. Playing up his Scots-Darien connection and a remote family tie with Robert Livingston, he married Margaret Livingston before the year was out. It was quite a rise for this ambitious son of an itinerant Scots cleric.[27]

Deciding to make his life in America, Samuel Vetch hoped to build a fortune and felt well on his way with an alliance to the Livingston family. John Livingston, moreover, thought enough of his brother-in-law to go into business with him. Shortly after his own wedding to Mary Winthrop, John appealed to his father and father-in-law for financial support to set himself up in partnership with Vetch and a Boston merchant, John Saffin, to establish themselves in the coastal and West Indian trade. It would be the first of many requests for help, and both fathers agreed; the marriage was still fresh, hopes were high, and relations good.[28]

As John Livingston pursued his ventures with Vetch, he and Mary also set up house in New London's North Parish on a huge parcel of several thousand acres, the New Yorker's share of a special land grant he held with several partners. The property was not far from the Fox farm, home to Samuel and Bathshua—and to their slave, Joan. It was in the heart of ancestral Mohegan territory, a portion of which remained in perpetual trust for the use and habitation of tribal members, assuring that the Livingstons would live in close proximity to Mohegan and other local Algonquin. On and off the dirt paths and roads of the North Parish, wigwams were a frequent sight. Striking out in the backwoods of Connecticut, John Livingston had extravagant hopes of replicating the manor of his youth on a smaller scale, "to make a fine country seat."[29]

He would follow his parents' example in other ways as well,

employing indentured and bonded servants of all stripes to a degree unusual for New England. Like most of his North Parish neighbors, he drew on the local Native population, especially Mohegan, to perform a range of tasks and errands. He called on Indians to deliver his letters to New York and once, "under a harsh medicine of [his] own invention," he had two Algonquin servants use hollowed animal horns to "suck out ye blood and ugly water which is settled [at his knees and ankles]" to treat chronic gout. For work on the farm, however, he would need the labor of African and English servants and slaves. At home, most New Englanders employed hired girls or perhaps owned a female slave to help with women's domestic work, but the Livingstons required more labor due to the size and comparatively high living standard of their household. Aside from employing female servants to clean, cook, and do laundry, gentlewomen in the family were accustomed to have a slave girl as a maidservant occupied exclusively with their toilet and personal belongings. Livingston men might also have had boys or men who served as valets.[30]

As the Livingstons moved into their mansion house at the North Parish property, everything seemed in place for a grand future. They had youth, property, and opportunity at their disposal—even the hard-earned good wishes of family members. Still, these many advantages seemed to hang around their shoulders as a yoke, driving John toward ever-more-grandiose and imprudent schemes. John wanted at a minimum to maintain his position in the world, but he was inclined to shortcuts and gambling to achieve that aim. New London's glittering couple also bore the taint of their rash and illicit romance amid a narrow social world with a long collective memory. John Livingston would face new challenges and responsibilities as he assumed the roles of husband and proprietor, but his methods were risky. If he failed, the same impulses that had drawn him into a perilous and self-centered liasion with Mary might easily drive him elsewhere.

MEN LIKE Fitz Winthrop, John Livingston, and even Joshua Hempstead might succeed in escaping charges of fornication. Others could not. In 1701, the freed African, John Jackson, was charged with the crime, though ironically he might have been the only one of the four involved not to have committed it—at least not in the instance that brought him to court.

Jackson's African-ness certainly played a role in the accusation, but it had not made him especially vulnerable; in fact, male African servants were rarely charged with the ubiquitous crimes of fornication and bastardy. Any financial punishment such as child support would have fallen to a man's master, and courts and communities were generally not eager to punish masters unduly for the actions of their servants. If resulting children were born to enslaved mothers, as was often the case, there was also no need for child support through a fornication trial, because these children were the property of her master. But Jackson's case fell well outside any predictable norms. Simply having John Rogers as his master made John Jackson an attractive target for the authorities. One way to get at the old dissident and his purse was through his longtime servant.

Katherine Jones was the daughter of an established New London family of English origins. She was twenty-one in 1701 when she was called before the county court to answer charges of fornication and bastardy and identified Jackson as the father of her baby. Jackson was unmarried (or perhaps newly married) at the time of conception, for he became Joan's husband around the time of his prosecution for fornication. Like most men and women accused of similar crimes, Katherine and Jackson faced nearly certain conviction. Their case differed from the usual reflexive fornication trial in one important way, however: Katherine's was a "mulatto bastard child." At the trial Jackson claimed innocence, but he was convicted like most accused fathers, and received a standard punishment: The court ordered him to pay one-half the cost of supporting the infant—whose gender was never mentioned—for four years until the child could be put out to service in a family. As Jackson's master, John Rogers was responsible for making the payments, a fact that had not escaped the notice of the court. Katherine, too, received a routine punishment—the choice between a three-pound fine or fifteen lashes of the whip.[31]

Jackson may have been the father of Katherine's baby, but there is a good possibility he was simply an easy scapegoat. His fornication trial may have been one small skirmish in the long battle between the Rogerenes and the authorities—one price of his close association with Rogers. Certainly John Rogers himself favored this interpretation. He believed that the magistrates cared little about identifying the child's true father, but a great deal about the affluence and dissenting principles of the defendant's master. Rogers attended Jackson's trial and, upon hearing the court rule, launched into a loud diatribe against the bench, claiming that the case was a veiled attempt to "unjustly and illegally" seize his own estate through his servant.[32]

Katherine herself appeared to hold no identifiable grudge against Rogers or his beliefs; in fact, the Jones family was part of John Rogers's social and spiritual circle. They were neighbors, and some of them, including Katherine's own father, Thomas, were Rogerenes. Thomas Jones had even been a codefendant with Jackson and Rogers in their 1693 conviction for breaking the Congregational Sabbath. Perhaps the legal authorities had pressured Katherine to name Jackson as the father; clearly her lover had been of African origin, and the number of men she could plausibly implicate was tiny indeed.

In terms of local anti-Rogerene politics, 1701 was a good year to target John Rogers. His conflict with minister Saltonstall, in particular, had reached a fever pitch, culminating in the publication that same year of *An Impartial Relation of an Open and Publick Dispute Agreed upon Between Gurdon Saltonstall, Minister of the Town of New-London, and John Rogers of the Same Place*—a public airing of their doctrinal disagreements. One particular battleground that gives a flavor of the nasty and personal tenor of their quarrels concerned the wearing of wigs. Since the 1680s, it had become fashionable among men of high station, including some ministers, to wear long curly periwigs that fell below the shoulder. Not everyone approved of the trend, however, many regarding wigs as pernicious markers of status and vanity.[33]

John Rogers believed that wig wearing actually violated scripture, an opinion that was shared by many conservative Congregationalists, including the Boston diarist Samuel Sewall, who loathed the new fashion. Salem's Congregational minister, Nicholas Noyes, who, like both Sewall and Wait Winthrop, had been a leading magistrate during the infamous witch trials of 1692–93, even wrote an "Essay against Periwigs" in 1702, reviling their use. Not surprisingly, the imperious Saltonstall was fond of wearing a periwig nonetheless. Rogers would trail the minister around town, derisively asking him if he thought wigs were worn in heaven. If Saltonstall reacted with anger or discomfort, Rogers would reel with laughter. Rogers's coup de grâce was to "donate" an actual periwig as a gift to the ministry to shame Saltonstall for his pride in dress and haughtiness in manner. Public pressure ultimately led Rogers to apologize, his letter of confession even entering the town records, but Saltonstall never forgave the insult, and hostilities between the two men continued to be decidedly sharp.[34]

Jackson's 1701 prosecution for fornication might therefore have been an irresistible means of retribution against Rogers, but there was another important reason to suspect Jackson's innocence. Katherine herself could have had a compelling personal motive to advance a bogus case. An unwed mother, she might have been frantic to protect her true lover from public censure, economic loss, and family disapproval. Only seven months after Jackson's final court date, another possible father came to light when Katherine married the "mulatto" Adam Rogers—the former servant of James Rogers, Sr., and likely a Rogers by blood. Perhaps her parents had opposed the union and Katherine had accused Jackson to protect Adam Rogers, with whom she envisioned a future. If her stategy had been to end up with Adam, it proved successful. Perhaps family disapproval ebbed after they saw that Katherine would not give up, or maybe there had been another pregnancy. In fact, the mixed African and English couple of Adam and Katherine Rogers went on to have a long marriage and many children of their own. Katherine's first "bastard" child, however, may have met an early death, as its absence from town records suggests.[35]

Setting aside the reliability of Katherine's allegations, Jackson never faced criminal charges of assault or rape because the court did not question that the relationship between an African servant and an English maid was consensual. The court acknowledged the resulting child's African origins, and inherently lesser status, when it described the infant as "mulatto," but its dispassion toward the pairing points to a certain flexibility about social mixing during this early period of New England history. What was possible and readily acknowledged without comment in 1701 court records—a reciprocal relationship between a man like John Jackson and a woman like Katherine Jones—would become socially unacceptable and presumptively aberrant by the end of the colonial period.[36]

Even more revealing, perhaps, was how the children of Katherine and the "mulatto" Adam Rogers became fully integrated members of English communities in the years that followed, their African ancestry going unmentioned in public records. This was not an instance of "passing"—the origins of these Rogers children were no secret to anyone in New London County who cared to know. Their gradual, matter-of-fact blending into mainstream English society suggested instead that in the early years of the eighteenth century, racial origin was not the final determinant in deciding who was and who was not a real New Englander.[37]

Whatever their implications or accuracy, Katherine Jones's accusations of fornication may not have been foremost in Jackson's mind in the first years of the new century. Around the very same time, he was focused on another momentous change in his life: He was getting married. This marriage probably took place in a house at Mamacock in the first few years after 1700—around the same time he fought fornication charges—with John Rogers presiding over a humble ceremony. The young woman Jackson chose to marry—assuming he had a choice—was Joan, Maria's daughter.[38]

Becoming a free man through manumission, Jackson probably remained a servant of some sort—indentured servant, wage worker, or itinerant laborer—for the rest of his life. Freedom could not erase poverty or prejudice, nor did it create economic opportunities where there were none. But freedom did permit Jackson to marry as his own man and start an independent family—even if that family had to straddle slavery to survive.

At the turn of the eighteenth century, African servants and slaves like Joan and John Jackson had a very limited pool of potential partners, especially if they hoped to share their Rogerene leanings. Usually dispersed in English households, servants and slaves had to overcome their physical isolation to form bonds with men and women of similar background and experience. Joan and John Jackson must have seemed a natural fit, drawn together by circumstance, faith, and the Rogers family connection. She was a native New England girl and he a new arrival, but both were Rogers family servants used to living among Rogerenes. They had probably even known each other since Joan was a girl.

There was nothing unusual about slaves and servants marrying in and of itself—with their masters' approval. The master of an indentured servant might logically object to his charge taking on the responsibility of a family, but the owner of a slave might prefer for a bondsman or -woman to enter into a stable marriage rather than engage in fornication, and any resulting children, of course, would belong to an enslaved mother's owner. In general, marriages, including slave marriages, were recorded in civil registers—in town records and in the books of justices of the peace, who typically performed the rites. That the Jackson marriage is noticeably absent from public records supports the conclusion that theirs was a Rogerene ceremony. Without a magistrate to preside over and record them, Rogerene dissenting unions escaped the public record and the usual recording process. If John Rogers kept his own tally of marriages among the brethren, it did not survive. For Joan and John Jackson, marriage represented a lifelong commitment and the beginnings of a joint family, but it would not mean that they could live together as husband and wife. Joan was still a Fox slave, so she could not join her husband at Mamacock.[39]

By the time the Jacksons wed, slavery in England's North American colonies was no longer the improvised convention it had been in the earliest days of settlement. At the outset, slavery in New England and the Chesapeake had not been so different. Beginning in the 1640s, colonists in both regions had used bonded workers to supplement English servant labor. By the 1660s in the Chesapeake, however, mortality rates had fallen and cash crops like tobacco and cotton made using slaves in greater numbers economically advantageous. While enslaved Africans were a major economic and demographic force in the Chesapeake by the end of the seventeenth century, New England slaves remained a relatively small demographic factor, reaching only around 3 percent of the total regional population by the middle of the next century, when figures became available. But it was a population concentrated in urban centers and along the coast. In Connecticut, for example, about one-eighth of all slaves lived in either Fairfield or New London counties, reaching the high single digits as a percentage of population during the eighteenth century. Nearby Newport and Kings counties held three-quarters of African Rhode Islanders. In Newport alone, 20 percent of the city's residents had African origins. Already by 1701, African bondspeople had become a familiar part of everyday life, particularly in the region's ports. The Jacksons were a married African servant and slave living apart, but they were also an ordinary New England couple, well known and easily identifiable among their neighbors.[40]

Like any young couple starting out, Joan and John Jackson could imagine the children they would have together, although such ordinary daydreams were darkened by the realities of slavery that surrounded them. Sometime around 1701, Joan bore their first child, a son called Adam. Absent a marriage date, the possibility that the Jacksons committed fornication prior to, or even prompting, their marriage remains open. The name of their firstborn was an unusual choice. Although Calvinist New Englanders favored biblical names, they rarely used "Adam," from the Hebrew word for "man." Intriguingly, the only other Adam easily identifiable in contemporary New London records was the "mulatto" Adam Rogers, the onetime servant and possible relation of James Rogers, Sr. There was a ritual of naming the first man and woman brought on board a slave ship "Adam" and "Eve," but the reasons behind the unusual naming of these two African-origin boys from New London with close ties to the Rogers clan—if there were any—remain a mystery.[41]

With her infant, Joan continued to live enslaved at Samuel and Bathshua Fox's while her husband worked as a Mamacock servant. The couple could probably count on seeing each other at least once a week on the Saturday Sabbath; perhaps John Rogers also permitted

Jackson to go to his wife and child in his off-hours. Around 1702, the divided family grew again when Joan became a mother for the second time, delivering a girl called Miriam. Near in age, the eldest Jackson children may have formed a close brother-sister bond. Together they shared a common childhood, training for lifelong work, but also clambering up the steep hill to the Fox house or twirling sticks in the brook below. Adam and Miriam would ever be treasured Jackson children—but they were also Fox slaves.[42]

IF JOHN JACKSON did not escape accusations of fornication, his master seemed to have fallen under permanent suspicion of the crime after his wife, Elizabeth, divorced him in 1676; still, it took more than twenty-five years for the authorities to find credible evidence against him. Rogers had taken the divorce from Elizabeth extremely hard. He never truly recovered from the loss of either his wife or his children, and he categorically refused to acknowledge the divorce as binding—even after Elizabeth married Peter Pratt in 1679. In fact, seven years after the divorce became final, Rogers made a heart-rending plea to the General Court for the return of his two children after their unprecedented award to their mother, but it was denied. One year later, the same court added insult to injury when it granted Elizabeth and her father the right to put John junior out to apprentice, an order Rogers vociferously protested.[43]

As the years passed, John Rogers—if the Rogers family is to be believed—remained steadfastly alone, living the life of an ascetic for more than two decades. Certainly he kept himself busy: leading the Rogerenes, managing his properties, appearing in court, and serving in prison, while also presiding over a complicated household at Mamacock filled with Rogerses, Jacksons, and other servants and followers. But if Rogers wanted to pursue dalliances at home with servants or slaves as he might have done in his youth—perhaps even with Maria—the authorities would have had little control over him.[44]

By the 1690s, though, Rogers's domestic situation began to change. Remarkably, both of his children, John junior and Elizabeth, returned to him as young adults, settling not only into the home of their birth but also into their father's unorthodox faith. John Rogers, Jr., in particular, became his father's ardent defender and his heir apparent in leading the Rogerenes. It is no small testimony to the power of Rogers's persusasiveness that even his children's half brother, Peter Pratt, Jr.—a son of Rogers's divorced wife who had been raised to abhor Rogerene teachings—also became a fervent follower, to his parents' deep dismay. Later, however, Pratt reconsidered and publicly denounced Rogers.[45]

The third marriage of Rogers's ex-wife, Elizabeth, in 1694, after the death of her second husband, Pratt (who, John Rogers, Jr., later claimed, fell into a "great Horror" before his death realizing he had married another man's wife), proved a turning point for John Rogers. For years, he had periodically harassed Elizabeth and Pratt, verbally and vociferously asserting his spousal rights to her. But after nearly twenty years and two subsequent marriages for Elizabeth, Rogers began to believe that he could justify remarrying—even if he would never do it by Connecticut's rules. Perhaps his long incarceration in Hartford had changed him. Authorities had held him there on various charges for three years, along with his follower and then-servant William Wright (who had been convicted with Bathshua of the meetinghouse burning). During that time, John Rogers, Jr., had campaigned to free his father, publishing a pro-Rogers pamphlet and distributing it across the colony. The superior court finally ordered old Rogers freed in October 1697 with a promise of good behavior.[46]

Wright appeared at the same session, but when the judges demanded that the servant agree not to perform servile labor on the Sabbath, he refused. In response, the court banished poor Wright from the colony, sending him "out to one of His Majesty's remote territories as a dangerous disturber of the peace," much to the devastation of his wife, Hagar, and the three children they now shared. At Wright's sentencing, Rogers bellowed in protest, landing himself back in jail for contempt of court until the fines he had incurred were covered through confiscations.[47]

By the time Rogers made it back to Mamacock after this extended ordeal, few in his family or faith would have begrudged him a second chance at earthly happiness; his choice of partner would try their goodwill, however. Perhaps Rogers did not plan in advance to have a sexual relationship with the young servant girl from Old England whose passage he paid in exchange for her indenture in 1699, but the arrangement does rather suspiciously resemble the seventeenth-century version of a mail-order bride. Whatever his original intentions, Rogers, who was in his early fifties, began a liaison with the young woman once she arrived at Mamacock. For her part, the servant, Mary Ransford, embraced her master and lover John along with his dissident faith. In the eyes of the Connecticut authorities, of course, their relationship constituted illegal fornication. Rogers disagreed.[48]

Even in a household of oddballs and characters, Mary Ransford stood out. If John Rogers's first wife, Elizabeth Griswold, was the devout daughter of a fine family, his second consort was a spitfire known for using assumed names and dressing in men's clothing. Once she threatened to throw scalding water on the town collectors who came to collect the minister's rate. Another time she quarreled with a Mohegan woman who heaved a piece of bark in her eye to fend her off. Ransford was sour-tempered, belligerent, and prone to violence, and her presence at Mamacock caused more turmoil within the Rogers family. Family members and servants probably resented the loud and uppity servant girl who had suddenly become their mistress and seemed to have the old man wrapped around her little finger. But no one in the household disliked her more than John Rogers, Jr., who found the thought of Ransford taking his mother's place intolerable. The two fought frequently and openly—caustic battles that seemed to leave both sides eager for the next brawl.[49]

The matter of Mary Ransford came to a head one June day in 1699. By then, many New Londoners were used to seeing John Rogers striding the streets of his native town, yelling at the top of his lungs. On this day, however, Rogers had the unpopular Ransford in tow, and his message was new. He and Ransford, he howled, were man and wife from this day forward. Using scripture as his guide, Rogers had concluded that a public announcement in the town streets was sufficient rite: Certainly he had no intention of following Connecticut law, which had taken his first wife and children from him. The couple had other reasons for coming to town: Mary had been summoned to appear before the county court to make a public apology for threatening to scald the tax collectors, and Rogers took the opportunity to execute his peculiar method of marrying. As the strange and unseemly couple—decades apart in age—tromped loudly through New London declaring their marriage, Ransford was probably already pregnant with their first child, a boy named Gershom, who was born in January 1700.[50]

New babies can be disruptive to a household, but well before Gershom arrived in January, Mamacock was already a chaotic compound that contained Rogers, his children, Ransford, and John Jackson, along with assorted other family members, servants, and hangers-on. Home to a complex and fractious extended family, Mamacock was also the center of a dissenting and still-persecuted religious movement, a reality that brought with it not only the constant exertions of baptizing and burying, prophesying and preaching, but also arrests, confiscations, trials, whippings, and imprisonments.

Household complications multiplied when John Rogers, Jr., brought home his own bride the very January that Ransford gave birth. That bride was well known and beloved by the family. Bathshua Smith was her bridegroom's first cousin, the daughter of Old John's adored sister, Bathshua Fox, from her first marriage. The girl was a familiar figure to the Jacksons as well, having lived around Joan since earliest childhood. It is hard to picture how Ransford and the young Bathshua shared the hearth, making small talk as they stoked the fire, when John junior could barely stand the sight of his "stepmother." The degree of their animosity was once captured in court testimony, when witnesses watched in amazement as Ransford railed against her "stepson," hurling "many wicked and notorious words, calling him son of a devil and son of a whore son of a bitch [and threatening to kill him] . . . though her neck stretched for it, she has but one life to live and would willingly lose that to be revenged on him." Even on the best of days, the household at Mamacock must have bristled with tension, with conflicts waiting to happen.[51]

Once Ransford gave birth to Gershom, the authorities saw their opportunity and prosecuted her for fornication. Not wanting to pay a fine for a child he considered legitimate before God, John Rogers appealed, and the sentence was ultimately rescinded on technical grounds. It does not seem that authorities were too eager to press the matter further—perhaps because they had made their point and maintenance of the child was not an issue. When Ransford gave birth to a second child in March 1702, however, the authorities must have felt compelled to intervene again, convicting Ransford and Rogers of fornication and bastardy and sentencing Rogers to pay the child's maintenance until age four (although one wonders to whom). In court, Rogers was defiant, holding his infant daughter Mary and giving "no direct answer to it either to own or deny."[52]

Faced with the prospect of continued fines and persecution, Ransford fled, alone, to Block Island, which was under the jurisdiction of Rhode Island. In May 1703, she made a final appeal to the General Court to allow her and Rogers to live as a family. When that failed, Ransford chose to remain on Block Island, eventually marrying and having another family there. Losing a wife for a second time, John Rogers appeared to come unhinged. He vented his desperation on his ex-wife, Elizabeth, and her new husband, Matthew Beckwith. Overcome with grief and rage, Rogers went to them, grabbed Elizabeth and warned Beckwith that he should never have "meddl[ed] with her." Beckwith had Rogers thrown in jail, where the old dissenter again languished for several months, refusing to post bond and guarantee Beckwith's safety. In a state of dread, Beckwith begged the court to keep Rogers confined, "for I have as much reason as ever to fear his attempts against my life."[53]

When Rogers returned to Mamacock by the end of 1703, the household was again changed, turned over in part to the demands of raising small children, even as the work of farm and faith continued. At fifty-five, Rogers had two young children to care for, Ransford's little Gershom and Mary. No doubt, much of the responsibility fell on the shoulders of his daughter-in-law and niece, Bathshua, who herself was now a mother of three boys under the age of three. At least Ransford's absence meant that the household was less divisive, allowing John junior's Bathshua to focus on the work at hand.

As John Jackson watched his master's second marriage fall apart, his own took a radical turn for the better. After he had married Joan, she had borne him two children, Adam and Miriam, but the mother and children still lived as slaves at the Fox farm. Sometime around 1702 or 1703, however, the Foxes followed John Rogers's lead and freed Joan from bondage. By granting Joan her liberty at the peak of her working life, and therefore her value, the Foxes recognized her loyalty and diligence. Perhaps they had begun to question slave-holding in principle, or sought to acknowledge a blood connection between Joan and the Rogers family. The Fox family may have been thinking of Bathshua's daughter as well; by allowing Joan to join her husband at Mamacock, John junior's wife, Bathshua, would have significant extra help tending to her five small Rogers charges, preparing food, cleaning house, and doing the wash. This much-needed help would have been especially welcome coming as it did from Joan, because the two young mothers had grown up together and therefore knew the solidarity of common effort.[54]

For Joan, the change was the most striking. On the one hand, at Mamacock her future children could live with both their mother and father. These new third-generation Jacksons would face obvious disadvantages as the progeny of freed slaves, impoverished and African, but they would still have something over John Rogers's children by Mary Ransford. That little pair, Gershom and Mary, carried the stain of illegitimacy in the eyes of society, while future Jacksons would be entirely legitimate, standing on the firm ground of their parents' long and stable marriage. There would be a chance for this new Jackson generation to gain a foothold in New England. But for Joan, who was probably only in her early twenties when she came to Mamacock, the price of this newfound liberty was extremely high. To live with her husband as a free woman and wife, she would have to leave her two eldest children, Adam and Miriam, behind in slavery. Forever.

Chapter Six

"ONE FLESH"

THE IMMIGRANT Robert Hempstead would barely have recognized the New London his grandson Joshua inhabited in 1700, nearly sixty years after his own arrival in southeastern Connecticut. The town had increased fivefold—forty fragile households had become two hundred strong, with no fewer than sixty new men coming to settle in the last twenty years alone. New London could now boast several inns, a fulling mill (where wool was cleaned and thickened in the process of making cloth), and a sawmill. Most newcomers were farmers and artisans, like Benjamin Starr, who moved into a house near the Hempsteads' on Bream Cove—a house so close to the water that at high tide he could unload goods from boats into his basement hatch. Others came with bigger plans—the Barbados-born Hallam brothers, John and Nicholas, arrived ready to trade and already among the wealthiest men in town.[1]

Just as in Robert Hempstead's time, meetinghouse hill was still New London's central hub, and its main street led down to the harbor and the Bank, where development had now begun in earnest. In 1700, the meetinghouse was new, a replacement for the one Bathshua Fox and William Wright had supposedly burned down a few years earlier. Along the waterfront, wharves continued to multiply, harboring mostly small- and midsize ships for the West Indian trade: sloops, brigantines, snows. New Londoners packed these vessels with barreled meat, grains, and livestock—especially horseflesh—bound for the islands, then welcomed them home from the return trip, loaded with molasses, rum, sugar, bills of exchange, and the occasional slave.[2]

This steady traffic in and out of New London gave Connecticut's southeastern port some measure of worldliness. Ships on the coastal trade called in frequently between Boston, New York, and Newport. Regular ferry service—often flat, raftlike scows powered by oars, poles, and brawn—took on local passengers and freight at key river points, especially to and from Groton across the river. By 1705, Groton was an independent town with its own congregation and minister. News and information circulated regularly even on this ragged fringe of the British Atlantic: Connecticut had no newspaper of its own, but New Londoners passed around other papers, especially the *Boston News-Letter* after 1704, and even the occasional cosmopolitan periodical like the London *Spectator*, brought in by post riders carrying mail or by vessels docking at the harbor.[3]

Amid the changes and the hubbub, however, general prosperity seemed to elude the rough-edged little community. Outsiders deemed the town worn and dull; insiders felt themselves perpetually on the verge of the next big break that never came. By 1700, it was already clear that early hopes of rivaling Boston or New York—both of which had already topped five thousand souls—would never be realized. Any original vision of echoing the London of Albion was now laughable. Although New London was a midsize port and a county seat, even the basic institutions of public life had a slipshod quality. The town lacked a courthouse for regular court sessions, so the meetinghouse often had to suffice. The nearby stocks and improvised prison were in constant disrepair, earning the town a fine from the county court as an incentive to improve. While Saybrook established what became Yale College (the school moved to New Haven in 1716)—New England's second institution of higher learning after Harvard—its southeastern neighbor was slow to open even a common school for its children, a neglect of basic education that brought with it another embarrassing fine.[4]

New London was destined to remain a poor stepsister among the port cities of the American Northeast, playing only a supporting role in New England's economic and political life. Unable to lay any claim to ascendancy, the town also languished as a social and cultural backwater, even by colonial standards. Eighteenth-century travelers regarded its "irregularly built . . . desolate" settlement of wooden houses as clumsy, brutish, and "mean." To the pedigreed elite of Boston or New York, even the town's betters appeared as "country people" and "lazy fellows." Locals, born and raised, were considered boorish "creatures" plainly out of place in genteel society.[5]

Within the scruffy little port, the harborside district at Bream Cove where the Hempsteads lived remained a particularly unpolished, working neighborhood—its graying buildings weather-worn, its air steeped with pitch from the Coit shipyards and with stink from the Truman tanning yards. It also welcomed newcomers, like Benjamin Starr, who brought with them new commercial activities and families even if they did not change the character of the quarter. The yeoman Holt family had settled across the highway from the Hempstead place in the last decades of the seventeenth century, becoming trusted near neighbors (William Holt was the neighbor who had testified against Susanna Truman in her fornication trial). The shipbuilding Coits built a new house by 1700, around the same time that Joshua and Abigail Hempstead reclaimed their family homestead overlooking the cove. Barely out of his teens, Robert Hempstead's grandson Joshua could be pleased with his newfound independence, ready to focus on the hopeful work of building a family and accumulating an estate to provide for them.[6]

Across town, the North Parish—home to the Fox farm, the Livingstons, and the English–allied Mohegan—remained relatively unsettled compared to in-town English neighborhoods like the one at Bream Cove. John Rogers's brother Samuel had been the first person to settle in the district on Algonquin land. Without a local meetinghouse, Congregationalists in the parish still needed to make the trip to town each Sunday to hear New London's minister preach, an arrangement that suited Baptists and Rogerenes just fine, especially the Rogerses and Foxes, who preferred to keep to themselves and gather privately in any case.

Like the General Neck, where Joan Jackson was born and raised, the North Parish was an easy refuge for those with views that ran counter to the prevailing Congregational "New England Way." Although Connecticut Colony had tried to maintain orthodoxy, the breakdown had already begun, and within a few short years Baptists would appeal successfully to the General Court to legitimize their meeting. By 1700, the Baptists and Rogerenes were no longer the only "dissenters" in town. In an ironic twist for New Englanders, even the Anglican Church—the original "mother" church—was enjoying a resurgence in the colonies. Both Virginia and Maryland had declared Anglicanism an official religion, and Episcopalian missionaries would soon attract adherents in Connecticut and New London as a wave of cultural and social Anglicization spread across the region—particularly among the "better sort," who associated high status with all things English. It would take more time for orthodoxy to cave completely, but the roots of its destruction were already visible, growing in families like the Rogerses and the Foxes and in pockets like the General Neck and the North Parish.[7]

FAMILIES ACROSS New London faced new opportunities and persistent challenges with the coming of the new century. For every young man starting out as a husband and a head of household—whether he was a Hempstead, a Jackson, or even a Livingston—there would be choices to make about what sort of patriarch he would be. Within the constraints of his station and circumstances, every man would have to decide how to provide for his family, fulfill his role as a husband, and take his place in the world. These three patriarchs would each face financial, legal, and personal challenges that would endanger their dreams and the lives they aspired to build for their families, but each would approach those hurdles quite differently.

For Joshua Hempstead, decisions about what sort of a man he would be appear to have come easily. He settled into the house at the lip of the Thames with his resilient little family and engaged readily in the hard, promising work of establishing a homestead. He married Abigail Bailey early and began to work to restore the life he had been

born to, the life his dead father and grandfather had planned and read-
ied for him. Now he could hang the heavy flintlock musket Robert
Hempstead had brought from England where it truly belonged—in
the house it had once occupied before death had dislodged it. Joshua
displayed the musket high on the summer beam—the central support
that girded the ceiling—in the hall, which was both his "best" room
and the room where the family spent most of their time. Outside,
Joshua immediately began cultivating the landscape, as two generations had before him. The fields, meadows, orchards, and yards were
all in need of his stewardship. Joshua would nurture the old domain,
enhancing and supplementing it in due course. Gradually, the house
could return to familiar rhythms and routines, its spare wooden
frame echoing with the voices of a fourth generation of Hempstead
children.[8]

It was a self-conscious, weighty time in Joshua's life, as he took a
wife, mastered his trade, and became an indpendent man politically
and economically. Although the first surviving pages of his diary
date from 1711, from their form and features they do not appear to
be the first pages that he actually wrote. It is possible that instead
he began the diary around 1700, when he first assumed his role as
a householder, husband, and soon-to-be father. He was certainly
already well practiced in writing by the turn of the century, and for a
man so attuned to bearing witness it would have been a rich moment
to begin to document both his world and his place in it.

The house that Joshua Hempstead inherited was the one his
father had built in the year of his own birth, a simple but serviceable structure with a ground-floor and upstairs chamber, a garret for
sleeping and storage, and a lean-to kitchen in back. At some point on
the eastern side, a lean-to shop was added; there Joshua would keep
many of his tools and perform the woodwork that could be done
indoors, especially in bad weather. During the early years of marriage, Joshua's life centered on building ships and working the land,
so that many of the daily exertions of creating a home fell to Abigail.
Her routine in the old house consisted of familiar rounds of female
work, labors that would have been largely second nature to her by
the time she became the mistress of her own household.

Everyday work followed a fairly typical pattern for New England wives and mothers like Abigail. She probably rose early, often well before sunrise, and revived the embers in the kitchen hearth that she had carefully tucked away the night before. Most women tried never to allow the kitchen fire to expire, hoping to spare themselves the effort of restarting it from scratch. Once Abigail had built up the flames, taking a few logs from the haphazard mountain of wood piled high outside the back door, she likely walked to the barn just north of the house to milk cows and feed chickens. After preparing a simple breakfast, perhaps milk and bread with a bit of tea or coffee, she would move through the forenoon straightening chambers and sweeping floors, doing the gardening or other housework, until she stopped to cook a hot dinner—the main meal of the day—which was typically served between noon and three o'clock. After dinner, she would wash up with water carried in from the well near the front door. In between these ordinary tasks and especially toward the end of the day, Abigail and women like her spun yarn or made and mended clothing, sometimes in the company of visiting women busy with similar work. Every evening Abigail would have prepared and served a small supper, and given the cows their second milking.[9]

Like other colonial housewives, Abigail also contibuted to her domestic economy in meaningful ways, whether by trading surplus home goods like cheese or preserves with other neighborhood women or by taking in boarders—adding an extra portion of food to the pot already on the fire. In all her work, Abigail was rarely alone. She soon had children underfoot, and even a young couple of modest means in early New England typically had help of some kind, perhaps even before their first child was born. For Abigail, help probably took the form of hired girls from the neighborhood, girls to whom she would have allotted some of the more disagreeable chores along with most of the spinning and child care. Her younger Hempstead sisters-in-law, Patience and Lucy, may have both also lent a hand as sisters or hired helpers. In 1705, in fact, Joshua's sister Lucy formally joined the household, choosing her only brother as her legal guardian. Joshua was her closest male relative—and certainly Abigail could have used her help—but Lucy's move also may have exposed lingering tensions between Joshua and the Edgecombes, tensions that would beg an outlet.

For Abigail Hempstead and most of the women she knew, one responsibility overshadowed every other. From the time she married at the end of her teens, Abigail became pregnant every two to three years. She nursed each baby roughly two years, only to begin the cycle again with a new pregnancy. So as she cooked and prepared food, scoured and sanded floors, washed and ironed clothes, Abigail also carried, nursed, watched, and tended to a growing succession of children that began with three fine sons: Joshua junior, Nathaniel, and Robert. Given the fairly narrow realm of Abigail's strenuous daily efforts, one might expect her home to be a model of cleanliness and order, the golden fruit of all her labors. But for all she accomplished, Abigail merely stemmed the continuous tide of oncoming disorder and filth from fields, livestock, hearth, and day-to-day family living. Her house, like those around her, remained a cramped, crowded jumble of activity and production that no amount of sweeping and scouring could surmount. Despite a housewife's best efforts, a New England home like the Hempsteads' remained a dark, smelly, dirty place that offered few physical comforts.[10]

Local records are eloquently silent regarding the Hempstead marriage, suggesting that Joshua and Abigail's union was a tranquil and successful one. During the years of their marriage, Joshua and Abigail appeared to fit comfortably into the roles prescribed for them as husband and wife, father and mother, together raising the children they hoped would inherit the product of their mutual work. Abigail embodied qualities he valued and expressed in the entries of his diary. She was "quiet"; she respected, obeyed, and supported Joshua. She was "sober" and "orderly," running her household efficiently by shunning waste and idleness. The good husband, Joshua provided well for Abigail and the children, in turn, working diligently and broadly to increase his estate. Their marriage appeared to exemplify aspirations expressed by Hempstead neighbors in court records. Good husbands and wives "were very kind and loving to each other," refraining from "any difference or anger or quarrel." An admirable husband was "very kind to his wife and his wife to him."

Couples like the Hempsteads who upheld community standards did
not find themselves on unwelcome display in local records.[11]

When Joshua Hempstead took possession of his father's house
and land, he had only recently emerged from an apprenticeship. His
training enabled him to practice his trade, but without a shipyard
of his own, the newly minted craftsman had to work the ships and
yards of others as a subcontracted journeyman. During these foundational years as a husband and father, Joshua performed "piecework," building ships—or rather portions of ships—for men like his
neighbor John Coit or ship captain John Hutton, who ran a yard near
Bream Cove. Occasionally, Joshua worked beyond New London in
more distant yards like Joseph Saxton's in Stonington. Subcontract-
ing lacked permanence, but it offered a variety that was useful to a
young man with ambition. Working for others, Joshua gained both
wide experience and useful contacts.[12]

When his eldest boys, Josh and Nathaniel, reached six or seven,
Joshua was able to bring them with him, leading them from the long
gowns of early childhood and their mother's care toward leather
breeches and the work of men. Like his father and grandfather,
Joshua Hempstead had no need to own a slave. For him, a growing
troop of sons supplied ample labor, at least for the time being. Nevertheless every Hempstead was accustomed to the company of the
town's nascent ranks of slaves, most of whom remained bound to
more privileged families like the Rogerses or the Winthrops.

The house Joshua and Abigail shared at Bream Cove typified a
New England domestic world that was both particular and collective. Its three rooms held countless moments of hidden intimacy, but
doors remained forever ajar, open and ready for quick conversions.
As the family changed and grew, this small domestic theater would
have to adjust to changing players and an ever-expanding repertoire.
While he turned the surrounding "Wilderness . . . a Mart"—to use
the wording of Woburn, Massachusetts, founder and author of New
England's first printed history, Edward Johnson—Joshua would feel
the old rooms bow and sway, assuming countless incarnations: infir-
mary, workshop, schoolroom, bedchamber, meetinghouse, court.
For its owner, a good deal of family life unfolded in and around

these walls. He was born in this house and there he would die. Once ensconced as a husband and father at home, however, a man of good character might also replay the paternal role for a wider audience as a father to his town.[13]

Working in the yards was one way Joshua pursued his family's interests and future. Another required challenging his mother and stepfather, Edgecombe. There had been no outward signs of strain in his relationship with the Edgecombes, but Joshua had harbored reservations about their handling of his father's estate. When he was thirteen, his mother had dipped into capital, selling off a two-hundred-acre farm at Mystic, the oldest section of Stonington, on which she took a mortgage. After Elizabeth married John Edgecombe about a year later, mortgage payments had gone directly to him. The arrangement must have rankled Joshua, although he waited until he was twenty-eight to register his dissatisfaction in any formal way. Perhaps he had tried first to come to a settlement with Edgecombe, before the demands of providing "portions" for each of his young sons forced him to take legal action. In 1705, when Joshua was about to become a father for the fourth time, he filed a lawsuit against the Egdecombes over the lost Stonington farm.[14]

The case was more complicated than it appeared. The will that Joshua's father had written on his sickbed ten years before his death had never been filed with the probate court. Joshua had been only five at the time, not old enough to have retained a copy himself. He might have had an ally in the wings, however, because it landed in his hands more than twenty years later. That ally could have been his uncle Robert Douglas, a venerable Scots immigrant and husband to his father's sister Mary—that first English child of New London—who had witnessed the will. In his nephew's suit Douglas gave compelling testimony verifying the will's authenticity, his voice and features conveying the singular gravitas of that first generation of settlers, the immigrants to whom children and grandchildren owed their very presence in the new land.[15]

Joshua's case went all the way to the General Court and, after many appeals and delays, resulted in his appointment as the executor of his father's estate; a second suit then allowed him to recover the farm. In this way Joshua became the owner of two hundred lush and grassy Stonington acres, prime grazing land, and his Edgecombe parents had to bear the cost of their mistake or misconduct. The records are silent about how the Edgecombes felt about this turn of events, but they left no evidence of any ill will toward their son, other than an unsuccessful petition to retry the case before the General Court, citing the costs they had borne in the care of Phoebe. For Joshua the recovery of his rightful inheritance was both gratifying and materially enriching. The farm would fit nicely into his plans for his sons' futures. In the meantime, he would make good use of it himself.[16]

Legal wrangling with the Edgecombes had earned Joshua a valuable property, but it had also afforded the provincial wright unexpected opportunities to step onto a larger public stage. Still in his twenties, Joshua had only recently begun to participate in New London politics when he found himself addressing the leading men of the colony in New Haven and Hartford on his own behalf. It was a precipitous, formative introduction to the broader world of law and politics that eased Joshua's gradual admission into a local governing class. When Joshua started out as a new husband and householder, his prospects for local prominence were in no way certain; many of Joshua's New London peers had comparable, if not distinctly superior, advantages. But not long after his first appearance before the General Court, New London's propertied men chose him to serve on two major town committees.[17]

In New England, local governance relied on freemen like Joshua who gathered annually in town meetings and elected one another to perform public offices and services. Many freemen served willingly, and the disinclined had to weigh reluctance against the certainty of paying a fine and the social cost of refusing. For the most part, freemen accepted the inconvenience and irritations of office, knowing that service conferred claims to authority and deference. It was also simply the right thing to do. Some like Joshua seemed to relish the role and the local prestige that went with it. Proving himself in lesser office, a man might even join a core group of local leaders whose political ascendancy was nearly total. By December 1709, thirty-one-year-old Joshua Hempstead was elected to the town's highest office of selectman. He had not reached middle age, but Joshua had already begun to join a core group of New London's most trusted leaders.[18]

IN THE years while Joshua Hempstead worked New London's yards and fought for his Stonington farm, the freed bondsman John Jackson also labored to safeguard his growing family. The means at Jackson's disposal were limited, but within the constraints of his poverty, his origins, and his servile status, he stepped purposefully into his role as patriarch. He had begun a new life with his Joan at Mamacock in the first years of the new century, and there he would build a home and family. From the start, the Jacksons were forced to confront separation and subjugation, but this would not stop John Jackson from trying to protect the children he could not raise, and to seek a family reunification. The legacy he provided his children could not be measured in acres or pounds sterling, but instead in the risks he took on their behalf, often in the face of overwhelming odds.

After he became free, John Jackson had apparently continued to work for John Rogers as a steady right-hand man—no longer his slave but still a trusted servant. Like the Hempsteads, the Jacksons passed most of this first decade together in relative tranquillity after the Katherine Jones fornication case was resolved in 1702, quietly building their family and household at Mamacock. Although the couple's precise living arrangements are uncertain, they probably occupied the house John Rogers had permitted Jackson to build at the farm near his own, paying some rent in the form of labor. At one point the Jacksons apparently shared their home with a local family of English origin named Camp.[19]

The Camps were a well-established English family in New London, related to the Rogerses by marriage—one Camp son had married a daughter of Bathshua Fox. For some period before 1710, a Camp couple rented a house jointly with the Jacksons on or near the Rogers farm. The only evidence of this multifamily household came from Abigail Camp, the wife of the couple, who later spoke about it in court testimony, though she gave no hint that the Jacksons' African heritage or slave origins affected her thinking about the arrangement. Certainly, there was nothing strange about English and African New Englanders sharing housing on unequal footing; that was, in fact, the norm. But to live as equals, as the Jacksons and Camps appeared to do, was an anomaly—perhaps another by-product of the noncomformity that prevailed at Mamacock.[20]

The relative calm the Jacksons experienced during these early years of the eighteenth century was due, in part, to Joan's new freedom. African New Englanders made up less than 3 percent of the population of Connecticut, but freed people were only a fraction of that number. Still, they were a familiar part of society, living with one foot in different worlds and often, like the Jacksons, with family members in both slavery and freedom. The Jacksons' route to free status—a master's grant of liberty in the prime of their working lives—was unusual at the time. One of few other locals to receive a similar grant was the "Negro Mareah," whom her wealthy master, the British-born merchant Alexander Pygan, released from bondage around 1690 when she was in her forties. But such early manumissions, especially outside the circle of Rogerenes, were few.[21]

A small number of New England freedmen were able to purchase freedom using credit or cash earned in the wage market during off-hours. One local man who did just that was Robert Jacklin, a contemporary of John Jackson who came to New London from Massachusetts in the first decade of the eighteenth century. Jacklin had been a valued slave to the Newbury physician Peter Toppan for more than two decades. Sometime after Dr. Toppan took a sharp fall and died in the early years of the century, however, his surviving sons allowed Jacklin to purchase his liberty. Jacklin turned up in New London, where he settled and started a family as the Jacksons had done, marrying a local woman who had grown up around Joan. Jacklin's wife, Mary, had been a child of the Algonquin Rogerene William Wright and his wife, Hagar, onetime servants to James Rogers, Sr., along with Maria and Joan. After William Wright had been convicted of the meetinghouse burning and banished, his "widow" Hagar had been left on her own to raise their three children, Mary,

Wait, and Sarah, under extremely difficult circumstances, though Hagar did manage to acquire her own plot of land. Nevertheless, Robert Jacklin gave Mary Wright a better life; they had three children, and Robert owned his own farm despite initial opposition from fellow New Londoners to his purchase of land. Eventually, the Jacklins moved to Colchester. Freed couples like the Jacklins or the Jacksons remained uncommon in early New England, but they were not unique.[22]

DURING THE peaceful years at Mamacock before 1710, John and Joan Jackson added four more children to their family. These siblings—Abner, Peter, Hannah, and John junior (called Jack)—would spend at least part of their childhoods on the Mamacock farm, where they may have learned the Rogerene faith. The daily working lives of their parents probably varied little from their former lives as slaves, and the Jackson children were exposed to the usual tasks and skills necessary for husbandry and domestic work. More unusual was that these children were growing up in the strange, exhilarating atmosphere of Mamacock with the children of John Rogers, Jr., as their likely playmates, and the old Rogerene leader himself as their likely spiritual teacher.[23]

Life inside the Jackson home at Mamacock remains largely hidden from view. John and Joan did not write, and they left no family records. Contemporaries who did write rarely mentioned them. One scant image does survive from around 1708, a time when there were three small Jackson children in their household. At that point the Jacksons were sharing their home with the Camps, and Joan was pregnant with her sixth child—the boy who would be her husband's namesake, Jack. She went into labor and someone from the household—a Jackson, a Camp, or perhaps even a Rogers—ran to a nearby farm to call on Ann Tongue. A member of the same Tongue family as Fitz Winthrop's longtime companion, Ann was a midwife, or at least experienced in attending births, and she came directly to stay with Joan during her travail. Ann Tongue would later recall that day, describing Joan as "the wife to a Negro man"—perhaps an indirect reference to Joan being part English, distinguishable from her entirely "Negro" husband. Old John Rogers himself provided a second rare sketch of the Jacksons. With approval and respect, Rogers described John and Joan during these tranquil years at Mamacock as "diligent and prosperous," although he did not characterize precisely how they lived or worked.[24]

TO CREATE a home and household together, John and Joan Jackson were forced to leave their two eldest children, Adam and Miriam, enslaved at the Foxes'. The hardship of separation had some consolations, however. The children were a relatively short distance away, and close bonds of family and religion between the Rogerses and the Foxes meant that there was regular contact. The Jacksons endured a split from their children that was precipitate and by definition involuntary, but their situation had some parallels to the separations English parents undertook when they put their children out to service. In the actual work they did, Adam and Miriam probably led lives resembling those of English child servants. They also had each other. The presence of a sibling was an unattainable comfort for many enslaved children.

The Jacksons maintained a sense of family in spite of the separation. Years later, one of Bathshua Fox's sons from her first marriage would recollect how during this period Joan Jackson came to the Fox household "from time to time" to nurse Adam and his baby sister "until they were weaned." Even if Joan had considered her children safe in service, freedom had meant losing the ability to provide them day-to-day mothering. Joan's trips to nurse her babies are poignant testimony to her efforts to mother her boy and girl nonetheless. Her eloquent strivings were not in vain. According to Bathshua's son, as Adam grew, he was "often times heard" to say that "John and Joan Jackson were his father and mother." Unlike so many children in slavery, Adam knew his parents and he wanted others to know as well. His words to that effect were a powerful declaration of who he was—even if the thoughts and feelings surrounding them remained obscure. These words, secondhand and paraphrased, were the only ones he spoke that were ever recorded.[25]

In contrast to the lives of most American bondsmen at the turn of the eighteenth century, Adam Jackson was relatively fortunate even in his enslavement. He had both of his parents and most of his siblings living nearby. What was especially rare was that Adam's parents were also free people who, through powerful connections to the Rogerses, could try to watch over him—even to shape his fate. Adam was a bondsman, but his parents' hopes and affections rested in him, their eldest son, no less than in a Hempstead or even a Livingston or Winthrop son. The Jacksons' prospects were humble, but they appeared solid enough in the first decade of the eighteenth century. John Jackson could hope to support the family he had created and to anticipate respectable work for each of his children. In his dreams and expectations, he relied on the help and influence of his master, Rogers, on whose sponsorship he had to depend. Soon an attack would strike at the heart of Jackson's delicate, hard-won family, however—a family already divided by miles and by slavery. And John Jackson's role as husband and father would be sorely tested.

IN ADDITION to his parents, Adam had his master and mistress, Samuel and Bathshua Fox, who, both despite and because of their ownership of him, acted as a surrogate "father" and "mother." Samuel Fox trained the boy in husbandry, the same work Adam's father did for John Rogers. Perhaps Fox also took Adam to Rogerene meetings, where he and and his sister Miriam might see and perhaps even sit with other members of their family. Working for his master, Fox, Adam grew up conversant with the geography of greater New London: the town, of course, but also Mamacock, where his parents lived; the General Neck, where his mother was born and Fox still owned land; and the North Parish, where the Foxes resided.[26]

From his fellmonger master, Adam probably learned to scrape and cure animal skins to prepare them for market. An inventory of Fox's possessions when he died revealed clues to Adam's life on the North Parish farm. At his death, Fox owned 358 pounds of tanned leather, an assortment of curried leathers, and a large number of sheepskins. With them, were a variety of tools and other raw materials, all evidence of his trade as a pelt dealer. The tanned leather included well over two hundred skins, enough to fill a hogshead bound for England with plenty left over to satisfy local needs. Although only low numbers of New England bondsmen received proper craft training, Adam would naturally have acquired some understanding of his master's trade in the course of his everyday work. Certainly, he knew the rudiments of the tanning process from watching or helping. He would have also observed as Fox's buyers and sellers, many of them Algonquin, came to trade. In the North Parish between the Connecticut River Valley and New London Harbor, Fox was well situated as a fellmonger. All around, wigwams peppered a landscape that was still home to Pequot—some of whom had been absorbed into the Mohegan or Narragansett after the Pequot War—and Mohegan.[27]

Adam Jackson's upbringing was not entirely different from that of his English contemporaries. Daily life for all boys revolved largely around work, accompanying male elders in farming, trading, and craftwork. Like men, boys worked six days a week, leaving the Sabbath—Saturday in the Fox household during Adam's childhood—for worship and quiet socializing. Like all children, boys of African descent probably received some religious education, listened to Bible readings, and perhaps even memorized catechisms. While Adam lived with the Foxes, the household contained just three books: two Bibles and a third unidentified volume (probably religious, perhaps even Rogerene)—texts that family members might know by heart.[28]

By the time of Adam's birth, English boys in the region could usually expect to attend some school, as Joshua Hempstead's sons would certainly do. At a minimum, they learned to read handwriting and printed material and to perform basic writing and practical arithmetic—fundamental skills considered unnecessary for African peers like Adam. Still, competencies varied appreciably, and some African New Englanders were able to defy the odds and attain a real measure of literacy.[29]

While Adam Jackson grew up at the Foxes', learning to read was probably not his first concern. Even if they did not experience harsh treatment themselves, young slaves like Adam and his sister Miriam would have been painfully aware of much grimmer potential realities than unequal instruction in literacy or even the trades. In early New

England, law and social convention did not condone extreme physical severity toward servants and slaves, but it existed nonetheless. Yet without fuller evidence, the extent and nature of extreme or even customary "discipline" are hard to determine. Connecticut statutes provided a general prohibition on the "cruelty and tyranny of masters." Implicit community values also did their work, enforcing accepted standards of treatment and discouraging unfettered violent abuse. Severe or life-threatening corporal punishment was probably not the norm in colonial New England, but there were always some masters who broke legal rules and unspoken convention. Adam and Miriam Jackson may not have experienced the extremes of abuse, but the threat of brutal treatment still lurked around every corner, over each horizon—if not with this master, then perhaps with the next.[30]

Local court cases give some indication of the outer limits of servant abuse. One extreme incident involved Benjamin Bump, an English youth in service, though not a slave. Whether a master was more willing to abuse a slave versus an indentured servant is open to question. On the one hand, a slave was more vulnerable and less likely to seek or obtain legal recourse. Usually he had no family to assist. But because a slave was valuable property, a master might be reluctant to damage his own estate. Bump's situation came to a head in 1720 when he appeared one day on a neighbor's doorstep, complaining that his master had whipped him severely and salted his back "with brine to stop the blood." Two men who examined the servant found that he had been "very much beaten and bruised all from his shoulders down as low as his mid thighs . . . [and] by the bigness of the stripes and scabs [that] it was done with a stick of considerable bigness." One neighbor had seen John Rood, Bump's master, "hang him up and whip him" with "a birch rod" "for a quarter of an hour," after which Bump ran away, "stealing two shirts and two scythes."[31]

Neighbors did not approve of the servant's flight, but they strongly condemned the master's brutality. They even recognized that Bump had some claim to the goods he took, shirts and tools being customary remuneration for servants who fulfilled their service. The case went to trial, and Rood pleaded not guilty, insisting his corrections had been "moderate." Rood's defense itself gave credence to accepted community standards of restraint, as did his request for a bench trial by the justices to avoid a jury and the judgment of his peers. The court found him guilty nonetheless, though his sentence was mild, its purpose to reassert basic standards rather than seek retribution. Rood paid a small fine of thirty shillings as well as Bump's costs of court and cure, and Bump was released from the indenture he found intolerable. The public airing of Rood's conduct achieved another goal: It eroded whatever good name Rood had and put townsmen on notice that he was a questionable master.[32]

Near neighbors knew the locale and embodied accepted standards, forming an important check on abusive treatment, along with other forms of deviance. In Bump's case, it was a neighbor who initially tried to enforce community morés after a bleeding Benjamin begged for help, claiming that Rood had "threatened to be the death of him and to geld him and to ram his stones [testicles] down his throat." When Rood came looking for his servant, his neighbor chided him as a "wretch for abusing [Bump] after such a shameful manner." Still, Rood would not budge, apparently replying that "he would abuse him so again and [the neighbor] too." When masters like Rood refused to abide by neighborhood standards, criminal law provided a final recourse.[33]

In New London court records, extremely abusive masters like Rood were rare. On those occasions when neighbors' vigilance failed and a master transgressed, however, things could go terribly wrong. During Adam's lifetime, at least one New London slave appeared almost certainly to have been beaten to death: a nine-year-old girl named Zeno. Her master was Nicholas Lechmere, the scion of one of the few New England families drawn from English nobility like the Saltonstalls. Nicholas's father was the English-born Thomas Lechmere, an embittered third son who countered his diminishing prospects by moving to the colonies and marrying a daughter of Wait Winthrop, a granddaughter to John Winthrop, Jr. In spite of his Winthrop match, however, Thomas Lechmere remained perpetually dissatisfied with his wealth and status. Perhaps his son Nicholas inherited his father's sense of entitlement, for he was driven to violent, uncontrollable rages that he vented on the poor child he owned.[34]

Nicholas Lechmere thrashed Zeno savagely with a "hunting

horsewhip upwards of two feet long . . . about her head, neck, and body." It took the nine-year-old three agonizing days to succumb to her wounds. Before her corpse even left the house, neighbors informed authorities they were "very suspicious" that Lechmere had killed the child: "[A] very great Concourse of People," Joshua Hempstead wrote in his diary, watched riveted at a hearing about "ye Cruel Whip[p]ing of Zeno." So many came to observe, in fact, that "the Court Chamber wod not hold all." Lechmere's neighbors had been aware of his sadistic behavior for some time but were hesitant to report it, perhaps intimidated by his high rank and connections. Never adequate for his father, that rank was probably sufficient to spare Nicholas from a capital charge. In the end, Lechmere's stand-ing, combined with a general, unmistakable reluctance to put men and women to death in the colony whatever the charge, shielded him from prosecution. A grand jury refused to indict, and Lechmere's escape from prosecution stood in sharp contrast to Zeno's excruciat-ing death, frightened and alone.[35]

The accusations against Nicholas Lechmere and his neighbors' keen interest in the case suggest that New Londoners viewed extreme violence against African slaves with curiosity and gravity. Another incident during Adam Jackson's lifetime confirmed this impression: In 1711, nearby Killingworth was abuzz with talk of the unexpected death of a "Negro woman" belonging to a local resident, George Chatfield. Thinking he could get away with a hurried, surrepti-tious burial, Chatfield had not informed authorities of the woman's untimely death as required by law. Chatfield believed that no one would take notice of this "contemptible creature" he had punished the night before for "her disorderly and turbulent behavior," but neighbors did pay heed and reported him to a magistrate.[36]

One set of neighbors found it strange that Chatfield had come into their house early on the morning of the slave's death, asking "as to what manner [the head of that household had] buried his Negro when he died." Other neighbors had watched Chatfield carry the body to burial with the help of another man's "Negro"—skulking partially hidden "through the lots the back way" to avoid "the high-way or the common road." Questioned, Chatfield admitted that he should have "call[ed] in some neighbors to see under what circumstances she died." In spite of his dubious behavior, the authorities lacked tangible evidence of wrongdoing and did not prosecute. Neighborly scrutiny nonetheless put masters on notice of the possibility of criminal charges. Even without a conviction, a master like Chatfield who defied community standards still risked casting a pall over his reputation and squandering this vital social asset.[37]

In all likelihood, Nicholas Lechmere would not have beaten an English servant girl to death, and surely Chatfield would not have buried an Englishwoman in secret, even one he had killed by force. African children were clearly more vulnerable than indentured English children who might have relatives to watch over them, even if from a distance. African children like Zeno were disconnected from any blood family, and often from a familiar culture or social world. Any family would have been powerless to act regardless. Fortunately men as brutal as Lechmere and Chatfield still appear to have been rare in early New London. If court records illustrate everyday experience, Zeno's terrible fate was unusual. Beyond community standards and legal constraints, masters must have considered their own economic self-interest when punishing a slave: An injured or dead slave was a bad investment.

JUST OVER the Rhode Island border in the Narragansett's South Kingston lived the Scots-Irish clergyman Dr. James MacSparren, a missionary for the Church of England who wrote unabashedly in his *Letter Book* about beating his slaves to "discipline" them. A learned cleric educated at Glasgow and Oxford is not the best source for determining local methods of punishment, but he was one of the region's few slave owners who wrote about disciplining his bondsmen. MacSparren was no "New England man," so his approach toward slave ownership might have differed. His Narragansett surroundings, too, where larger-scale plantation-style slavery was the norm, might have fostered harsher rule than in other parts of New England. The sophisticated Boston businesswoman and travel-journal keeper, Sarah Kemble Knight, apparently judged Connecticut slave owners to be far too cozy and overfriendly with their slaves (according to the edited version of her journal). "Too Indulgent (especially ye farmers) to their slaves: sufering too great familiarity from them," she pronounced with disapproval. Typical or not, MacSparren provides an account of physical punishment that he, a respected clergyman, considered reasonable.[38]

According to his own unself-conscious report, MacSparren favored whipping as a form of correction. When his slave Hannibal had spent all night out fornicating, MacSparren "stript and gave him a few Lashes till he begged." The minister's New Englander wife, being a "poor passionate dear," found the whipping insufficient and gave the unfortunate Hannibal "a lash or two" herself. Hannibal ran and hid after the lashing and, upon finding him, MacSparren had a blacksmith fit him with pothooks—a metal collar designed to restrict movement though not enough to prevent him from working. Less than a month after the first beating, the cleric judged Hannibal insubordinate and disobedient to Mrs. MacSparren, and again the man received several strikes. In using the lash, masters and mistresses like the MacSparrens copied a standard criminal-law sanction. Reenacting an "official" whipping at home, masters might have felt an implicit endorsement, both in the form of punishment and in their authority to mete it out.[39]

Unlike the criminal law, slave owners were not legally empowered to impose the ultimate sanction of death against slaves they deemed incorrigible. When whippings proved unable to "reform" Hannibal, for example, MacSparren resolved the situation by sending the man away to live with another master at some distance. Within a few months, the clergyman ordered the strong-willed bondsman sold, probably never to be seen or heard from again in South Kingston. A slave who did not bend to his master's will risked losing familiar surroundings, friends, and relations, even—as Hannibal might have—the woman he loved.[40]

New Englanders expected slaveholders to behave within certain limits, but they required slaves like Adam Jackson to abide by a more exacting code of conduct, explicitly written and implicitly understood. Masters prized obedience and diligence in African slaves, but these were also qualities men desired in servants, children, and wives.

Along with faithfulness and industry, masters valued an "orderly carriage," the quiet submission to authority. Providing a character reference, one master praised how his bondsman had "lived with him and his sons above twenty years and carried himself orderly."[41]

If a slave did carry himself "orderly," English masters and townsmen might feel affection for "a good old Servt & Christian," a mixture of attachment and respect that was sometimes even tinged with admiration. In his diary, Joshua Hempstead broke his usual pattern of terse entries to elaborate when such a person died. To the shipwright, the qualities that set these men and women apart were their faithfulness and diligence, but always in combination with long service. Thus he would write of the ninety-year-old Cush, "a faithful Slave in his family" who died after a lifetime of distinguished service, that Cush "was a Servt to [Gurdon Saltonstall's] Granfather . . . who died near 50 years ago & then to . . . Saltonstall." Writing of Peter, a slave belonging to his friend and neighbor John Coit who sometimes worked also for Joshua, the diarist praised "a very faithfull Laborious Servt." At the death of an enslaved Algonquin woman he had known since childhood, Joshua eulogized "an Honest faithfull Creture" whom he "hope[d]" had been "a good Christian."[42]

South Kingston's Anglican minister, MacSparren, who dryly recorded lashing Hannibal, wrote with considerable fondness of another slave, "my dear Servant Stepney," after Stepney drowned in a "fatal Pond" called the Narrow River. MacSparren described the young man, whom he had baptized as a boy with his own hand, as "my fine Negro Stepney, the best of Servants." MacSparren's feelings about Stepney were inextricably linked to the youth's usefulness and MacSparren's self-interest: "Stepney, poor Boy, is dead and I have no Servant I can now so well depend on to go and come quick and [do] his errands well." For the cleric, Stepney's obedience was intrinsic to the attachment he felt for him.[43]

Just as criminal law might prevent the extremes of masterly abuse, it also provided a final counter to slave "misbehavior." Connecticut lawmakers began to establish a legal regime surrounding servitude in general as early as the 1640s. By time of Adam's birth, legislators created criminal legislation that applied specifically to Africans,

whom they deemed "very apt to be turbulent, and often quarrel-
ing with white people, to the great disturbance of the peace." The
breach of the king's peace was a traditional criminal infraction, but
in a 1708 statute, Connecticut law created the special sanction of a
thirty-stripe whipping for any "Negro" or "mulatto" caught "breaking the peace" or "offering to strike any white person." There were
also special sanctions for an enslaved person "being abroad in the
night season" without express permission from his or her master.[44]

A number of civil laws also focused on restricting the economic
and social activities of the enslaved, due to either their African origins
or their civil status. Like wives, indentured and enslaved servants
were not permitted to engage in trade "without their owner's leave"
and could accumulate capital only with their master's consent. African New Englanders could not travel at will. Enslaved people were
forbidden to pass beyond the bounds of the town of their residence
without a written permission from their master. Any slave found
outside those limits "without a pass" was a de facto runaway. The
free person of African origin likewise needed a pass attesting to his
free status when traveling outside the town of his official residence.
Colonists in early New England regarded anyone of ostensible African origin as a likely slave and a potential threat to a peaceable and
orderly community.[45]

The concentration of slaves in households across the region followed a familiar general pattern, with most enslaved people, like
Adam and Miriam Jackson, living in households with a small number of slaves and sharing close quarters with slaveholding families
and other servants. In parts of New England, however, there may
have been subtle local differences that broad patterns cannot capture. The Boston gentlewoman Sarah Kemble Knight appeared to
write suggestively in her jaunty journal of a particular intimacy she
encountered between masters and slaves in Connecticut, her edited
journal commenting disdainfully on the custom of masters allowing
slaves "to sit at table with them (as they say to save time), and into the
dish goes the black hoof as freely as the white hand." For most Connecticut colonists, however, such ordinary familiarities would have
been an unremarkable part of everyday life by 1700.[46]

As Adam Jackson grew up quietly at the Foxes', he might have been able to know the worst extremes of slave life at some remove. Living in one household since birth, Adam had a chance to grow in the affection of his master and mistress and to prove his diligence and loyalty. Nothing in the historical record suggests he did otherwise.

ONLY A few miles from the farm where Adam Jackson lived in slavery, John Livingston inhabited a very different vision of manhood from those embodied by either Joshua Hempstead or John Jackson. Livingston was the son and heir of a hugely successful self-made man, and both of his parents had given him automatic entrée into circles of privilege and opportunity. Unlike Hempstead or Jackson, Livingston did not aspire to rise much beyond the social and economic heights of his father, although he most certainly did not want to lose the advantages he had been born to. Self-interest—rather than family or community welfare—was Livingston's principal guide. He wanted to inherit and even hoped to add to his fortune, but he was disinclined to pursue conventional forms of work—whether in land management, mercantile affairs, or public service—to achieve his aims.

Apparently, John had not inherited a taste for proprietorship from his mother, Alida, who ably managed the family manor, for once he acquired the North Parish farm, he turned impatiently to other interests, becoming largely an absentee landowner. Along with the farm, John also distanced himself for long periods from the young bride he had wooed so urgently, leaving Mary alone and increasingly isolated. Instead, he chose to follow in his father's mercantile footsteps by pursuing his trading partnership with Samuel Vetch, although he seemed to lack Robert's business judgment and acumen.

By nature, Livingston was prone to gamble and speculate—staking a great deal for a chance at quick and high returns—and his approach toward business with Vetch was no different. Rather than content themselves with legal commerce, the brothers-in-law decided instead to play a dangerous game, trading illegally with England's enemy, the French in Newfoundland. If successful, this risky—even unscrupulous—plan to sell costly French goods in American cities held out the promise of steep profits. For John, success could mean a store of capital on which he could draw to pursue other ventures; it might even reassure his father that John was a worthy inheritor of Livingston Manor. Smuggling was by no means unusual, and some officials had been known to turn a blind eye. Nevertheless, if Livingston and Vetch were caught, they faced the possibility of public disgrace, financial ruin, and even criminal prosecution.[47]

Together, the brothers-in-law bought a sloop and christened it the *Mary*, after John's new bride. The sloop's first voyage was a great success, and John Livingston probably felt elated as he sold off their illegal cargo—French wine and brandy—in the colony of New York, while Vetch embarked on a second run. On the return voyage in November 1701, however, the sloop ran aground at Montauk, Long Island. Locals were surprised to come upon the *Mary*, entirely unmanned and appearing as a ghost ship. The mystery was soon solved, however, for Vetch, who showed up within a few days, had left an incriminating notebook on board that clearly identified the responsible parties. The crew had, in fact, disembarked to seek help after the *Mary* first ran aground at Fisher's Island, and the ship had simply floated away. This intriguing fact carried no sway with colonial authorities, however, who could not ignore such a blatant flouting of the law. They seized and condemned the *Mary* with its entire cargo, including "eighteen cask of brandy and ten hogshead of claret, six chest of sundry goods . . . a box of beaver skins, a peg of scarlet cloth." Vetch and Livingston went on trial for illegal trading, and, as a result, both the *Mary* and its contents were confiscated to the tune of two thousand pounds—a colossal loss from which both men would find it difficult to recover.[48]

While Vetch continued to fight the confiscation, Livingston tried to absorb the blow and move on. The reputational and financial setbacks were considerable, and Livingston needed a path to salvage both. As a child of privilege, he faced a set of constraints on his working life, because the occupations he might pursue while also still maintaining his social position were limited. For a young man destined for a patroonship, the list of options was surprisingly short:

He could be a merchant, a gentleman farmer, or a public servant— perhaps even a scholar—but not much more. Given his performance in academics and trade, and his lack of aptitude for gentlemanly husbandry, Livingston now chose the only viable alternative: public service, inspired less by a sense of duty to country than by expediency and self-interest. Characteristically he was drawn to the riskiest option. When another Indian war—Queen Anne's War—provided a chance to join the the fight and redeem his name, he seized it.

Like most able-bodied men, Livingston was already a member of his local militia, having attained the rank of colonel by 1704, when he decided to assume a command. Men of high status were routinely appointed to officerships without regard to their military fitness; Livingston appeared to have been an exception, for he appeared well suited to service. One of a series of conflicts between the British and the French between 1702 and 1715, Queen Anne's War was the colonial iteration of the War of the Spanish Succession, in which the two imperial powers and their Native American allies fought over control of the American continent. For New Englanders, the front that most engaged and imperiled them was the fight with French Acadia, a region that included part of Quebec, the Maritime Provinces of New Brunswick, Nova Scotia, and Prince Edward Island, along with present-day Maine north of the Kennebec River. Confronted with English encroachments on Acadian territory in the first years of the eighteenth century, French-allied forces decided to fight back in earnest.

The far north was familiar ground for Livingston, who had grown up in the thick of Indian diplomatic circles; his father had been New York's long-serving Commissioner of Indian Affairs and his uncle, Peter Schuyler, was a Mohawk-speaking politician and leading figure in Anglo-Indian diplomacy. When Connecticut decided to contribute to the English war effort, Livingston assumed the command of a militia company made up in part of Mohegan and Pequot. Many of these soldiers Livingston recruited himself, perhaps even from his own North Parish neighborhood—to fight on the colony's behalf. Apparently Livingston had a talent for persuading men to join up; in a letter to Fitz Winthrop, New York's then-governor, Edward

Hyde, Viscount Cornbury, angrily accused Livingston of stealing Indian recruits from his native Albany when assembling his company there—a charge of which he was likely guilty.[49]

Livingston's success at recruiting from the New London area was not simply a matter of personal charm and connections. Since King Philip's War, New England Algonquin had ceased to be a viable military force, so that men from traditional fighting families who had managed to survive had few opportunities to engage in battle. Because Algonquin women customarily performed all agricultural labor, with men engaging in war and hunting, the expedition to Canada had an obvious appeal over work as a farmer or indentured servant in an English family.

Events in the winter preceding Livingston's departure for Canada provided local Algonquin a more immediate inducement to serve, however. One snowy day in late 1703, the Barbados-born merchant Nicholas Hallam had gone to the North Parish to survey the boundaries between New London and the Mohegan. There he encountered a pathetic sight: a group of thirty or forty half-clothed, impoverished Mohegan men, women, and children gathered at the Norwich River crying and wailing openly. Governor Fitz Winthrop had driven them from their customary planting fields a day earlier; he would soon order their annexation to support the expansion of the town of New London. The Mohegan would respond by appealing directly to the Crown, resulting in legal maneuvers that would drag on for decades. Fitz's 1703 landgrab was part of a broad policy of Native dispossession, but that winter it also made the North Parish especially fertile ground for military recruitment.[50]

In February 1704, Livingston and his men were stationed near Deerfield, Massachusetts—then a small frontier outpost that found itself on the front lines—when French and allied Mohawk, Huron, and Abenaki forces attacked the settlement in what the English would later call the Deerfield Massacre. They killed more than fifty inhabitants and captured more than one hundred, including many children. Livingston led his company in pursuit, but he failed to catch up with the French-allied party as they led their captives on a harrowing trek to Quebec, an ordeal that killed another twenty-one

Deerfielders. Among those who made it to Canada were the town's minister, John Williams, along with his five children, including a seven-year-old named Eunice. New England scrambled to respond, and as governor of Connecticut, Fitz Winthrop sent his son-in-law on a mission to seek an alliance with the Iroquois against the French. It was Livingston's "first adventure . . . in a public capacity," as Fitz put it, and the young officer performed well, even if he was unable to bring the discussions to a conclusion.[51]

Horrifed by the assault on Deerfeld, New Englanders made the return of the captives a diplomatic priority. John Livingston had not been in the field very long, but he had positioned himself well enough, with the backing of his father-in-law, to be chosen in early 1705 to negotiate terms with the governor of French Canada, the Marquis de Vaudreuil. In his second major public role, Livingston exceeded expectations, returning to Massachusetts triumphantly in June and bringing with him four released captives, including three children—one a Williams.[52]

War service had required Livingston to be away from New London and from Mary for nearly a year—a long absence that must have been a strain on their young marriage. The Deerfield survivors recognized Mary's sacrifice in emotional letters of gratitude, including one from minister Williams, who could barely find words to express his appreciation, even though one of his children, little Eunice, remained behind—still captive. Upon hearing of John's arrival in Boston that June, Mary immediately rushed to join him, reaching the city at "10 o'clock at night" for a joyous reunion.[53]

After a celebratory time in Boston, John and Mary Livingston returned to New London and the North Parish, but life there must have felt monotonous and insignificant to John after the many heady months of waging war and engaging in important affairs of state. During his absence, Mary had been left to manage the farm operations as well as a coterie of farm and household servants—a daunting task even for an experienced property owner and merchant, and certainly one for which the young mistress was ill equipped. She and John had probably hoped to conceive a child upon his return, but no child arrived. Their inability to produce an heir must have weighed

heavily on the couple, especially as they watched other young families around them grow. Coming home also forced Livingston to confront the reality of his finances: the debts he had accumulated and
the condition of his estate. He probably directed his attention to the
management of the farm and to smaller ventures in trade, but this
was not the life he had imagined for himself.

John probably did not see the possibility of undertaking any
major mercantile activities. The *Mary* fiasco some years earlier had
been extremely costly for him, and he no longer had the ready capital. In contrast, his brother-in-law Vetch had continued to trade illegally, becoming mired in legal disputes and earning a minor criminal
conviction in Massachusetts, compelling him to flee to London in
1706 to petition for exoneration. Once there, Vetch found that his
personal agenda dovetailed nicely with the prevailing political
winds. New Englanders had been clamoring to retaliate against the
French for the Deerfield raid, exerting particular pressure on Joseph
Dudley, the governor of Massachusetts. (This was the same Dudley
who had fled to England in the wake of the Glorious Revolution
after his all-too-enthusiastic service for James II's Dominion of New
England. He had since returned in 1702, having been appointed governor by Queen Anne. In the interim, the cunning political opera-
tor had switched his allegiance from James II to William III, and
then earned the further enmity of his fellow colonists while on New
York's governing council by playing a major role in the conviction
and execution of the popular rebel Leisler.) Although many New
Englanders, including Wait Winthrop, were indignant at the political resurrection of this native son, whom they regarded as traitorous,
they needed his gubernatorial backing to fight France, and Dudley
demurred lacking direct approval from London.[54]

In the English capital, Vetch assumed a leadership role in the lobbying campaign to win Crown support for an invasion of Canada—a
prospect that appealed to him because it combined military adventure with the dream of Scottish empire dear to his patriotic heart.
Vetch had nursed Scottish imperial ambitions ever since the Darien
Colony failure, even though these would now require English backing due to the parliamentary union of Scotland and England in 1707.

Back in Connecticut, John Livingston must have read and heard of Vetch's activities with some envy and regret. Few of the plans he had made as a hopeful bridegroom had come to fruition—he had no children and his estate was in a shambles. As 1708 approached, Livingston was ready to seize new opportunities and take new chances. He would soon find two possible means to achieve his ends—each of them a considerable gamble.[55]

IN THE winter of 1707, John Livingston's father-in-law, Fitz, visited Boston to attend two important family events: His widowed brother, Wait, was remarrying, and Wait's son, John IV, was marrying for the first time. John IV had scheduled his wedding close enough to his father's so that his uncle Fitz, still the Connecticut governor, could attend both celebrations. Soon after his brother's wedding, however, the sixty-nine-year-old Fitz became gravely ill. He succumbed before John IV could be married, his death throwing a dutifully somber cast over the nuptials.[56]

Back in New London, Fitz's death meant a shift in the local and colonial power structure. Minister Saltonstall was elected to the governorship of the colony in 1708, leaving a vacancy at the First Congregation. The town brought in Eliphalet Adams, a level-headed, Harvard-educated cleric, who was also an accomplished linguist, proficient in an Algonquian dialect along with Latin and Greek. Adams settled into a long and rewarding tenure.[57]

For John Livingston, Fitz's death dangled the prospect of financial recovery with his wife, Mary, set to inherit. Despite his father-in-law's unorthodox home life with his live-in companion and Mary's mother, Elizabeth Tongue, Fitz had been a traditionalist, even a regressive one, when it came to family property. In his will, he had followed the English custom of primogeniture, which favored eldest sons and males and kept large properties intact. In New England, by contrast, providing a share to each child, though often an extra portion to the eldest son, was already common practice. Primogeniture, of course, matched the self-conception of third- and fourth-generation Winthrops as New England aristocracy, but Fitz had no sons of his own, so he chose his nephew, John IV, as the object of his bounty.

An unappealing young man bestowed with an outsize version of the long Winthrop nose, the Harvard-educated John IV was bookish like his grandfather and dogmatic like his great-grandfather, but he lacked John junior's brilliance and John senior's great moral calling. He was also arrogant and self-centered, characteristics that endeared him to few contemporaries. By this fourth generation in New England, the Winthrop shine had lost quite a bit of its luster.

Like Livingston, John IV had also made an illustrious match that began with dissension, even veiled rancor. His bride, Anne Dudley, was the granddaughter of the second governor of Massachusetts and the daughter of Wait's despised political rival, then–Massachusetts governor Joseph Dudley—a man Wait once described as a "venemous serpent." Like Livingston, John IV had endured his family's objections to the marriage, but had ultimately prevailed—Dudley family status outweighing Winthrop disdain. Still, the Winthrops remained wary of their new in-laws.[58]

After Fitz's death, Mary's mother—his consort, Elizabeth Tongue "Winthrop"—joined the Livingston household on their North Parish farm, while Wait, who was named coexecutor with John Livingston and minister Saltonstall, moved back temporarily to Winthrop's Neck to settle his brother's affairs. As a familiar quagmire of claims and counterclaims against the estate began to take shape, Livingston saw his chance to protest his wife's portion. Mary's inheritance, of course, had been part of Livingston's own marriage calculus, but he now needed funds more than ever. Watching this infighting from his home in Roxbury, Massachusetts, Joseph Dudley was not pleased to see his daughter's future fortune jeopardized, and he wrote to Wait to express his dissatisfaction: "It is so contrary to what I have long time been assured." For Wait, however, the bickering was familiar territory; he and his brother Fitz had wrangled for many years with their sister's widower over the distribution of their own father's estate (that brother-in-law had even appealed his ultimately successful case against them all the way to the Privy Council in London). For John Livingston, it was a calculated risk; he would potentially destroy his relationship with his wife's family for the chance at a big settlement. One can only imagine how Mary and her mother, Elizabeth, felt, living together with John as he quarreled openly with Wait and John IV and contested their dead patriarch's will.[59]

On the other hand, Livingston enjoyed the popular support of New Londoners in his fight with the Winthrops; locals naturally favored the rights of their native daughter, Mary, over her interloping Boston cousin. Livingston's tactics were underhanded if effective, as he sued Winthrop tenants for "unpaid" rents already collected by Wait, trying to force him to settle. By April 1709, he seemed to have achieved his goal when Wait grudgingly entered into an initial agreement. Then Livingston appeared "very placid and handsome," as he smugly signed papers and treated all to "a handsome supper." But the agreement did not hold, and it is unclear whether a new settlement was ever achieved.[60]

Livingston may not have won his gamble, but he did earn the permanent resentment of Wait and John IV as he continued to be a thorn in their sides—even making claims to Winthrop's Neck itself. Wait and John IV derided him with unflattering nicknames, with Wait calling him "the Mohawk"—a jibe at his Albany roots and the Livingston family's long involvement in Indian affairs. They also mocked Livingston for putting on airs. He became "Don Quicksot," the easy and pompous drunk, and they found Livingston's references to Robert Livingston's manor as "our Mannor" affected and grating.[61]

JOHN LIVINGSTON'S pursuit of his father-in-law's estate was not the only wager he made to reestablish himself as a patriarch. Not long after he challenged the Winthrops, he allowed his dynamic brother-in-law Vetch to lure him into another grand proposition, one that dangled the prospect of both glory and lucre. It would require Livingston to leave home again, but Mary's failure to give him a child had apparently diminished her claim on her husband's time. While Livingston was squabbling in New London, Vetch had used his experience as a smuggler to present himself as a Canada expert in the British capital, producing his own invasion blueprint. Through a combination of diplomatic skill and astonishing bravado, he proposed this plan in 1708 before the Board of Trade and secured the support of the British monarch herself. Vetch partnered with Francis Nicholson, a seasoned soldier and the former lieutenant governor of New York during Leisler's rebellion, whom Queen Anne chose to lead the expedition.[62]

Vetch, Nicholson, and eleven British officers returned to New England in April 1709, ready to launch a well-financed summer campaign after recruiting sufficient colonial troops among the English and Native American populations. Vetch set up his campaign headquarters in Boston, where he brought his wife, Margaret, and their young daughter, Alida. Livingston did not take much persuading to sign on as a major and commander of the Connecticut contingent, a largely Indian unit he would lead in the anticipated assault against Quebec. The Canada venture held the possibility of honor and also considerable wealth: If New England's fighters were successful, they expected a payday in the form of conquered property taken in plunder. As an officer, Livingston could also expect a high position—and a government salary—in any new settlement. But the expedition required a large up-front outlay. Commanders like Livingston had to supply their companies using their personal credit, with the expectation of Crown reimbursement. Livingston was therefore gambling not only with his life but also with his already diminished resources.[63]

John Livingston and his men joined an advance guard of regiments that gathered at Woodcreek, the site chosen for a military camp in northern New York. Arriving there in May 1709, Livingston's company hunkered down through what he called "hard and difficult service," constructing canoes and building a crude fort while they awaited the arrival of a promised British war fleet that would enable the assault on Quebec. After three months of waiting, Livingston made a quick trip to Boston in September, hoping to ascertain that reinforcements would be imminent, but there was nothing new to learn. He returned quickly to his Woodcreek post, growing increasingly desperate. By then, conditions at the garrison had deteriorated, hastened by shortages of provisions and the outbreak of disease. And winter was coming.[64]

Livingston did not know it then, but during the long summer

they had languished at Woodcreek, Whitehall had changed course. The devastating news did not arrive in New England until October: The Crown had canceled the Canada expedition, and colonials would bear the cost—tens of thousands of pounds sterling and much more in political and human capital. John Livingston barely made it out of Woodcreek alive. Some seventy Connecticut men out of a contingent of four hundred did not; the survivors scrambled home, and many faced months of lingering illness. Livingston was one of the returnees; he went back to the North Parish to regroup, resigning himself to another winter there.[65]

In spite of these setbacks, many New Englanders would not relinquish their Canada aims so easily. The reversals of the aborted invasion had left Samuel Vetch's reputation in New England once again in tatters, so when colonial leaders decided to plead the case for invasion once again in London, they chose instead Vetch's expedition partner, Francis Nicholson. With Nicholson came an unusual contingent: John Livingston's uncle, Peter Schuyler, escorted four representatives from New York's allied Five Nations of the Iroquois to voice their support. After months of lobbying, Nicholson and his companions accomplished their goal, receiving royal approval for a limited expedition against the fort of Port Royal, with Vetch named future commander of the conquered garrison—a prospect that for Livingston meant the assurance of high position. As Nicholson's delegation was feted in London, John Livingston waited, eager for news.[66]

While he had been at Woodcreek, Mary had wondered if she would ever see her husband again. The farm had languished without a master in his absence, the task of running the large operation beyond her scope. Despite the sacrifice of family life and the outlay for expenses, there was probably no question for Livingston that he would sign on to the second Canada expedition on Acadia's capital, Port Royal. He had already staked his reputation, his health, and his credit on the ultimate success of the venture. And he was running out of options. In the meantime, he continued to take out his frustration on his father-in-law's estate, drumming up local support for his claims. When spring arrived and the revitalized expedition took off, John Livingston left New London with a new consignment of recruits.[67]

The costly failure of the first Canada expedition muted New Englanders' support of a second run against Port Royal. But their spirits rose when colonial forces took the settlement easily on October 16, 1710, and renamed it Annapolis Royal after their queen. Vetch and Livingston must have been elated when Vetch was made colonial governor of the new province of Nova Scotia, and wealth and position finally appeared within their grasp.[68]

Only days after the victory, however, Nicholson chose Livingston for a dangerous mission—an overland trip from Port Royal to Quebec to negotiate a peace and prisoner exchange with the Marquis de Vaudreuil. By now, Livingston was a seasoned soldier and negotiator, but it was a treacherous journey with the Canadian winter at their heels. Livingston and his small party set out immediately and made a promising start, but they were soon forced to abandon their canoes and continue on foot through the bitter wilderness. For weeks, they walked without provisions, eating moss and leaves, with Livingston documenting their travails in a small notebook.[69]

As her husband wandered half dead through the far north, Mary Livingston must have been beside herself with worry. Her aging mother and sometimes her unmarried sister-in-law—John's younger sister Johanna—kept her company at the house, but no one could offer real assurances that all would be well. Not only had she no child to provide purpose and distraction during the long months of vigil, she had probably also begun to feel a painful soreness in her breast that resisted treatment. Her relief must have been palpable when she learned that John had emerged miraculously from the woods and arrived safely in Quebec that December after a two-month ordeal—healthy enough even to complete negotiations for a French surrender. Despite the distance between them, it was a high moment in their lives.[70]

SOMEWHERE IN the house at Bream Cove, locked in a box or a desk, was a neat stack of papers to which its owner turned nearly every day. Like the house around him or his children in their beds, these thin sheets of paper were a great constant in Joshua Hempstead's life. On a September Saturday in 1711, he wrote a few lines on the first of these pages to survive: "Fair & Lowering. I workt at ye Ship about ye Stern except 3 hours or less a making 15 foot Rails for ye Stern. Arrived Braddick from Albany [and Selenks] for L. Island. Richd Rogers child buried Infant." Awkward and unfamiliar, even faintly unwelcoming, the words picked up inauspiciously in the middle of a story. No grand entry into the life of a man, they are as good a beginning as any. On those pages and hundreds like them, Joshua wrote of everyday weather, work, and local affairs. As the sheets accumulated, he sewed them together in quires or sections. Gradually and in increments, they formed a whole that would be entirely, exquisitely of his own fashioning, precious not for the eloquence of its words or the richness of its binding, but as the summary expression of a life in thought and—most especially—in deed.[71]

Today most diary writing is highly personal and revelatory, giving an intimate, intensely private view into an author's inner life. In early New England, however, truly inward-looking diaries were quite rare. Of these, most belonged to college-educated clergymen who used journals to document and interpret their spiritual journeys. Few yeoman and artisans had the education or inclination to engage in personal reflection through writing. In this respect, Joshua Hempstead was typical. His was a terse style that from the distance of several hundred years can appear stilted and detached, even jarringly unemotional. The remoteness of his prose did not reflect any lack of feeling, however, it simply echoed a genre and a time that maintained sharp divisions between emotion and written daily expression.[72]

Joshua was a scribe by nature. As a child, he wrote early and well, and by young adulthood he had achieved basic mastery of several genres: legal, epistolary, and diurnal. Through his diary, Joshua connected himself through time and ritual to men and a few women across centuries past who also aspired to greater understanding through diurnal writing. At its most basic level, his diary keeping reflected the rise of literacy in the Anglo-American world since the Reformation. Since the sixteenth and seventeenth centuries, literacy skills had filtered down into the middle ranks of English society, as individual believers sought to cultivate an unmediated relationship with God's word. Early New Englanders were a self-selected group that enjoyed higher literacy rates than even their Old English contemporaries. Diaries also served very practical functions as backup or substitute account books. Legal and economic relationships were becoming increasingly complex and rationalized, making more accurate and complete records of all sorts desirable. Although no substitute for unadulterated accounts, a diary like Joshua's could have similar uses, its record of transactions even admissible as evidence in a court of law.[73]

Joshua had reasons for keeping a diary that ran deeper than mere practicality, however. For more than a century, Englishmen had been journal writing in new and meaningful ways. Joshua chose a serial structure, using the date and day of the week to organize his entries. The choice consciously invoked ancient modes of public chronicling used for centuries. Domestic relationships were not simply private matters in colonial New England. With few activities taking place beyond the scrutiny of coworkers, kin, and neighbors, personal relationships between husbands and wives, parents and children, and masters and servants were of direct concern to a man's neighbors, and this communal interest had very real consequences. If a man foundered economically or even morally, the support of his household fell by mutual obligation to his fellow townsmen. Likewise, adult children who neglected an aging parent could expect to feel the full force of community reproach, urging them to fulfill their duties so that neighbors would not have to assume them. For Joshua and diarists like him, keeping a publicly inspired journal had less to do with any new sense of individuality augured by the Enlightenment than an innate recognition of the collective nature of everyday life.[74]

Imposing structures on time, Joshua's diary keeping also expressed a sense of historical meaning. The diary was itself a history—not just of an individual life course but of an immediate surrounding world. As such, the diary faithfully documented births, baptisms, marriages, epidemics, disasters, and celebrations in and around New London. For the most part, Joshua presented these as factual listings that together formed a community chronicle—an ancient, quasi-public genre used in the medieval monasteries of Europe. Like monastic chronicles, the diary too served a spiritual purpose. Laying bare the patterns and disruptions in daily existence, the diary was an implicit reference to God's hand in the affairs of men.

Behind the diary's quantitative, cumulative organization lay Joshua's own command of numbers and the obvious pleasure he took in enumerating his surroundings. Joshua was among a growing number of contemporaries who prized factuality, measurement, and quantification. As a shipwright, surveyor, and trader, Joshua applied relatively complex mathematics and geometry in his daily life. His natural desire to quantify did not simply meet the demands of his work: It also emanated from within him. Like other men informed by Enlightenment ideas, Joshua had begun to aspire to a more rational and systematic understanding of the world. Keeping a diary was a supreme act of quantification, a habit that suited a man who regularly consulted the heavy watch that always rested in his front pocket during an era when many of his neighbors remained content to tell the time by watching the sun or listening for the meetinghouse bell. Quantifying often served a practical purpose, but Joshua also felt gratified by the mere act of counting. Whether weighing the carcass of a slaughtered steer or counting cocks of hay after a hot day of mowing, he knew the satisfaction of measuring and numbering a job well done.[75]

One contemporary genre strongly influenced Joshua's diary. The almanac was an indispensable yearly manual for men who worked the land in both Old and New England. Utilitarian handbooks, almanacs were glorified monthly calendars that combined accounts of sunrises and sunsets, lunar phases, zodiacal dominances, and court sessions with short essays on astronomy, weather, and chronology. The connection between almanacs and diaries was explicit: Almanac readers routinely used the handbooks themselves as diaries, with some printers leaving space on the page expressly for that purpose. When he noted the weather, crops planted, or court and meetings attended, Joshua quite knowingly paralleled the almanacs he and his neighbors consulted to plan the farming year.[76]

Just as an almanac gave form to weather and farming cycles, Joshua's diary structured his ordinary daily labors. When he was not plotting the patterns and changes of community life, Joshua wrote most often about his work. Given the diversity of his labors, ordering his time and efforts after the fact was both useful and satisfying. Already in the diary's first surviving pages, Joshua depicted his remarkable range. During September and October 1711, he mended windows, built ships, served on town committees, repaired fences, pressed cider, slaughtered animals, husked corn, surveyed land, made furniture, and stacked hay—then wrote about it in his diary.[77]

As Joshua bore meticulous witness to his own life and the life of his town, he rarely mentioned another part of the domestic scene that took place just over his shoulder. Abigail, along with the cleaning, cooking, washing, milking, and cloth and clothes making that consumed her days, is nearly absent from her husband's diary. Her absence had nothing to do with lack of affection or regard. Her everyday activities simply had little place in a diary that was part almanac and part account book for her husband's work. Neither did they belong in a chronicle that sought meaning in the accumulated patterns of life and death, the natural and supernatural. In fact, it was only when Abigail, a highly competent helpmeet, broke established routines that she landed in her husband's careful entries.

As the first decade of the new century came to a close, Joshua Hempstead seemed well on his way to achieving the happy prosperity that had eluded his father, Joshua senior, and grandfather, Robert. He was a master craftsman, propertied householder, and community leader. He had even, whether he knew it or not, begun a book for the ages. By now, his agreeable young wife, Abigail, had produced three more healthy boys: Stephen, Thomas, and John. The older boys—Josh, Nathaniel, and even Robert—had begun to share meaningfully in their father's work. One by one the younger ones would join them. After a long absence brought on by the death of Joshua senior and the dispersal of the family, Hempsteads had reawakened the house and lands of their forebears, reasserting their presence on a place that would bear their name for generations to come. Already Joshua had many ideas for its improvement. But there would be time for all his plans. This next decade would be the hardest of his life, yielding a sorrow so deep it would bring him to his knees.

Chapter Seven

"SHE WAS TAKEN AWAY FROM ME WRONGFULLY"

I<small>N THE</small> spring of 1710, the future at Mamacock looked quite bright for John and Joan Jackson. They were living under the same roof, and half a lifetime in slavery could have made ordinary days and ordinary work on their master's craggy farm at the edge of the Thames something to savor. Coming to Mamacock, Joan had been forced to leave two children in slavery, but her firstborn son and daughter remained nearby and were not in physical danger. As John and Joan worked for the Rogerses, they had been able to have and raise four more children in relative calm, avoiding any troubles with the authorities or their neighbors. Joan was even now pregnant with a seventh child. They owned virtually nothing, but in purely economic terms their lot was not so different from that of other members of New England's unpropertied classes. If prosperity and abundance were unattainable, the Jacksons could still be well satisfied in possessing an estate more dear. They had their children and they had each other.

There were similar families in town: Other freedmen and freedwomen eking out an existence as laborers and servants. Like John Jackson, Thomas Bohan (known as Tommy) was a freedman who worked in husbandry and had a family nearby. Tommy's wife joined the First Congregation, and she and Tommy had a large family together. Robert Jacklin worked as a farmer, had a wife and three children, and even owned his own farm in the North Parish. The Jacksons could also identify with bondsmen and bondswomen in the area, whose numbers had grown steadily since the earliest days of settlement.[1]

Whereas John and Mary Livingston had stumbled into misfortune as they strove toward further heights of status and affluence, John and Joan Jackson, living quietly at Mamacock, received adversity as an unwanted birthright. There had been trouble brewing for some time among the Rogers siblings. John Rogers's brother-in-law Samuel Beebe (married to his sister Elizabeth) was a Rogerene in good standing, but Beebe and others in the family had been nursing grievances about money—in particular, about the administration of the patriarch James senior's estate. Elizabeth was the youngest child of James Rogers, Sr., and Beebe felt that his wife received short shrift in the distribution of her father's estate; they blamed the executors, John Rogers and Bathshua Fox, for mismanagement and unfair treatment. Despite the decades that had passed since James Rogers's death and the long-dead patriarch's express written wish that his children never contest his will, Beebe chose 1710 as the time to lodge a claim in court against his father-in-law's estate with John and Bathshua as executors. In families with substantial property like the Winthrops or the Rogerses, inheritance disputes were not infrequent, but Beebe's charge was different. The amount in question was quite small, hardly worth fighting over in a wealthy family, given the legal and emotional costs. But the stakes were striking. According to Beebe, John Jackson's wife, Joan—born a slave in the James Rogers household—was rightfully his.[2]

Beebe's real motives for pursuing Joan twenty-three years after his father-in-law's death are elusive. Some kind of ill will had developed between the Beebes and their Rogers siblings, a family conflict that played out in disputes over property. Certainly Beebe's claim was not born of need. Perhaps John Rogers had even offered to settle the case and Beebe had refused. Beebe was one of New London's richest men, owning enough property in Connecticut and on Long Island, including Plum Island (then part of Southold) where he resided, to earn him the moniker "Beebe the Great." Religion also offered no motive to fight, as the Beebes were dedicated Rogerenes. It was true that servants were in short supply in the New London area at the time, but certainly there were easier and less costly ways to acquire one than by stirring up an epic family battle. However, Beebe also knew that obtaining Joan would open the door to claiming every one of her children, and this knowledge provided added financial incentive, dampened only by the uphill road of conducting multiple lawsuits. Win or lose, Beebe could be certain of one thing: Fighting over living property—over people—was an especially potent way to exert power over one's relatives.[3]

A close look at Beebe's claim suggests that his assertions were thin. James senior had indeed bequeathed his daughter Elizabeth Beebe ten pounds in his will, but he had directed his invalid widow to pay the legacy "only . . . with the advice of my son [and executor] John." Beebe now claimed that in the intervening years, the widow Rogers had in fact directed John and Bathshua in writing to pay Elizabeth's ten-pound legacy in the form of two copper kettles and "my Negro girl called Joan, daughter of Maria, who is apprised at seven pounds ten shillings." Beebe produced an alleged deed of gift signed with a *C*-shaped mark, and while it was common for others to draw up legal documents for those who were unqualified or could not write, the widow Rogers had been a bedridden invalid even before her husband's death; it is highly probable that she was both physically and mentally incapable of executing such a deed. Unsurprisingly, the witnesses to the document were Rogers's brother Jonathan and his wife, Naomi, who were also unhappy with John and Bathshua's administration as executors.[4]

Beebe won his initial claim, though it was subject to appeal. The case began a prolonged legal battle, but for John and Joan Jackson it would become the fight of their lives. By the early eighteenth century, the Rogers and Jackson families had become so intertwined through domestic, legal, and religious bonds that Beebe could damage the fabric of the former by tearing apart the latter. In time, however, John Jackson could also exact a toll on Beebe for these manipulations.

Most likely, Jackson had some warning from the Rogerses of

Beebe's suit for ownership of his wife, so the freedman was not surprised when a constable knocked on his door on June 9, 1710, looking for Joan. Jackson told the officer that she was not at home, and he did not argue with him. Having a father in jail would do his children no good. Although it is not certain, Jackson himself may have sent her to hide—probably with help from the Rogerses. The officer searched for Joan around New London nonetheless, eventually apprehending her and two-year-old Jack over the river in Groton. From there, he conveyed the unhappy pair across the Sound to the Beebe house on Plum Island, just off Orient Point.[5]

Although the decision was subject to appeal, Beebe had won the first round in his legal claim; Joan was now required to become a slave in his household, against her will and the grant of freedom she had long enjoyed. Again she did domestic work for a family who owned her, towing Jack around as she cleaned, cooked, washed, and spun for the large Beebe household, which included some of the Beebes' nine children—including a daughter named after Bathshua Fox.

The Beebes may not have needed to use force to compel Joan to submit. Pointedly reminding her of the vulnerability of her children could have given her sufficient motive to comply. Although she had lived around Rogers siblings much of her life, Joan probably knew her new mistress, Elizabeth Beebe, relatively little. Elizabeth had left her father's household and New London to marry Samuel Beebe when Joan was only a young child. Perhaps this unfamiliarity explained why the Beebes, unlike other members of the Rogers clan, regarded the Jacksons purely as property to be bought, used, and sold.

Elizabeth Beebe's siblings, John Rogers and Bathshua Fox, had more complicated feelings toward the Jacksons. If they had regarded Joan simply as property, they might have just handed her over to make peace within the Rogers family. Instead, they maintained in court that Joan had been a gift to Bathshua during their father's lifetime and therefore never part of his estate, even if the grant was never formalized in writing. Perhaps John and Bathshua (before her death in 1711) found conceding to the Beebes morally objectionable, believing that the Beebes had manipulated their mother or even committed outright fraud. But their objections appeared to run deeper than legal positioning, family politics, or economic self-interest. Whether or not they were related to Joan by blood, John Rogers and Bathshua Fox showed concern for her welfare. Their fight with Beebe may even have expressed a new way of thinking. For Rogerenes, Baptists, and their denominational cousins, the Quakers, years of religious communion with slaves, servants, and free people of color was beginning to affect established notions of hierarchy. John and Bathshua, the Rogerene brother and sister, were among the first New Englanders to feel and act on the pangs of an emerging awareness that slavery might be wrong.

John Rogers and his Rogerene movement had not articulated a coherent ideological position against slavery in 1710, but Rogers's evolution may be detected through the lives of the Jackson family. Although the seeds of change were already in place before 1700, when Rogers freed John Jackson, the Rogerene leader's approach toward slaveholding remained highly ambivalent. John Rogers owned, worked, and profited from slave labor, but he also forcefully safeguarded the Jackson family when he saw fit—a protection that went well beyond a vigorous defense of his property rights. Rogers's position was obscure, but the impact on the Jacksons was not. Just as they could trace their enslavement to the Rogerses, what liberty they would ultimately acquire they also would owe, in no small measure, to the same family.[6]

With her taking by Beebe, Joan Jackson found that the year 1710 had turned bleak. She had to give birth to her seventh child, a girl called Rachel, while she was held against her will in the Beebe household. On certain days, in certain spots, Joan Jackson might have looked across the Sound at the opposing coast and pictured her husband and children on the other side. Unlike Mary Livingston, however, whose husband had willingly abandoned her, Joan cradled evidence of her husband's devotion in her arms every day. Still, how could he ever rescue her when she had been seized by an Englishman of such wealth and prominence? It was almost beyond imagining.[7]

*   *   *

IN FACT, it took John Jackson less than a year to strike back against Beebe, a slow unfolding of months during which he waited out the winter and arranged with his master each stage of a bold and meticulous plan. Not until the first hours of May 29, 1711, could they finally act. On that day, Jackson stood watchful and uneasy on his master's boat, as he and John Rogers maneuvered it across the dark waters of the Sound. In one sense, Joan's taking was merely the latest affront in a long list of injuries, stretching back to before his first arrival on the shores of this chilly land, fresh from the terrors of an ocean passage. In another sense, however, Jackson was a wholly different person now—both in his own eyes and in those of the law—with more automony than he could ever have anticipated. Whether this unusual history left him enraged or exhilarated on that fateful night, Jackson needed to push the old shadows aside and fix his mind on the task at hand. He had children on both sides of the water. Jackson and Rogers needed to reach Long Island well before sunrise, before the working day began and the likelihood of discovery became too great.[8]

Under the best of circumstances, traveling back and forth between the Connecticut coastline and Southold on a small boat in one night was a daunting proposition, a minor feat of nautical audacity. The course was treacherous, a maze of rocks and strong currents that could easily bring down a lesser craft. Safe passage required careful preparation and not a little luck. It also relied on seat-of-the-pants calculations that early American sailing men could perform by instinct. Jackson could not have done it alone, and it was John Rogers who provided the help he needed. Although he was sixty-two by this time, Rogers still proved a formidable ally. Age had brought with it physical limitations, but there was still no one better at righteous battle or standing his ground. Rogers had given much more than moral support, supplying his labor, boat, and the backing Jackson needed for the risky endeavor. Without the old radical, Jackson could have never attempted such a trip.

On May 29, Jackson and Rogers left New London after midnight, casting off in secret from Mamacock's rocky jut. They had timed the departure precisely. The full moon was two days away, but that night it would shine just as bright to the naked eye, giving them light enough for the passage. They navigated warily, perhaps overshooting their destination to make a less problematic landing. From there, they stashed the boat and walked to the well-appointed house of Samuel and Elizabeth Beebe. Quietly Jackson broke in, perhaps forcing his way into the back kitchen or climbing a side ladder and slipping through an upstairs window. He may have been to the house before—even visited Joan and his children. Or Rogers might have told him the best way to get in without waking the household. The danger was considerable; if Jackson was found out, he faced at best a certain criminal conviction for breaking and entering or burglary and the possibility of being branded, fined, and whipped. Once inside, he groped through the darkness until he found Joan where she slept, their boy Jack and baby Rachel probably resting beside her.[9]

Reunited at last, Jackson lay down with Joan. They had waited for this moment nearly a year, Joan trapped at the Beebes' and Jackson biding his time at Mamacock. Even now, the future remained highly precarious, but for these stolen moments, at least, they were together. In Joan's ear, her husband probably whispered the plan to take them to safety, and shared news of their children in New London: all well. Conscious of the passage of time, they soon rose and carried their two young children to the boat and Rogers. From there the small party made the difficult crossing back to Connecticut, straining to reach home before four, when the sun rose high and bright in the morning sky.[10]

Having accomplished this seemingly impossible rescue, Jackson and Rogers arrived back at Mamacock in the waning dark of May 30, heady with their success. As the day unfolded, New Londoners saw Joan and the children at John Rogers's house and next door at his son John junior's. One local "heard Jackson ask . . . Negro Joan to go home"—probably back to their own Mamacock house. Later, the same man saw the Jacksons there. At some point during the day, Joan may have received some word through the Rogerses of her eldest children, Adam and Miriam, who were still living in the North Parish and were around eleven and nine at the time. Certainly eight-year-old Abner and his younger siblings, Peter and Hannah, all three of whom lived at Mamacock, had been able to see and embrace their mother, brother, and new baby sister. Any reunions would have been bittersweet for all concerned, however, as everyone knew that Samuel Beebe would not take lightly either the loss of "his" slaves or the affront of their taking. Back on Plum Island, upon awakening to find Joan and the children gone, Beebe knew exactly whom to blame, and he reacted with speed and fury. He notified the authorities immediately, accusing Jackson and Rogers of stealing his property.[11]

Jackson and Rogers had anticipated Beebe's quick response, however. When a New London constable appeared at Mamacock that very afternoon, ready to arrest them and to seize Joan and her babies, both mother and children were long gone. Finding only John Jackson, the constable and his assistants took him into custody, walking him to town to face prosecution. Along the road, they encountered none other than John Rogers coming from the opposite direction. The seemingly chance meeting allowed them to arrest the Rogerene leader. It also permitted the two conspirators, the ex-slave and his master, to speak—a conversation later recalled for court by a constable's assistant.[12]

"Is she hid?" Rogers asked.[13]

"Yes," Jackson replied.[14]

The four-word exchange confirmed it. Jackson and Rogers had arranged for Joan to flee, but her whereabouts, for the time being, remained a mystery to the bewildered New London constable.

Although Jackson and Rogers had reason to be pleased, they still faced a legal onslaught that would require a different kind of bravery. The frustrated magistrates tried to find evidence of guilt by grilling the Rogers family and servants. They questioned John Rogers, Jr., who avowed he had never heard his father or Jackson "say anything about bringing off Joan from the Island." John junior did admit that he had watched John Jackson "go down toward the boat" with his father, but denied seeing "John Jackson with Negro Joan . . . at [his] father's house" the next day. Quite implausibly, John junior also claimed not to remember if his father or Jackson had told him how Joan had come from Long Island. Perhaps it was not an outright lie, but John junior was probably happy to obstruct corrupt justice through dissembling, as his father did routinely. Elizabeth Williams, probably a Rogers servant at the time, was a bit more forthcoming. At John junior's house the morning Joan arrived, she admitted that she had seen Joan enter, but Jackson and Rogers senior had not been with her. The conspiring pair had remained guarded in front of the servant girl and revealed nothing to her about how Joan had come—probably because they knew quite well that she would later have to testify.[15]

When magistrates questioned old John Rogers, Sr., the dissenter freely admitted being at Beebe's house the previous day. Asked if he had transported Joan to New London, his response was cryptic: "Twas none of my business; I have nothing to do with that." He admitted seeing Joan at the Beebe house (but not the children) and then to seeing her at the Jacksons' the next day.[16]

Beebe's case against Rogers and Jackson came to trial that September. Before the court, Rogers freely accepted responsibility. He "declared publicly that he brought Negro Joan from Long Island." Jackson, who occupied the lowest rung of free society and had a wife and young children who needed him, could not afford to be so brash; he reacted to magistrates' questions with calculated unresponsiveness—a strategy he and Rogers might have rehearsed beforehand. Asked if Joan and the children had come over in the same boat with him, Jackson simply declared, "They must prove it," referring to Beebe and his counsel.[17]

"How did she come to be at John Rogers' house that very day?" probed one of the magistrates.[18]

"You must ask her," was the freedman's retort, knowing full well that Joan was in Rhode Island, beyond the magistrate's jurisdiction.[19]

Then Jackson did something remarkable. In a world accustomed to deference toward one's betters, he boldy asserted his rights as a freedman and husband in open court, declaring, "She was taken away from me wrongfully." For a penniless freedman in 1711, such a statement was a show of resolve and self-assertion that was nothing short of astonishing. He had flouted a court order by "stealing" Joan back, and now he challenged the bench face-to-face with open defiance. Although no official response was recorded, those assembled at the court must have been incredulous at his audacity.[20]

The two accomplices chose a bench trial by the judges, rather than a jury. Perhaps they hoped to emphasize the injustice of an inevitably unfavorable judicial decision. Or had they simply hoped to avoid the popular animosity toward Rogers and his Rogerenes that a jury was sure to express? To no one's surprise, the court found them guilty, ordering each to pay a fifty-shilling fine and one-half of treble damages plus costs to Beebe—to be reduced to one-half of double damages of forty pounds upon Beebe's retrieval of Joan and the children. They were entirely guilty of taking Joan, Jack, and Rachel from Beebe, of course, but they regarded Beebe's original claim to them as fraudulent, no matter what a court had said. Hearing the sentence against them, Rogers and Jackson were brazen in their defiance. According to the Crown attorney then present, both defendants "fully and slanderously declared that said sentence was rebellion against her Majesty [Queen Anne] and that it was injustice." Their words so raised the ire of the judges and this chief prosecutor that the court found Rogers, whom they regarded as the instigator, guilty of contempt on the spot.[21]

While awaiting appeal on the theft conviction, both Rogers and Jackson had to post bond of sixty pounds to guarantee their good behavior in the interim. A hefty sum by any standard, the amount for Jackson was three times the market value of the enslaved wife and two children he tried to retrieve. Again the Rogers family rallied to his cause, with Samuel Fox and John Rogers, Jr., serving as Jackson's sureties and promising to pay if the freedman failed to behave.[22]

At the time they posted bond, Samuel Fox owned Jackson's two eldest children, and John junior—for reasons that are not entirely clear—had come to own the three middle Jackson children, all of whom were living at Mamacock. It may seem paradoxical that Jackson's guarantors held five of his offspring in slavery, while also backing his struggle to regain his wife and two youngest children. But the Rogerses and Jacksons may have seen little irony in the actions of these Rogerene masters—in their simultaneous enslavement, defense, and rescue of the Jacksons. Fox and Rogers ownership of Jackson children appeared to lend slavery at least tacit approval, but ownership itself had other important implications that contemporaries immediately grasped. The Jackson children were minors who needed to be protected from Samuel Beebe both legally and physically. They were much less vulnerable to him as the possessions of powerful Englishmen who could ably defend their property rights in court than they would have been as the children of a poor, marginalized freedman. It was not impossible that the Jacksons and their Rogerene masters had in fact made some kind of arrangement, whereby the children would provide youthful service in return for legal protection from Beebe in childhood and a future grant of freedom.

Why would the Rogers family have offered or accepted an arrangement so unusual for the period? The most obvious reason was a possible, though unproved, blood connection between Joan Jackson and the Rogers clan, but religious objections to slavery may also have played a role. The Rogerses may have also felt a sense of duty to a family who had served them for over three generations. Still, the degree to which John Rogers and other members of his family supported Jackson and his cause, putting both property and person at considerable risk, defies easy explanation. The bond between Rogers and Jackson, whatever it might have been, extended beyond either ownership or obligation.

After Joan's flight to Rhode Island, Samuel Beebe did not merely pursue Jackson and Rogers by pressing charges in court. For him, the insult was personal—personal enough for him to leave the comfort of his Plum Island roost and go after Joan Jackson himself. He hired two men to join him in hunting her and the children down, following their trail through Connecticut and into the neighboring colony. John Rogers may have tried to arrange Joan's path to liberty, passing her from hand to hand through sympathetic channels of Baptists. But with the help of the Rhode Island authorities, Beebe did find Joan—probably in Narragansett, where a Connecticut runaway might hope to escape detection amid the slave-laden estates and Algonquin settlements.[23]

Carting Joan back to New London, Beebe probably had no intention of brooking the reluctant slave again in his own house. Instead of bringing her home to Long Island, he quickly got rid of her, selling her almost immediately to another large landowner. In the space of less than two weeks, Joan, Jack, and baby Rachel had escaped slavery and fled to a transitory freedom in Rhode Island only to be dragged back to Connecticut and separated again from their husband and father by yet another transaction—another degree of enslavement. Exhausted and disheartened, Joan and the children must have had to muster everything they could to come to terms with this new landscape of their bondage: the palatial North Parish farm of a new master and mistress, John and Mary Livingston.[24]

THINGS HAD not been going well at Annapolis Royal for John Livingston since an initial peace was reached in October 1710. In a reversal of policy, London now forbade New England troops from appropriating the captured property of Acadian settlers, eliminating that long-awaited financial reward for Livingston and his men. Without the prospect of profiteering, the rank-and-file recruits wanted to go home. Vetch, who still dreamed of a permanent colony, ordered the men to hold the garrison and await replacements. Company commanders like Livingston were stuck in the middle. He remained with his men much of the winter in tiresome routines of drilling, boredom, and privation in the filthy, overcrowded garrison, with only the frequent quarrels between New England and British troops to interrupt the monotony. To make matters worse, because he had personally outfitted his men as a company commander, every day that passed meant that John was going deeper into debt, with the likelihood of Crown repayment growing increasingly dim. When spring finally approached in 1711, disease struck the garrison, and men began to fall by the dozens. Annapolis Royal, on which John Livingston had staked his name and his future, had become a death camp. At this point he, too, fled back home to New London, desperate to find a solution to his financial and political dilemma.[25]

Along the way, he stopped in Boston and visited with the Vetches. Once at home in March, he wrote his first surviving reference to his wife's illness in a letter to his father, Robert. His report was optimistic: "My spouse is well (except her breast, which I am encouraged is no cancer, nor worse)." Her treatment was also in place, for their doctor had "promised to stay with her 'til it is cured; it is better than it was." John had been aware of her condition during the winter in Annapolis Royal, but he did not plan to remain with her now to see her through her continuing treatment. He was returning soon to Boston, he told Robert, whence he would embark for London to lobby for the Canadian war effort—along with his own repayment. He expressed his hope that Robert and Alida would be "kind to my spouse in my absence."[26]

In fact, Francis Nicholson was already in London, using his influence to seek additional Crown support—this time to build on the taking of Annapolis Royal and mount a full-scale invasion of Canada. If it came off, it would be Livingston's third major Canada mission in just a few years. When news arrived that Nicholson had secured the queen's support, Livingston called off his own trip and appeared instead to have spent much of the early summer of 1711 based in New London. Mary's condition was worsening dramatically, and she was not responding to treatment. John may have been unable to cope emotionally with her deterioration; rumors would later emerge that the Livingston scion, never the most attentive husband, was spending time in the company of another, unmarried woman in Boston.[27]

Just why Livingston agreed to take part in Beebe's legal pursuit of the Jacksons during this period is not known. Court records list him as Beebe's attorney—not a lawyer per se but a legal agent to represent his rights at law, a position that may have required him to appear in court on Beebe's behalf. Perhaps Beebe, who lived primarily on Long Island, compensated Livingston for serving as a stand-in in the Connecticut courts. Or maybe Beebe had promised him that Joan and every one of her children would be Livingston's if he pursued the case. Certainly native-born servants like the Jacksons would have been highly useful on the Livingston farm.

While the surrounding circumstances are mysterious, it is certain that Joan's new Livingston master was in New London on June 13, when her sale and that of her two children were entered into the town land records. On the same day, in fact, Livingston also filed suit for Beebe against John Rogers, Jr., and Samuel Fox, demanding the remaining Jackson children, including Adam and

Miriam. Livingston was also in New London one week later, when Francis Nicholson, who had just returned with royal funding for a large land force and the promise of major naval support, arrived in town and convened a war council along with Vetch and the region's governors.[28]

That intervening week was an eventful one for the Jacksons. Initially, it would have appeared to John Jackson that he had no recourse to protect either Joan or his youngest children. Then a reprieve of sorts came just one day after Livingston bought them—an opportunity that stemmed in part from the same court that had done the family damage. John Jackson had no money to pay the more than twenty pounds he owed Beebe from his conviction for stealing Joan, so the court ordered Jackson to work off the amount, as was entirely customary. It was also usual for a winning litigant like Beebe to have the right to assign the term of the loser's labor to anyone else. In this instance, Beebe transferred his rights to Livingston, and Jackson signed an indenture contract with his new master for a term of four years and ten months.[29]

When Jackson indentured himself to Livingston, he hoped to join his wife and work off his debts, but he also harbored a more ambitious aim. Jackson expected his service to Livingston to permit him to accomplish a goal unattainable for most New England freedmen: acquiring land. In the indenture agreement, John Livingston had agreed to confer one acre of agricultural land to Jackson for each year of service. Had their bargain proceeded without a snag, Jackson could have accumulated a minimal holding of more than four acres, which would have been worth about twenty pounds. Such a parcel was too small for a family sufficiency, but it would have been a good start for an ex-slave nonetheless.

It is not hard to imagine why Beebe assigned his rights to Livingston, wanting nothing to do with Jackson—a man who had already given him a great deal of trouble. Livingston's aims are less clear; he had no history with Jackson, but as the owner of the man's wife and children he may have expected that Jackson would be highly motived to stay and work on his farm. The added arrangement of letting Jackson work for land may have been a strategy to bind him and his family even more securely to the Livingston farm. The more children Jackson had with Joan, the better for Jackson's owner. Livingston was also accustomed to tenant farming from his upbringing on Livingston Manor, and may have regarded his arrangement with John Jackson in a similar way.

The contrast between the freedman John Jackson and his new master, Livingston, was especially sharp. By New London standards, Livingston was a cosmopolitan adventurer. Whatever his difficulties, he still possessed the grandeur of his family name and manorial heritage, not to overlook his own military bearing. John Jackson, notorious for his association with John Rogers, was an unpropertied African, a common freedman, and a laboring husbandman who had pulled himself out of slavery to form a home and family. But their differences were not simply a matter of class and opportunity. Livingston had squandered many advantages through recklessness and greed, abandoning his young wife for long periods of time—even to struggle alone with a cancer that was killing her. Jackson's troubles, on the contrary, were directly attributable to his African origins and his family's enslavement. Rather than leaving his wife and children to their fate, however, he continued to fight for them in whatever ways he could.

For the Jacksons, the Livingston farm represented a different world. This was no Mamacock, the motley Rogerene enclave devoted to religion, family, and farming. John Livingston would never have been content to have an ordinary New England farmstead in any case. Instead, Livingston Manor was the model for his estate, and John still had hopes of one day replicating the patroonship of his birth on a smaller scale.

Having trained for husbandry with John Rogers, Jackson was probably considered unqualified for work in Livingston's mills and therefore would have continued instead to perform the familiar labor of a farmhand. Joan, too, found a different world of service where Livingston gentlewomen had slave girls as maidservants occupied exclusively with their toilet and belongings. Given their numbers, the Jacksons and other Livingston slaves and servants also probably lived in separate quarters or outbuildings in the manor style, set apart from the Livingston great house and family.[30]

The North Parish house and lands—home to Winthrops and Livingstons along with a retinue of servants—must have impressed John and Joan Jackson with their scale and prestige, but they entered life on the farm at a strange and gloomy time. During a June 21 war council, their master had received his marching orders; the assault on Canada was imminent. The British fleet was expected in Boston in a few days, and Livingston needed to get back to Annapolis Royal. Their mistress, Mary, was already gravely ill and worsening by the week. Within about a month of the Jacksons' arrival, both their master and mistress were gone. The Livingston farm may have appeared grand and imposing, but it was a rudderless ship.[31]

John and Mary Livingston left the farm by July, each on a vital undertaking. Together they went first to Albany and Livingston Manor. There, John left Mary with his parents—who, despite their initial opposition to the marriage, now took a genuine interest in their daughter-in-law's welfare—and then returned to his garrison to await the British fleet. Mary probably had little opportunity to miss her husband, however. By September, she had gone with her father-in-law, Robert, to his Pearl Street town house in Manhattan, where she was confined to a bedchamber. Barely out of her twenties, she was already suffering appallingly with breast cancer. Mary had tried resolving poultices and plasters, but the tumor had defied every attempted cure. The pain had finally become so intolerable that it drove her to agree to the most extreme intervention available: surgery.[32]

For Mary's medical procedure, Robert Livingston brought in the Albany physician Dr. Jacob Staats, whom the family held in the highest esteem; according to John, "the best surgeon by far" in the colonies. Two physicians assisted him. Aside from the expertise these colleagues might bring, Staats needed their dexterity and strength to stop the bleeding and to hold Mary down. Undoubtedly, they were both eager to observe the extraordinary procedure, which would put Staats's considerable medical skills to the test. With little to dull Mary's pain, the Albany surgeon excised her tumor as quickly as he could, removing most of the afflicted breast as well, although, as Robert reported, he "saved her nipple." No matter how efficiently the surgeon worked, the operation took the longest minutes imaginable, leaving the suffering Mary "full of pain," according to her father-in-law. Not unusual in the major cities of Europe, Staats's surgical undertaking was rare in the colonies, perhaps even the first of its kind. (One of the most innovative physicians in the northeast, Boston's Dr. Zabdiel Boylston—known for his pioneering work in promoting smallpox innoculations—did not perform a mastectomy until 1718, seven years after Mary's treatment.)[33]

Through all this, John Livingston was in distant Canada. It was his father, Robert, who watched at Mary's bedside after the surgery. His description to Alida of those first terrible hours was brief and understated: "She has had a bad night; I have sat up with her." The operation was a success, but previous treatments had ruined her chances, he told his wife: "She could have lived for two years [had she been operated on sooner], the doctors say. And she has been cheated by Dr. Laboree [her Connecticut physician]. Thank God it is over." When the initial danger passed, Robert continued to issue reports on her condition in family letters. Hopeful signs came when doctors rebandaged the wound, which was then an elaborate procedure. "She has been bound up now for the second time and looks well." To Alida, Robert wrote of his disapproval of John's inattention: "I hope her husband will come and see her." By the end of September, Mary was able to return home to New London, passing by way of the manor to see her mother-in-law. Robert's fears proved to be accurate: The surgery bought Mary some time, but it could do little more than prolong a grueling march toward certain death.[34]

In Mary's absence, her cousin, John Winthrop IV, had moved to town, finally taking possession of the great patrimony her father, Fitz, had bequeathed to him. Although John IV was eager to defend Livingston's claims against the estate, he was also a reluctant heir. In fact, he had done everything he could to avoid coming to New London. Unlike his father, Wait, he had no fond childhood memories of the place, but his lands needed management so he was forced to leave Boston and move his young family to Winthrop's Neck.[35]

That fall, the Jacksons, too, were adjusting to a new environment— a vacant world with an absent patriarch, a dying mistress, and an inept overseer, if Livingston's complaints are to be believed. And yet the relative disorder at the farm may have provided the Jacksons small, unexpected liberties: a break in the workday or a chance to socialize with other men and women in service. With luck, they even had time for visits with Adam and Miriam, now achingly close at the Fox farm. Perhaps they were permitted to go to the Foxes' later that fall when Bathshua Fox, the mistress who had owned and freed Joan, became sick and died—leaving the eldest Jackson children with one less bulwark against Samuel Beebe.[36]

EITHER JUST before or during the trip home from New York in late September, Mary had received the news from Canada. While she had been awaiting surgery in New York a month before, the British fleet had been making its way up the perilous St. Lawrence River, with Livingston and his men waiting impatiently at Annapolis Royal, when a severe storm struck bringing disaster with it. Massachusetts governor Joseph Dudley wrote his son-in-law John Winthrop IV of "ye dismal and awful account of our fleets miscarriage in Canada river, 8 English transports being foundered, & by the computation they sent us have lost 800 or 1000 men." With the loss of the fleet, the new expedition was now abandoned.[37]

By October, most of the New England troops in Canada had deserted, fleeing home on the first available supply ship. Livingston, too, returned to New London briefly: the first time he had seen Mary since her surgery. But he was back in Annapolis Royal before the winter was out, having accepted Vetch's commission to hold the garrison with a small contingent of Mohawk troops whom Livingston had recruited. Surely he felt a sense of duty to Vetch and to his men, but there is another, less charitable, interpretation: The posting allowed him to escape the unfolding nightmare at home. He wrote tellingly to his father in February 1712, while in New London again on a brief furlough: "My poor spouse continues still very ill and what the upshot of it will be, god knows; there is but little hope of her recovery as I can see but the Dokter gives us some encouragement. My sister Hanna is well." Robert and Alida had sent seventeen-year-old Johanna to help keep Mary company and care for her, but there was an unmistakable coldness in John's assessment of his wife's prospects of survival. It is likely that John had determined she would not live and was moving on. He spent most of 1712 away.[38]

During that same year, John Jackson would have labored in his absent master's fields while Joan worked in and around the rooms, gardens, and barns of the great house. Livingston could spare himself the spectacle of his wife's horrifying decline, but for the rest of 1712, Joan would have to watch the excruciating trials of the mistress about ten years her junior. Already by August, John Livingston's sister Margaret Vetch reported that "[Mary] was given over by her doctors who all despaired of her recovery." By November, Johanna wrote her parents that Mary was "very ill" and had switched doctors, though her brother John seemed more concerned with his own "recurr[ing . . .] illness"—gout—as well as with getting Mary "to send his horse down to Boston for him to come home."[39]

Aware of her mistress's suffering, Joan Jackson had her own new personal tragedy to bear. Her baby, Rachel, the child born during their captivity in Beebe's house on Long Island, must have died during those same months—as the baby's absence from subsequent records indicates. Still, Joan could take heart that all of her other children had survived, when so many other mothers around her were much less fortunate.

Cruel ironies had brought John and Joan Jackson back together, just as they would tear John and Mary Livingston apart; John Jackson's conviction for stealing Joan from Beebe had ended up reuniting husband and wife nonetheless. By contrast, John Livingston foundered on the shoals of opportunity and privilege through his own cupidity and recklessness, and social status had not spared Mary from cancer. The Jacksons surely felt scant comfort seeing their young mistress endure such a bitter stroke, in spite of the injustice they suffered at her hands. Mary wasted away, abandoned by the husband who had once professed everlasting love. As she did so, the governor's daughter was forced to bear witness to an unattainable bounty, just out of reach. With her own body ravaged by cancer—one breast already gone—Mary would see Joan, the pitiable "mulatto" against whom she committed a supreme wrong, swell before her in health and expectation, big with the eighth Jackson child.[40]

* * *

IN EARLY 1713, while a slave at the Livingston farm, Joan Jackson endured her eighth labor and delivered a healthy boy: Jeremiah, nicknamed Jerry. About the time of Jerry's birth, John Livingston returned hastily home. He had not seen fit to be with Mary through her surgery or to stay with her during the worst of her suffering, but he did make it back—if only barely—to be there at her last breath.[41]

Mary died in January. In the end, the trappings of wealth and station that had been insufficient to bring her happiness or to restore her to health even delayed her final rest. Just as John Livingston had made her wait in life, he let Mary's corpse lie in the house unburied for nine long days, postponing the funeral until suitable finery arrived from Boston to display the family's mourning. When Mary's burial finally took place, more than three hundred people attended, snowshoed pallbearers braving a heavy blizzard.[42]

As usual, John Livingston was less careful in managing the private side of his life and finances. He neglected to pay his wife's final medical bills—treatments that included repeated, excruciating redressing of her wound and "14 potions of Physick . . . English saffron 9 potions . . . spirits lavender . . . spirits vitriol [watered-down sulfuric acid]," not to mention eight potions of the costly purgative Gascoigne's powder, containing crabs' eyes, the black tips of crabs' claws, pearls, bezoar (an emetic to induce vomiting, made from antimony and nitric acid), and white coral. He also declined to escort his now eighteen-year-old sister Johanna (who had spent more than a year caring for Mary) back to the manor and her parents, though she felt "very desirous to be at home." Instead, he left her in the North Parish with Mary's anguished mother, Madam "Winthrop," where she waited for months before finally escaping to Boston to stay with the Vetches in the late spring.[43]

IN ALL the years that John Livingston had owned the North Parish farm, he had done relatively little to improve its vast territory, spending much of his time away. Back at the farm in the spring after his wife's death, Livingston lamented the condition of his estate: "All

my business lay here at sixes and sevens." His long absence, together
with Mary's illness and death, had left the farm operations in a ruin-
ous, neglected condition. In particular, he found the servants and
slaves, John and Joan Jackson among them, overindulged and under-
worked. Livingston complained at length in letters to Albany, trying
to rouse his father's sympathy: "I am now under a thousand difficulties concerning my little estate. A house full of servants and at a great
charge and nobody to take care of them in my absence, except an
overseer, which you well know how they manage."[44]

Some of his troubles he now blamed on Mary's grieving mother,
who still lived at the farm: "As for the old gentlewoman [as Livingston sarcastically referred to the innkeeper's daughter], she is good
for nothing but to spoil servants . . . and a very ill-tempered woman.
I thank God that I have no more to do with her only to allow her
thirty pound a year during her life." John soon moved her back to
a house on Winthrop's Neck, but one wonders—if his censure of
his mother-in-law's excessive kindness to servants was correct—if
any of that tenderness had been shown to the Jacksons and their
baby, Jerry.[45]

After Mary's death Livingston's attitude shifted, and he began to
turn his attention to the underdeveloped property with new enthusiasm. Perhaps his imperial disappointments and the mounting debt
he had incurred in military service led him to alter course, but his
grandiose plans had the distinct flavor of a man planning an estate
for his family—a legacy for an heir. This transition had implications
for the Jacksons as well. The neglected farm became a great work-in-
progress that Livingston envisioned as a hive of activity, with fields
and mills producing goods for local and overseas markets.

Livingston's relationship with Elizabeth Knight was not his
first thoughtless amorous adventure, but this one would earn him a
degree of real opprobrium. While Mary was dying, her husband had
made good use of his frequent visits to Boston by starting a romance
with Knight, the daughter of Sarah Kemble Knight, the widowed
businesswoman and travel writer, whom a Boston newspaper called
"ingenious and well known."[46]

Even as he was "tormented with the gout," John had pursued

Elizabeth Knight while he was married, conduct that appalled his sisters, Margaret and Johanna, who now watched the courtship from close by in Boston. To make matters worse, the Knights—though people of some means—were far beneath the Livingstons in strictly social terms. Still, the Livingston family was more concerned with the shortcomings in Miss Knight's moral character than her inferior social credentials. In the same way that the family had examined his first wife and her Winthrop parents' unorthodox union, they now turned their scrutiny onto the Knights and found both mother and daughter wanting. Margaret and Johanna, in particular, hammered their brother and parents with united and resounding disapproval from Boston.[47]

Although Mary had been dead only five months, Margaret wrote her father in June that Knight's "wedding clothes are already amaking . . . [for] I hear [they] have also appointed the day." Then came the kicker: "[John] told me himself as much while his late consort was yet alive about which indeed I shall always think on with abhorrence for in my opinion a woman that will encourage a man in such a matter during the life of his wife is not to be looked on as one of a very good principle; some indeed talk very odd of unlawful familiarities which is best known to himself." Young Johanna, who had spent so long caring for her now-dead sister-in-law, was equally reproving, if more succinct: "[Elizabeth Knight] is a woman of very stone character." She reminded her parents, too, of the difference in social position, lamenting, "Brother despairs our family to make it equal with Mistress Knight from which I know a very ill thing." But it was for the older sister, Margaret, to deliver what she hoped would be the fatal blow: Elizabeth Knight is "a woman of neither note or good family . . . [even] of a stained character." Whether Margaret referred solely to Elizabeth's illicit relationship with her brother or to some other blemish remains unknown.[48]

John felt betrayed by his sisters' opposition—becoming furious with Margaret, in particular, for some time—but he remained unchastened in his pursuit. He wanted Miss Knight, and he aimed to have her. Did he not deserve happiness after all he had suffered in his first marriage? In the face of his resolve, the collective Livingstons begrudgingly relented, and Robert and Alida gave their consent. On October 1, 1713, the Livingston heir married Elizabeth Knight in Boston, her predecessor having spent but a few short months in her New London grave. By spring, the master had returned to take up residence in the North Parish with his new, if slightly tarnished, bride. Shortly afterward, in April 1714, Elizabeth suffered her first miscarriage. The new Livingston bride may have even been pregnant when she married; certainly the North Parish would have been a good place to hide such a fact.[49]

For John, who had already lived through one childless marriage, the end of this first pregnancy was particularly ominous—a signal perhaps of an emerging fact. While families all around him added child after child, John Livingston could not seem to produce even one. Instead of gaining an heir, the Livingston household added a new mother-in-law, the widow Knight, who moved in with John and Elizabeth that spring, just as the tiresome widow "Winthrop" had done before her. Soon "Mother Knight" was also contributing to her son-in-law's till, lending him money to advance his military and investment schemes and maintain a certain lifestyle.[50]

For John Jackson, the return of Livingston, after having been so long under the ambiguous rule of an overseer, might have meant a loss of freedom. Inside the great house, Joan Jackson and the other household women had answered for some time to no authority other than a youthful Johanna Livingston and an elderly "Winthrop" mother-in-law (whom John regarded as soft on servants), and when these surrogates departed, to no one at all. The arrival of a new, Boston-bred mistress of dubious character—followed by her mother—must have been a considerable adjustment. Perhaps Sarah Kemble Knight, who had complained of loose divisions between Connecticut masters and slaves in her travel journal, insisted that her daughter, Elizabeth, try to enforce a strict divide and discipline between the Livingston family and her new charges.

As he anticipated and then realized his union with Elizabeth Knight, Livingston began to implement his plans for the farm. His design was to expand the "great house and garden and pastures for my horses" beyond farming and create a multifaceted, proto-industrial enterprise, encompassing farm production, manufacturing, and trade—much like Livingston Manor itself. Wheat and corn from his fields John would now turn to flour in proprietary mills abutting a large millhouse—"42 feet wide [by] 21 feet and 20 feet . . . tall"—built in 1714. The millhouse was well placed for trade, able to accept sloops for loading at any time during the year. The North Parish was sheep country, and John's new ventures included sheep raising and processing wool in a proprietary fulling mill. He even planned one day to hire a clothier to prepare manufactured cloth for sale as finished product. John detailed his ambitions and pretensions for the farm in letters to his father, Robert. The site he had described unremarkably as "my farm in New London" in the year of the Jacksons' arrival now became "Mount Livingston."[51]

Livingston's workforce—which, in characteristic Livingston fashion, he drew from indentured and bonded workers of all stripes— was varied by New England standards and would have been new to the Jacksons. Aside from employing Algonquin servants and African bondsmen, Livingston even tried to bring some of his parents' tenants to Connecticut, writing his father in 1712 to acquire "two or three Palatine boys and a girl" as servants to be drawn from the manor's refugee settlers from Germany's southwestern Palatinate, though there is no record if they ever came.[52]

Livingston also differed from most of his New London neighbors in the scale and the semi-skilled industrial nature of the work his men performed. When his proprietary mills were running at full throttle in early 1714, John had no fewer than twenty men at work in them. While some of these were probably English or Algonquin day laborers, others must have been servants or African-origin slaves. Although his farm records do not survive, Livingston also needed to employ men outside the mills to work the land and raise animal stock; this and his frequent absences explain why he had broken with New England custom by employing an "overseer" in the manner of the plantation or manor to supervise his workers.[53]

John Jackson had managed to reunite himself with his wife and youngest children by selling his labor to John Livingston. For several years, he even nursed the hope that he might become a landowner himself. In 1714, however, his family was again shattered. This time it was not Samuel Beebe who was responsible; instead the Jacksons found themselves the indirect victims of British imperial politics.

In spite of his grand visions for his farm and his family, John Livingston still labored under a mountain of debt from the advances he had made to the Crown as an Annapolis commander. Having backed Vetch's aborted Canadian expeditions, John Livingston had fallen on the wrong side of royal advantage. For a long time, he continued to hope that reimbursement would come, writing his father in July 1713 that he expected Nicholson to arrive any day with the funds. By December, he had become desperate and began to plan a last-ditch effort to travel to London and plead his case in person.[54]

In January 1714, John Jackson was nearly two years and seven months into his indenture. According to his original agreement with Livingston, he was due at least two acres for the time he had already served. Those terms surely stayed at the forefront of Jackson's mind as he labored for Livingston. They barely registered with his master, however, who was preoccupied with his own financial problems and had begun to make arrangements for his London trip.

Some of the "housecleaning" that Livingston undertook in anticipation of leaving for England was the liquidation of various goods and property to raise cash. The following month, he rented out the farm to Capt. Peter Mason, a member of the Stonington family of celebrated Algonquin interpreters and negotiators, "with all ye stock and servants for two year and ye mills only reserving to myself ye great house and garden and pastures for my horses," as Livingston explained to his father. For unknown reasons, the Jackson family was not part of this arrangement: Instead, Livingston decided to sell them outright. Jack was now around five; Jerry was about one.[55]

On the first of day of 1714, Livingston delivered Joan and little Jerry "by his own hand," according to the deed, to the slave markets of Boston. To John Jackson it must have been a devastating blow. Livingston and his agents made the sale, soliciting buyers to inspect the human merchandise—mother and child—at a tavern, coffee house, or private home. They could have, and surely did, market Joan as other women were being advertised: a "very likely Negro Woman" able to "do all manner of Household Business." It was a Framingham yeoman by the name of John Stone who looked over the sad pair and made their purchase for fifty pounds.[56]

Jack had reached—if only barely—an age serviceable for farm and other labor, so Livingston decided to sell him as a distinct lot, separating him from his mother, father, and siblings. He sold the child to Winslow Tracy, a young man of a respectable Norwich family who was just months away from marrying. Tracy, who would become the father of six sons, thought the enslaved Jackson boy would prove useful in the work of his farm, enabling the soon-to-be bridegroom to establish his own competency.[57]

Within weeks, John Jackson had witnessed the remains of his immediate family torn utterly asunder, while other families—English families—built their domestic prosperity on the labor and personhood of his flesh and blood. It may have been several months into early 1714 before he even learned where Joan and Jerry had landed— whether in Massachusetts or beyond. No doubt he had to rely on his old master, Rogers, to ferret out their whereabouts.

Old John Rogers had personal reasons to empathize with Jackson's plight. Though he was a man of wealth and property, Rogers had also had wives and children taken from him by law. After more than another decade alone, Rogers was trying to form a third marital bond at the very moment that Jackson was fighting again for Joan and his children. The woman Rogers proposed to was Sarah Coles, a widow from Oyster Bay, Long Island. Sarah, who must have shared or at least tolerated Rogerene beliefs, had heard rumors that Rogers had driven his second "wife," Mary Ransford, away. To convince Sarah of his good faith, Rogers took her to Block Island to visit the remarried Ransford and hear directly the story of her flight from New London. A magistrate then married Coles and her sextagenarian bridegroom on the very day they had parleyed with Ransford.

John Jackson faced much bigger hurdles in attempting to reunite with his wife and family. It would have been understandable for Jackson, seeing Joan and their youngest children taken from him again, to resign himself to grief and to defeat. He could also have chosen to soldier on alone, as Rogers had done for so many years. Or he might have simply moved on, as Livingston had, turning his back on his terrible loss. But Jackson was determined to fight back, resolute against all logic and possibility. The family clash that had begun between factions of the Rogerses—with the Jacksons caught in the middle—would reverberate long into the future.

Chapter Eight

"THE WAYS OF PROVIDENCE"

LTHOUGH THE Jacksons faced particular burdens, every family in colonial New England confronted the possibility of sudden destruction. Just as John Jackson was tested, the amiable shipwright Joshua Hempstead would have to decide what kind of husband and father he wanted to be. The Hempstead family experienced no persecution under color of law, but it was torn apart by the ravages of successive illnesses that shattered the family's very foundations. For two generations, Hempstead children endured the early loss of a parent.

The first decade of marriage had been good to Joshua and Abigail Hempstead. Joshua spent those years hard at work, providing for his family in the shipwright's trade, shuttling between different yards and projects. It had taken him more than a decade as a journeyman before he was able to strike out on his own. Then in 1713, with a small store of capital and a new adze from New York, Joshua rented a yard from a Bream Cove neighbor and began his first "ground-up" construction of a boat—probably a sloop—called the *Joseph*. Running his own small yard, the father of eight—now including two little girls, Abigail and Betty—hired local ship carpenters and used his two eldest boys, Josh and Nathaniel, as helpers. When he and Abigail took in Ebenezer "Ebe" Hubbell after Ebe's shipwright father died, the boy joined them in the yard.[1]

Joshua was well liked, and given his skills and contacts, business flowed along nicely. By 1715, the brewer and tailor Solomon Coit—an Edgecombe neighbor and member of the shipbuilding Coit family—had contracted with Joshua to design and build another sloop. Securing his success as a wright, Joshua began to trade in earnest—a clear sign that he hoped to move beyond the work and pay of a tradesman.[2]

Since his boyhood, Joshua's path toward the shipwright's craft had given him entrée into an ancient artisanal wood culture. In manhood, becoming a shipwright also provided a natural link to the commercial economy. Craftsmen like Joshua saw no contradiction in pursuing a trade in the shop and a competence in the field, while also engaging in gainful trade with the Atlantic mercantile world. It was a small distance to travel from fabricating "horserooms" on the latest vessel to stocking those rooms with a horse or two of one's own when the ship was ready to sail. Though a builder, Joshua also routinely loaded vessels with trade goods for profit: livestock, candles, bee's wax, tobacco—even oats borrowed from a neighbor. He began small, making modest "venture[s]" by buying cargo space along with a shipmaster's time and judgment to complete the transaction at the other end of a voyage. In late August 1713, for example, he sent "a Ram by [Captain John Mayhew] & £13: 4s: 03d in Silver" to Barbados. Two and a half months later he received "1 h[ogs]h[ea]d Rum 8 lb Pepper & 4 yds Cherry dery [fabric]" in return.[3]

Such ventures provided profits, and they also created new opportunities to help his extended family. Part of the silver he sent with Mayhew belonged to his sister Mary, wife of the mariner Green Plumb and a mother of four children. Mary's husband had set off on a voyage to the West Indies and had not been heard from in five years, so she was trying to manage alone. Helping out a sister in need involved more than simply adding her account to Joshua's own. There were also the little, uncompensated tasks necessary to see her share through. Four months after Joshua sent the ram and silver out, he could be found at a town warehouse, "drawing Sister Marys part out of my h[ogs]h[ea]d" of rum, assuring with his own hand that the presumed widow got hers. With her husband long gone, Mary could rely on her younger brother.[4]

These small successes in trade made Joshua Hempstead want a bigger piece of the traffic. By 1714, the Bream Cove shipwright had begun to invest directly in sloops, usually taking on a small fractional share and spreading his exposure between vessels and voyages. While farming and building ships could provide a decent living, they were low-margin, labor-intensive activities. Joshua had ambitions to move beyond competency and to accumulate enough wealth to buy land for his sons. Trading, even on a small scale, offered the opportunity of higher profits, although the risks of market, weather, and accident were greater. As partners, Joshua chose men he trusted and had known all his life, often members of his extended family.[5]

It was the *Samuel*, a tidy little sloop built in 1714 by his stepbrother Samuel Edgecombe, in which Joshua took his first share: one-sixteenth. Such joint ventures were not simply arms-length transactions, but active, tangible investments that required Joshua to get his hands dirty. As the *Samuel* made its way to and from the Indies, Joshua and his partners were kept busy "making up acctts," "unloading ye Sloop & dividing" cargo, "fetching . . . 2,000 Staves," hiring shipmasters, and maintaining the vessel. Their takings came in various forms, including salt, molasses, rum, and sugar—goods Joshua slipped into Ben Starr's cellar right off the boat, then sold and exchanged over time on the local market.[6]

By 1716, Joshua's prospects abroad appeared yet more promising, and his contentment at home was apparent. Two of his sons were already beginning to follow their father's trade. Joshua had attained some financial security so his boys would not have to face early apprenticeships as he and his father had done. Meanwhile, Abigail had fulfilled the best aspirations of any upright New England girl as an excellent domestic manager and fruitful mother—widely acknowledged as a "good wife," as Wait Winthrop once wrote of her. In 1716, she was pregnant with their ninth child, at the age of thirty-nine. As a mother she had reason to feel particular happiness and gratitude. At a time when parents could not expect all their children, perhaps not even one, to reach adulthood, Abigail had been exceptionally fortunate. During the years of her marriage, she had given birth to eight healthy children, and every one of them had survived the perilous stage of infancy. That July, all of them surrounded her: Josh, seventeen; Nathaniel, sixteen; Robert, thirteen; Stephen, ten; Thomas, eight; John, six; Abigail, four; and Betty, two. Together, they offered ample evidence that this pregnancy, too, would probably proceed smoothly.[7]

Joshua and Abigail Hempstead had had a potent reminder of their good fortune the previous winter and spring. During those cold months when families remained holed up in cramped houses, a measles epidemic had hit New London. Measles, like smallpox and diphtheria, was an implacable killer during this period, for which there was no effective remedy. In the midst of any outbreak, men and women tried to continue their daily routines, but these were often interrupted to care for the sick, visit the dying, and attend funerals. Even when a particular household or family was spared, its members still experienced any epidemic directly and intimately as friends and neighbors of the afflicted. When word arrived, friends and neighbors ran to help the sick and dying. They watched with their own eyes, prayed with their own words, and nursed with their own hands. They scoured the town for medical help, and when medicine and prayers failed, friends and neighbors consoled the bereft. Finally, they accompanied the surviving family members to the burying ground, standing by as the latest victims entered the earth.

In 1715, Joshua and Abigail had watched the disease closing in around them, progressively consuming families. On February 12, Jonathan Hill asked Joshua to make a coffin for nine-year-old William, who had died the night before. Local families often asked Joshua to make their coffins, which usually took him less than a day—it was by necessity quick work, since unembalmed bodies did not last long. Entrusting a loyal neighbor like Joshua to make a loved one's coffin might also have given some comfort. For Joshua, crafting coffins could be a productive channel for bereavement. When Hill needed a coffin for his boy, Joshua went directly home to his tools and pine boards. Hurriedly, he assembled the simple flat-sided box in his lean-to workshop, a black hexagon that would follow the outlines of William's body. As the box took shape, its maker looked with new eyes on the healthy body of his own nine-year-old, Stephen, so like the one he had measured for burial. Hammering boards, he could think of dead William, "ye same age of our Stephen," and count his blessings.[8]

The next day had brought further cause for Hempsteads to pray and be thankful. Eleven-year-old Jonathan Hill, Jr.—about the same age as Joshua's son Robert—succumbed after his younger brother. The Hills had not yet interred William, and now Joshua set to work making a slightly larger twin to William's coffin. Soon the two brothers, along with the hopes of their parents, were "buried in one Grave," their coffin maker looking on. The boys' little sister, seven-year old Ruth Hill, was so ill she could not come to see the burial. Still reeling from the deaths of their sons, the Hills then lost Ruth—the same age as Joshua's Thomas—the day after the funeral. Keenly aware of the encroaching risk, Joshua wrote ominously in his diary that the child had been a healthy little girl only one week before.[9]

The Hills were not the only family to suffer such a heavy toll. One day after Ruth Hill's death, another young daughter of New London, Ebenezer Dennis's six- or seven-year-old girl, also perished. The following evening, February 17, after many hours reworking ships at the harbor, Joshua attended the child's funeral. The next night her grieving mother, Sarah Dennis, gave birth, but the infant was dead by morning. Exhausted and ailing, Sarah Dennis listened for the second time in the space of two days as mourners gathered around the entry of her house to walk another child to the grave. It was more than the stricken mother could bear. She held on only until the family returned from the burying ground. That very night Joshua received word from Sarah's husband, Ebenezer: Would he make his dear Sarah's coffin? Joshua began work immediately and watched the black box enter the earth the very next day.[10]

For the twenty-eight days that followed, Joshua alternated between shipyard employments and watching the sick and dying.

Although he continued to work and to write, the entries in his diary began to fray at the edges, straining under the weight of the surrounding calamity. Some days Joshua neglected to work—or perhaps, to record what work he did do, focusing instead on deaths and funerals. Perhaps he was also too distracted to look up and out across the water, for he abandoned his usual habit of noting the comings and goings in New London Harbor. Still, as the disease closed in on his family, the diary's very existence, its semblance of constancy, gave solace.[11]

When the disease finally entered Joshua's house on March 23, it slipped through a back door. Rachel, one of Abigail's hired girls, had not appeared that morning. As the day progressed, Abigail's worst fears were confirmed: Rachel had the measles. Even though the girl had not come to her mistress's house that day, Abigail and Joshua knew when they put the children to bed at night that it would be only a matter of time. In less than a week, Joshua was staying home from the shipyard, lingering to watch over Abigail, the first to become sick even as she nursed little Betty. The next Sabbath, Mr. Adams was too unwell to preach. No Hempsteads attended meeting either. Those in the family who were not ill were sorely needed to care for the afflicted.[12]

Joshua remained well. Perhaps an earlier bout with the disease had given him some immunity. Until the middle of May, he continued to work fitfully at the harbor. The sloop *Samuel*, in which he was an investor, arrived loaded with goods from Barbados, and Joshua attended to the cargo. Amid the usual talk of work and local events, he laced the diary with clipped references to his domestic turmoil. The seemingly innocuous "I was about home most of ye day," carried somber meaning as "Nath[aniel] broke out ye measles" and "Abiga[i]l is very Ill." On the tenth, Joshua noted "a Gen[era]ll Fast," an official day of prayer and atonement for a populace in the throes of a devastating epidemic.[13]

Joshua must have been very anxious for Abigail, although he would address his worries only indirectly in the diary. When John Chappell's "Daughter Christian a young woman . . . had ye measles & died Suddenly" on April 9, he surely considered the peril to his own wife. On the twenty-eighth, Abigail lost her father in Southold, but was too sick to attend his funeral. In May, however, she suddenly showed signs of substantial improvement. Joshua wrote, "34 days Since ye measels [*sic*] broke out on her," she rose from her bed "to go alone." It was the beginning of a full recovery.[14]

A year later, as Abigail's ninth labor approached, collective memories of sickness and death in New London were still raw. But the timing of this child's birth was good, even promising. Women's intense work of spring and summer would soon be over: The house was likely cleaned, the garden tended, cheese made. Abigail's husband, too, was anticipating a birthing of his own—one that had also taken many months to realize. Shortly after the previous year's epidemic and not long before the conception of their ninth child, Joshua Hempstead had entered into a contract to build a sloop. Again his partner was tailor-entrepreneur Sol Coit of the shipbuilding Coits. Aside from overseeing its construction, Joshua also took a one-quarter stake in the vessel. In the months after the contract was signed, Abigail's abdomen grew big with the last Hempstead child as Joshua's sloop, later christened the *Plainfield*, took form in a shipyard nearby.[15]

By the summer of 1716, both the baby and the sloop were nearly ready. On a hot July 28, Joshua called "al hands a Graving" to the yard, including seventeen-year-old Joshua junior and sixteen-year-old Nathaniel, to grave the ship's bottom. (One of the final steps in preparing a boat to embark, graving was a wearisome task that involved burning off accumulated matter and then sealing the sides with hot tar.) Two days after Joshua tarred the *Plainfield*, Abigail went into labor. Having borne eight children, she knew what to expect, likely waiting until she was well along before she "mustered ye women," to use her husband's martial turn of phrase. On July 31, the women of the neighborhood would have received word—perhaps from a breathless Hempstead son—that Abigail was near her time. They dropped what they were doing and went to her. Fortifying food and drink probably awaited them, for no one knew how long they would need to attend. When she gave birth in her chamber, Abigail drew on a midwife and a congregation of women for help and strength.[16]

While the women gathered around Abigail, Joshua left the house to collect timber. He needed wood to lay a log path leading from the shipyard to the water's edge. Across it he would draw the *Plainfield* to launch. If he did come home during the course of the day to check on Abigail's progress, he did not write of it. Perhaps after eight healthy births, Joshua, the expectant father, could afford the luxury of a certain nonchalance. Joshua may also have preferred to keep busy rather than sit helplessly at home hearing every sound coming from the next room. Around sunset and surrounded by her neighbors, Abigail gave birth to Mary, a hale and hearty girl the family would call Molly.[17]

One day after Molly's birth, her father launched the sloop he had built throughout her mother's pregnancy. During the three days afterward, Joshua put finishing touches on the *Plainfield* and traveled to Fisher's Island to salvage a mast from a wreck that lay there. At home, Abigail likely drank restorative tea and rum and kept largely to her bed. Little Molly began nursing, although her initial forays were probably on a breast other than Abigail's. The premilk of new mothers was thought to be impure.[18]

During the days after Molly's arrival, Joshua mentioned neither his new daughter nor her mother in his diary entries. Instead he wrote of his progress on the *Plainfield*, so close to completion. Not until August 4, when Joshua spent another entire day "in ye [ship]yard about Town" did he refer to them again. Coming home to sup that night, he found Abigail "very Ill." From there on, her descent was precipitous.[19]

Joshua spent that desperate night trying to save her, bringing in the best medical men New London had to offer. The first to come to Abigail's bedside was the relative newcomer John Winthrop IV, who, like his father and grandfather, offered medical treatments and "used means for her Relief." Despite John IV's efforts, "relief" was probably the last thing the weakened mother felt as she endured his well-intentioned ministrations. The cure he brought was probably the famed Winthrop remedy, "rubila," developed decades earlier by John Winthrop, Jr., which induced fierce vomiting and diarrhea. John IV had inherited the secret formula and he mixed the potion regularly, often sending it to relatives, friends, and innumerable admirers and supplicants.[20]

When Joshua asked John IV to come to him on the night of August 4, it was Winthrop's expertise but, in particular, his rubila that he anxiously sought. This same "Physick," or medicine, Joshua could recall, had brought his son John back from a dangerous sickness four winters past. Perhaps it might now save his wife. In spite of these hopes and the harsh purgings the medicine elicited, Abigail's condition did not improve. A little before midnight, Joshua used the only weapon remaining in his arsenal. He sent for Mr. Jeremiah Miller, the local schoolmaster.[21]

Miller had graduated from the school that became Yale in 1709, having studied medicine. He had settled in New London to practice his profession and had taken on the role of schoolmaster in 1714 to supplement his income. Like John IV, Miller was one of the few college-educated men in town and thereby had the theoretical and anatomical training necessary to engage in phlebotomy, or bloodletting, a therapy performed exclusively by educated male practitioners. Joshua and Abigail had faith in Miller. One year earlier they had sent their son Thomas to live with and receive schooling from him. Around midnight on the fourth, Miller let blood in Abigail's foot.[22]

The appearance of Winthrop and Miller at Abigail's ultimate hour was noteworthy. Medical practice in early New England was customarily women's work. Male physicians, trained by apprenticeship and later at institutions of higher learning, did not begin to dominate until the late eighteenth century. During Joshua's lifetime, basic medical care for ordinary New Englanders remained firmly in the hands of women, typically midwives, especially when ailments concerned pregnancy and childbirth. Joshua's decision to consult male practitioners demonstrated his desire to pursue every means to save Abigail, but it also connected him to circles of scientific knowledge and education—not to mention social standing and political power. Joshua's progressive outlook on medicine, like his pursuit of journal writing, revealed his aspirations to achieve a more empirical, learned understanding of the world.[23]

On August 5, despite the best efforts of family, neighbors, and available medicine, Joshua's "Dear Wife Died about a half an hour before Sunrise." Writing of her death, her husband described no symptoms and named no disease, as he often did when locals died. Probably neither Joshua nor anyone around him knew exactly what had taken her so quickly. The cause may have been childbed, or puerperal, fever, then an untreatable streptococcal infection that was a common cause of death soon after delivery. Like Abigail, a mother stricken with the fever often first gave birth to a healthy child, only to develop a severe infection shortly after. Once the infection took hold, an eighteenth-century sufferer descended quickly and all but inevitably toward a painful and feverish death.[24]

Throughout her illness, family, neighbors, and friends would have gathered around Abigail at her bedside, staying up day and night to watch over her. When she died, she left few identifying markers outside the lasting impression on the faces and hearts that surrounded her. As her sea-captain neighbor Joseph Coit put it at the death of his adult daughter, "at her deathbed the bystanders were the greatest sufferers." In such bystanders, Abigail's memory remained very much alive, however. One of them took down the last words of this "loving and devout mother"—as she lay dying, on a scrap of paper that would be passed from hand to hand across time. Abigail did not live long, but Hempsteads would remember her, even nine generations later, as a mother who had faced death's prospect with her children's spiritual well-being uppermost in her mind.[25]

"Oh, my dear children," Abigail warned, "avoid evil company, & let your minds be on things above, & not on things below . . . you are born to die, & yt in a little time, for ye day of ye Lord is at hand & will suddenly overtake you . . . remember ye words of your dying mother."[26]

Would her words be strong enough to carry them through the long motherless years that lay ahead? The sorrow of uncertainty, of not seeing her children grow up, was Abigail's agony. Yet if she doubted her husband's capacity to bear this dreadful stroke, she need not have. Joshua would keep her memory and her wishes alive in their children's hearts, just as he preserved her words and her example in a small slip of anguished dictation.

After the awful night of her death, Joshua remained "at home al day." Although it was the Sabbath, he did not attend meeting. Instead, he prepared for the funeral and consoled his children while grieving his own terrible loss. Women from the neighborhood, his mother and sisters probably among them, would have come to lay Abigail out. Just as they had visited her house to exchange milk or wool, women would now wash her body, trim her hair, and clothe her one last time in a hastily sewn shroud of white linen. After they had finished, the women would lay her out in an open coffin or directly on a table in the hall, covering her partially with black cloth. Joshua and the children probably stayed mainly with her, as mourners came to extend condolences and sit up with the corpse. In the evening, Joshua managed the walk up to the burying place overlooking the harbor and shipyards where he worked. His was the sorrowful errand of selecting the site for Abigail's grave and paying the sexton to dig it.[27]

On the morning of Monday, August 6, Joshua faced and greeted the last of his visitors. By noon, rain had begun to fall in steady streams as mourners gathered in and about the hall, peering through outside windows once the room was full. Around one o'clock, the party collected at the front door and entryway as the pallbearers raised Abigail's coffin to their shoulders and began the slow march toward the gravesite. The small, dark company made its incremental course up the dirt road, gathering apologetic stragglers along the way.[28]

The story of what happened next was passed down through the Hempstead family for generations. According to family lore, Joshua junior, the firstborn Hempstead child, was struck particularly hard by his mother's death. As the funeral procession began to collect near the front of their house, the seventeen-year-old looked on from where he stood at the drinking well, grieving bitterly. He continued to watch as the black of the casket traced an unsteady course above the heads of the column of men. Down the worn path the coffin hovered, trailing southward from the house to the highway. It was time for the family to follow, but the boy stood fixed in place, unable to move. Later, family members retold, "grief so swelled in his heart that he burst a blood vessel." Joshua junior collapsed onto the ground, lying there until some of the mourners retreated and carried him inside. At home, the boy remained inconsolable as the rest of the family interred his mother's body at two o'clock. He soon grew "very Ill . . . with a Sore Throat & fevar," pointing perhaps to a new or different cause for his decline, but his beleaguered father could not commit himself fully to his eldest child's care. Molly, just days old, needed him most.[29]

The night following Abigail's funeral, it continued to rain heavily. In the midst of the downpour, Joshua bundled up his poor "babe" and walked gingerly along the same muddy path he had taken earlier to bury her mother. They trod over the crude bridge south of the house and then the few more steps to their Truman neighbors. Perhaps when Joshua passed an old pear tree "of my Grandfathers planting" in the first hard years of settlement, the recollection eased his heavy spirit. At the Trumans', where Thomas and Susanna still lived, their sister-in-law Mary (the wife of Thomas's brother, Joseph junior), was expecting them. A nursing mother herself, Mary Truman had agreed to feed the Hempstead newborn until her father could find Molly a permanent wet nurse.[30]

The relief Joshua felt at securing temporary care for baby Molly was all too brief. Three days after burying Abigail, her husband resumed work on the *Plainfield*. When he came home from the yard that evening, he found Joshua junior now gravely ill, his condition having worsened considerably. He watched and nursed his son for hours as the boy took "Extream bad about Midnight." Once again Joshua sent for Jeremiah Miller, who "Readyly gat up Came to See him & tarryed al night using Such Means as he thought most proper." One more night and into the next day Joshua stayed at the child's bedside. Then came the dreaded hour when his "Dutyfull Son Joshua Died about Noon like a Lamb being 17 years & 20 days old a patren of patience." Redoubled in his grief, Joshua Hempstead watched and waited again as neighbors and kin came to lay out the body and offer their sympathies. Once more he walked to the burying ground, now to set his firstborn next to Abigail in her fresh grave.[31]

Stricken though he was, Joshua came to meeting the very next day on a different kind of errand. In his arms Joshua held his infant, Molly, whom he had brought for Mr. Adams to baptize. The week that had passed had been the most harrowing of his life. But in his diary Molly's father used less than a page to make a terse record of her birth, and of the deaths of her mother and brother. An unusual boldness in the lettering and a simple penline frame around the entries were the only acknowledgment of the extraordinary sorrow his words described.[32]

In the face of so much loss, Joshua still had to resume his daily activities and obligations almost immediately. His work on the *Plainfield* continued, and toward the end of the same month that had claimed his wife and son, the *Samuel* arrived from Barbados with a load of goods. Meanwhile, at home, Joshua was grappling with bleak alternatives. Now the sole parent of eight children from one week to sixteen years in age, he had to determine how to care for them. He had no doubts about keeping his five boys, who ranged from six to sixteen, at home with him. Each of them, even the youngest, John, had begun to assist their father in his work and would prove increasingly useful in oncoming years. Thinking of little Abigail, his eldest daughter at just age four, Joshua wondered if she might also stay with him. With help from neighbors, sisters, and hired women, he must have reasoned, he would be able to provide enough female guidance for his little girl. The thought of losing another Abigail might simply have been too much. He decided to keep his dead wife's namesake at home, no matter the challenges. He would have to send his youngest daughters away, however. He understood that a father alone could not care for children as small as Molly and her two-year-old sister, Betty. He needed to find families where he could place his little girls—at least for the time being.[33]

Eight days after Abigail's funeral, Joshua carried two letters to the harbor and asked shipmaster Samuel Gardiner to deliver them to Long Island. One was to Thomas Tallmadge in Easthampton, who was married to one of Abigail's sisters. The letter would have told of everything Joshua's family had recently endured, especially of the deaths of their sister and nephew. Receiving it, Thomas and Mary Tallmadge passed the sad news on to family and friends. A second letter went to the Salmons who lived in Southold. Hannah Salmon, wife of William, was the third Bailey sister.[34]

After Salmon learned the sorrowful news, he entered it in the long chronicle he kept that tracked Southold births, deaths, and marriages. The drive to record and remember was one that the weaver

William Salmon shared with his Hempstead brother-in-law. But the deaths of his sister-in-law and nephew cracked open the contained, local world Salmon had faithfully represented since 1696 in his chronicle. His two entries—"August 5—Sister Hempsted at New London" and "August 10—Joshua Hempsted"—were among the very few that strayed beyond Southold's bounds.[35]

Nineteen days after his letters left New London, Joshua received a visit from the Tallmadges. They arrived in New London the night of September 12, lodging most likely in the hall where Abigail's body had recently lain. For the next five days, they visited with Joshua and the children, brightening spirits and accompanying the family to meeting. During the Tallmadges' stay, Joshua worked as little as possible in order to spend time with them. Each day, Mary Tallmadge might have paid special attention to little Betty. Perhaps the child even found a comforting resemblance between her maternal aunt and the mother she had so recently lost.[36]

Forty-two days after her mother's death, two-year-old Betty left the only home she had ever known. Her father had arranged for her to stay with her aunt and uncle Tallmadge in Easthampton. Thoughtfully, he sent a big brother, eight-year-old Thomas, on the trip over to ease Betty's adjustment and "keep her Company a while." For Joshua, the parting was a painful one, filled with the awareness that it might easily become permanent. As he watched his "pritty babe Elizabeth" "Carryed away" on the boat bound for Long Island, he could not bring himself to turn away. Instead, he and ten-year-old Stephen kept the small party in their sights, watching the boat's course by walking from the harbor where it embarked all the way to Goshen on the General Neck—a distance of nearly four miles. Then, from the beaches of Goshen, the very place where decades earlier John Rogers might have first baptized his Rogerenes, he and Stephen watched the boat until, barely in sight, it reached the shores of the Island. By holding Betty in view, Joshua tried to protect her from harm, even to keep her somehow with him. He would make sure to visit his little girl regularly, but the separation from Betty— so difficult to bear that bright September day—would prove to be a long one.[37]

It was less than a month, though, before Joshua looked in on Betty in Easthampton for the first time. In mid-October, they spent a weekend together, and after the visit, Joshua and the Tallmadges went to the Salmons' in Southold. There two remaining Bailey sisters and their husbands talked again of Abigail and most gravely of the newborn daughter she had left behind. During the two months since her mother's death, little Molly had remained just over the brook from her father at their Truman neighbors. Mary Truman had cared for her ably, but the arrangement was temporary. It was to one of Abigail's sisters that Joshua hoped to entrust his littlest "babe." In the house of a maternal aunt, he felt, his daughter would be treated as one of their own. With Betty already situated at the Tallmadges', it was to the Salmons that Joshua now turned. Would they take in Molly—their tiny motherless niece—just two and a half months old?[38]

The Salmons agreed, offering their home and family to Molly, and within two weeks her father brought her to them. The November crossing proved difficult, including a missed landing and a night in the cold. Throughout the ordeal, Molly rested in the arms of Mary Truman, the trusted neighbor to whom she owed her life. The trio finally arrived in Easthampton, where they spent nearly a week, due to bad weather, visiting with little Betty and Aunt and Uncle Tallmadge. When the weather cleared, they brought Molly to Southold and left her at the Salmons'. By arrangement, Joshua agreed to a compensation of three shillings sixpence per week for Molly's care. The rate reflected a premium on the bare-bones two shillings sixpence of weekly support that courts typically required fathers to pay to support illegitimate children. To cover Molly's expenses, Joshua sold forty acres of land, receiving both cash and a bond payable to William Salmon. For Joshua, taking leave of Molly appeared easier than parting with Betty had been. Molly had spent most of her short life at the Trumans', so father and daughter had had little chance to know each other. Joshua's relief at seeing his infant finally safe and well settled, after such a difficult start, might have outweighed any sadness he felt at letting her go.[39]

By sending his two small daughters away to live with relatives,

Joshua observed accepted custom that he believed would best serve
the children's interests. Even if he had wanted to, Joshua could not
have cared for the girls and maintained his work, civic responsibilities, and commercial interests. This obvious truth had less to do
with their gender than their infancy. Joshua's young sons were old
enough to accompany their father in his daily activities or to follow
the direction of older brothers in his absence. A father might also
piece together enough female supervision to keep a slightly older
girl, like their sister, Abigail, at home with him. Little Betty and
Molly still required the kind of intensive hands-on care that in early
New England only women and girls, whose work revolved in and
around the household, could provide.

It was typical for a widower with small children to turn to nearby
married women and relatives for wet-nursing and child care, as
Joshua did. James Fitch of Norwich, who lost his wife after childbirth during Joshua's boyhood, had also relied on a local woman
who came and "suckle[d]" the child (although in Fitch's case, the
woman had first nursed the ailing mother, who believed in breast
milk's curative powers). In New England and throughout the early
modern world, nursing mothers were everywhere. Most women had
long and active reproductive lives, extending from their late teens or
early twenties into their fourth decade. Pregnancies came at frequent
intervals, and babies nursed for around two years. A widower therefore could turn to a close neighbor, like Mary Truman, to nourish
a motherless infant. For longer-term care, relatives were the most
reliable option. The widower George Denison of nearby Westerly,
Rhode Island, faced a calamity similar to Joshua's in 1724, when
his wife died leaving an infant son. Knowing he could not care for
the boy, Denison turned him over to close maternal relatives—in
his case to in-laws who agreed to take in their grandson as a matter
of course.[40]

There was also nothing strange or unseemly in paying for a child's
maintenance. Families who took children in for wet-nursing and care,
even close relatives like the Salmons, usually received compensation.
(In fact Molly's ever-practical father, retrieving his daughter after
eighteen months of nursing, duly and proudly recorded the weight
she had gained, even noting the cost per pound as if she were a prize

calf: "She hath gained by weight 11 ¼ lb. tht is £1 5s 2d p[er] lb.")
George Denison's father-in-law, Joseph Minor, refused any due compensation to care for his daughter's baby precisely because he wanted to raise the boy as his own son. He told Denison, "I don't desire you to give me anything for bringing up the child, for I will take him as my own." In place of payment, the grandfather expected Denison to relinquish the rights and privileges of fatherhood. In the same way, a father like Joshua who paid for child care affirmed and secured his rights to that child—rights that included the child's labor.[41]

Once his two youngest were in care, Joshua was able to move beyond the immediate crisis of Abigail's death. Meeting his girls' urgent needs had consumed much of his thoughts during the three months since he had lost his wife and son. With Betty and Molly securely placed, their father was left with the hollow ache of his own grief. With it came the awful awareness of the long future that stretched before him, the sole parent now of eight children. A week or more after his wife and son had been buried, Joshua had likely kept his bereavement on view in the black of his mourning clothes, eventually perhaps reduced to an armband of plain black crepe. Of inner longing or despair, Joshua revealed nothing in his diary. Given all that he had suffered, the words he did write were flat in their strict adherence to the diary's impassive form. However, signs of Joshua's anguish over the loss of his wife survive in hidden places in the diary.[42]

Traces of Joshua's grief may be found in his references to the deaths of other mothers who left young children behind. When his stepsister, Sarah Edgecombe Bolles, "Died ths morning before Daylight aged 58 years & past," Joshua felt the need to add: "Left 8 Sons & 2 Daughters growing." Factual on its face, this last phrase mirrored Joshua's own ordeal. Similarly, Joshua echoed his experience when he wrote of "the wife of abel Moor[e] near Lyme line [who] Died this morning In child bed having had Twins and both living & 7 Children before." Joshua seemed to find kinship or consolation in the suffering of other widows and widowers. His clipped reports of the losses around him were as close as he came to expressing grief about Abigail in the diary.[43]

Perhaps the most compelling sign of Joshua's love for Abigail, and of his sorrow over her death, was the extraordinary choice he made once she was gone. He probably came to his decision gradually, as a soft backdrop to his everyday life, eventually embracing it with wholehearted conviction. Joshua was the rare widower who did not seek another wife—in a world where widowers with small children nearly always remarried, and usually with some haste. Widowers who wed quickly were not coldhearted: They were answering a real practical necessity. Aside from profound emotional solitude, parenting alone posed enormous practical and economic difficulties that few fathers were equipped to shoulder. A widower faced a huge shortfall of domestic industry in the form of cleaning, washing, preparing food, making cloth, and sewing clothing, not to mention caring for small children. A wife's work was labor that few men could manage without. Typical was the reaction of Solomon Coit, the shipwright Joseph's brother and Joshua's sometime business partner. Like Abigail, Coit's wife died shortly after giving birth in 1713. Before thirteen months were out, Coit took another wife. When this second wife then died during the measles epidemic of 1715, he remarried again within just ten months.[44]

Joshua may have struggled over the decision to remarry, as some widowers did. There was the very real concern that a new wife would not be a good stepmother to beloved children. Fathers also faced the important worry that having additional children with another wife would not only distract her from caring for those already born but also deplete a limited estate. Joshua cared deeply about providing for his children's futures; adding more dependents would have strained his ability to do so. His exisiting brood would probably not have hurt him in the marriage market, however. Then as now, some women looked on widowers with small children with particularly sympathetic eyes, finding them all the more appealing for their familial distress. For most widowers who wrestled with reservations about remarriage, however, the weight of domestic burdens without and of loneliness within ultimately led them to claim another woman for a wife. Joshua was the uncommon father who chose not to.[45]

Although Abigail's ever-devoted husband never wrote why he decided to remain single, his diary gave certain clues about broader qualms he may have felt about remarriage. He clearly seemed to admire those men and women who, like himself, carried on alone after losing a spouse. Joshua took special notice in his diary when a longtime widow or widower died, as though they deserved particular acknowledgment. Memorializing their all-too-familiar solitude and fortitude, Joshua recognized kindred spirits: "Richd Morgan aged about 66 or 7 died of a Consumption. he hath lived Single Since his wifes death above 20 yr"; "I was at the funeral of old Ms Solely Late of Boston. . . . She has been a Widow 58 years & was upwards of 93 yr old"; "the Widow Mary Comstock aged about 83 Died. Widow of Kingsland Comstock who Died with the fall from a horse above 50 years ago." In his reserved, implicit way, Joshua wanted to acknowledge the loyalty and sacrifice of these long-enduring spouses.[46]

Conversely, Joshua obliquely disapproved of inordinately quick remarriages, as when an uncle's widow remarried within two months of her husband's death, or a widow Webber waited less than six weeks to find a replacement for her dead husband. He seemed to reserve a more pointed, if still indirect, censure for marriages with large age gaps, like those of the septuagenarians John Fox and Henry Delamore, both of whom married women half a century their juniors.[47]

If Joshua himself made any romantic forays in an attempt to remarry, however, his efforts must have been halfhearted or short-lived. Joshua's social world abounded with opportunities to find a wife and, by any contemporary standard for his station, he was an excellent catch. He was a master craftsman with a marketable trade, possessed of a respectable and growing estate. Politically, Joshua was a man on the rise, having already been elected to the first town office of selectman and to the General Assembly representing New London. In a society in which one's good name was the best currency of all, the name of Joshua Hempstead was held in the highest regard. When New London needed a man of upright character and indisputable honesty, Joshua came immediately to the collective mind. He served as a constable, a grand juror, and on innumerable trial juries. He was chosen as a guardian to orphaned children, an appraiser of valuable estates, and an arbitrator between parties in conflict. In his more intimate relationships—when children were sick, spouses died, and houses caught fire—family, friends, and neighbors turned to him. If he had wanted to, Joshua Hempstead surely had ample opportunities to remarry.

Though Joshua chose not to take another wife, he probably did not pursue an illicit sexual relationship in its place, at least not over the long term. In close-knit New England, it would have been difficult for a locally prominent man to maintain both his good name and a sexual liaison outside marriage. The risks to his reputation, including an out-of-wedlock pregnancy, were substantial. Though not a major offense, fornication or sex with an unmarried woman was a crime that remained at best socially undesirable, especially during the first half of the eighteenth century. Leniency toward offenders prevailed in the latter half of the century, but that leniency was directed toward the young—in particular toward couples who subsequently married.[48]

Adultery with a married woman was a felony that carried harsh sanctions, a fact of which Joshua was conspiciously reminded just three years after Abigail's death when, as a grand juror, he helped indict a Plainfield physician, Dr. William Bloggett, for adultery with a magistrate's wife. Joshua observed Bloggett's conviction and his punishment in person, as the doctor was "whipt 25 Stripes & Branded on ye forehead with A & a halter on his neck [there] to Remain forever." Even if Joshua had been willing to risk such a relationship, finding the time and place for intimacy would have been a challenge. Joshua had his hands full raising his children and earning a living. His unusual status as a widower also meant that all eyes were watching, making the possibility of a protracted forbidden relationship all the more difficult.[49]

Joshua never allowed another woman to take the place of Abigail, "the Wife of my youth," in either his heart or his home; his children would have no stepmother. Instead of finding a new helpmeet, Joshua threw himself into his work. As a widower, he now needed to pay others to do the housework and child care Abigail's death left undone, and he could ill afford to lose the momentum he had built as a shipwright and trader. His shipyard work was just beginning to yield fruit in commerce, and Abigail's death may even have pressed him to assume greater risk. In January 1717, Joshua decided to retain a quarter interest in the *Plainfield*, amounting to £160.[50]

This sloop had been his second "ground-up" construction, the same vessel he had shepherded into being during Abigail's final pregnancy. That spring the widowed Joshua upped his one-quarter-share ownership in the *Plainfield* after it returned from Barbados. In July, he also made a bold attempt at a "spec" sale—an uncertain gamble that held the prospect of high returns, or losses. He took his now eldest son Nathaniel and sailed the *Plainfield* first to a lumberyard at Lyme's Four Mile River where they "Loaded [it] wth 16260 foot Plank," the raw stuff of his profession. Then father and son sailed on to New York Harbor, where, on what was probably the first visit for both, the Connecticut shipwright sold his sloop and all the lumber in it. It was a daring enterprise for two men from the provinces and, after their success, they stayed on for a couple of weeks, taking in the formerly Dutch town before returning home as passengers, ready to distribute the sale proceeds to the *Plainfield* investors.[51]

Investments in shipbuilding and trade did more than draw Joshua into the broader commercial economy and provide a sufficiency for his motherless family. While Joshua strove to be "a very just Dealer," he also held another object quite dear to his heart: to "Trade . . . Much by Sea & Land with good Success for many years & only by his own Industry acquire . . . a great estate." Joshua had ambitious plans to provide amply for each of his children when they came of age, and for that he would need to attain a degree of wealth and property. Venturing in ships and trade allowed Joshua to accumulate some capital, capital that he could eventually direct toward investments in land and lending that required little labor and no physical risk. That capital may also have permitted the master craftsman to give up the trade he had performed since boyhood.[52]

In 1717, Joshua reduced his work in the yard significantly; within a year he had relinquished pursuit of his craft in any meaningful way. It was probably a strategic shift. Arduous and often dangerous, shipbuilding was work best suited to younger men. Perhaps Joshua, having accumulated adequate capital, saw more desirable opportunities elsewhere, whether in land, lending, or civic service. His timing suggests another reason: The typical aspiration for a master shipwright at the peak of his career was to run his own yard, employing others to do the bulk of the hard labor and reaping profits from selling ships and cargos. But it was nearly impossible to operate a shipyard, to provide accommodation and provisioning for apprentices and other workers, without the help and work of a wife. Abigail's death had dashed any plans her husband had entertained of running his own big yard, as the Coits did.[53]

Joshua knew it was time to turn his attention to other things. Confronted by the loss of his partner soul, he had chosen an unusual, almost singular, path. He focused on his children and worked to reunite his family. His course would require patience and self-sacrifice, but it would not be without its rewards. In it there would be much to admire—a life crafted through fatherhood and service—but nothing in this new chapter would ever mend the breach in the last. Joshua Hempstead would never fully recover from the loss of his Abigail.

Chapter Nine

A HIGHER COURT

IN 1714, when John Livingston sold Jackson's wife and son and leased out from under him the farm he tilled, John Jackson contemplated the limited options available to him. Objectively speaking, he stood near the very bottom of New England's social hierarchy, and his enemies were among the most powerful in the colony. The freedman could easily have been defeated by his own powerlessness and by the forces rallied against him—drawn from the top of the social pyramid. But Jackson's self-assessment was quite different from his society's low estimation of him. And he had learned much more than husbandry from John Rogers.

Jackson would have recognized that the chances of John Livingston now honoring his indenture agreement were slim, given his master's lease of Mount Livingston and his expected departure for England. Jackson had hoped to secure land from that agreement—another dream that now appeared to be slipping from his hands. Perhaps Jackson had even confronted Livingston, or the farm's new lessee, Peter Mason, to reassert his rights and had come up empty-handed. But he did not leave things there.

Colonial patriarchs often turned to the legal system to resolve family disputes. Joshua Hempstead had sued his mother and stepfather to recover his dead father's Stonington farm, and Winthrop men often came to court to assert their rights against family members and in-laws. For most African men in the colonial period, however, their only experiences of the legal system were as chattel or as criminal defendants—objects in a botched sale or violators of the English legal code. Jackson's experience was entirely different and perhaps unique. Having lived much of his life around John Rogers, Jackson was accustomed to seeing his old master and the Rogerenes go to court to stand up for their convictions—even to face arrest, fines, and imprisonment without flinching. Jackson himself had been prosecuted for Rogerene beliefs; and even when he had faced ordinary charges of fornication in 1702, he and Rogers had greeted them with defiance rather than submission. Whether or not Jackson considered himself one of the Rogerenes, he had internalized their ethos: He recognized a higher authority than earthly justice and did not accept society's judgment of him.

Confronted again by the loss of his family in 1714, Jackson reacted not as a penniless, marginalized freedman but instead as an entitled patriarch and free man who asserted his rights without hesitation and without regard to the consequences. It took Jackson two years to mount his attack. The historical record is silent as to what he did during that period, but it may have taken Jackson some time to extricate himself from Mount Livingston, and once he did, he probably remained based in the New London area. Mamacock seems the likeliest place for him to have gone. He had children there, and given their long connection, Rogers and his son John Rogers, Jr., would hardly have abandoned Jackson at that point.

To survive Jackson may have been able to work for the Rogerses, as he had in the past, or he may have contracted out his labor as an indentured servant or sold it as a day laborer. He was then in his mid-forties at least, and his marketability as a farm servant was fast diminishing. Property holders would be less and less willing to choose Jackson for hard physical labor if they could hire a younger, stronger man. During the many years he had already spent with John Rogers, Jackson may have accompanied his master during his travels—to Newport, Boston, and other destinations. Rogers had continued to pursue mercantile activites to some degree, and he had extensive social and religious contacts, particularly throughout Rhode Island. Rogers also self-published a number of books and tracts during his lifetime, and these publications gave him additional reasons to travel, especially to Boston. Like any traveler, Rogers sometimes delivered letters and packages for others in the locales he visited, on one occasion even bringing "a piece of silk" to the Dudleys in Roxbury for one of the daughters of John Winthop IV who was staying there. Performing such small reciprocal courtesies was common during this period, and would have trumped any political or religious rivalries, even personal dislike. If Jackson had journeyed with his old master, as certainly was plausible, he would have attained a degree of worldliness that was highly unusual for an ordinary New England farmhand, particularly an ex-slave. It may also partially explain why, in the years following his departure from Mount Livingston, he took up a new occupation.[1]

Probably around 1715, John Jackson began to travel the coastline from New London to Boston, working as a peddler and selling goods he carried on his back or pulled along in a cart. It was an existence steeped in poverty, uncertainty, loneliness, and rebuff. Colonists distrusted peddlers, viewing them as an unscrupulous underclass who cheated customers, traded illegally, and undersold reputable merchants. The good Englishmen and Englishwomen of Boston, Newport, and in between regarded Jackson, as a "Negro" peddler, with particular disdain. As he traversed New England, Jackson would have done the best he could to profit from selling small items—making use of New London connections, delivering mail to acquaintances, and hoping to rustle up business—but often getting a door slammed in his face. It was an uphill road for a man on the cusp of what was considered old age, and it was only a matter of time before he would have to give up this line of work, too, for he would not be able to walk the paths and highways of an unreceptive New England forever.[2]

John Jackson may have come by the idea—and the wherewithal—to become a peddler from travels with Rogers and perhaps even from deliveries and services he had seen Rogers perform. But the wandering life served other functions for Jackson; it may have allowed him to visit his far-flung family—Jack and Miriam in Norwich, and Joan and Jerry in Framingham. Peddling goods along the way would have helped finance such visits.

His traveling also permitted him to begin to fight back—perhaps with additional help from the Rogerses. Because Joan and Jerry were in Massachusetts, it was there that Jackson needed to go. However he got there, he was in Cambridge on February 4, 1716, when he met with a magistrate and obtained a writ against Joan's new owner—the Framingham yeoman John Stone. Jackson's demand: "Her trial for her freedom."[3]

Until then, John Jackson had received only hard treatment from English courts, but he must have harbored some hope of a fair hearing when he brought suit in Massachusetts. Jackson again claimed Joan's freedom on the grounds of her original release from slavery by the Foxes—the same grounds on which he and Rogers had lost to Samuel Beebe in the Connecticut courts. But Massachusetts was a different jurisdiction—far from the Connecticut judges and power brokers whose dislike for his old patron, John Rogers, colored their objectivity. Jackson was right. In a first trial in a lower court, the freedman won—successfully arguing that Stone detained his wife "in slavery unjustly" as a "free woman." Not surprisingly, Stone appealed, and a new trial date in the Superior Court of Judicature in Cambridge was set for July 1717.[4]

Talk of Jackson's presumption spread across New London, making its way to the Livingston dinner table and eliciting expressions of disbelief over his "designs to sue for his said wife," as John Livingston's mother-in-law, Knight, put it. Having guaranteed title when he sold Joan to John Stone, Livingston was now obligated to help in Stone's defense. If Stone lost, the Framingham yeoman would be able to sue Livingston to recover his loss. During this period, while his former servant had taken up peddling and engaged in a battle to recover his family, John Livingston's life hovered in a peculiar sort of limbo. Although Livingston had seemed ready to set off for London in early 1714 when he sold off Joan and Jerry and leased out his farm, he was still kicking around New London more than three years later, facing his own diminishing prospects.[5]

Unable to appear at the trial due to a bad episode of gout, Livingston nevertheless "resolved not to lose her patiently" and pulled every string he could. He wrote to Connecticut governor Gurdon Saltonstall, who was then in Boston, asking him to assist Joan's hapless buyer, Stone, and even to serve as a witness, if necessary. He penned another letter to Stone, assuring him of Saltonstall's enthusiastic support. He also wrote directly to John Valentine, the superior court judge who would decide the case, requesting him "to do whatever lies in him for the servicing of the interest."[6]

Having secured Saltonstall's support, Livingston probably felt assured of Jackson's loss at trial, but Valentine was a man not so easily handled. Although he was a well-known Boston lawyer near the peak of his career, Valentine had reached his magisterial position the hard way, turning to the law late in life after exhausting other options and then working his way to the top without any formal education or training. Although he had become a leading figure in Boston's legal community and would soon secure appointment as attorney general of Massachusetts, John Valentine—like Jackson—had remained an outsider and was not well liked. Born in England, Valentine was a staunch Anglican who perhaps compensated for his outsider status by cultivating an air of haughty superiority that rankled New England's Congregational old guard. The feeling was mutual, however, for Valentine had no qualms about riling conservative Puritan sensibilities.[7]

By modern standards, Livingston's behind-the-scenes manipulations constitute obstructing justice. Eighteenth century observers, however, would have seen them as de rigeur maneuvering among the gentlemanly caste. A judge in Valentine's position might even have felt no ethical qualms about taking Livingston's wishes and assertions into consideration. It seemed very unlikely, on the eve of trial, that a lowly African freedman, with or without John Rogers's backing, would have a chance against Englishmen of such means and connections.

But John Livingston had miscalculated if he believed the judge was in his pocket. Considering Jackson's case, Valentine found himself in a highly unusual position. The judge had rarely if ever seen a plaintiff quite like the one now before him: a propertiless freedman from another colony, demanding his rights and challenging all com-ers. If nothing else, one had to admire the man's nerve. Perhaps the thought of ruling against the entrenched elite even gave Valentine some pleasure.

Whatever his reasoning, Valentine was confident enough to follow the law. He remained unmoved by Livingston's claims and contacts and instead delivered Jackson the unimaginable victory: Joan was free and his decision was final.[8]

Jackson would not be the only man to win a freedom trial in New England's courts, but he was different from most successful plaintiffs. Those who won liberty at law usually did so on the grounds of Algonquin lineage—not on the legal particulars of a deed of gift, as in Joan's case. Obtaining her freedom as Jackson had done was a very rare triumph indeed. It had been more than six terrible years since Beebe had first taken Joan away from Mamacock, but Jackson finally had his wife back for good. What satisfaction the couple must have felt when the sheriff collected her from Stone.

In the midst of his suit to recover Joan, Jackson also used the New London courts to redress a different wrong. In the months between when he first filed his case in Cambridge and Valentine's final ruling, Jackson sought to hold Livingston—the man who had bought and sold his wife and child—accountable for having reneged on his contractual promise of land to his indentured servant. Asserting his legal rights as a free economic being, Jackson sued the prospective patroon for breach of contract, forcing his former master to appear in court and make a settlement with him—the details of which do not survive. Livingston probably agreed to some form of pecuniary compensation (which, given Livingston's track record, Jackson may have had difficulty collecting). If he received funds, Jackson surely used them to support his family and his legal fight. From that point on, however, any real hopes Jackson had of owning property slipped away for good.[9]

For the Jacksons, nearly every victory would be hard fought and grudgingly conceded, and Valentine's ruling was no exception. Stone was forced to surrender Joan, but he simply refused to give up Jerry, the child he had purchased with her, when the constable came to collect them. To get the boy back, Jackson would have to take further legal action; for the time being, John and Joan were forced to return to New London while leaving the child—now around four—alone and enslaved in Framingham.[10]

Once back in Connecticut, Joan gave birth to their ninth and last child, a boy named Jacob. The family may have lived at Mamacock, for Jacob became the property of John Rogers, Jr., like his three siblings—perhaps also to provide youthful service in exchange for Rogers's legal protection.[11]

While Jackson continued his legal fight for Jerry, Stone took the child to Boston from Framingham in November 1717 to have his small person inspected and appraised, ascertaining the boy's monetary worth so that he might calculate his loss if he were taken: thirty pounds. For two more years the Jacksons endured a disheartening, legal back-and-forth with Stone. Finally, however—in August 1719, when Jerry was around six—Judge Valentine ordered Stone's arrest if he did not relinquish the child. When a sheriff arrived at Stone's door, the furious yeoman again "utterly refused to deliver said boy," obliging the officer to "apprehend and seize said boy" and deliver him to his waiting father.[12]

Jackson's battles in Cambridge and Framingham were only two fronts in his war for his family. After he returned home to New London, and while he still fought for Jerry, John Jackson filed suit to recover Jack, the other child whom Livingston had sold away. Records concerning Jack are few, but the boy, described as "molatto" like his mother, had been living as a Norwich slave since Livingston sold him to Winslow Tracy. In June 1718, Jackson took Tracy to court, claiming that he unjustly detained the boy from his parents. Although John Rogers's backing of Jackson is not always clearly visible in the records, it appears here in black and white. Rogers provided Jackson with the bond necessary to file the suit against Tracy. In fact, it seems likely that Rogers provided some or even all of the financial wherewithal Jackson needed to pursue litigation for his family, with Jackson perhaps paying him back in labor. Certainly the freedman did not have the means to have paid his legal expenses by himself. Furthermore, Jackson was almost certainly illiterate, so Rogers and his son, John Rogers, Jr., might also have assisted him in putting together the documentation he needed.[13]

In his case against Tracy, the lower court found against Jackson;

it would have been difficult, if not impossible, for the freedman to obtain justice in Connecticut. As the case worked its way through the courts—with Jackson losing at each stage—Samuel Beebe inter-evened and asserted his own claim on Jack. Jackson appealed in late 1719, with the backing of John Rogers, Jr. Old John was back in jail, having again stormed the New London meetinghouse in September of that year with "his crew" of twelve, disrupting Mr. Adams's ser-mon and yelling fiery condemnations. Their November trial was a fiasco, with Rogers bellowing at the justices, "That's a lie," "That's a devilish lie"—a colorful performance that earned him an immediate conviction for contempt. In the meantime, assorted Rogerenes, male and female, broke open and vandalized the New London jail and prison yard—even carrying away the prison door.[14]

Whatever possibility there had been that Jackson might prevail probably withered with these last Rogerene taunts. John Jackson might have saved Jerry from slavery, but he could not do the same for Jack. The outcome might have been worse than even he expected, however. The child remained enslaved, but it was apparently Samuel Beebe, Jackson's old nemesis, who ultimately became his owner. For many years afterward, there was no trace of him in New London.

In the end, even Judge Valentine, the champion of Jackson's Mas-sachusetts legal victory, eventually lost the inner strength he had shown in upholding the rule of law in the Jackson case. Some years later, the good judge inexplicably "hanged himself, att home, in his upper chamber, with his sash" from his robe, in the words of a Bos-ton chronicler. The suicide of this prominent member of America's first Anglican flock stunned Boston, and Valentine's friends and family were left dazed and diminished—reduced to haggling for a churchyard burial with concessions of insanity.[15]

WHILE JOHN JACKSON fought for his family in the courts, John Livingston's schemes seemed to be sputtering to a halt. His marriage to Elizabeth Knight had initially promised a second chance for a family and heir, but she, too, had failed to give him a child. His plans for Mount Livingston were at best on hold, for the farm was now in the hands of its lessee, Peter Mason, and his military career appeared

1. The son of Connecticut governor John Winthrop, Jr., Fitz-John Winthrop (1638–1707) was born in Massachusetts and spent part of his childhood in New London. After failing to enter Harvard, he left for England to serve in the army that ultimately ushered in the Restoration of Charles II in 1660. Fitz eventually returned to America and New London, where he engaged in public service and formed an unorthodox union with Elizabeth Tongue, a local innkeeper's daughter. Elected governor of Connecticut in 1698, Fitz served until his death. His only child, Mary, married John Livingston. In his will, Fitz left his real property to his nephew, John IV.

2. Fitz-John's brother, Wait Still Winthrop (1642–1717), spent part of his childhood in New London before settling permanently in Boston. He enjoyed a long public career, during which he served as a gubernatorial councilor and militia general, eventually achieving the position of chief justice of the high court of Massachusetts, the Superior Court of Judicature. Wait's son, John IV, settled in New London.

3. Born in Scotland and raised in Rotterdam, Robert Livingston (1654–1728) joined New York's colonial elite through success in trade and civil service, along with an advantageous marriage to Alida Schuyler Van Rensselaer. Wealthy and self-interested, Robert was the proprietor of Livingston Manor near Albany and the father of John and Margaret (who married Samuel Vetch).

4. Born into an illustrious family in Massachusetts, Gurdon Saltonstall (1666–1724) became New London's Congregational minister after receiving two degrees from Harvard. In New London, the high-handed Saltonstall became a locus of attacks by John Rogers, Sr., on the "established" Congregational ministry. After the death of his friend Fitz-John Winthrop in 1707, Saltonstall was elected governor of Connecticut, a post he held until his own death.

5. The only child of Fitz-John Winthrop and his longtime companion, Elizabeth Tongue, Mary Winthrop Livingston (c. 1676–1713) grew up in New London and married John Livingston in 1701, before settling in New London's North Parish. This rarely published portrait was probably one of a pair made of Mary and her bridegroom, John, sometime around their wedding. No portrait of her husband survives, however, and Mary's likeness was returned to her natal Winthrop family when she died childless, after a long and agonizing battle with breast cancer.

6. The only surviving son of Wait Winthrop, John Winthrop IV (1681–1747) graduated from Harvard in 1700 and married Anne Dudley, a daughter of Massachusetts governor Joseph Dudley, Wait's political enemy. After inheriting from his uncle Fitz, John IV grudgingly settled in New London. When his father died in 1707, John IV engaged in lengthy litigation with his only sister, Anne, and her husband, Thomas Lechmere, disputing Anne's inheritance. Although he ultimately prevailed in court, he did so at the expense of his wife and children, whom he abandoned in Connecticut to pursue an appeal in London before the Privy Council in 1727. He never returned. Historians usually refer to John as "John F.R.S" as a tribute to his membership in the Royal Society—his only real distinction.

7. According to family accounts, this European firearm is likely that of Robert Hempstead, the immigrant. It may have hung on this beam in the hall of the Hempstead house for centuries.

8. Exterior of the Hempstead house.

9. John Jackson's surety appearance bond (May 31, 1711). After John Jackson "stole" his wife, Joan, and two of their children from Samuel Beebe on Plum Island, he had to face Beebe's charges in court. Jackson turned to Samuel Fox and John Rogers, Jr.—both of whom owned his children—to post the sixty-pound bond to secure his appearance. John Jackson's unusual, circle-shaped "mark" is clearly visible.

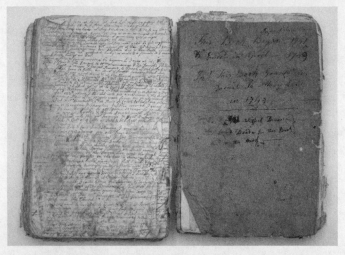

10. A portion of the extraordinary diary that shipwright and magistrate Joshua Hempstead likely kept for more than forty-seven years.

11. The principal room in the Hempstead house, the hall likely held a bedstead, a table, and a small number of chairs that could be moved near the hearth for warmth. Most domestic activity took place in the hall where Joshua sometimes held court, laid out corpses before burial, ate meals, or performed indoor work. Some members of the family also would have used this room as a bedroom. The bedstead depicted is a Hempstead family piece from the period.

12. This page of Joshua Hempstead's diary includes the shipwright's entry from September 27, 1727, in which he announces, "Adam is come ys morn"—Adam Jackson's arrival in the household.

13. "Letter to the Editor at John Rogers's Death" (1721) in the New England Courant. John Rogers's life and horrifying death are lampooned in an anonymous letter to the editor. The letter, which drips with contempt and derision, was likely written by someone in the Saltonstall-Winthrop circle.

They write from Newport, that several Persons have been taken ill with the Small Pox there, who are remov'd out of Town to prevent its Spreading.

Extract of a Letter from a Gentleman at New London to his Friend in Boston, dated Nov. 24. 1721.

SIR,

I Find the Death of John Rogers, the Baptist Teacher of this Place, is mention'd in one of your publick Papers; and if you think the under-written Account of his Carriage (when near his End) will oblige the Town, you may communicate it. The old Man by his Presumption, has brought such Distress on his Family, as I believe is not to be parallel'd in Boston: Some of them, particular his Blacks, are so obstinate as to deny themselves the use of Means when sick, it being against their Opinion. As for John's Errors, I hear of neither Recantation nor Confirmation; but when ill, he seem'd as if astonish'd, to think the Small Pox (a Punishment for the Wicked) should be sent to him. All I can learn he said, when Mr. G——n first told him the Small Pox was out upon him, was, That he was in the Hands of God, and had no Fear upon his Spirits; and for several Days he was possest he should not die; till at last Strength failing, and all Hope of Life being taken away, he kneeled down (for he could not ly in Bed) and prayed, That IF God had seen any thing amiss in him he would forgive him; and that he would either keep his Wife from the Infection, or carry her thro' it. And so died John Rogers the Baptist; who while he lived said more than was desired, when he came to die said less than was expected; And as he led his Followers, so he left them in the Dark, where I think, (if no good Man ever died of a Common Calamity) we must e'en leave him.

The same Letter adds, That a certain Man at Stonington (who has a Wife and several Children) lately castrated himself; which has occasion'd abundance of Waggish Talk among the looser Sort of the Female Tribe, who are so incensed against him, that some of them talk hotly of throwing Stones at him, if he lives to come abroad again. He is very much swell'd, but seems rejoyc'd at what he has done.

On Monday Morning last died here Mrs. Elizabeth Yeomans, Consort of John Yeomans, Esq; of the Small Pox.

We are assur'd that the Small Pox is at Lime in Connecticut.

Custom House, Boston. Entred Inwards.

14. Relatively warm in winter and hot in summer, the garret of the Hempstead house would have been filled with stored provisions. It also likely contained beds for the young men of the household, including Joshua Hempstead's older sons, Adam Jackson, and other male servants or visitors.

to have come to a dead end—buried under the still-unpaid mountains of debt from his Canada missions. He received support from his new mother-in-law, but there was a limit to both her resources and generosity, and she could not afford him the lifestyle he desired. Although he was only thirty-seven, John's health was also deteriorating fast. The hereditary gout from which he had suffered for years was worsening; as he complained to his father, it sometimes kept him "in intolerable pain and distress" for weeks on end.[16]

John had implored his parents to use their money and influence to secure him a reputable military command in New York—closer to the manor and to them—but Alida did not think her eldest son deserved further help, and she made her disapproval known to her husband. "Our son writes to buy him a captain's commission," she informed Robert by letter. "He should do that himself." John's brother-in-law and former partner, Samuel Vetch, could offer him nothing. Vetch had become persona non grata in New England after the Canada fiasco, and his onetime collaborator Francis Nicholson had become Vetch's sworn enemy. Appointed colonial governor in Vetch's place, Nicholson now called into question Vetch's financial accounting of the expedition and garrison. Under threat of arrest and imprisonment in Boston, Vetch had already fled to London by the spring of 1714—the same year Livingston sold Joan Jackson—hoping to find vindication along with reimbursement for his own loans to the Crown. His wife and children were left in Boston, unable to afford the grand new house they had been building right on the Commons. To add God's judgment to their dejection, the house was struck by lightning that July, with a "principal rafter . . . split from the top to the purloin."[17]

Unlike her brother John, Margaret Vetch had children to care for; even so, she received no relief from her Livingston parents, who were "so far from giving her the least assistance that [they . . .] never so much as answered her letter," as her husband wrote to Robert from England with disbelief. It was plain greed, according to Vetch, that prevented the Livingstons from aiding their daughter.[18]

Facing his own financial and personal downfall, John Livingston—like John Jackson—sought legal redress. With refusals of support from the Crown and his own parents, Livingston turned to the only other deep pocket available to him: his dead first wife's relatives. Mary had been dead since 1713, but he would continue to take swipes at his former Winthrop in-laws for much of the decade, using direct and indirect lawsuits against Fitz's estate so that Wait and John IV might provide a settlement simply to get rid of him. Even while Mary had been alive, Wait and John IV had found Livingston's attitude toward them "very rude." John IV had no intention of compromising now, and instead took the well-trodden path of fighting over every pence.[19]

After so many delays and setbacks, John Livingston did finally leave for England in November 1718, four years after he had begun to plan his departure. In London, he joined forces with his brother-in-law, Samuel Vetch, in a joint effort to rescue their fortunes and once again seek repayment from the Crown for their Canada loans. (Margaret had joined her husband there in 1717.) But this last-ditch effort also failed. Livingston succumbed to gout far from home—at the seat of imperial power in Westminster. Sick, childless, and heavily in debt, plagued by personal and professional misfortunes, he was only thirty-nine. In a will written hastily from his London sickbed, John Livingston provided "decent and complete mourning" attire to the Vetches "in consideration for the great love and esteem I have for them." He had been a failure in business and in politics, suffering from bad judgment and bad luck—and his personal life had offered no redemption. His stake in his father's Livingston Manor went to his brother, Philip, and John—who might have reigned supreme over a healthy portion of New York—became an almost entirely forgotten member of his illustrious family. Livingston histories now barely mention him.[20]

When he died, he abandoned his wife, Elizabeth, to his debts. His estate inventory back home in New London was brief, but it included some of the accoutrements of the gentlemanly status that had mattered so much to him: silver plate and a japanned cabinet that imitated Asian-style lacquer. Elizabeth was also left with a field tent—a remnant of a military career that had ended in loss and failure, but had also represented John Livingston's finest hour.[21]

John's parents turned their backs on his widow the moment their son died, even harassing her to pay off his debts to them. Elizabeth was able to rely on her own mother, however, who continued to prosper in business in New London and Norwich until her own death in 1727. Elizabeth never remarried, and she lived into her forties when she expired suddenly one morning after an ordinary breakfast, screaming, "I am Dying!"[22]

The Vetches stayed in London, but perpetual penury eventually took Samuel to King's Bench prison for debt. He died in 1732 at the age of sixty-four—his health and spirit ruined. The resilient Margaret fared better. Plagued herself by debts in England, she made her way back to Manhattan and an inheritance from her now-dead parents, including a house on Pearl Street. There, being an able businesswoman like her mother, Alida, Margaret lived out her life, enjoying moderate success as a trader—an accomplishment that had proved so elusive to her husband and brother.[23]

IT WAS probably a relief to John Winthrop IV when John Livingston left New London for England, embittered as Winthrop was toward his cousin-in-law after Livingston's many legal assaults against Fitz's estate. With John IV, however, there would always be new villains to fill the void—and even old friends could become enemies. John IV had fought Livingston at every step—a pattern he followed with tenants, neighbors, and even the town of New London, so that locals before long came to resent the condescending Boston Brahmin.

After he settled on Winthrop's Neck in the summer of 1711, it took only a few years for the Winthrop heir to squander half a century of goodwill and loyalty toward his family due to his litigious nature and universally overbearing manner. His attitude managed to alienate even Gurdon Saltonstall—himself no stranger to conceit—who had at first been disposed to defend his departed friend Fitz's heir and nephew. But John IV blamed New London and its inhabitants for his troubles, and he filled letters to his father, Wait, and his brother-in-law, Thomas Lechmere (who had married his sister, Ann, in Boston), with reports of his perceived persecutions. Lechmere, a spoiled English aristocrat trying unsuccessfully to maintain his family as a Boston merchant, proved an especially receptive audience.[24]

Forced to remain where his property resided, Winthrop IV and his wife, Anne, had made do, sending their children off to study and socialize in more promising locales among the less degraded, while they remained trapped in New London, surrounded by "the most sorry and mean persons perhaps in the world, indeed to the last degree." In 1715, they entrusted their daughter Mary to her grandfather Wait in Boston so that she could attend a proper school. At home in New London, some said, the Winthrops took out their frustrations on household servants by withholding ordinary benefits and threatening to deport them to harsher service in Virginia.[25]

A bright moment came in May 1716, when John IV, then a father of four daughters, rejoiced at the birth of a son and namesake. But the happiness would not last. The infant fell sick during his first winter, leaving John IV and Wait frantically consulting each other about possible remedies. To save his grandson, Wait sent iron ore to be "hung at the pit of the stomach" and hair from an African lion "to be applied under the arms." The origins of this last remedy are somewhat curious, since lion's hair would not customarily have been available even to the richest New Englanders. In 1716, however, the first live African lion to be exhibited in America was in Boston; the sea captain Arthur Savage had it on display at his Brattle Street home, where it was kept under guard by one of the captain's "Negroes." Wait had persuaded the lion's keeper to nip the hair quickly from the creature's back. But these remedies, however exotic, proved unhelpful. The "lovely sweet babe" died at nine months, leaving his stricken father "bowed down in grief." To express his sympathy, Judge Samuel Sewall sent a vial of tears from Boston.[26]

The loss of his son only exacerbated John IV's anger and frustration toward his life in New London. He saw himself as the victim of terrible misuse: "The barbarity, cruelty & inhumanity they have treated us with always has been intolerable and now more insufferable." To his father, Wait, he lamented, "Let me and honest men rather live in Turkey than amoung such rude & insolent people that will do what business & notorious abuses they please under color of law & Justice."[27]

IN THE meantime, Thomas Lechmere had his own difficulties. He had been trying for years to earn a proper living as a merchant, but he had little sense for business and before long found himself mired in debt. He also lived perpetually beyond his means, so that his wife, Ann—John IV's only sibling and mother of the five Lechmere children—was in constant fear of ruin. In 1716, Lechmere even ventured home to the family seat in Worcestershire, England, hoping his widowed mother or elder brother Nicholas might give some material support. Instead, he was humiliated. After reproaching him directly for his spendthrift ways, his mother, Lucy Lechmere, sent a sharply worded letter to his father-in-law, Wait, censuring him for failing to provide sufficient assets to the young Lechmeres. Meanwhile, Nicholas Lechmere had continued to rise to dizzying heights of fortune and position in England, becoming solicitor general of the nation in 1714 and attorney general in 1718.[28]

Nicholas's success gave his Boston brother a sense of superiority over New England men, but also left him with an unvarnished envy. To Thomas, it seemed a considerable injustice that he had to watch others enjoy their fortunes while he was reduced to scrimping pennies and enduring his mother's criticisms. The fact that his brother-in-law, John IV, always groused about his life, while sitting atop the Winthrop fortune—even complained to his father, Wait, of his New London impoverishment by declaring "we are reduced to 3 knives and but 2 forks and are in poor condition"—was salt in the wound.[29]

Relations between the brothers-in-law had only recently soured. Their correspondence had been warm and affectionate when Lechmere returned from his humiliating trip to England in 1717 and took special care to send John IV English grape seeds and fruit stones "from the finest cherries in the world." In fact, the brothers-in-law had much in common: Both were husbands and fathers with young children, and both came from privileged upbringings that left them ill equipped for the realities they faced. Both felt like exiles, trapped by circumstance. John IV was stuck in New London, resenting his surroundings and the day-to-day management of a complicated inheritance. Lechmere had had to leave England and his aristocratic home for an alliance with the Winthrops designed to sustain him economically, but he was reduced to trying to scrape by through his own efforts in an unfamiliar city. For John IV and Lechmere, it was the death of Wait Winthrop, however, that eventually turned them against each other.[30]

In November 1717, Wait died in Boston at the age of seventy-five. His friend Judge Samuel Sewall eulogized the Winthrop patriarch in his diary: "Last night died the Excellent Wait Winthrop, esqr., for Parentage, Piety, Prudence, Philosophy, Love to new England Ways and people very Eminent." He then noted pointedly, "His Son not come though sent for." John IV did not get himself to Boston to bid farewell to his father, but he did come afterward to orchestrate his funeral—the most lavish New England had ever seen. There was even a place for Wait's slave, Mingo, who led a riderless horse in the procession. Though the funeral was overstated, Wait had earned Sewall's tribute. He may not have had the intellect or vision of his father or grandfather, but Wait had become one of the most committed public servants of his generation, serving New England in various judicial, political, and military roles. Unfortunately, however, despite the fact that Wait had long been chief justice of Massachusetts, he had failed to execute a will—an oversight that sowed animosity among his heirs.[31]

After Wait's death, financial arrangements in the family continued informally with John IV in charge as executor of the estate. Under the intestate laws of Connecticut and Massachusetts, John IV's only sibling, Ann Lechmere, was entitled to one-third of their father's real estate, while John IV, as eldest son, received either a double or two-thirds share. John IV had no desire to sell assets to make a proper division, so he simply passed along funds according to his inclination, with the Lechmeres, buried in debt, becoming increasingly exasperated.[32]

Sitting in his own Boston house in March 1720, Lechmere composed yet another letter to his brother-in-law, John IV, in New London. He was feeling the strain of his financial situation, which had become dire enough for him to contemplate another trip to England and another humiliating appeal to his family.

Before he sealed his missive, however, the Englishman added a small note—a reference to the familiar figure waiting outside the door of his house. The dispatch would travel "per John Jackson ye negro peddler." Although Lechmere no doubt shared the Winthrop family enmity for Jackson's master, apparently those feelings did not prevent any of them from allowing their letters to make the cross-colony trek in the freedman's pouch, just as it did not stop them from entrusting goods to the old dissenter John Rogers, as when the latter carried "a piece of silk for [John IV's] daughter Beck" on another occasion.[33]

Under threat of arrest for nonpayment of debts and complaining to John IV about selling household goods to buy bread for his children, Thomas Lechmere slipped away to England and his wealthy family again in 1721. In his absence, Lechmere-Winthrop relations reached a new low, with Ann Lechmere, who remained in Boston with the children, expressing her dismay that her brother was not moved "to afford me some of the sweepings of the mill your swine fed on to keep me and my poor children from perishing." To counter the accusation of a "hoggish disposition," an affronted John IV dispatched Ann the less than magnanimous sum of ten pounds, reminding her ungraciously of the thirty pounds he had sent eight months earlier.[34]

Fortunately for Thomas Lechmere, however, the timing of his 1721 trip to England proved to be perfect. His brother Nicholas had recently become a man of great fortune by marrying the daughter of an earl and he would be elevated to the peerage immediately after Lechmere's stay, becoming Lord Lechmere of Eversham. The soon-to-be peer now saw fit to help his profligate brother, if only to avoid embarrassment to himself. He pulled strings to obtain a sinecure for Thomas that enabled him to assume, through no merit of his own, the role of surveyor general of customs for the Northern District of America that June. Thomas Lechmere could never hope to breathe

the same exalted air as his ennobled brother, but he could now hold his head high in Boston, settling into a life of relative stability and colonial comfort. He would later even obtain a plum job as customs collector of New London for his son whom he had strategically named Nicholas after his powerful uncle—the same young man who distinguished himself while in that capacity by beating nine-year-old Zeno to death with a horsewhip.[35]

IN ENGLAND, Lechmere may have been nothing but an impecunious younger son, but in the small world of New England his background and unearned sinecure put him near the top of the social pile. Most New Londoners would have viewed him as a distinguished dignitary. By the same token, a respected yeoman—a master in New London—appeared a virtual peasant in the "best" drawing rooms of Boston. New England's size meant that social classes were forced into a certain level of intimacy—in households, meetinghouses, and simply on the street. This broke down some barriers, no doubt, but class prejudices remained powerful, especially at the upper end of the spectrum. Although the collective Winthrops found Hempstead politically and practically useful when navigating life in New London, calling on his services as a selectman and agent, behind his back they would regard the Connecticut yeoman and his ilk as one step up from animals in the yard.

These tensions were on full view at the Lechmeres' when Joshua traveled to Boston on business in the spring of 1723, accompanied by a New London lawyer named John Pickett. Whatever the differences between Thomas Lechmere and his brother-in-law, their disdain for their social inferiors proved an enduring bond. Writing to John IV after Hempstead's visit, Lechmere bemoaned spending time with the tiresome provincial blowhard, for " 'twas long before could see Hempstead taken up with his business." Hempstead revered the Winthrop family, and was surely nervous mingling with the fine English gentleman. To Lechmere, however, the shipwright's repeated toasts to John IV's health merely appeared fawning and excessive—a high-flown excuse for another round—and his table manners were nothing short of appalling. While Hempstead likely took pains to be on his best behavior, Lechmere lamented having to dine with "those creatures"; apparently even Pickett, a Yale graduate who had been ranked first in his class in terms of family social status, had failed to pass muster. Lechmere commiserated—rather insensitively—with John IV: "How you can live among such, I know not."[36]

Whatever prominence the earnest diarist might achieve at home, it carried little weight on the streets of Boston or New York. But Lechmere's jibe about Hempstead's taste for the bottle was rank hypocrisy. Years later, when the surveyor general himself died at eighty-two, a Boston printer and chronicler eulogized him thus: " 'Tis conjectured by those who knew him, that a quantity of Maderia [sic] Wine equal to what he has drank, would be sufficient to float a 74 Gun Ship."[37]

ONLY A few months after Hempstead's visit to Boston, the financial struggle between Lechmere and Winthrop took a dramatic turn. That summer, John Winthrop IV was anticipating his own trip to Boston, his native city. Not only was the thought of being away from the petty indignities and boredom of life in New London cause enough for celebration, he was also tickled to have received an invitation to attend festivities occasioned by the recent succession of George II to the throne of England. Never one to hide his modest talents under a bushel, John IV took the opportunity to speak before the assembled crowd of dignitaries in verse. The *Boston News-Letter* captured his grandiloquent bungle, which included lines of breathtaking presumption: "Live. Mighty King! All Protestants do Pray; / This New World too, Under Your Feet I Laye." Though he held no public office, either elected or appointed, John IV felt that he was the right man to bestow the American continent upon the new imperial monarch.[38]

The editor of the *New England Courant* did not share John's self-assessment and devoted much of the August 19–26 issue to lampooning the large-beaked Winthrop for "his inimitable Genius to Extempore Poetry" and asking, "Whether his Snout a perfect Nose is, / And not an Elephant's Proboscis." Although his reaction to the coverage does not survive, there is little doubt that the prickly, hot-tempered John IV, who put great store in his personal dignity, would have been both mortified and incensed by this new evidence of New England's unworthiness. During the same visit to Boston, he stayed several weeks at the Lechmeres', where, in the bosom of his family, he could soothe himself with reassurances of his own standing.[39]

It was therefore a particularly rude awakening when, as his horses waited on the morning of his return to New London, John IV was served a summons to appear before the probate court to answer charges that he had mishandled his father's estate. His Lechmere sister and brother-in-law had lost patience with waiting for Ann's rightful share. Infuriatingly, neither Winthrop's familial host nor hostess had bothered to mention the impending suit during the course of his visit. John IV complained indignantly to his wife, Anne: "I was unexpectedly stopped in my intended journey by some of my nearest relations who I hitherto thought I might have trusted my life and my all in their hands, but I now find those that dipped in the dish with me have betrayed me." Within the year, the Lechmeres filed a case in Connecticut claiming Ann Lechmere's portion of Winthrop lands in that colony as well.[40]

With an attack from his nearest and dearest, matters now reached a full boil. John IV convinced himself that the Lechmeres had underhandedly challenged his administration of Wait's estate, and he became adamant that in return he would deny his sister, Ann, any part of their father's lands. To do so he had to challenge colonial intestate law itself, arguing that New England's custom of granting a share to all siblings violated primogeniture under English common law.[41]

Chapter Ten

"A PESTILENCE INTO THAT LAND"

W HEN A smallpox epidemic devastated Boston in 1721, many feared that it was a sign of God's judgment. The disease had swept through the town several times since the earliest days of settlement, but it had never struck as hard as it did that year—throwing the bustling little city of about twelve thousand into panic and crisis for months. The first outbreak came around April, but as the summer advanced, the death toll began to mount precipitously. One victim died in May, then eight in June. By July, Gurdon Saltonstall expressed compassion to a Boston correspondent along with his fears for New London, which had still been spared. In the unleashing of sickness, however, Saltonstall saw the "anger of God against his People." When twenty-six more Boston sufferers perished in August, the terrified city was in an uproar, becoming, in Cotton Mather's words, "almost an Hell upon Earth."[1]

Mather himself was struggling to allay the suffering by advocating inoculation—then a novel treatment in Europe and America, although long used in Africa and Asia, and one Mather had learned from his own slave Onesimus. Mather had solicited the help of one of Boston's best-known doctors, Zabdiel Boylston, who tried out the regimen—which involved transmitting a weak strain of the virus by putting infected pustules from a victim into a healthy person—on his own six-year-old son and on his slave Jack and Jack's two-year-old, Jacky. Although the procedure was highly effective, it aroused intense suspicion and opposition among Boston's clerical and medical establishment, who then fed the fears of the general populace. One of the staunchest opponents was the printer James Franklin, who, with the help of his younger brother Benjamin, voiced his vitriolic hostility in his new *New England Courant* and caused a sensation.[2]

During that punishing summer, Boston largely shut down. Shops closed, the harbor stood still, and many residents fled to the countryside. In September, smallpox claimed another 101 victims, and the selectmen had to restrict the incessant tolling of funeral bells. Over the course of the epidemic, nearly half of the city's population became infected. A boat trip away, New London had yet to feel the pain of contagion.[3]

At the peak of outbreak, however, one hoary resident of the Connecticut town inopportunely decided it was the right time to visit the beleaguered city. Seventy-three-year-old John Rogers wanted to check on the progress of a book he was having published in Boston, and did not fear for his safety, having had previous exposure to the disease. When he finished his business, he stayed in Boston to visit sick friends, despite the danger. Even with immunity, however, there were risks. It was not hard to spread the disease; one could do so even through unwashed clothing. Rogers's controversial decision to take that chance provided ripe fodder for his detractors, who saw evidence of recklessness and hubris. Whatever his reasoning, he reaped a bitter harvest for his actions.[4]

After leaving Boston, John Rogers returned to Mamacock, where his extended family of children, grandchildren, servants, and fellow Rogerenes awaited him. He was home less than two weeks before the first signs appeared: fever, aches, and a purplish rash around his midsection. Were it only for himself, Rogers could have easily borne his dreadful miscalculation, but as inflammation devoured the surface of his body, he could not escape the terrible truth that this time it was he, and not his establishment enemies, who had brought this destruction into his family.

The disease spread rapidly through the compound, sickening

no fewer than thirty members of the combined households there. Before long, Mamacock was declared a public health emergency, requiring selectmen to institute a quarantine and restrict access to the farm—a measure that appeared effective in halting the spread of the epidemic. Adhering to the tenets of Rogerene belief, however, many at Mamacock—in "particular his Blacks," according to a letter published in a Boston paper, and no doubt including the Jackson family—refused medical treatment, favoring faith healing and the laying on of hands.[5]

Old John Rogers died of smallpox on October 17, 1721. His storming of the New London meetinghouse and resulting stint in jail two years earlier had proved to be his last stand. It was an excruciating end, his wasted body covered with pus-filled sores, doubtless appalling to the families at Mamacock sealed off in their suffering from the outside world. Rogers's death coincided with a peak in mortalities in Boston—411 dead in October became 249 in November. When December brought only 31, many residents who had fled the city began to come home. But there would be no return to normal at Mamacock. John Rogers's final act had been to infect his entire collective family and to take two members closest to him to the grave. His beloved son John junior would face the cruelest test of devotion to the father he idolized: the triple blow of losing his father, his wife, and his eldest son in quick succession.[6]

Rogers's body was not yet cold before his enemies began to take pleasure in the seeming vindication his death represented. "Old John Rogers has his death for his presumption," Thomas Lechmere wrote to John Winthrop IV. In a letter published in James Franklin's *New England Courant*, an anonymous foe—a "Gentleman at New London"—defamed Rogers, "who while he lived said more than was desired." The letter attacked him both on civic and religious grounds, not only decrying Rogers's endangerment of the public and his own family but also disparaging him as a leader who "left [his followers] in the dark." As it listed his faults, the anonymous screed also revealed some details of Rogers's death. At the end, his skin was so inflamed that he could no longer lie down. Among his last words were a prayer that his wife, Sarah, would be spared.[7]

For his enemies, John Rogers's end was not simply a matter of just deserts but a sign of divine retribution—the audacity of his trip to Boston merely an echo of the radical individualism that had given him strength to lead a group of dissenters in the first place. But while the death of the Rogerene leader might have been a cause for relief and merriment among his embittered rivals, it was a gut-wrenching blow for Rogers's family and followers. That his grandson and daughter-in-law (and niece) Bathshua—followed him to their deaths compounded the horror.

If these deaths signaled a sea change at Mamacock, the Jacksons may have been among those who felt it most acutely. The younger Bathshua had grown up alongside Joan. For good or for ill she had also been a constant female presence in the lives of the three Jackson children born at Mamacock during the years their parents were compelled to be absent. Her sudden death, along with her eldest son's, would have been shocking for Abner, Peter, and Hannah Jackson. In the wake of John Rogers's burial on the shores of the Thames, however, John and Joan had to face a different sort of grief: With the old man's death, they had lost forever their most powerful, if ambivalent, ally.

JOHN ROGERS'S detractors probably felt that the death of the Rogerene leader, and God's will so clearly demonstrated thereby, would permit New London's religious life to achieve a state of relative calm—and that even dissenters might take a quieter, more conventional approach to voicing their differences with the "New England Way," as colonists referred to their brand of Congregationalism. And indeed, as years passed, the Rogerene movement began to dwindle. Some followers moved away, establishing small settlements in New Jersey, while those who remained gradually lost their numbers. Still, to the inevitable dismay of New London's governing class, John Rogers, Sr., had bequeathed a broader legacy than his particular faith.[8]

During three decades at the head of the Rogerenes, he had succeeded in establishing New London as a center for religious dissent and diversity—a rare triumph in doctrinaire Congregational Connecticut. After reluctantly giving harbor to the Rogerenes and to the broader Baptist movement at the end of the seventeenth century, New London became the first Connecticut community to welcome the Anglican Church in the 1720s. Before midcentury, this home to Baptists would also secure its place as a center of the religious revival of the Great Awakening. The Winthrops and Saltonstalls notwithstanding, colonial New London showed a receptivity to extremism, whose roots can be traced directly to John Rogers and his followers.

When John junior became the new leader of the Rogerenes and head of the Rogers family, he also took on his father's enigmatic role as simultaneous owner and "protector" of the Jacksons. Like his father, John appeared to feel a complicated mix of legal, familial, and religious ties toward the Jacksons—ties that in his mind did not controvert his owning Jackson children. He would behave toward the Jackson family much as his father had done, with a dual sense of duty and proprietorship. Four of the Jackson children—Abner, Peter, Hannah, and more recently Jacob—were his slaves. The likelihood that the Jacksons had consented to allowing their children to remain property to protect them—even though the children should have been free by birthright—is supported by the fact that Samuel Beebe did, in fact, continue to press his claim to them, litigating against the Rogerses and Jacksons well into the 1730s.[9]

Because John Jackson was in no position to support his young family, his children would have faced compulsory indentured servitude had they not been someone's property. But the theory of a mutually beneficial agreement is perhaps most persuasively supported by the fact that John Rogers, Jr., eventually freed three out of four of the Jackson siblings. In 1723, just two years after his father's death, Rogers recorded in the New London land books his pledge to release Hannah Jackson after ten years, recognizing her "faithfulness and good service." Her brother Peter likely received a similar promise around the same time—and Jacob, the youngest Jackson, likely some time after that. For reasons that are unclear, only Abner appears to have received no offer of freedom.[10]

AT THE time of old John Rogers's death from smallpox, not everyone in New London proved as uncharitable as the anonymous *Cou-*

rant writer who lampooned him. Although Joshua Hempstead did not condone Rogers's extreme beliefs or his disruptive behavior, the evenhanded shipwright noted the Rogers tragedies soberly in his diary. On October 10, 1721, he wrote, "old John Rogers hath got the Small Pox. he came from Boston." Seven days later, "old John Rogers died with the Small Pox," and one day after that, "old John buried." Given that it warranted an entry, Hempstead may have even attended the funeral and paid the exasperating old man the respect he was due. Then, on November 6, "young [John] Rogers the 3rd died with the Small Pox, he was near 21 years old." Joshua may have felt particular empathy for John Rogers, Jr.: It had been only five years since he had lost his own wife and eldest son in less than a week.[11]

In any case, at the time of the calamity at Mamacock, Joshua Hempstead had little time for recriminations. He was preoccupied with concern about his elderly mother, Elizabeth. Eight days after John Rogers's death, Elizabeth Edgecombe visited the house on Bream Cove that she had shared with her first husband so long ago to ask her son for help. She probably brought Phoebe, her mentally disabled daughter, who at forty-five still required her mother's nearly constant attention, since she was unable "to help herself either with food or raiment," as her brother put it. Phoebe had always lived with her mother, but the arrangement had become more difficult when John Edgecombe had left Elizabeth a widow at the age of sixty-nine, just six months before. At first, the two women had managed on their own in the Edgecombe house at the center of town. Mrs. Edgecombe had been left the customary widow's "thirds," which meant that she and Phoebe had the use of one-third of the Edgecombe house and lot; Edgecombe had also given his "loving wife Elizabeth a feather bed and bolster and pillows" with a pair of sheets, a blanket, a pot, and a kettle for her use and comfort.[12]

In spite of these provisions, however, Elizabeth Edgecombe found that she was unable to maintain the property without assistance. In the Bream Cove house that October, she watched as her son wrote out the terms of a contract, the deal they had struck gradually emerging on paper. In exchange for "maintenance during [Elizabeth's] natural life," Joshua purchased her one-third dower rights and would work the land and manage the property in her stead. As with infants, caring for the elderly was usually compensated among family members.[13]

The bargain permitted Phoebe and her mother to continue to live at home, but the arrangement proved short-lived. Within three years, Elizabeth found that she could no longer manage Phoebe's care. In the fall of 1724, Joshua sought and received legal guardianship over his sister, probably bringing her to live with him. She would not survive another year, however, likely succumbing to complications related to her condition. The month after Phoebe died, her brother "brot down Mothers Bed & Household Stuff" and moved Elizabeth in with him at Bream Cove.[14]

Even as Joshua worked to meet the needs of his extended family, being a father to his own children remained the central mission of his life. Since Abigail's death, Joshua had thrown himself into raising them with singular devotion. As the children grew, this meant shepherding them through late childhood and early adulthood using a combination of tender fathering, work and social training, and generous financial backing. While widowerhood did not unduly impair fathering to sons, it strained mightily a father's ability to raise daughters. Like any father, Joshua had initially left the daily care of his three girls to their mother, Abigail. When she died, he had turned to close surrogates for the care of his toddler and infant, while daring to keep his five-year-old girl at home with him. When the girls were young women, however, they all came back to him, and he again needed to find additional female attention and guidance. As his daughters approached marriageable age, Joshua placed them in reliable households to meet eligible young men and become the objects of courtship. Like their parents, Joshua's girls married young, quickly taking on the roles of wife and mother.

While his girls would need to orbit around a number of familiar households, Joshua gave his boys a longer tether at home. One of the most important commissions of any father of sons was to instruct them in productive work. Although Harvard had been around since the 1630s, and Yale was established by the early years of the eighteenth century, Joshua never considered higher education for his boys, though he knew and associated formally with men whose sons attended college, such as the Millers and the Winthrops. And only a handful of colonial sons sought an education beyond their native shores. For boys from the yeomanry like the Hempsteads, part-time schooling at a town-maintained school or in the home of a local tutor—along with craft training—was the only education they expected. Whatever their aptitudes, Joshua's boys would need to be satisfied with the local prominence and landed prosperity available to men of everyday experience and common understanding. They could expect to become independent and productive men of the town, but no more.

When choosing for their sons, many early American fathers aimed to diversify occupations, spreading skills and resources to expand family economic networks. But in a town like maritime New London, dominated by one industry, there was room for sons of one family to enter related or even identical trades. Here shipping and associated craftwork like coopering, shipwrighting, sailmaking, blacksmithing, and rope making could sustain an unusually high proportion of local boys, allowing Joshua to indulge his natural preference for the craft he knew best. Of his six sons, Joshua had intended that at least three—Joshua junior (who died in 1716), Nathaniel, and Stephen— would follow him into shipwrighting.

In preparing his boys for work, Joshua followed a hands-on, companionate approach toward fathering. A long apprenticeship beginning around age thirteen was an obvious and practical option, but Joshua instead chose to keep sons at home as much as he could. Joshua saw part- or full-time apprenticeships as vocational training, but not as a means to delegate his paternal role. As his boys neared mastery in a trade, he sent them out to work and received their earnings, but even then he was reluctant to hand them over completely. Parsimony might have influenced his emphasis on home training: He could train the boys cheaply himself and then hire them out on his own account at a higher rate. Home training was also a way to shield sons from the absolute authority of other men.[15]

For Hempstead sons, independence came through hard work and application, but also with strong paternal backing. Aside from giv-

ing them sustenance and training , Joshua aimed to endow his boys
with assets accumulated over decades to establish households and
families. Unlike some early American fathers who used property
as a means to exert authority over adult sons, Joshua showed little
interest in controlling his adult sons' affairs. Instead, he desired his
boys to become established and was prepared, even eager, to provide the financial wherewithal to help them get there. As a result,
each of Joshua's boys except Stephen started families relatively early,
as Joshua himself had done. Once independent, however, the boys
could still turn to their father when difficult financial, legal, or family problems arose. For Joshua, fatherhood remained ever a life's
work. Like the diary he wrote with his hands and the land he marked
with his industry, his efforts as a father would leave behind a deep
and lasting imprint of his days on this earth.

In Joshua's plans for his sons, each boy held a particular place.
The eldest surviving son, Nathaniel, for example, was to remain at
home for life. Born in 1701, Nathaniel had spent much of his boyhood with his now-dead brother, Joshua junior, together helping
their father in the fields and the yard. As boys, they often appeared
as a pair in their father's diary, mastering various tasks. At eleven
and thirteen, they dug holes and spread dung to prepare for planting.
At thirteen and fifteen, the brothers stacked hay. Once they reached
their late teens, their father could largely depend on them to do the
work of men. They became two of their father's primary hay mow-
ers, performing this exceptionally demanding task in which young,
stronger men excelled. In late childhood, both Joshua junior and
Nathaniel also attended school, sometimes living a few months at
a time with a schoolmaster. Nathaniel spent most of his tenth year
away at school, for example, accompanied at that time by eight-year-
old Robert. While his eldest two sons were young, Joshua had still
actively practiced his trade and naturally had brought the boys into
the trade with him. With his firstborn, Joshua appeared to teach him
informally, allowing Joshua junior simply to accompany him to the
yard and learn. Second son Nathaniel sometimes tagged along, too,
helping with basic tasks like trimming (balancing the load in a boat's
hold) and graving a ship's bottom.[16]

Even before the death of his firstborn, Joshua had made arrangements for Nathaniel's future. Through his connections to Abigail and her Bailey family, Joshua had come into possession of some property on Long Island near the Tallmadges. According to his original plan, this estate was to fall to his second son. Until he could inherit, however, Nathaniel needed practical work experience as a shipwright. When the boy was fifteen, Joshua sent him to live briefly with tailor-entrepreneur Solomon Coit, establishing a pattern of occupational training that he continued. Joshua chose a trusted friend he had known since earliest childhood, a contemporary with whom he had close business and personal connections and who lived next door to his own mother, Nathaniel's grandmother. Instead of a formal apprenticeship, Joshua chose a short-term living arrangement that was part of a lifelong economic relationship with Coit in which the boy's work was just one small entry. When Nathaniel began work at Solomon's, Joshua and Coit were in the midst of building the *Plainfield*, so the boy could help in building Coit's share of the sloop—the price of his labor then debited to his father's running account.[17]

Living at the Coits', Nathaniel continued to help his father with his own share of the *Plainfield*, working "about jobbs" and about "timber for the horse [awning]," finishing the "horse rooms" to hold one of New England's biggest export products to the West Indies. He also began to work as a shipwright on other boats, though probably still on his father's behalf. In April 1717, for example, Nathaniel was employed by his stepuncle, the shipwright Samuel Edgecombe. A month later he worked on a flat-bottomed scow belonging to Mrs. Elizabeth Hallam, the wealthy widow of Barbados-born Nicholas Hallam (and his future mother-in-law).[18]

While Joshua had expected his two eldest sons to follow his example in training for shipwrighting and husbandry, Joshua envisioned his third son, Robert, a blacksmith, the indispensable trade likely held by their immigrant forebear. When Robert turned fifteen in 1718, Joshua sent him to apprentice in his mother's hometown of Southold. With the death of his eldest son, Joshua had needed to shift his plans for younger siblings: Nathaniel became the eldest and heir to Bream Cove; therefore Robert would inherit the Long

Island property. Joshua preferred having his children close by, so he was reassured to think of Robert surrounded by Bailey relations—especially the Salmons and the Tallmadges, the families who had helped him raise his daughters, and with whom he remained close all his life.[19]

Family lore preserved through the twentieth century tells of Robert living and studying with Benjamin Youngs, a local magistrate and longtime town recorder—the propertied grandson of the Norfolkshire minister who founded Southold. But Hempstead family history seems to have forgotten that Robert first trained and worked as a blacksmith in Southold, perhaps even while he lived at the Youngses'. Robert had the support of his father, Joshua, who gave him land to settle on, along with a fine Boston-made blacksmith's vise when Robert outfitted his own shop in 1724. His life as a blacksmith even made a small cameo appearance in a local criminal case, when Southolders asked him to fabricate leg irons to hold an Algonquin man accused of theft. Once Robert established himself as a blacksmith in Southold, his father assigned to him the training of his younger brother, John, the sixth son, sending him over to learn the smithy's trade as well.[20]

Joshua's fourth son, Stephen, began his early life just as his brothers did, although he would ultimately venture farthest from home. As a youth, Stephen followed directly in his father's footsteps, gaining mastery as a shipwright through years of trailing his father in his daily work. Joshua hired Stephen out to work at fourteen for a brief stint herding sheep for the town shepherd, but it was not until the boy turned eighteen and had achieved a relatively high degree of competence as a wright that Joshua engaged him for an extended period of shipyard work. Stephen went first "to work with" Dan Hall, a New London shipbuilder, from whom Joshua received forty-five shillings per month and Hall's commitment to "instruct . . . in the trade." Although Stephen's work for Hall represented a kind of short-term apprenticeship, Joshua did not turn his son over entirely; after spending most days working with Hall, Stephen would nevertheless "Lodge & Sup at home" each night. Nor was Stephen's time entirely Hall's. Joshua called on the boy when he needed extra help carting firewood or fetching staves. In turn, when Stephen became ill in Hall's service, it was his father, not a master or mistress, who nursed him back to health. Then, with Stephen "vomit[ing] much" and "a Pain in his Right Breast," Joshua brought in Dr. Jeremiah Miller to "let him Bleed . . . and Bathed . . . his Breast with ointment of [the curative herb] Marsh Malloes."[21]

After Stephen's nine-month service with Hall, Joshua was able to hire out the nineteen-year-old as a full-fledged shipwright to his neighbor, John Coit, now at the much higher monthly rate of three pounds ten shillings. Still, Stephen was to "Lodge at home & diet night & Sabath day," spending every evening and Sunday in his father's house. As Stephen worked with Coit, probably assisting in the building of a particular ship, the price of his labor rose again, allowing Joshua to hire him out to the Groton shipwright Jonathan Williams at the rate of four pounds per month, a sum Joshua took in kind rather than in cash.[22]

The early decades of the eighteenth century were an interesting time to be a New London shipwright. The shipping trade was in the midst of a period of expansion. Before the eighteenth century, most ships built in New London were sloops—small, one-masted, fore-and-aft rigged vessels suitable only for relatively short voyages and rarely carrying more than fifty tons. Only occasionally did New London shipwrights build larger vessels such as a brigantine, snow, or brig. The 1720 arrival of Capt. John Jeffery, a master shipwright from Portsmouth, England, who set up a yard on the Groton bank, augured a change in the industry. Just as Stephen was beginning to work as a shipwright, Captain Jeffery began building a seven-hundred-ton ship, the largest ever constructed in the Americas. During his training with Hall and Coit, Stephen could look across the river and see "the great Ship," as his father and the rest of the town called it, rise out of Jeffery's yard by the ferry landing. Within two years, he and the rest of the men at Coit's yard would take the day off to join "a great Concourse of People" to watch it being launched. For many young men building the town's ships, the sight of an enormous vessel bound for the Indies and even Europe stirred up feelings of restlessness and wonder. Some dreamed of more than life in the yard.[23]

For Thomas, Joshua's fifth son, there would be no life beyond the fields and yards of New London. Of all the Hempstead boys, Thomas left the smallest trace in the pages of his father's diary, in spite of regular appearances at Bream Cove to help his father with the work of the day. Thomas's faint image in his father's entries did not reflect any lack of affection, however. As with Joshua's beloved wife, Abigail, those closest to the diarist did not enter its pages if they stayed put and suffered no misfortune.

WATCHING CHILDREN become adults was a long-sought recompense for Joshua as a father and single parent. In 1723, after both Nathaniel and Robert had reached majority, their father formalized the readjustment in his assets necessitated by his eldest son's death and made Robert the owner of his Long Island property while giving Nathaniel a stake in Stonington lands, along with the Bream Cove property. Nathaniel waited only nine days after the transfer before he published his intention to marry on the meetinghouse door for all to see. Mary Hallam (also called Molly), daughter of the widowed Elizabeth and the wealthy merchant Nicholas, would be his bride. The wedding took place on July 18 "in the Evening between 7 & 8 Clock in Ms Hallams Hall," Mr. Adams uniting the couple in front of a large gathering of family and friends.[24]

Most New Londoners simply used a justice of the peace to marry, since Congregationalists viewed marriage as a civil contract, not a religious sacrament. When Joshua himself became a magistrate, he would do a brisk business in such ceremonies. But when it came time for his own children to marry, Joshua wanted the learned Mr. Adams to perform the rites whenever possible. Most likely his choice had less to do with the depth of his religious feeling than his high personal regard for New London's minister. Neither did Joshua object to the prestige Adams lent to any occasion, distinguishing the families of the bride and groom. After the ceremony, guests celebrated with gusto, "many people held the Entertainment till between 12 and 1 Clock" in the morning. Revelry resumed the next day and lasted until late, the groom's exhausted father finally taking his leave "about 12 Clock."[25]

After Nathaniel's marriage, references to him in his father's diary changed subtly. One month to the day after the wedding, Joshua simply wrote: "Nath 6 days this week." The distinction was subtle, but undeniable. Before Nathaniel might have "Sheerd 111 [sheep]," and "Mow[ed]" on his father's behalf, but these "six days" had a new meaning. Nathaniel was now independent, and his time and labor no longer belonged to his father. Their working relationship would now conform to the continuous system of exchange Joshua maintained with any number of other men, entering the pages of each man's account book in a perpetual tit for tat.[26]

After visiting with relatives through September, "Nathll & wife come home." With that terse preamble, Joshua introduced a new family into the household at Bream Cove. It was a tight squeeze with only two real chambers and a third-floor garret, space they often shared with Hempstead siblings and hired servants. The newlyweds probably slept in a Hallam bedstead in the hall with only their calico curtains and valance for privacy, their father Hempstead resting in the room just above.[27]

Robert soon followed his brother's example. By the end of the same year, he had taken possession of Bailey land in Southold. With his father supplying the lumber, he raised a commodious house on Cooper's Lane, a road named for the family of his maternal grandmother and a stone's throw from his mother's birthplace. Soon he also took a wife: Mary Youngs, daughter of his master, Benjamin. For Robert, Southold had indeed become "home."[28]

Next-in-line Stephen went to visit Robert after he wed, but as Stephen drank toasts to his brother's happiness, he must not have envisioned himself married. After his time spent around yards and sailors, Stephen felt the lure of the sea. When he turned twenty-one in 1726, he signed on "with Burrows for 50s p month for Mertineco [Martinique]." This was a common path for a New London boy, attracted by the chance to see the world and accumulate some capital—not through wages but by taking on a portion of cargo to trade for his own account. With luck, skill, and good health, a young man like Stephen Hempstead—who probably never envisioned a lifetime at sea—might even put together enough resources to buy into a boat or purchase property at home.[29]

Joshua never wrote what he thought of Stephen's decision, but he was well aware of the risks. Seamen were especially vulnerable to injury and death through random shipboard accidents and epidemic disease, along with the ordinary danger of falling overboard—a simple misstep that typically led to drowning, as most men could not swim. Hempstead neighbor captain Joseph Coit described the trials and privations of his own first voyage to the Indies thus: "[I] was taken with the small pox [and short-term blindness] after which had the distemper exceeding bad, [serving] on a small sloop, not one fowl or drop of wine on board or anything else that was comfortable except good Cheney oranges which kept me alive." If a sailor survived such perils, he was still subject to storm and shipwreck. In bad weather New Londoners like Joshua waited anxiously for sons, fathers, and husbands to come home, hoping against hope that the worst would not come to pass. Still, a voyage to the West Indies was relatively short—eighteen to thirty days' passage if all went well—so that a young man like Stephen could justly believe he would beat the odds.[30]

For his first voyage, Stephen engaged to perform the "work and duty of a foremast man" at the monthly rate of fifty shillings. His pay was on the higher end of worldwide English merchant shipping, probably reflecting both the high mortality of the West Indian trade and Stephen's carpentry skills. While large ships might organize labor into a hierarchy of positions, small sloops of the sort Stephen knew had no such division of labor. On these ships there were only three basic positions: A novice sailor like Stephen began "before the mast." After several successful voyages, he could hope to hire himself out as a mate. And after another round of voyages as a mate, together with a bit of capital, a mate might rise to the rank of master—a commander supervising the ship's navigation and business with supreme authority, frequently as part owner. In his more than twelve-year career, Joseph Coit made nineteen voyages: three as foremast man, five as mate, and eleven as master.[31]

Although Stephen went to sea as an ordinary foremast man, his shipmaster surely valued his skills as a trained shipwright. Most small boats did not have a designated carpenter, so a man like Stephen could perform repairs when necessary and sometimes receive a higher rate of pay. Aside from his wage, Stephen also received his "'customary usage' in the 'necessaries of life.'" He even negotiated "one barrel privilege out and home," entitling him to this fixed amount of cargo space, free of freight charges. Although he began with the privilege of just one barrel, Stephen might later bargain for a larger proportion of a ship's hold.[32]

New London seafaring men had common experiences with English sailors across the Atlantic world, but their lot was also distinctive and local as well. While mutinies, harsh discipline, and desertion were endemic in the English merchant fleet, these were unusual occurrences on ships emanating from an insular port like New London. Because local shipmasters drew their labor largely from the yards and farms of the town, crews were often made up of young men who had known one another since childhood—men who had friends and relations in common and lives and families to return to. Unlike most English seamen, New London sailors were not the poor and dispossessed without prospects at home. Many like Stephen simply saw their time at sea as a short-term gamble, one that might yield a lifetime of stories, not to mention the snug comfort of a house and family on New London's shores.[33]

DURING THE 1720s, as Joshua Hempstead shepherded sons and daughters into adulthood, John Winthrop IV prepared to abandon his seven children. After his litigation with his sister and brother-in-law Lechmere began in 1723, it dragged on for months and then years—punctuated by a number of partial decisions and even leading the Connecticut General Assembly to fine-tune its intestate statute in May 1726, which bolstered the Lechmere claim. As he saw the New England legal system uphold the American custom of shared inheritance among children over English primogeniture, John IV came to regard his fight with the Lechmeres as a grand battle between the son of New England's great founding family and his ungrateful country. When he lost to the Lechmeres in Connecticut's superior court in March 1726 and Thomas Lechmere was awarded adminstration of the estate, John IV became apoplectic—even borrowing a page from John Rogers's playbook and causing enough of a disturbance protesting in the General Assembly that he was arrested for disorderly conduct. Life "among such a rude and ungoverned wicked crew" had become impossible for John IV. His final recourse was to set sail for England, leaving his wife and seven children behind in New London.[34]

The Privy Council in London served as a court of last resort for colonial appeals. But it was impractical, expensive, and rare for a colonist to file an appeal there, and the council was also under no obligation to hear a case. John IV pulled as many strings as he could to have his case admitted in February 1727. Exulting in the change of scene in the British capital and buoyed up by the promise of a fresh hearing, John IV was happier than he had been in years. Back home at Winthrop's Neck in New London, however, Anne Winthrop and their seven surviving children, then aged four to eighteen, found it difficult to share in their father's excitement. They missed their husband and father terribly, and Anne was daunted by the work of caring for children while overseeing the management of John IV's vast holdings of largely undeveloped land.[35]

Anne's letters to her husband are difficult to read, as she poured out her distress in measured doses, fearing his ire: "my eyes are consumed with grief and heart killed with sorrow for you." Meanwhile John IV was living comfortably in London, an expensive proposition he expected his Connecticut holdings and besieged wife to support. As the legal process continued, months in London turned to years, with John IV ensconced in the home of a female cousin, while his abandoned wife and children were reduced to genteel poverty in Connecticut. His letters to his family became infrequent as Anne Winthrop struggled with mounting despair and constant money troubles. In March 1728 she pleaded with him, "Is it not better to come home and enjoy a little than to fling away the greater part because we cannot have the whole?" By then, though, John IV had already received the result he had long dreamed of. The king in council had ruled in his favor, striking down the Connecticut intestacy statute, a decision that had implications for inheritance law across the colonies. Aside from its broader legal implications, however, the decision restored the whole of the now-diminished Winthrop landed estate to him alone.[36]

John IV had spent a fortune in legal, travel, and living expenses to pursue his claim, but these and the catastrophic emotional costs to his family did not perturb him as he gloated in victory. The Winthrop scion celebrated with travels through the English countryside, watching the graduates as they took their degrees at Cambridge and then visiting the ancestal Winthrop home in Groton, where he was feted "with dancing music and myrth." With all England at his disposal, John IV must have begun to forget the sound of his children's voices and even the sight of their faces. To the father of seven, there seemed little reason to return to deadening, maddening New London—with or without the Winthrop estate.[37]

Chapter Eleven

"ADAM IS COME"

T HE FIRST days of September 1727 found Joshua Hempstead walking the house and lands of the Samuel Fox property in the North Parish, taking notes and jotting down figures— the sharp New England air recalling summer even as it foretold fall.[1]

Old Samuel Fox was dead at age seventy-six, and the local probate court had chosen Joshua Hempstead, who was known as a fair and honest dealer, to assist the executors in recording and dividing the fellmonger's considerable estate. The work was uncomplicated and familiar. Although Joshua had grown up working in fields and clambering up and down the scaffolding of half-built ships, he was drawn to legal work. Nearly a decade had passed since he had entered one of New London's many shipyards as a builder, having abandoned the shipwright's craft after Abigail's death. When he was not caring for his children, he turned to a wide range of gainful pursuits—trading goods, surveying land, cutting gravestones, making coffins, and providing legal services. Useful about town, the well-liked Joshua had become a man whom family, friends, neighbors, and local government singled out for his ability and commitment to serve the common good. By nature he possessed the rare capacity to convey a mollifying tone, even under the most contentious circumstances. When a sick neighbor needed care, the meetinghouse wanted rebuilding, or an estate—like old Fox's—required valuation and distribution among potentially quarrelsome recipients, New Londoners turned to Joshua.[2]

As September progressed, the work at the Fox farm moved slowly, interrupted by Joshua's frequent trips home to Bream Cove, some eight miles away. Toward the middle of the month, the weather turned surprisingly hot, and Joshua fought off a recurring malaise made more debilitating by the heat. While tabulating Fox's bonds and currency, he felt his mouth go dry and his large frame shudder with the familier chills that no amount of rum could quash. At forty-nine, Joshua had long suffered with a particular "ague and fever"—probably malaria, which was then common in both Old and New England. By this time he could anticipate its predictable cycle: the portentous chills followed by uncontrollable fits, vomiting, dysentery, high fevers, and lingering sweats. The attack he suffered that September struck hard enough for him to seek out a bed at old Fox's. He lay there the night of the thirteenth in a delirium.[3]

The following morning, Joshua returned home to pull hops and cut letters into the plain flat stones that would stand at the head and foot of Fox's grave, but he was forced again to surrender to "fitts." Within the week, though, Joshua rejoined the appraisal, helping to divide property between the dead man's widow and grown children from three marriages. There were no disputes over the inheritance. The cash, paper, plate, and even promises of payment Joshua found easy enough to tally and distribute. During the apportioning, he also made a proposal—one that would benefit the estate and spare executors the effort of a later sale. There was an unwieldy item among Fox's movable goods in which Joshua acknowledged an interest. The appraiser had made note of the item long before he came to Fox's that September, but perhaps he had decided to act as he walked the old man's lands—even as he had lain in the house suffering with fever.[4]

Close proximity and the passage of time had given Joshua ample opportunity to consider the young "Negro" man named Adam Jackson who had lived as a slave with the Foxes since his birth about twenty-seven years earlier. The executors accepted Joshua's timely offer of eighty-five pounds for Adam—five pounds down and the rest in one year with interest. The price was relatively high and readily accepted, justified by Adam's New England upbringing, his skills at husbandry, and his reputation as an affable, useful, and obedient servant. By September 26, the yeoman farmer and former shipwright could leave the Fox farm satisfied with a deal well struck. Along with his expectations of the bargain, Joshua took home three pounds of honey—partial payment for his work on the estate and on the stones for the old man's grave.[5]

A day after the division was complete, Adam Jackson walked the eight miles to town—a detail recorded in his new master's diary. Adam was alone, traveling along familiar roads and highways that were little more than rough dirt paths. Although the town had grown considerably since 1700, New London remained a relatively modest settlement in 1727. New shops and housing had opened up along the main street, and the Bank continued to expand with wharves and commercial buildings. But only one major addition to the central hub could be counted: Timothy Green, a member of an established Boston printing family, had come to town and set up a printshop just up the hill from Joshua, which eventually became Connecticut Colony's first official printer. Green's shop provided a new center of information and sociability in town, giving locals unprecedented access to a variety of new publications, including pamphlets, sermons, and all of the colony's lawbooks—essential reading for any man hoping to get ahead.[6]

Walking through New London, past the meetinghouse and burial ground, Green's shop and the town pound, a native son like Adam encountered men and women who could instantly place him, just as he could them, in an instinctive geneaological shorthand. Locals knew one another's parents and families, one another's stories—just as they surely knew Adam's reason for passing through town that day. Turning onto the highway to Bream Cove, Adam walked down toward the productive if inelegant neighborhood at its edge. To his back was the only home he had ever known—if a master's house can be a home. Ahead lay New London's busy harbor and shipyards and the house that would be his future. He had almost certainly seen its old weathered frame many times before. As he entered the yard the smell of neighbor Truman's tanning vats might have reminded him of the powerful scent he carried in his nostrils from old Fox's pelts. Adam closed the gate and walked the worn path to the door.

THE SAME morning that Adam Jackson walked across New London, eleven-year-old Molly Hempstead had probably dressed before light and tripped sleepily along the path from her father's house to the barn to take the morning's milk. Although men could milk in a pinch, the English viewed this ancient rite, repeated every dawn and dusk, as quintessential woman's work. Familiar female hands and tones soothed the cows, encouraging milk to flow. English fathers typically included a healthy milk cow with a daughter's marriage "portion" so that a young bride could provide milk and cheese for her family. Although her own wedding day was years away, Molly was already adept at the work. The child had been trotting up and down the same path to milk for as long as she could remember.[7]

A newborn when her mother died, Molly had lived in Southold, where she was nursed by her aunt Salmon for a year; then her mother's sister sent her along for another six months to an elderly Easthampton widow who ably weaned the child. Molly's eighteen long months on the North Fork were more than enough separation for her father: Although he and her siblings faced daunting challenges caring for the toddler at home, Joshua seemed to jump at the chance to bring her back. Molly's sister Betty remained with her aunt and uncle Tallmadge in Easthampton. Three years older, Betty had quickly joined the productive members of that household, so her father had no reason to uproot her again.[8]

When Molly returned to New London she spent the next four years at home with her father, though his diary registered little of the doings of his youngest child during this period. She spent most of her time with women and girls, including her older sister, Abigail, and the steady stream of neighborhood women and hired girls who maintained the household during Joshua's widowerhood. With Molly immersed in female company, Joshua's diary distilled her early years at home into another characteristic sequence of mishaps, signposts along his daughter's progression through the perils of childhood. The result was a staccato rendering of infancy: a "feaver & ague" at three, a severe scalding at five (her brother Nathaniel's "dis[h] of hot milk" spilling down her back and neck); a nasty fall from an upstairs window at six with a hard landing "into ye [open] Cellar door way," injuring badly a growing knee and hip. Each of these and other times her father came to her bedside and nursed his motherless daughter back to health.[9]

When Molly turned seven a new stage began. First her father sent her for a few months' schooling at the home of a local family, the Couches. Women of Joshua's generation had inconsistent literacy skills, and Molly's father wanted his girls to have a solid grounding in reading and writing beyond any instruction he might give them at home. At eight, Molly spent four months in Stonington with Thankful Smith, who taught girls basic reading, writing, and arithmetic with other useful skills at her "dame" school. By the time she turned eleven in 1727, Molly had also lived at the home of an uncle, her father's half-brother, the Norwich joiner Thomas Edgecombe. The child may have simply helped out informally, although she may also have worked as a "hired girl," her wages going to her father. With four little ones at home under the age of six, Thomas Edgecombe's wife, Katherine, must have found her young niece a godsend.[10]

On September 27, Molly had been back from her aunt and uncle Edgecombe's less than a month. Making her way from the barn to her father's kitchen that morning, she could feel the raw warmth of the milk pails—piggins, to use her father's antique term—rise up against her knuckles. Inside the house another Molly listened for the child's steps. Molly Hallam Hempstead had been married to Nathaniel for four years. Apart from Joshua's aged and declining mother, this elder Molly at just twenty-two was the only grown woman living in the household. That September morning the two Mollys met in the back kitchen to prepare the morning's meal—probably the common New England breakfast of cornmeal mush sweetened with new milk fresh from the piggins. For men and children alike, they might serve hot coffee or tea and hard cider to drink—water was considered unhealthful, and it often was.[11]

While the elder Molly took charge of the cooking, she could depend on her young sister-in-law to keep an eye on her boys, three-year-old Josh and baby Natty. These were the first Hempstead grandchildren, and it was only fitting that the eldest boy should be named Joshua. At a minimum, the Mollys could expect all six of the house's occupants at breakfast, apart from the baby. Fifteen-year-old Abigail was on Long Island, where her brother Robert and sister Betty lived, but she would be home within a fortnight. Stephen was at sea. Nineteen-year-old Thomas and seventeen-year-old John, who both lived on and off at the house while they worked around town, might have also joined the family that morning. Especially during the demanding seasons of planting and haying, Thomas and John helped their father, bedding down in the cramped garret or even tumbling into the small trundle at the foot of his bed.[12]

Hempsteads came to breakfast from different parts of the house. Nathaniel and his wife would most likely have emerged from their bedstead in the downstairs hall, flanked by little Natty and Josh. Lying just above them in the second-floor chamber he had occupied for nearly three decades, Joshua could hear every word they spoke. In failing health, mother Edgecombe inhabited a snug back room above the kitchen where warmth from the cooking hearth eased the aches and chills of old age. During that fall, however, she kept mostly to her small chamber. She would not live out the year.[13]

The morning routine that September day probably gave no sign of expectation, but the household did anticipate a new arrival. At some point that morning or in the days before, Joshua might have told Thomas and John to make a place. Up in the garret next to hogsheads of salted meat, bins of grain, and stacks of husked corn, the brothers made room for Adam Jackson, setting up a small mat or bed alongside their own. Basically unfinished storage space, the garret offered few luxuries; musty, rank, and home to more than its share of vermin, it still had certain positive attributes. In summer, its many windows permitted a welcome cross-breeze. And when the weather turned cold, as it did that September, the garret was the warmest part of the house, the scant heat of the chambers below collecting snugly in its eaves. Looking out from the south side, the view toward the port and harbor was also fine.

Later that same day at a high corner of the house, John and Joan Jackson's eldest son threw down his few belongings and took it all in. At best, his first days held nagging uncertainties. At worst, they might be harbingers of new and lasting misfortune. If he brooded too long, Adam's mind may have spun with the possibilities. No matter what good word he had of master Hempstead, he could not know the treatment he would find as his bondsman. Would he make a place for himself here near his own family, or would there be another sale into a complete unknown? Alert to his master's call, Adam had to swallow hard on his doubt and hasten downstairs to find out what Joshua would have of him.

Joshua's account of Adam's arrival was succinct: "Adam is come ys morn." The young man lived another five days with the Hempsteads before he appeared a second time in his master's diary: "Ad Cleaned ye Corn he Thrashed yesterd." The curt entries did little to convey all that had gone into Adam's coming. They gave no hint as to how Adam really made his way: whether he longed for the North Parish, for parents and siblings dispersed across town, or even for a familiar master now dead. They also told little of how Joshua integrated Adam into the work of the farm or the life of the family, even less how Joshua felt about owning a man. Whether they were inclined to reflection, neither man had much time to ruminate—corn needed to be cleaned, animals tended, and wood hauled for the winter.[14]

Every New England household needed the labor of its able members for its head to reach the goal of "competency"—an imprecise state of household economic autonomy that stood somewhere between scarcity and abundance. In spite of the obstacle of his widowerhood, Joshua Hempstead in 1727 could contentedly claim this sparing state of comfort as his own. Yet the communal duty to work the land fell harder on some than on others. Enslaved New Englanders like Adam worked as human property, bought and sold entirely to labor, their very industry becoming a dissonant virtue that conferred moral worth while it underpinned enslavement. Captive to a life of perpetual, unfree labor, Adam Jackson entered the unfamiliar governance of a new master, but he also came home to a world of work he understood almost innately. This much, at least, would be the same: There were things he knew with his hands that no one could take from him.[15]

THE WORLD of work would always be familiar ground to Adam, no matter the changes or subjugation he endured. Separated in legal and social terms and in their relationship to the work at hand, Adam and Joshua would nevertheless share an inevitable connection to the natural environment and to the materials that comprised the raw stuff of their labors—dirt, wood, crops, or even the weather itself. For free and servile New Englanders who worked the earth, few materials were more ubiquitous and uncooperative than the rocks underfoot. Day by day, the hard, tangible logic of stone created a medium of interaction for every husbandman—whether he was piling up stones to enclose a yard, digging them out to ready a field, or giving them a place in the built landscape. When Adam came to Bream Cove in 1727, work's substance might have provided a meaningful and stabilizing force. As he passed through the pain and upheavals of perpetual servitude, the rocks he felt and worked with nearly every day would remain a constant.

New England is an especially rocky region, made so by glaciers in its prehistoric past. When advancing glaciers arrived at what became New London and dropped precipitously into the waiting ocean, they left behind boulders of such size and number that the area became, even by New England standards, a strikingly stony locale. Nearby Stonington, in fact, offered tribute to this local characteristic in its very name. Building stone walls to divide and protect land and livestock was an activity in which every working husbandman was experienced to some degree. A practical necessity, the stone wall or fence was also a declaration of hard-wrought mastery over the land, one that appeared to later generations as an evocative symbol of foundational values. By the time Adam arrived on Joshua's lot, it was already filled with stone walls of his master's fashioning, a mishmash of rings and lines across a worn terrain. Together the two men carried on the constant work of wall making and repair, shielding land and livestock from loss but also gratifying themselves as builders when they created durable monuments to their labor and skill. After finishing a wall, a maker could look and muse approvingly, as Joshua did, "placed every Stone my Self."[16]

Among workingmen making walls, the oldest and most experienced became expert, able to place stones in a wall just right. When a man aged and lost physical strength, he still retained the eye of a veteran. An acknowledged old hand, Joshua enjoyed reserving for himself the careful work of placing stones. Building a section of "Stonewall" "before the Door" of the house in 1739, Adam and Joshua's then-fifteen-year-old grandson, Josh, did the heavy work of carting stones to the site. There Joshua, schooling his twelve-year-old grandson, Natty, in stone, put boulders knowingly into place. Such divisions of labor capitalized on the strength of youth and the expertise of an elder. For builders like Joshua and Adam, walls stored memories of weather, company, and time of life. A few, like one near the cove built during a stretch of fair weather that same year, 1739, memorialized incidents that broke ordinary routines. One evening, Josh tossed stones to his grandfather, who put them deftly into place. The boy flung one too hard, and it bounced, landing on Joshua's two fingers and leaving them "masht . . . very much."[17]

Stone walls were just one facet of a deeply embedded stone culture that engaged New Englanders like Joshua and Adam throughout their lives. For men who worked the land, as most did, stones were a constant refrain to the day's labor, punctuating the pitch of the shovel, the thrust of the hoe, and the steer of the plow. Stones, as fences and foundations or even as entire dwellings, formed boundaries and provided shelter. Perceived as markers, they could confer ownership, place, and name. At the outer limits of a human connection to stone, men beheld mystery and danger—even specters of the otherworldly in a rocky prospect.

Stone was integral to New England domestic worlds. Alongside walls built from field and quarried stones, men used stone to support homes. Stone shored up walls, protected porches and cellars, and allowed for heat—and cooked food—in fireplaces and chimneys. All around, stone trimmed the edges of New Englanders' domestic environment, providing a last bulwark between the destructive forces of nature and the decay of less permanent materials. With stone, Joshua braced the cellar at the southwest corner of the house; with stone, he mortared the chimney, perched carefully on the eastern side of the roof.[18]

Trimming the ends of domestic space, stones mindfully chosen also created entries to interior space. The enormous stepstone at Joshua's front door gave form and footing to the threshold of his house. In the winter of 1737, Joshua and Adam rode out to Gungywamp Hill (well known for its large, flat stones and Native American stone ruins), where they selected a smooth, seven-foot specimen. Chaining it to the horses, they towed the block down to the hill's base. And there it lay for many months at the foot of Dart's hill, an unremarkable sight to the unaware, but already connected in Joshua's thoughts to the house at Bream Cove. Only after four years, did Joshua have Josh and Natty bring the stone home by a team of oxen, and then it lay to one side on the lot another three months until its owner made it the entry point of his house.[19]

A familiar tableau in the New England landscape was of men simply "diging Stones" to ready soil for plowing. Joshua and sons Nathaniel and Stephen had taken part in one such portrait, depicted in Joshua's diary in March 1719, moving three abreast and sweeping the ground slowly and steadily with hands and tools, each figure taking rocks from his swath of field and heaping them to the side. Once piled, some stones stayed in place; others Joshua hauled, dragged, or carted away to use or pile elsewhere.[20]

Stone work was an unremitting routine of digging and hauling, but it also provided some of the most dramatic moments in men's working lives, joining them together to perform great feats of strength and stamina. Removing large boulders required colossal physical effort. Pried free, these memorable boulders could reappear, assuming new roles in the domestic scene. On one late autumn evening, Joshua, with eight oxen and one horse, hauled a massive rock to the orchard meadow behind the house. There he put it to good use, sinking it as rock bed for a new cart path. On another midsummer morning, Joshua, Adam, and fellow New Londoner Joseph Lester gathered on a hill northeast of the house to pry out "a very Large Stone" using a wedging system. Within days, the stone became part of a wall between the front meadow and the cove.[21]

Walking just beyond the stony northeast corner of his lot late in life, Joshua would stumble upon the bloodied body of Wetherell Denison, New London's long-serving town clerk, lying dead in a snowbank. Denison had a large bloody gash at the back of his head. Had he fallen from his horse on a woozy ride toward town? Tracking the clerk's last minutes in his mind and with his feet, Joshua followed a nearly five hundred foot trail of blood up and down the rocks, his breath steaming in the cold air. First, Joshua surmised, Denison had leaned against a stone wall, wiping blood from his head onto its stones with a hand or a kerchief. Then he had staggered another five hundred feet until he collapsed amid the rocks. Stones familiar from boyhood were immediately transformed into the place where Denison had lain dead and bloodied.[22]

Other rocks triggered similar associations. On a winter afternoon two years after Denison's collapse, the elderly, "male[n]cholly" Benjamin Beebe, a member of the extended Beebe family, walked gloomily along a path between the homes of his two grown daughters. Along the way he turned back, then veered entirely off the trail to a ledge of rocks that shielded him from view. Sitting on a stone "as if . . . in a Chair," Old Beebe tied fishing line between his neck and his coat "fastned to his Staff," then stuffed the coat into the branches of a sturdy bush overhead. Leaning forward into the "warm Springlike" air, he "Stopt his breath," "Slipping of[f]" and killing himself.[23]

Some rocks assumed otherworldly dimensions. New London was home to the enormous "Swiming Rock" of Poquoyog that moved "unacountably," its motion suggestive evidence of "Supernataral Power." The rock attracted considerable attention among locals. On three separate occasions, Joshua took his brother-in-law, a friend, and two leading residents to view and measure it. Like another nearby landmark of wood—"the Tree that was Remarkably Split with the Thunder & Lightning"—the "Swimming Rock" remained an attraction for several years, a local oddity that defied rational explanation and caused onlookers to marvel.[24]

Stone formations dotted Joshua and Adam's landscape, creating natural markers that they used to orient themselves around the lot. There were also structures of their own making, like the stepstone at the front door and the "Island of rocks" that lay northeast of the house. Though it may have begun as a natural swell of rock, that "Island" evolved into a mountainous heap of unwanted stones added to or picked from by workingmen according to need and inclination.[25]

IF THE rock "Island" was haphazard, other stones men placed with great care. When the English came to settle New England, many brought with them the tools of a relatively new art and science, tools they would need as much as the plow or hoe to assert their dominion over the land. In Europe, modern surveying, which required the use of applied mathematics and geometry, had begun in the sixteenth century as the pursuit of scholars and intellectuals. By the time of New England's settlement, surveying was well established across the manors of Old England and would become a potent force in creating new property and new law in North America. Many English immigrants, including perhaps Joshua's grandfather Robert, and certainly his stepfather Edgecombe, a county surveyor, conveyed their skills—along with their tools—to sons and nephews, so that the art of surveying passed from generation to generation in families.[26]

Joshua, too, became a county surveyor, marking boundaries with a variety of stones and other signposts. Among these standard property markers were surveyor's meerstones—small monuments to English legal culture and cultivation whose square tops (sometimes carved with an owner's initials) often peeked out at the edges of English land. Meerstones were close cousins to the milestones that measured and marked distances on highways, some of which Joshua also placed with his own hand. While meer- and milestones shared a formal, graven appearance, other boundary stones were strikingly random. There was the heap of stones with a stick jammed in it, a

"Rock with Stones on it & Small Cracks in it," the "heap of Splitten Rocks [that] Stands up Edgeways," or the "very high clump or heap of rocks." Still other markers were of wood rather than stone, like the chestnut tree marked *TA* for its owner, or the white oak marked *SR* with three sides "chipped with an ax." Every husbandman like Joshua and Adam knew the marks that defined the land where he lived and worked.[27]

Other stones in the landscape told stories of people and the passage to eternity. A stack of these Joshua kept behind the house near the family's large woodpile. Just as ordinary field rocks pervaded farm labors, smooth stones like these, beginning in the 1720s, became a small but steady part of Joshua's artisanal life. A few years before Abigail died and Adam came, Joshua began to buy and stockpile unlettered gravestones on the lot. There they sat until, once or twice a year, a death close to home resulted in an order. Then Joshua would stay "at home al day Marking Gr[ave]stones," cutting letters and numbers into stone under the ample shade of the locust tree near the front door where he liked to work. Once marked, Joshua's stones stood in local burying grounds, easily recognizable as his for the unmistakable vernacular of their plain lettering and a distinct tilt in the number 7.[28]

The work of cutting stones to remember the dead complemented Joshua's penchant for capturing experience in words and numbers. Gravestone imagery during the period was very elaborate, richly expressing Puritan faith with depictions of doorways to eternity, coffins, winged death's-heads, and soul effigies. Imagery also changed over the course of his life, reflecting variations in iconographic sensibilities. But Joshua's work was unadorned, in plain Connecticut style. Like most men who made gravestones, Joshua did so part-time. Unlike the most skilled practitioners, though, Joshua did not carve and illustrate in stone, but only "cut" or "marked" bare or precarved blanks with letters and numbers.[29]

Among New England's foremost carvers and the originator of the so-called Merrimack River School—an indigenous style that spread from Essex County, Massachusetts, to southeastern Connecticut— was John Hartshorn. A transplant from Haverhill, Massachusetts,

Hartshorn had joined a daughter in Norwich after surviving the 1708 French and Indian raid, in which he had lost his wife, son, and three grandsons. Hartshorn had carved stones for the victims of the raid, giving them his distinctive look; small stones bearing blank gazing faces, surrounded with rosettes, flowers, stripes, wheels, and whorls, and often showing their price on the side. Joshua's younger sister Lucy married Hartshorn's nephew, so the New London shipwright naturally turned to his old and expert "uncle Hartshorn" when he needed stones for purchase.[30]

Gravestones came in pairs: Headstones and considerably smaller footstones that framed graves like an eternal bedstead. Joshua bought small loads of unlettered stones from suppliers in Middletown or from Hartshorn in Norwich. From Hartshorn, for example, Joshua might buy a load of ten on "spec" or a pair destined for a specific customer, giving the old man "Mony . . . blue fish" and "wool" in exchange. For a pair of decorated, unlettered stones, Joshua paid wholesale prices of around ten to twenty shillings, although both costs and prices rose dramatically over time. Stones lettered over the course of days, weeks, months, or even years, Joshua could sell by the pair for around twenty-five to forty shillings, but sometimes for as much as three to six pounds—prices that usually included set-ting stones at the gravesite. (One such "Set[ting] up" took place two months after Adam's arrival, when Joshua put in place the stones for Adam's old master, Samuel Fox.)[31]

For decades, Joshua worked on two to three sets of stones per year, serving a variety of customers among his large acquaintance-ship, many of them relations. Occasionally, he even lettered a tomb-stone, whose large slabs lay flat on pillars atop the graves of New London's elite, such as that of the merchant-magistrate Richard Christophers, at whose funeral "the great Ship [in the harbor] fired 26 great guns ½ Minute distance," but whose gravestones Joshua did not finish for another six years (almost to the day).[32]

Samuel Bill, a New Londoner who worked the Connecticut coastal trade, had to wait even longer for his wife's stones after she died "with a Dropsie" in 1740. Nine years later, the Bream Cove ship-wright finally finished lettering her headstone—though he did not get around to setting it at the gravesite for another four years. When Adam finally carted Mrs. Bill's stones to place at the burying ground, Joshua recalled having finished them "2 or 3 yrs ago. & now this Day [Samuel Bill, the purchaser himself,] Died." Had Bill's impending death prompted the long overdue delivery? Although Joshua once cut eighty-one letters in just a day and a night, he usually took his time and let a grave lie bare or with temporary wooden markings for some time.[33]

Joshua's crude lettering style was immediately recognizable in plots across New London County, but neighbors did not hire him for his superior workmanship. Joshua's distinctive handiwork on a stone might have had a different local cachet, not evident in its dull aesthetics. Doubtless the lack of refinement in his work did not trouble the practical Joshua. Engraving letters into stone was simply one of an assortment of crafts to which he applied staple skills learned as a wheelwright's son, a tanner's stepson, and, above all, a master shipwright. Together these pursuits provided additional income and a buffer to the ups and downs of weather and farming.

At first thought, cutting gravestones might appear an unlikely sideline for a shipwright. But in England what became the trade of undertaking was originally the work of woodworkers and carpenters, who made coffins. In this light, Joshua's gravestone cutting is fitting. Through his forties, Joshua the woodworker had also made coffins for neighbors and relations—Trumans, Douglases, Plumbs, and Foxes—at the rate of one or two a year. Coffin making was a quick job, performed while a corpse awaited burial. It was also intimate work, tied to the contours of the body of the deceased and the grief of the bereaved. (In 1725, Joshua had needed only "about 10 foot of bords" for his younger sister Patience Hodsell: She was less than five feet tall.) Sometimes he went straight from comforting at a bedside to fashioning a coffin. He gave up the work, for the most part, by the late 1720s. Then he returned to it briefly in 1733 for an infant grandchild, blacksmith John's son, making most of the tiny coffin, "all but the Cover," one fair September morning.[34]

One of the costliest pairs of stones Joshua ever sold were for the grave of Frank Provido, a young "negro man." Frank was slave or servant to Joseph Powers, a propertied ferryman and shipmaster who had moved to New London from South Kingston, Rhode Island. Young Frank Provido appeared to have been a well-known personage in town largely because of his father, "Old" Frank, another Powers servant. Their master esteemed young Frank enough to spend more than three pounds on stones for his grave—a grave that may have stood at the low end of the burying ground near the river, where some of the town dead with origins in Africa appear to have been accommodated. Frank's stones lay around Joshua's house-lot more than six months—time enough for Adam to wonder what his own grave might merit.[35]

Chapter Twelve

BREAM COVE AND BEYOND

OR JOSHUA HEMPSTEAD, buying Adam Jackson made sense in practical, economic terms; Joshua was an aging landowner who needed help doing the work of the farm. But his decision to become a slaveholder affected and buoyed other aspects of his life. Owning Adam bolstered his career as a public servant and even his role as a dedicated father and grandfather. As Adam became integrated into the work of the farm, even taking a primary role, Joshua would be able to devote more of his time to serving both his grown children and a growing community.

Joshua had taken advantage of his role as appraiser when he bought Adam in the first place—the youth never even making it into Samuel Fox's estate inventory. But the timing of his purchase was more than happenstance. Rarely, in fact, did Joshua leave anything important involving his family and household up to chance. The yeoman shipwright followed the dictates of his church and the minister he revered and likely took the existence of slavery for granted. For Joshua, owning a man was a pragmatic decision with important domestic—if not moral—implications.

At forty-nine, Joshua was old to be a first-time slaveholder. Most colonists who wanted and could afford to own another man did not wait until late middle age. As a widower Joshua certainly needed extra hands to run his household and farm, but up until the mid-1720s his five sons had provided the bulk of additional labor to support the family's needs. As his boys began to take their places in society as independent men, however, Joshua had to find a reliable replacement for their work. Approaching his fifties, Joshua had fulfilled many of his dearest aspirations for himself and his children—achievements that had been stolen from his grandfather and father by an early grave. As the aging yeoman looked with satisfaction on his prospering children and now-plentiful estate, he allowed himself to turn further outward, comfortably answering the call to become more active in public affairs—a call that had grown louder with the passage of time.

Losing Abigail had created an emotional void in Joshua's life, but it also may have opened up the possibility of a different kind of fulfillment in serving the public good. Given the number and variety of official and unofficial posts he held, Joshua was clearly a popular and well-trusted townsman. He possessed a kind of leadership distinguished by patience and gentle persuasion rather than intimidation. Without a wife waiting at home, Joshua was perhaps uniquely suited to answer New London's increasing demands for his attention. He needed only to cover the essential work of his farm. Purchasing a slave meant that Adam Jackson could fill that need, and even provide some insurance against old age as Joshua's physical powers began to wane.

Buying Adam was not the only milestone in Joshua's fifth decade that promoted his civic career. In the year leading up to his purchase of Adam, Joshua had taken another important step—one that also came late in life compared with most of his neighbors. In 1726, he finally joined the membership of the congregation he had attended since infancy. While church membership was not a prerequisite for high local office, it was evidence of one's status as an upstanding member of the community. Although Joshua's generation had experienced an overall decline in church membership, most men who aspired to become members did so earlier in life—usually between twenty-five and thirty-five. But as the prime years for church admission came and went, Joshua had let them pass him by.[1]

Joshua never explained his delay in this regard, but he did leave a few clues. Even as he assumed a place of prominence in local governing and legal circles, Joshua was clearly less zealous in taking a leadership role in the Congregational Church. He was a believer and dutiful congregant in a world where faith was assumed and regular attendance mandatory, and Joshua's relationship with his church tracked, in many ways, a broader history of New England Congregationalism. Joshua had grown up in the Congregational Church—like most of his generation—by virtue of the halfway covenant, the diminished, compromise status that was a tacit acknowledgment of religious decline. While a husband and father, Joshua watched many of his peers from the town's oldest families join the church. Even his wife, Abigail, joined as a full member in 1709, following the not uncommon path of a wife leading her husband. Still, although Joshua had Mr. Adams baptize his infant children, he did not follow Abigail into the church. Even the terrible year of 1716, when he lost both wife and son, did not induce a religious experience sufficient to prompt him to seek membership.[2]

On the second day of September 1726, enrolled brethren of the First Congregation met to consider admissions procedures, while Joshua was setting up gravestones on a neighbor's farm in Stonington. The meeting perceived "that there are Diverse Persons Among us, of good character and deportment, who stand off from joining our Communion, because it hath been insisted upon that a Revelation of your Experiences, should be brought by." Apparently the prospect of relating a conversion experience before the entire congregation was deterring potential communicants. In a move toward inclusiveness, the brethren relaxed this requirement: "Where any have a very great scruple and difficulty upon their spirits to comply with this custom," they would not need to do so.[3]

Joshua Hempstead may have been one of those "of good character and deportment." If he had had "a very great scruple" or some "difficulty upon [his] spirits" that prevented him from revealing his faith publicly, he did not confess it in his diary. Perhaps he had never undergone a conversion experience, for it seems unlikely the affable town leader, well accustomed to public speaking, would have been daunted by an appearance before the congregation. Whatever his reasons, the September 1726 modification resolved his reluctance, and by that November he could write, "I was took into the Church."[4]

It had not been quite as simple as that. In a rare instance of stinging personal conflict for Joshua, one church member and propertied New Londoner, John Morgan, had voiced "Objections agst my being admitted to ye Church. [The minister and elders] Considered his Allegations & my Defence & Judged them groundless & me Inocent by their full determination with one Consent." Morgan's actual accusations remain a mystery, but court records reveal that Joshua had arguably wronged him years earlier, unfairly using his official influence to exact a bit of payback from Morgan. At that time, Morgan had sold a one-eyed bay horse that rightfully belonged to Joshua. (The horse had originally been Morgan's, but was later conveyed to a third party who sold it to Joshua, with Morgan apparently never having agreed to the original transfer.) It was a common sort of dispute that men routinely settled through civil litigation, arbitration, or simply heated conversation. Something provoked Joshua's indignation, however, and he took the extreme step of instigating a criminal action against Morgan.[5]

Rather than simply lodging a criminal complaint as an alleged victim, however, Joshua instead choreographed a grand jury indictment so that the prosecution appeared to be a communal rebuke rather than simply a personal conflict. (Then a selectman, Joshua accomplished this by writing out a presentment in his own hand and then getting a grand juror to sign it—a measure, perhaps, of the pressure a local official could exert.) A jury convicted Morgan for taking and selling the horse (a fact Morgan had never disputed), and Morgan was ordered to pay Joshua treble damages of six pounds, along with costs and a fine to the county treasury. Six pounds was a hefty sum to pay for an apparent misunderstanding, and Morgan probably never forgave the incident. When Joshua came up for church membership a decade later, Morgan may have thought it was time to return the insult.[6]

Once Joshua did achieve membership, he was content simply to remain a member in good standing. He seemed uninterested in becoming a deacon, a church elder able to lead the meeting in the minister's absence. Though he attended meeting and was a dutiful Christian, his diary leaves the impression that religious faith was not a driving force in his life. Rather he maintained an accepting, pragmatic attitude toward faith, apparent in his tolerance for men and women with other beliefs. For Joshua, differences in theology were eclipsed by ties to individuals—familial, neighborly, or commercial. Throughout his life, Joshua remained close to his Baptist cousin Benjamin Fox (a member of the large Fox family), for example, and had no trouble appreciating the faith and piety of members of other denominations. When the Baptist minister Joshua Rogers "Hanged himself in his own Hovel at [Black Point, a point of land in Niantic]" (after he impregnated his wife's sister and was found out), Joshua truly lamented the downfall of this "Baptist Teacher, an ordained minister & a very Sober orderly man." Likewise, when the young wife of Jonathan Rogers, Jr., died, Joshua venerated her as "a Pious woman a Strict observer of the 7th Day Sabath." Joshua was even accommodating in his everyday interactions with Rogerene neighbors. Their storming of the meetinghouse in 1716, with Joshua in attendance, had not stopped the diarist from surveying land for old John Rogers a month later.[7]

Becoming a church member and a slaveowner did not secure Joshua's civic career, but these milestones did ease his ascent. That public career depended on Adam and his work at home; there would be no corresponding calls to service as a magistrate or town officer for this other third-generation son of New London. The closest aspiration Adam and other African inhabitants of Connecticut might harbor was to become a "black governor," a ceremonial leader elected each June by enslaved New Englanders to "govern" by ceremony and serve as a sometime mediator of disputes. Such elections, especially in the latter half of the eighteenth century, could be quite festive, with slaves holding large celebrations and wearing finery that mimicked a master's status. Masters, for the most part, appeared to tolerate and even support such events as a relatively harmless diversion and outlet. Adam contented himself with staying largely within the lines prescribed to him, keeping himself well versed with the borders of his master's fields, and with the paths and byways leading into and around New London. He would lead in silence in the field, amid the rocks and furrows, the chopped trees and animal pastures: places he knew like the back of his hand.[8]

Other members of the Hempstead household also benefited directly from Adam's arrival. Nathaniel had crowded his family into the old Bream Cove house for five years, but with some ten people now sharing that limited space it was bursting at the seams. Nathaniel planned his own addition, a new side of the house that would roughly double its previous size. But earning a living and raising two small boys had left Nathaniel only just "finished geting his [house] Timber" when Adam entered their lives. Adam's labor would prove a particularly welcome prospect for Nathaniel. Within weeks of his coming, Joshua recorded his son and his slave of about the same age working together, "Mowing," and "in ye wood getting Timber to Ring Cartwheels." With Adam in the household, Nathaniel would be able to raise and finish clapboarding his new half of the house within the next year, just before the onset of winter.[9]

Joshua continued to rise in public life, but his civic career reached an important culmination within a year of his purchase of Adam. Beginning at the turn of the century, Joshua had regularly held office in New London, including stints as constable, rate maker (tax collector), school committeeman, county surveyor, and repeatedly as a governing selectman. With other leading men of the town, he also took several turns as a deputy or representative to the General Assembly. But no legal or administrative office was arguably more central and powerful in the daily lives of ordinary New Englanders than that of justice of the peace—a position Joshua attained beginning in 1728 and continued to hold for the rest of his life. As in Old England, the justice of the peace was the local magistrate with jurisdiction over petty offenses and the authority to hold hearings for cases to be tried in higher courts. He was the local face of Crown justice, a neighbor empowered to enforce the king's peace. In the event of a crime, for instance, the justice of the peace was often the first person to whom colonists turned for redress. Although justices formed a part-time lay judiciary (they received no salary but did collect fees for service from the county court), their services stood at the foundation of public life.[10]

Unlike Old England, the scarcity of gentry with legal knowledge or formal education meant that magistracies often fell to a lower echelon of men in the colonies. While a yeoman shipwright with no legal training or college education might be passed over in Old England, such a man in Connecticut, having proved himself in lower office, could become a prime candidate to serve. The lack of legal manpower in New England also meant that justices of the peace like Joshua probably wielded greater individual authority than did their Old English counterparts. While English magistrates' "sessions of the peace" required a bench of at least two justices, magistrates in Connecticut routinely presided alone over one-man "justice courts" that formed the backbone of judicial process in the colonies.[11]

By the time Joshua, the civil servant, became a magistrate, he had a wealth of practical legal experience. Aside from regularly attending court as an observer, Joshua had served on innumerable petit juries in criminal and civil trials, on grand juries considering indictments, and on coroner's juries determining cause in unnatural deaths. Each of these—along with the statute books provided free of charge to magistrates by the colonial government (and printed up the road at Green's shop)—meant that Joshua and men like him were entirely capable of effectively meting out low-level legal process.

Alone and often at home, the justice of the peace issued arrests and search warrants, summoned witnesses and deposed them, often presiding over bail hearings and in particular over initial proceedings in the common crime of fornication, asking local girls to name the fathers of their illegitimate children. Though he did exercise both civil and criminal summary jurisdiction—in which his decision was final—the stakes in these cases were low, never exceeding any amount or penalty over forty shillings. Like other justices, Joshua usually held court in the hall of his house, fitting sessions in between family life and other kinds of work in the field and yard. If necessary, however, his was also a portable court that traveled with the person of the justice, able to take form in prisons, taverns, and private homes—sometimes even the homes of criminal defendants or victims. As an offshoot of his public role as a civil servant and magistrate, Joshua also engaged in a certain amount of "lay lawyering," performing legal work for pay. Like magistracy, lawyering was not yet professionalized in early New England, so that laymen like Joshua, possessed of a certain amount of legal know-how and influence, could serve in lawyerly roles that ranged from writing legal documents to advising neighbors in legal conflicts. They were excluded from formally pleading before a court, a legal practice that required admission by the bench of the court and some degree of training.[12]

There was no standard way to become a lawyer, although an apprentice- or clerkship with an experienced attorney was the time-honored method. Harvard and Yale did not yet teach law, and the founding of the first Anglo-American law school in Litchfield, Connecticut, was still many years away. In England, men of the middling ranks had long acquired practical legal training at London's Inns of Court, but that expensive option existed for only a tiny minority of New Englandmen. (That elite group, incidentally, included Paul Dudley, John Winthrop IV's brother-in-law, who became Massachusetts attorney general in 1702 and eventually its chief justice and was considered among the best legal minds in the colonies.) As a result, ordinary literate men sometimes filled the void, doing legal work of various kinds. Joshua was one such "lay lawyer," a civil servant and magistrate who wrote innumerable deeds and wills, mediated civil disputes, and represented family and neighbors. On many occasions, he even appeared as an "attorney" for a civil litigant in court—taking on a role closer to the modern power of attorney, acting in place and on behalf of a party, rather than as professional legal counsel. (When John Livingston took on Beebe's suit over the Jacksons, for example, he most likely acted in this capacity.)[13]

As a part of his civic service to New London, Joshua also made himself of use—legally, administratively, and personally—to the Winthrop family. Joshua was genuinely charmed by his brushes with the colonial elite, connections that raised his own social tender. The diarist was a strong believer in deference and hierarchy, and he viewed his service to New England's "first" family as an obligation—

both as a townsman and a colonist. Apart from this sense of duty, Joshua also enjoyed basking in the Winthrop glow, a light that still shone bright in the eyes of the provincial shipwright.

After John IV left for England, Anne Dudley Winthrop turned to Joshua as one of the few New Londoners she could count on for help. Although he sometimes had to oppose Winthrop interests in his various official and judicial capacities, Joshua provided innumerable services to John's beleaguered wife, addressing her reverentially as "Madam" and acting at various times as her business agent, legal representative, property manager, and handyman. Theirs was an upright business relationship, but one steeped in social deference. Joshua had a deep respect for New London's "first lady," and modern speculations that there was more between them are unpersuasive. Adultery was a deadly sin and capital crime; moreover, the daughter and grandaughter of governors and a woman of impeccable reputation, Anne Winthrop would have regarded the yeoman shipwright from the Connecticut backwater as an inconceivable match.[14]

ALONGSIDE JOSHUA'S increasing participation in the affairs of his town, Adam's presence at Bream Cove also permitted his master to continue his parenting of adult children and his involvement in their lives. During Adam's second year at Bream Cove in 1729, Joshua sent his fifth surviving son, John, to his brother Robert on Long Island for a period of craft training. With Adam at home, Joshua was better able to spare this youngest son and filial worker. From his brother, John learned the blacksmith's trade and kept a keen eye on the charms of eligible Southold girls. By that time, twenty-six-year-old Robert was well established with a house, shop, and family, established enough to take his younger brother on as an apprentice. For their father, Joshua, sending John to learn the smithy's trade from his brother must have been the next-best thing to training the boy himself. Back at Bream Cove, twenty-eight-year-old Nathaniel had settled nicely into his new half of the old house with his wife and two boys, and the little family now awaited the birth of a third child. His twenty-year-old brother, Thomas, sometimes stayed on their father's side of the house to work, apparently in preparation for a life in husbandry.

At the beginning of 1729, the remaining Hempstead son, Stephen, was away at sea on a voyage bound for the island of Madeira, the Portuguese outpost off the coast of Africa. Stephen had already made three trips to the Indies since Adam's arrival two years earlier—the first to Martinique, a second to Antigua, and a third to Barbados. He had never planned to take the 1729 trip to Madeira until he suffered a personal setback. After his third voyage, his father had made a substantial investment in Stephen's future, purchasing him a one-third share in James Hodsell's sloop for ninety pounds. (Hodsell was Stephen's uncle James, the widower of Joshua's sister Patience.) A close relation and elder, Hodsell appeared a sound choice as a first business partner. Joshua did not simply provide capital, however. In keeping with his hands-on approach to fatherhood, he helped Stephen equip the sloop, permitting the young man to set sail soon after as master for the very first time. At the launch Joshua even tarried on board, helping Stephen to maneuver it toward Newport before returning home alone in a small sailboat. He soon grew apprehensive, however, noting "a fierce Storm & much Rain." As it turned out, Joshua's fears were well founded. Meeting severe weather off Martha's Vineyard, Stephen was forced "to Run on Shore to Save their lives which wr in great Hazard."[15]

It was his father who went to rescue Stephen. Hearing news of his son's predicament, Joshua had set off immediately for Point Judith on the Narragansett, riding his black mare and picking up a horse for Stephen along the way at their Stonington farm. Stephen had been lucky to escape with his life, and even though Joshua ultimately salvaged the ship, the venture had been a failure. Perhaps it was Joshua who advised his son not to risk it a second time, for Stephen never tried his hand at being a shipmaster again. Instead, he contented himself with remaining a mate, as he did when he left for Madeira within two months of the debacle.[16]

By the approach of summer in 1729, Stephen was back in New London, perhaps bringing with him samples of Madeira's strong, sweet wine for his father to taste. Arriving home, he found John away with Robert in Southold and the household at Bream Cove humming along agreeably with Adam and Nathaniel hard at work. It must have been a relief to return to a mild New England spring after the heat and intensity of the islands and shipboard life.

On a fair May day not long after Stephen's return, however, there was an accident at Bream Cove when "a Cow wch having Newly Calved being Angry" went wild. The animal, Joshua wrote, "Ran at me Struck me in the face Locked my teeth & Cut my lip & hurt my Arm & Leg. She Ript of[f] Mollys Gown & tore her Stays but did her no hurt." The damage was limited, but the incident was disturbing, and it seemed to set in motion events that spiraled quickly downward.[17]

While recovering from his mauling, Joshua descended into his old "fever & Ague." The case was so severe that he suspended the diary for nearly a month—a rare lapse. As the days turned into several weeks, dread replaced the calm resignation Joshua had initially felt in yielding to his recurring ailment. Just as it had in 1715, measles had now arrived in New London, and this time it would rip through the house at Bream Cove, afflicting nearly everyone in it.[18]

Joshua became so unwell he could not "ly down night nor day," his mind bleary with pain and thoughts of nearby children ailing "Exceed[ing] bad." Thomas was felled: On July 4 "my dear & dutyful Son died about 4 in the Morning being Aged Twenty one years (Apr. ye 14.) Two months & Twenty days." Like many colonial fathers, Joshua noted the exact age of his lost child, but he was too sick to attend the boy's hasty funeral the following evening. Within four days of the family burying Thomas, his father finally left the chamber where he had lain more than a month, stepping feebly into the yard. The next day he gave his grief a fuller airing with a gingerly walk "to the upper End of the Lot & back." Then a fresh and bitter blow razed any prospect of girding body and spirit. Despite the attentions of Dr. Jeremiah Miller, "Son Nathll who Lived with me Died about Ten of ye Clock at night. a Dear & Dutyful Son Aged 28 years 6 Months & 3 days." In the space of five days, he had lost two sons.[19]

Nathaniel's end was particularly agonizing, leaving behind "a Sorrowful Widow 2 Sons & She near her time againe." Joshua garnered enough strength to arrange and attend Nathaniel's funeral, assuring that his eldest son would be "decently Interred." New Londoners flinched at the now all-too-common sound of the meetinghouse bell, ringing out each new victim of the disease, this time the young Hempstead husband and father. For the twilight burial Joshua gave mourning gloves to sixteen honored attendants, marking the occasion of his son's life and his death. While Joshua watched Nathaniel's body enter the ground, women gathered around his son's suffering widow just down the hill in her darkening chamber where she was in the midst of her third wrenching labor. By nine o'clock, day had turned to night and Molly had given birth to her first girl, the child's young father lying fresh in the ground.[20]

Sons Thomas and Nathaniel Hempstead were buried just twenty days when their father received more alarming news. In Southold, sons Robert and John had also taken sick—probably with the same disease that had killed their brothers. Joshua left immediately to care for them. Arriving at Robert's house, he found his elder son already on the mend, but John still gravely ill with "a high fever & much in his nerves Twitching & Trembling in his limbs & his Tongue Swelld or numbed that he could Speake plain Scarcely Speak at all." Having already endured the losses of Nathaniel and Thomas, Joshua was determined not to let him go. He tended and watched over the boy with the skill of an accomplished nurse: "I followed him with a [clyster, or enema] Every day & gave him Cold water to drink often in Small Quantitys a Jell or more at once as often as he Craved it & . . . his fever began to abate & . . . his Tongue Cleared at once wch was Covered over with a Thick hard Scurff & as black as a Shoe well nigh." After more than two weeks at his son's bedside, Joshua returned home certain—at least for the time being—that he would not lose another child.[21]

Joshua's fathering of his sons did not end when he carried their coffins to the grave. Young Thomas died with little property, but it fell to his father to distribute his few possessions. Four months after the funeral, Joshua "helpt John down [from the garret?] wth his

Cheast yt was Thomas's." In it were "Tho[ma]s best Suit of Cloths & Wigg & Shoes &c." that would now be his brother's. Many months after that, Joshua could be found walking through town, paying off Nathaniel's debts, protecting his son's good name, his estate, and the widow and children he had left behind. It was just the beginning of what a father would do for a dead son.[22]

NOT LONG before Joshua had circuited the town to pay Nathaniel's debts, he had walked a similar course on a much more pleasant errand, his four-year-old grandson, Josh—who had lost his father, Nathaniel, less than a year earlier—ambling at his side. The boy and his grandfather had come to see a rare sight. Edward Burlesson, a severely crippled showman, puppeteer, and onetime schoolmaster, had arrived in town driving two teams of oxen pulling a wagon mounted with a cage. In it was a genuine lion, sometimes billed by Burlesson as "the lion of Barbary." (Strangely enough, this was the exact same lion whose fur had been used to treat John Winthrop IV's dying baby, John, in 1717; the animal had since spent time in the West Indies before returning to New England and arriving in Joshua's neighborhood.) On a tour of New England, the lion was housed in the Winthrop stable and could be viewed for a fee across from New London's Point of Rocks. For the grandfather and his young grandson, it would have been a special and memorable outing.[23]

The day they saw Burlesson's lion, the tender bond between grandfather and grandson was already on display. After the child's father died, his widowed mother, Molly, had struggled to survive without her husband, moving her three small children back and forth between the homes of her parents and her father-in-law. This precarious arrangement had ended in March 1733, when Joshua accepted legal guardianship of Josh and Natty, their mother retaining custody of baby Molly. Their fifty-four-year-old grandfather was already the most constant male presence in the boys' lives, best suited—in spite of his age—to guide them toward manhood. Given the entailment of the Hempstead home property, little Josh—as the eldest son of Joshua's eldest surviving son—had also become its heir. By agree-

ing to take on Josh and Natty, Joshua freed their widowed mother
to remarry without fear of relegating them to second-rate status in
another man's home. Just ten days after formalizing the guardianship, in fact, Molly married a Hempstead neighbor, the hatter Joseph
Truman. This must have seemed like an ideal arrangement for all
concerned, because the union kept her and little Molly living immediately next door to the boys.[24]

These two fatherless grandsons gave Joshua's life renewed purpose. They also in some sense replaced the sons he had lost. Bereaved
colonial parents often commemorated a dead child by naming a subsequent sibling after the departed. One of Joshua's sisters, a child
named Phoebe, had died in infancy, her name later given to her disabled sister. For Joshua, the loss of his two eldest sons, along with
young Thomas, had been wrenching. Then another Joshua and
Nathaniel had come to him in the form of two grandsons—both still
young enough to become "my 2 boys." Parenting these two cherished
sons of a son gave the grandfather another chance at fatherhood.[25]

Long before he became their legal guardian, Joshua had been Josh
and Natty's loving grandfather. Within a year of Nathaniel's death,
Joshua had broken with his usual custom and skipped Sunday meeting to care for a sick Josh. That same year, he brought Josh several
times to Stonington—less for the limited help the six-year-old could
offer shearing sheep or mowing hay than for the companionship and
instruction he could give the child. When the boys stayed with their
maternal grandparents, they occupied Joshua's thoughts and he felt
impelled to visit. With their father gone, he also consciously fostered
Josh and Natty's ties to their extended Hempstead family, taking
them to visit aunts, uncles, and cousins.[26]

With an open heart, Joshua adopted his two grandsons in all
but law, devoting his time and energy to raising them to adulthood. It was no little sacrifice, recommitting his life in a singular
way to another generation of children, just as he had when Abigail
had died. But much had also changed in Joshua's circumstances in
the ensuing years. He had grown children now who could lend a
hand when necessary. He also enjoyed a serenity that came with age
and estate. Adam Jackson was also now in the house and in the field

and could contribute to the work of nurturing and training his master's grandsons.

During the early years of their instruction in the work of men, Adam became one of Josh and Natty's principal companions, teaching them requisite skills and ensuring they completed the task at hand. When they worked alone with him, Josh and Natty fell under Adam's charge. Though a slave, Adam still possessed the delegated, earned authority of experience and expertise, a sway that, under ordinary circumstances, included some direction of livestock, land, implements, and even coworkers. Now that authority sometimes extended to his master's grandsons. The phrase "Adam and ye boys"—whether they were carting dirt, hilling cornfields, pulling flax, raking salt hay, or digging stones—became a persistent refrain in Joshua's diary. In the years that followed, Joshua could write confidently, "Adm & boys gathered Corn" or "Adm & the Boys Raked Salt Hay at the flatts," knowing that Adam would see that the boys learned, and that work was finished.[27]

WITH ADAM'S help, Joshua's later years were filled with fatherly contentment. Having endured hard trials, Joshua had garnered enough strength and property to raise five boys and three girls without their mother. He had borne the deaths of three beloved, "likely" sons, losses that made the children who remained all the more dear. For an aging widower who had crossed grave waters, the latter years of fatherhood offered moments of exquisite fulfillment and thanks. Well-earned satisfactions came on typical days and on special ones, but they brimmed over when children and grandchildren came together, nourishing Joshua with ample evidence of all his labors.[28]

Molly's wedding day in 1736 was one such time when Joshua bore witness to the fruit of his parental accomplishment. His youngest, Molly, was the little babe he had carried to nurse in a driving rain after her mother died, and the second to last of his children to marry. By the time she took a husband, her eldest brother, Robert, was already the father of five. Their brother John had recently married another Southold girl, Hannah Salmon—his first cousin and a daughter of the same aunt and uncle who had cared for Molly as an infant. After his apprenticeship and marriage, John had returned to New London and converted Joshua's lean-to into a freestanding blacksmith's shop near the cove. Then he and Hannah moved into the side of the house that his brother Nathaniel had built and occupied before he died. John and Hannah had lost a son in the house, but they now were blessed by a small daughter named after her mother. Then, just months before Molly's wedding, John purchased a house and lot nearby and, with his father's help, established his own household.[29]

Molly's sisters had also married. The eldest, Abigail, had strengthened the family's Stonington ties by marrying Clement Minor, a merchant and scion of a prominent local family. Abigail and Clement established themselves on a verdant countryside property not far from Joshua's own Stonington farm. Living alongside a well-used thoroughfare, the Minors managed a shop and warehouse where they sold trade goods.

Betty had finally returned home to her father and New London in 1731. She had been gone for fifteen years since her mother had died, spending every moment "Since Shee was Caryed about 6 weeks after her mother died" on Long Island, where the Tallmadges had ably cared for her in Easthampton. Given the length of her stay, the original nursing arrangement must have developed into a working relationship whereby Betty learned domestic skills and provided her labor in exchange. After her return to New London, Betty had married Daniel Starr, the son of Hempstead neighbor and the county's longtime sheriff, Benjamin. (It was Ben's cellar that Joshua had used for storage in years past.)[30]

The year after Molly wed, their brother Stephen, the sailor, would also marry a neighbor child, Sarah Holt, the daughter of William who lived just across the highway (the same William who had testified against the inventive Susanna Truman in her fornication trial so many years before). Stephen and Sarah made a home in the newer side of their father's house, just as Nathaniel and John had done before them. Stephen's choice of Sarah meant that Molly would be the only Hempstead child to reach beyond the locality to marry, joining herself with Thomas Pierpont of Boston. On the day of her wedding her diarist father made a rare note of the pleasure he took in that moment: "my youngest daughter Mary was married. . . . Abigail was here from Stonington and Rob[er]t and his wife & Children that I had the Satisfaction of Seeing all my children most of my Grandchildren together."[31]

Chapter Thirteen

"THEIR CHILDREN'S CHILDREN"

IN THE 1730s and 1740s, generations of living in close proximity, often in the intimacy of small households, had left families in New London and New England intricately bound together through ties of blood, work, religion, and law. There was no avoiding this elaborate web of interconnection into the third and fourth generations, and decades-long legacies of household servitude, captivity, and slavery only complicated this domestic tangle. While every family wrestled with fortune, families on the margins—African, Native American, poor, or outwardly mixed—faced particular challenges in trying to endure, often under cover of English households. While the first generations of New Englanders might strive to live in households that were little commonwealths, their children's children would break out in unforeseen, unpredictable ways.

Although he had faced parental loss over multiple generations, Joshua Hempstead still lived at the center of English yeoman society, a position that in combination with his own hard work and fortitude had enabled him to achieve an ideal of New England manhood by midcentury, and to lead his family to economic and domestic prosperity. But he was able to fulfill his admirable commitments to children, grandchilden, and community in part on the back of Adam Jackson, his labor, and the family Adam might have had. Patriarchs on the English margins could not follow Joshua's course, no matter how hard they strove and toiled. John Jackson had embraced his status as a freedman and a free man, and refused to accept reenslavement, engaging instead in an audacious struggle to free and unite his family. Within one generation, however, many of his aspirations for his children had been overcome by poverty, servitude, and prejudice. His eldest son, Adam, would never even entertain freedom and would have to reconcile himself to life as a New England bondsman—the very life his father had cast off so dramatically.

Other families at the margins—families that the Jacksons and the Hempsteads encountered routinely—would react differently. Some children of Indian war captives, who had worked and lived quietly in New London for most of their lives, would reject their parents' resignation to forced servitude when they became adults, choosing instead to assert the freedom that the previous generation would or could not seize. In New London and elsewhere, there were even certain English whose parents had fled captivity by the Indians and the loss of English belonging, but who now found themselves unable or unwilling to embrace their own Englishness.

In 1738, two years after her bright wedding day, Molly Hempstead gave birth to a second son, her diarist father noting with relief, "my Daughter Pierpont was Safe Delivered of a Son this morn after 7 a clock." Molly had traversed a difficult childhood, but as a young woman she would welcome her children into the security of a promising marriage, a certain degree of material comfort, and a large colonial family. Molly had spent years of her life in the homes of others, as a ward, helper, or perhaps servant—that first brutal separation taking place within days of her birth when her father took her to a neighbor to nurse. Having overcome these hurdles, Molly must have felt a special gratitude as she welcomed this second son with her husband, Thomas.[1]

Another daughter of a well-known area family, Kate Garrett, was just a few years older than Molly. She, too, had been sent out of her natal home as a child, though perhaps not as an infant. Kate was a member of one of the few remaining Pequot families that, like most local Algonquin families, had fallen on hard times. During her childhood, English settlement had continued to encroach on Indian land through the early decades of the eighteenth century. Algonquin in the New London area, who had already suffered from the demographic and cultural losses of war and dislocation, were running out of options. Individuals and families confronted limited choices: With agricultural land dwindling, many sought employment as day laborers or indentured servants in English settlements; some, like Kate, were consigned to a lifetime of service and acculturation. When she was a small child, her family had decided—or it was decided for them—that Kate would be better off living in the home of Saybrook's minister, Samuel Worthington. From her own account, Kate found good treatment there. The Worthingtons taught her to read and write and provided her with religious and domestic training.[2]

In the first years of Molly Hempstead's marriage, Kate also found herself pregnant with a son. Joshua marked the life of Kate's child, too, but in a very different way than he would his grandchild. On the morning of May 3, 1738, Joshua walked up the hill toward the meetinghouse as throngs of other colonists flocked to town with him. They came to hear Mr. Adams deliver an extraordinary, emotional sermon, but many took a keener interest in what would happen after the midday dinner. That afternoon Kate Garrett would be hanged at meetinghouse hill before the large gathered crowd.[3]

Kate, a servant girl living in her master's house, had found herself single, poor, and pregnant, probably from an illicit consensual relationship. (The pregancy could have been the result of rape, although she never accused an attacker, and her own account of events suggests otherwise.) Fearing discovery, Kate had concealed her pregnancy and when her labor began, she hid that as well.[4]

Kate gave birth alone and, like other poor and powerless young women across the centuries, felt no alternative but to do away with the infant she could not explain or care for, smashing his small skull and hiding the child in the Worthington barn. When her mistress became suspicious, Kate denied having given birth, but Temperance Worthington found the baby still clinging to life under some rotting hay. Kate was charged with murder. The court found her guilty and sentenced her to death: to be "hanged up by the neck betwixt the heaven and the earth until she be dead, dead, dead."[5]

By the standards of colonial society, Kate's execution was severe though not extraordinary punishment for her particular crime. New England justice was not generally overeager to exact the highest penalty against criminals, even murderers, but for the young women accused of infanticide or neonaticide (murder of an infant within a day of birth), it often reserved a special fury. Infanticide was particularly disturbing, in part, because it represented an unholy combination of sexual deviance, motherhood, violence, concealment, and caste. Connecticut law required the bodies of stillborn infants to be examined for evidence of murder, and concealing the death of a bastard child was a capital crime. From the perspective of a disenfranchised girl like Kate, however, infanticide was perhaps just the darkest extreme in a very limited range of options.[6]

Whether she was aware of it or not, her clandestine killing of the child followed an established method among Algonquin women to deal with unwanted infants. There were even special places in the local landscape—like the "Bastard Rocks" near the old Stanton house in Stonington—where such secret Indian births (and deaths) took place. Among the Indians such killings were kept secret but could be tolerated as socially desirable or even necessary.[7]

Many in the crowd who watched Kate hang were sympathetic to the distressed girl's plight, in spite of her crime. When he spoke that day, Mr. Adams had felt the need to admonish the gathered assembly against excessive compassion, even remarked disapprovingly on the foot-dragging he had observed in bringing the young woman to judgment. After her conviction and as she waited months to die, Kate gradually turned to God, joined the First Congregation, and expressed her faith and remorse. As he watched Kate's end, Joshua could think of his own daughters forming families and delivering babies and count himself among those who felt empathy for the "poor Woman . . . Dispatched out of this world," daughter of a once-great Pequot family. Although English law and society were typically unconcerned with marriage, out-of-wedlock sex, or even infanciticide among free Algonquin, when ostensibly Christianized Algonquin married or had sex within colonial settlements, as Kate Garrett did, they brushed up against English institutions and interests and had to pay the consequences.[8]

Kate's violent end was an extreme result of a common problem: Men and women in servitude, especially those of Native or African origins, faced particular obstacles in forming and maintaining families within English households. Twenty-seven when she died, Kate—unlike Molly Hempstead—had not been able to marry, lacking the opportunity, her master's permission, or both. A single servant girl living in her master's house and moving quickly beyond her marriageable prime, Kate was particularly vulnerable to engaging in illicit sex or becoming the object of sexual exploitation. Once she became pregnant, she faced at best a prosecution for fornication and the loss of her child to servitude at an early age. The one option that remained out of reach was to keep her child and raise it independently.

KATE'S EXPERIENCE clashed starkly with Molly Hempstead's, but there were other families on the margins who fared better—men, women, and children who also straddled the dividing lines of freedom and slavery, ethnicity and culture, and who endured any number of captivities. John and Joan Jackson were one such couple, but there were other enslaved and serving men and women, both African and Indian, who were able to forge families and lasting relationships, even within English households. Although some marriages between slaves may have been informal, many were legally sanctioned, performed by justices of the peace or local ministers. In his role as a magistrate, Joshua Hempstead married a number of enslaved couples at his house at Bream Cove, perhaps within sight of Adam Jackson. One of these marriages was that of James and Dinah, slaves to John Rogers, Jr., who also lived at Mamacock like Adam's parents and siblings. (In 1753, Joshua would even appraise the couple—still together—for their master's inventory, finding Dinah "full of infirmities.") With a master's formal consent, Joshua presided over other bonded grooms and brides, including "Negro" Exeter, a slave to Joshua's ship captain neighbor Joseph Coit; "Negro" Susan, Jonathan Prentice's slave; and "Negro" Jordan, slave to John Ledyard of Hartford with "Negro" Lily, another Prentice slave. Although an enslaved husband's rights to his wife and children would be limited necessarily by the terms of their bondage, the right to marry, at least, was commonly observed and exercised.[9]

Just how enslaved families—or families with one parent in slavery and another in servitude, as the Jacksons had begun—passed their days under their masters' roofs often escapes the historical record. Forced to blend into the larger households, such families still appear to have maintained a distinct sense of kinship and belonging. A chance entry in Joshua's diary describes "a Sad Accident" one December in the English Hurlbut household: "The Stick on which the Tramels Hung broke & a Large kittle of Wort [a malt infusion for making beer] fell & Spilt on the Negro man Cesar who had his own Child of about 10 months old in his Lap wch was Scalded that it died before next day. Cesar & one more of his Children much Scalded above there knees." This brief entry cast a remarkable portrait of Cesar, holding one baby in his lap and keeping another child at his side as he worked at his master's hearth. Like Joshua, Cesar was a hands-on father who cared for his children. Like John Jackson, Cesar probably also left no doubt in his children's minds who their father was, whatever servitude and separations they had to endure.[10]

AMONG THESE families on the fringes and at the hearths of early New England were many whose members could trace their origins to different continents. Ultimately, men and women at the bottom rungs of English society had to marry and form families opportunistically—choosing from the small array of partners available to them and paying little heed to the niceties of common origins or histories. The long-standing marriage of the English Rogerene Katherine Jones (who accused John Jackson of fornication) and "mulatto" Adam Rogers was among a minority of these mixed unions that came to be viewed as English. The Jacksons, too, were a blend of African and European, with Joan the daughter of an unknown English father. The most common ethnically mixed marriages, however, were likely between Algonquin and Africans like the Rogers servants William and Hagar Wright. Just as Justice Hempstead married the enslaved, he also presided over a number of these blended unions, although always with the obligatory masterly consent for servants. Families he joined with his own hand included "Negro" Stippany, a servant to Pelatiah Bliss, who wed "Ann an Indian woman" and "Negro" Simon, a servant to Andrew Lester, who married "Agnes Holderidge an Indian woman."[11]

African men outnumbered African women in New England, so pairing with Algonquin women was arguably a demographic necessity. But African men, especially the enslaved, had another powerful incentive to choose Indian women as mates. After the 1670s and the end of major Indian conflicts, the children of Algonquin women were free under colonial law. For most New England bondsmen, obtaining manumission as John Jackson had done would never be a realistic possibility, but exploiting this escape hatch in the legal system certainly was. Because children inherited their legal status from their mothers, a bondsman who procreated with a free woman would have free children. African men across New England regularly followed this course—pairing with or marrying Algonquin women whose children enjoyed freedom by birthright. Even freedmen could hope that the status of subsequent generations would not be questioned if they married an Algonquin.[12]

For Native women the equation was different. Algonquin women turned to African men, even slaves, to form families for demographic reasons as well: Indian men were in short supply after a succession of wars, disease, and enslavements. Some Algonquin women may also have preferred to form families with African men—even slaves, in the hope that they might one day obtain their husband's freedom— and escape traditional Algonquin gender roles in which women performed the hard work of planting and harvesting, while men roamed to hunt, gather, and fight. Others may have even sought to avoid the practice of polygamy to which some higher-status Algonquin men had access.[13]

Such unions with African men were not without risks for Native women, however. Coming from a matrilineal society, Algonquin women faced the potential loss of their place within that society. In the late eighteenth century, Native concepts of tribal and racial purity would also begin to crystallize. As the progressive dispossession of Algonquin lands continued to threaten local tribes, some, including one faction of the Mohegan, would react by limiting membership by lineage. Though Algonquin may not yet have fully articulated a restrictive definition of Indian-ness in the early years of the eighteenth century, Native people may have already sensed its coming.[14]

PERHAPS THE best-known and longest-lived African-Algonquin union in New London was the marriage of York and Rachel. Their long and fruitful bond illustrates an extraordinary chapter in slavery's early history, one with strong parallels to the lives of the Jacksons. Like John Jackson, African-origin York was brought as a slave to New London in the 1670s or 1680s, probably from the West Indies. He first served the wealthy and volatile Alexander Pygan in Saybrook and New London—the same Pygan who later freed "Negro" Mariah. The English-born Pygan was a man who followed his own lights, freeing a slave when few did and often brushing with the law—shooting a horse, alienating his future wife's affections, selling liquor to Indians, and behaving at home with impassioned ill temper. After Pygan died in 1700, York passed to his master's teenage daughter, Lydia. Within a few years, Lydia married minister Adams who, like most Congregationalist ministers, saw no moral conflict in owning slaves, though he did feel a duty to christianize his "charges."[15]

York's wife, Rachel, had a very different past from her husband. She was one of numbers of Algonquin captives after King Philip's War who contributed to a surge in Algonquin service in English households in its wake. She was also among those wartime captives who had been bound to temporary service in a family, but whose service had slipped into permanence even after she became legally free. Like many servants in her position, Rachel did not challenge her continued servitude, perhaps discouraged by the difficulty or even reluctant to exchange the certainty of a life she knew for an unknown. Liberty—for anyone with a history of enslavement—could prove elusive, and it had its risks.[16]

In 1676, as an orphaned captive of around ten, Rachel was placed into service with Capt. John Prentice, a shipmaster in the West Indian trade, and his wife, Sarah. The Prentices had five daughters, whom Rachel no doubt helped to raise. As an adult, Rachel married York soon after he had joined minister Adams's household. Like the Jacksons, Rachel and York had to live apart, although their two households were not far from each other. In the first decade of marriage, Rachel bore seven children: Simone, Bilhah, Zilpha, Hannibal, York junior, Scipio, and Dido.[17]

Although Prentice's will directed that Rachel's children be freed between the ages of thirty and thirty-five, it also divided the children among his five daughters. Therefore when the master died in 1715, the children were taken from their mother: Simone went to Hartford and Bilhah to Colchester. Hannibal stayed local, while Rachel herself, along with York junior, Scipio, and baby Dido remained with the widow Prentice until their future owner, a minor Prentice daughter, came of age.[18]

A few interesting details of Rachel's life have survived—making her one of the few captives whose fate can be known with some individuality. Having been raised primarily among the English, Rachel adopted many English ways and values, just as Kate Garrett must have done a generation later. Rachel was a woman of strong Christian faith, and she reared her children to share those beliefs. Mr. Adams himself baptized "Rachel an Indian-woman & her Daughtr Dido" when Dido was around ten. The minister later married her son Scipio to an "Indian" woman named Hannah, and Dido, too, eventually married in the Congregational Church. While the fates of her other children remain unknown, both Rachel and Dido did ultimately become free, as Prentice had directed. Like John Jackson, Rachel nevertheless continued on as a Prentice servant. Her husband, York, remained a slave to Mr. Adams until the bondsman's death, but York was able to leave this world knowing that his children at least had a foothold in freedom. When Rachel died, New London's most assiduous diarist drew on a lifetime of memory to give her an unusual, affectionate eulogy, even commenting on her uncommon girth: "Old Rachel formerly a Servt to Capt John Prenttis Decd was buried in the Evening. I Supose She was near 80 years of age. She was a Captive taken in the Narhaganset war in 1675. I have know her about 60 year. I think She was as big when I first knew her as Ever. She always lived in the family & had many Children by her Husband (york . . .). She was an Honest faithfull Creture & I hope a good Christian. She was one of our Church for many years past." Her daughter Dido, whom Joshua described at her death as "½ Indian ½ negro . . . a free Molat woman . . . about 40," outlived Rachel by only five years before she too was buried in New London ground, "froze hard."[19]

THERE WERE other captives like Rachel who lived both enslaved and free in New London's households, adding their own layers of cultural complexity to the colonial domestic scene. These men and especially women had been caught up in the ethnic maelstrom of early New England. The families they created strongly resembled the Jacksons in their everyday experience, if not their outward appearance. Most of their particulars were hidden from English records, but the extraordinary tale of one such family emerged by chance one day in June 1739, when the blacksmith Samuel Richards showed up on Joshua Hempstead's doorstep looking for legal process. He came to complain about the loss of his slave, but brought with him the rare life story of another child captive and her son. Theirs was a characteristic account of Native anguish, endurance, adaptation, and renewal.[20]

Betty, as the English called her, was a member of the Pequot band that had suffered so prodigiously since colonization. Like York's wife, Rachel, Betty had been a child in 1676. A refugee of the war, she found herself in New London with other captives under the authority of the then-governor, John Winthrop, Jr. The governor had not allowed his knowledge of medicine and language, or his love of learning, to get in the way of his efforts to protect New England. He planned to send the wretched party to slavery in the West Indies, where—if Betty survived the voyage—she could expect to be worked to death. As she and the other prisoners awaited this unhappy removal, a local woman, Mary Christophers Bradley, came to inspect them. The English-born daughter of a merchant-shipowner and the young wife of the shipmaster Peter Bradley, Jr., Mary Bradley strode along the familiar wharves searching determinedly for a useful girl when her eyes fixed on Betty. Mary appealed directly to the governor and prevailed; he allowed her to keep Betty and sent another unfortunate captive in her place to fill out the allotment. Through Mistress Bradley's arbitrary intervention, Betty remained in Connecticut, enslaved at the Bradley house in the center of town for an intended term of ten years.[21]

A decade of service did not deliver Betty to the freedom she had earned, however, though it did bring change. Her Bradley master died in 1687, and her mistress, Mary, remarried, taking Betty to the household of a second mariner husband, Thomas Youngs of Southold. At the Youngses', Betty married a "Negro" slave in the household called James. They had at least one child, a boy described as "molatto . . . or mustee," born around 1712. Named Cesar, this child grew up a servant with the Youngses, although he would later fancy himself "Cesar Le Grand" or "Cesar the Great." Betty lived and died a servant and slave—unaware, uninterested, or simply compliant when it came to the unlawfulness of her enslavement. Sold off from the Youngses, her son Cesar instead became a slave to the Yale graduate and Middletown lawyer Jabez Hamlin.[22]

When the blacksmith Samuel Richards subsequently bought Cesar from Hamlin in 1739 for £110, he thought he had made a savvy purchase. Though rather proud, Cesar was also native-born and -trained, and at twenty-seven he was in the prime of his working life. Richards had ventured poorly, however, because Cesar deserted him within a fortnight. Hoping his slave would return after a short fling, Richards gave Cesar two days' leeway before he came knocking on Joshua's door to complain.[23]

The confident Cesar Le Grand had remained local after his

escape, appearing in the hall of the Hempstead house the very day that Joshua issued his arrest warrant. For the next two years, Cesar also bravely defended his freedom in court, citing his dead mother's status as a war captive. John Curtis, a failed minister who became one of the colony's few experienced lawyers, represented Cesar on appeal, even putting up a £200 bond to secure his client's appearance at trial. When the litigation ended, the unlikely pair of Curtis and his "mustee" client emerged victorious, and Betty's free status received a posthumous acknowledgment—too late for her, but in time enough for her boy Cesar.[24]

THERE WERE others like Betty and Rachel inhabiting the homes of early New England, caught up in the chaos of diaspora after colonization. One was "Carolina" Ann, an "Indian woman" purchased as a slave "at Newport [straight] out of a vessel" around 1700. Her buyer was William Gardiner, a wealthy Narragansett cordwainer (fine leather shoemaker) and planter known by the nickname "Wicked Will." Gardiner sold Ann to his yeoman brother Stephen, who later moved her to Norwich, where she served at least twenty years, helping her master and mistress raise a family of twelve children. To the household "Carolina" Ann added three of her own, a boy and two girls: "Molatto" Cesar, along with Ann and Phyllis, both described as "Indian." (Whether the children had different fathers or simply "looked" different is anyone's guess.)[25]

One night after decades of service, "Carolina" Ann simply ran away, taking her children with her. Soon arrested, the family had a defense: The mother Ann was a Mohawk "born free." Their lawyer, Ebenezer Backus of Norwich, brought in two expert witnesses to prove their case: Kellogg brother and sister, Martin junior and Rebecca, a sibling pair with whom Joshua Hempstead was friendly.[26]

Like "Carolina" Ann, the Kelloggs had also been captives, although of a quite different sort. The brother and sister had been among those English colonists captured in the Deerfield Massacre and forced to march to Quebec. While many of these Deerfield captives, especially the adults, had longed for redemption to New

England through ransom or escape, others felt differently. Children, in particular, adjusted readily to life among their captors, enjoying tender treatment and wholehearted adoption into families according to long Iroquois tradition. Among the English, the most famous of these "unredeemed" captives was little Eunice Williams, who became entirely acculturated at Kahnawake, a settlement of Catholic Mohawk near Montreal, refusing her clerical father's unremitting efforts to persuade her to return.[27]

Like Eunice, eight-year-old Rebecca Kellogg and her eleven-year-old sister, Joanna, became full members of Kahnawake, adopting Catholic and Mohawk ways. Eunice and the Kellogg girls all grew to adulthood in Kahnawake and formed families. The Kellogg brothers, Joseph and Martin (twelve and seventeen at their capture in 1704), returned to New England, although neither seemed to fit in entirely: They became military men and interpreters. Joseph stubbornly pursued his sisters' return. Joanna refused, but Rebecca relented in 1729 when she was in her thirties, on condition that her family, a son and husband, accompany her and that she not be prevented from returning to Canada. Once she arrived in Massachusetts, however, her brother Joseph got the General Court to dispatch her family, sending them on a mission and paying off her husband and son with forty pounds each. Rebecca remained, facing an unfathomable adjustment to a life and family that were at best unfamiliar to her. When magistrate Joshua Hempstead took her deposition in the 1743 case of "Carolina" Ann, the purported Mohawk, Rebecca Kellogg was moving between the homes of her two brothers, Joseph in Massachusetts and Martin in Wethersfield, Connecticut, also not quite fitting in among the English.[28]

On the eve of trial, Rebecca and her brother Martin each interviewed "Carolina" Ann in Mohawk in an effort to determine her true origins. Martin took particular care, quizzing her at night and then asking the same questions the next morning. To Rebecca, "Ann answered in Mohawk without shutting her lips . . . peculiar to the Mohawk tribes." (The language has no labials—no consonants formed by the lips.) Ann passed their examinations, and the Kelloggs were able to confirm her claim, judging her "one of the Huron which nation is one of the five nations" of the Iroquois League, a confederation of New York–area tribes. She and her children won their case and went free.[29]

It is possible, however, that Ann might have been a "Carolina" Indian after all. The Huron or Wyandot were not of the Five Nations, although their language, Wendat, was a regional lingua franca that League members could understand. There was a Sixth Nation after 1722, the Tuscarora, an Iroquois people who had migrated centuries earlier to the Carolinas, but had faced return to New England as captive slaves in the aftermath of conflicts culminating in the Tuscarora War from 1711 to 1715. Perhaps it was really Tuscarora that Rebecca heard out of Ann's open lips and tried to place, settling finally on Huron—a timbre once removed, though still intelligible.[30]

Both Rebecca Kellogg and "Carolina" Ann were captives, torn between cultures and conversant in both. The English identified Ann, like any "Negro" slave, immediately as "other." Under her English shift and skirts, she still bore Iroquois body art: "a strake on one of her legs down her shin and in her gartering place, flowered after the Indian fashion." There were traces of Indian-ness, like this tattoo, not so easily removed—scrubbed away. (Traces of Africa could be just as persistent, like the "country marks"—identifying "negro scars"—sometimes visible on faces arriving at New London Harbor.) But what of Rebecca Kellogg? Did her English cousins perceive the "twenty-four years among the Mohawk" in her hair, her dress, and the way she talked and moved?[31]

Rebecca's old Deerfield and Kahnawake playmate, Eunice Williams Kanenstenhawi, certainly caused a stir whenever she visited New England later in life. When news arrived that she was in New London one day in 1734, locals like Joshua Hempstead could not resist gathering to stare at the "french Woman . . . Taken 30 years ago." To the onlookers, both English and even Indian appeared then were erased, replaced with "french." New Englanders like these— Old Rachel and "Carolina" Ann, Rebecca Kellogg, and "mulatto" Joan Jackson, together with their children—played roles, integral and marginal, in New England society. Each had a place, yet each remained a permanent enigma.[32]

As it turned out, the enigma that day in 1734 for gawking New Londoners was even more mysterious than it appeared. The "french" woman they stared at, looking for traces of the minister's daughter, was likely not Eunice at all—but an imposter whose real identity remained unknown. The real Eunice did not come back to Massachusetts until some years later, when she came to visit her New England family. The other figure on display was something else entirely: a conjured imitation of not quite English, not quite Indian, not quite French—an idea of the onetime Williams girl.[33]

LIKE THE refugees of war, the Jacksons, too, were a family on the edges of the English mainstream. Perhaps only the patriarch, John, had experienced a sudden captivity in a different culture, but all the Jacksons nevertheless faced the challenges of forced servitude, separation, and prejudice. Unlike the Indian war captives who were his contemporaries, however, John Jackson had fought the enslavement of his family every step of the way and succeeded beyond all measure. And unlike the children of war captives who broke out of their parents' unlawful bondage, John Jackson's eldest son, Adam, chose instead to reconcile himself to a lifetime in slavery.

Adam made a certain peace with his fate, but living separately in slavery made keeping ties with his family much more difficult. No document has ever surfaced to show Adam seeking out parents and siblings, nieces and nephews, but he did have chances to maintain relationships with his family, and he probably took them. Over the years working for Joshua, Adam spent entire days at Mamacock, where his master owned land. When he plowed fields, drove cattle, and mowed, raked, and stacked hay along Mamacock's shores, Adam could have also taken the opportunity to connect with family members living nearby, especially his Mamacock siblings. From Bream Cove, Adam could still track Jackson milestones. He probably knew the day in 1730 when, three years after Joshua bought him, his own mother, Joan, matriarch of the large Jackson brood, had "died with the dropsy." Adam had lived with Joan only a short time as a small child, but she was no less a mother to him.[34]

By the time Joan died, the old Jackson couple had become enough of a fixture in the town's social landscape for her passing to merit an entry in Joshua's diary, just as old Rachel the captive had warranted. A year later another link fleetingly appeared: Adam spent a "fore[noo]n" mowing hay with his widowed father. That fact had entered Joshua's diary because the Jackson patriarch worked as a day laborer for his son's master. Had there been other days of work, or evening visits, that never made it into writing? Perhaps John Jackson was heartened that day when he mowed with his eldest son, but the work was grueling for a man in his sixties, and his presence hinted at desperation. Adam, the capable son, could have shouldered an extra patch of ground if his father struggled, but he could do little more for him. Unlike Joshua, who could invite his dying mother to live in his house, Adam had little real care to offer his father. For the most part, Adam had to content himself with being a spectator in his family members' lives, remaining at some distance from their struggles and their turmoil, but also from their company and from freedom.[35]

With Miriam, his sister and childhood companion, Adam may have maintained a relationship in spite of enslavement and distance. Miriam, too, had been sold away in the 1720s from the North Parish—she, with her husband, Cuff, had gone to become the property of Nicholas Lathrop in Norwich. There Miriam bore two children, a fact made clear to posterity only through one of Beebe's relentless lawsuits when he claimed these Jackson grandchildren, too. But if Adam had felt closest to Miriam because of their childhood, he perhaps knew his brothers Jerry and Jack the least. It was Jerry whom Beebe had dragged to Southold with his mother and who later lived as a child slave in Framingham after some time on the run and at the Livingston farm. Jerry finally won his freedom in 1719, having endured an ample dose of anguish by the time he returned to New London.[36]

Adam also had little access to his younger brother Jack, born at the Livingston farm, where his parents had been forced to live in servitude. When Jack was still a small child, Livingston had sold him off to the Tracy family of Norwich. John Jackson sued the Tracys for his son's return, but Beebe intervened, pressing once more his old claim on Joan's descendants. In what must have been an especially cruel twist of injustice, the court readily awarded the boy to Beebe, the wealthy Rogers nemesis, and Jack must have spent his late childhood and early adulthood as Beebe's slave. Not only would Beebe's reentry into the Jacksons' intimate life have been an especially bitter pill to swallow, but Beebe would live much farther away than the Tracys did, eventually moving to Newport and taking Jack with him.[37]

In 1731, twenty-three-year-old Jack became the subject of a new court case. During a visit to his family's home ground in New London, he had made a bold break from Beebe and refused to return, claiming his freedom. Predictably Beebe had come after him, suing for his human property in court. By then, it had been ten years since old John Rogers's death, but the Jacksons could apparently still count on Rogers backing. When Jack needed to post £150 bond, John Rogers, Jr., did so on Jack's behalf. Perhaps more surprising, by the 1730s enmity against the Rogers faction had apparently waned enough for Jack to find a small measure of justice. Beebe's case was eventually dismissed, and Jack did become free. Unfortunately, the details of his life after this triumph are murky. In 1732, when a New Jersey mariner brought a debt action in Newport against "John Jackson of Newport, Labourer, Free Negro," he may have provided a final clue to Jack's fate.[38]

It was no accident that Jack had chosen New London for his escape. Even after the deaths of Bathshua Fox, old John Rogers, and his own mother, Joan, family ties between Rogerses and Jacksons were still strong enough to give Jack something to run toward. And once he returned to Newport a free man (if he did), he himself might have provided the draw for another Jackson brother.

Jacob was the last Jackson to be raised at Mamacock, but he may not have lived there much past the age of fifteen. During his teens, he perhaps lived with and worked for the baker Samuel Rogers, old John's brother and a leading resident of the North Parish. John Rogers, Jr., might have manumitted him, and Jacob may have gone to Newport. Years later "Jacob Jackson, a Free Negro Man of Newport, labourer," was accused of squatting in a house belonging to the widow Jane Rogers (another family connection?). Near New London and with plenty of work at its busy harbor, Newport seems an obvious place for the free Jackson brothers to have settled. For

Adam, enslaved at Bream Cove, on the other hand, Newport was a county, a colony, a world away. For him, any Jacksons there would be out of reach.[39]

Living under the wing of the Rogers family remained a double-edged sword for the Jackson siblings who stayed on at Mamacock. They had lived enslaved for most of their youth—economically useful and needing legal protection—until John Rogers, Jr., must have followed through on spoken or unspoken promises of manumission—or at least on some of them. As always, freedom would exact its own toll on these Jacksons. After Adam's sister Hannah (whom Joshua described as "Molato," like her mother) completed ten years of adult service, it appears that John Rogers, Jr., did honor his promise to free her in recognition of her "faithfulness and good service." Hannah continued to live in New London, though surely in service, perhaps even at Mamacock.[40]

Peter Jackson gained freedom from Rogers at around the same time. He, too, stayed close by, perhaps working as a day laborer, and appearing in court records in 1735 as a debtor in the trifling amount of fifteen shillings. Peter defaulted in the case, so the court ordered his possessions confiscated to pay his creditor. The list was short. Peter owned three large objects: a chest, a bed, and a locked basket. The contents of Peter's chest and basket were unrecorded and "unknown," presumably containing clothes and other personal items, perhaps even the papers to prove his freedom.[41]

The unfavorable court ruling was the least of Peter's problems, however. Only a year earlier, he had lost his young wife, Hagar, a slave who belonged to Madam Elizabeth Tongue "Winthrop" (until her own death in 1731), leaving him the only parent to their two daughters, Eunice, then four, and Rose, then one. These girls, who were surely servants or perhaps even slaves, were two local Jackson grandchildren whom their uncle Adam might have visited and known.[42]

Among the Mamacock Jacksons, Abner stood apart—the only Jackson sibling raised there never to become free. Why John Rogers, Jr., treated him differently is unclear. Perhaps because something else set him apart: Of all the Jacksons, Abner appears to have been the only one to learn a craft in addition to husbandry, making him one of few enslaved master artisans in the county during the colonial period. Abner was a cooper, an expert in one of the most challenging forms of woodcraft and a trade that ran in the Rogers family. Two of old John Rogers's brothers, Jonathan and James, ran cooperages, so a slave trained in the family business might have been an especially useful asset. Ironically, his superior skill may have been what kept Abner in bondage, as subsequent generations may have therefore been less willing to part with him. Abner never appeared in Joshua's diary, but of all the Jackson siblings, it was he who shared with Adam both a life of perpetual slavery and a lifetime in New London. Whether these two Jackson brothers were able to foster a meaningful relationship, however, remains hidden.[43]

It was real desperation that appeared faintly visible in John Jackson that day in 1731 when he mowed as Joshua Hempstead's day laborer, alongside his eldest son, Adam. After his beloved Joan, his wife of more than three decades, had died the year before, the old "negro peddlar" declined quickly, bent by the weight of age, poverty, and grief. In 1734, Jackson's situation had become so dire that it attracted the notice of New London's selectmen. "Grown old and infirm and in danger of falling into decay," Jackson needed to be taken in hand. Adam was surely aware of his father's precipitous deterioration, but he was powerless to help. Since 1702, masters who freed their slaves were required by statute to care for them in sickness or old age, and after 1711, towns could be held liable for masters who did not fulfill this obligation. In accordance, the selectmen ordered John Rogers, Jr., as the son of Jackson's former master and executor of that master's estate, to take over the cost of Jackson's care. The three selectmen, all justices of the peace, conducted this business in person, going to Mamacock one "very hot" day to visit the homes of Jackson and Rogers junior. One of these town fathers was Joshua Hempstead, who might later have told his slave Adam what he had seen that day, though he would feel no need to mention such a thing in his diary. John Jackson lived out another three years, then died, "an old Negro man" around the age of seventy.[44]

Chapter Fourteen

"ADAM WORKED ALL DAY"

IN SEPTEMBER 1739, a group of Catholic slaves of likely Congolese origin carried out a major insurrection that tore through South Carolina. The armed conspirators plundered the countryside, killing colonists and burning plantations in their wake. Militiamen soon supressed the violence; the perpetrators were killed, executed, or sent to slavery in the West Indies, but the fear of revolt was not so easily squelched. Colonists mounted the heads of decapitated rebels as a warning to others, and the South Carolina legislature passed greater controls on its majority slave population. The so-called Stono Rebellion would be the largest slave revolt in the English colonies before the Revolution, and an encouragement to smaller insurrections that followed in Georgia and again in South Carolina. Much closer to New London in the spring of 1741, New York suffered a series of fires that many feared would bring that city to its knees. Suspicions fell upon a supposed conspiracy to overthrow Manhattan among slaves and the working poor, who burned buildings and killed inhabitants. The conspiracy's existence was itself uncertain, but the retribution against suspected insurgents was ruthlessly clear. Scores were tried and executed, most of them hanged or burned at the stake.

On the worst day of the Stono Rebellion, Joshua wrote in his diary, "I went Down to the flatts & helpt Adam Load 19 Cocks of Salt hay." The men had gone to retrieve these canonical mountains of hay, cocks that had sat and dried for some time until they were ready for transport. Once they carted them home, Adam and Joshua would use the hay as mulch for fields and fodder for cattle. It was hard work, but a far cry from the violence that scorched to the south. Surely the New Londoners heard of the turblulent events in other colonies; New York, of course, was less than a day's boat ride away. No doubt Joshua would later read the torrid stories of what had happened as newspapers made their way to New London's harbor.[1]

Whatever Joshua and Adam thought about such rebellions, these opinions did not seem to affect their day-to-day work or their relationship. The turmoils did not even warrant a mention in Joshua's diary. Over the years in Joshua's service, there were moments when Adam chafed at the burdens of his condition, but the times he allowed himself to act outwardly on those feelings were few. He would never engage in open rebellion, and there is no evidence that he ever raised a hand in violence toward another man. The closest he came to revolt were some hours of shirking work or cavorting with friends. It happened one spring day after more than a decade's service to his master Hempstead, for example, when Adam spent most of the day away from Bream Cove, without work and without permission. What had begun as an ordinary frolic with fellow servants had gotten out of hand, leading the Groton constable to take Adam and his companions into custody to dampen their enthusiasm.[2]

While Adam and the others cooled their heels in informal detention, a lax watchman dozed off, allowing Adam and the "company of Negroes" to make a run for it. Not relishing the reception that awaited him at Bream Cove, Adam decided to put off the inevitable and play truant for a day. Joshua did not record how he greeted his wayward servant when he returned, although he duly noted Adam's lapse in his diary.[3]

That Adam Jackson spent time diverting himself in "a Company of Negroes" was not extraordinary. There was enough room in the New England workweek to permit a certain amount of sociability, even for servants and slaves. Large covert gatherings were technically unlawful, especially at night, but a certain amount of informal mingling was generally tolerated, as long as it stayed within certain bounds. Getting rowdy or excessively drunk crossed the line—as did not showing up to work when leisure time was over. A few years before, in fact, another group of "10 Negro men" had been taken into custody "for being out unseasonably in a frolick at old Wright's." (Joshua would have likely referred to the then-elderly Hagar Wright as "Old Hagar," so perhaps this was her son Wait, who would have been in his forties. Wait's father, William, had been banished from the colony.) They received a short trial, and the "3 tht went without Leave was whipt & the 7 yt [that] had leave, dismist with paying their part of the Charge 5s 3d Each."[4]

In his diary, Joshua kept his description of Adam's own jaunt to Groton very brief. He did not mention drunkenness, but the presence of alcohol would hardly have been surprising in hard-drinking, cider-soaked New England. Even a slave going on the odd bender would probably not have been a cause for great alarm among most masters, though inveterate drunks had to be put in line. Just how much access Adam had to alcohol is uncertain, but at a time when water was considered dangerous and unhealthful, a servant who had to drink while he worked might have been able to sneak away a pint or two, or perhaps even more. In later years, the seasonal task of making the Hempsteads' hard cider often fell to Adam, in fact.[5]

None of the particulars of Adam's Groton escapade are especially noteworthy. What stands out about his day of bold defiance was that it was one of the few times during decades of service when Adam Jackson disappointed Joshua in any meaningful way. Unlike the bondsmen of the Stono or New York rebellions, Adam's was a small, isolated fling with defiance—a brief hiccup in a lifetime of steadfast diligence and acquiescence. And so the incident itself poses a deeper question: Who was the man behind this lifetime of unbroken service?

MOST OF what is knowable about Adam comes from Joshua's diary, a restrained source that presents obvious challenges and bears the insurmountable problem of being the creation of the man who owned

Adam. Joshua never intended to characterize his slave—or anyone else—in his diary. He was very concerned about documenting work, and as a record of Adam's working life, the diary is rich. Yet as a journal of Adam's enslavement, the diary is by definition a chronicle of Adam's objectification. With all of its shortcomings, however, Joshua's diary still remains one of the great records of everyday life in slavery and renders Adam one of the best-documented enslaved men in America's English colonies.

The diary even manages to tell an elusive story about Adam the man—in what it says and does not say, depicting Adam as a nearly seamless example of hard work and constancy. Complaints or criticisms of Adam or his work are rare, and Adam exhibits few signs of overt resistance in its pages. Adam avoided conflict, choosing instead to follow a no less venerable path of industry and acquiescence. Perhaps he found satisfaction in his work—unbiased labor that permitted him to assert his own sense of mastery over the land, if not to win respect from workingmen of all kinds. Perhaps this quiet approach to decades of servitude reflected Adam's general attitude toward life.

Adam, John Jackson's eldest son, remained notably absent from criminal and church records, preferring to stay within the lines of accepted and unexceptional English norms. He seems never to have attempted to run away, even though young unattached men were most likely to run, and certainly his deep family ties to New London were a powerful incentive to stay. But unlike so many servants and slaves, including his own parents and siblings, Adam probably never formed a family of his own. In his master's diary no wife or child, not even a lover, ever comes into view. Master and slave had very different reasons for turning their backs on marriage, but it was an undeniably rare pairing—two unyielding singletons in a world where marriage was all pervasive—one an aging widower with a house and heart full of children, the other the abstemious, long-suffering servant desirous of peace and the absence of tragedy.

Adam was probably stoic by nature, and his experiences only reinforced that tendency. By the time he arrived at Bream Cove in 1727, he had already known plenty of loss and turmoil. Born into slavery away from his father, he had been old enough to grieve when his mother left him to join John Jackson at Mamacock. During the long years of separation that followed, Adam endured loneliness and isolation, coupled with fear and powerlessness when his mother and siblings were thrown back into slavery by Beebe. Before he turned thirty, Adam had seen enough of family destruction and uncertain freedom to last a lifetime. As a man, he would follow a quieter path, a life that did not court further desolation. The one certain way to avoid the pain of losing a wife or a child was never to have either.

To be sure, Adam had watched his parents fight for and win considerable freedoms, but he had also seen the heavy price they had paid for it. From his life of muted service to Joshua, he had watched his free parents propel themselves forward only to be battered back time and again by forces beyond their control. He had watched, too, as his five free siblings were dragged about the county and the colony, carving out hardscrabble lives that remained largely ignored in English records. Torn apart by law and by necessity, the Jackson family became their own diaspora writ small, a scattering that had begun the very moment the family had formed—the moment John and Joan were joined at the turn of a new century, servants to two masters. During Adam's lifetime, the Jacksons always hovered precariously at the edge of English society—never united but never entirely destroyed.

Unlike his parents, Adam rose early each morning and accepted the role that was prescribed to him. Good behavior allowed him certain liberties, perhaps even to keep his bonds of kinship with his parents and siblings, if he so wished. As vulnerable as they might be, Jackson blood ties were the only thing Adam undeniably possessed. Prevented from living with parents or siblings, Adam would almost certainly have had chance encounters in the town or along the road— moments when his life in slavery collided with theirs. They were times he may have anticipated and treasured when they occurred.

IN 1739, Adam Jackson cut down half of one of the oldest English-planted trees on Bream Cove. This "great yellow Apple Tree yt Stood East from the house" was the very same one that Robert Hempstead the immigrant had planted hopefully "about 90 years agone" when he staked out a place for his young family. Hempsteads still inhabited the waterfront plot as Robert had envisioned, but the English yeoman had probably never considered the prospect of an African New Englander hewing its limbs nearly a century later—or of his grandson owning a man. Much had changed in those many years, but other things had remained the same. A bondsman might now live in the "new" house at Bream Cove, already more than half a century old, but the third and fourth generations of Hempstead men were still working the land, just as Robert the immigrant had once done. And although Adam Jackson cut the ancient apple tree, it was Joshua who trimmed it a week later.[6]

Adam left his mark all over the house-lot, from slashes in trees to furrows in the field, but in his work the bondsman had to submit to his master's broad vision of the world. It was Joshua who decided when wood was hauled, where a stone fence would be built, what they planted and when. All of their labors served a strong and productive Hempstead household with Joshua at its head, enjoying property and competency while providing for children and grandchildren. Adam did not have to share his master's vision of the world or of family, but he did have to understand it.

Nevertheless, no imposed vision could totally subsume Adam's own picture of his surroundings. Adam could incorporate the English view of things taught him since birth alongside a different imprint, a dimension apart, persisting in and around the blocks of English-owned land with which colonists identified so strongly. Adam's internal map traced footpaths between and behind those blocks of land, creating a cartography drawn by human landmarks— the mother three miles away, the sister in Norwich, the friend next door.

Adam's domestic and psychic arrangement as the sole slave in a household would have been very familiar to so many New England bondsmen in all but the most elite, urbane households. He had to endure the seemingly constant presence of one or more Hempsteads, and the accompanying prickly mix of trial and benefit that went along with that intimacy. Being a lone slave did not mean that Adam was isolated from a wider world, however. His very work as a bondsman put him in regular contact with a wide spectrum of New England society, from African-origin slaves like himself to the highest circles of the colonial elite.

Joshua's diary allows a rare view into Adam's daily activities over more than three decades, a unique and sometimes unexpected portrayal of an early American bondsman that defies easy stereotypes. Adam was not isolated or socially removed. As Joshua's bondsman, he worked with at least eighty other laborers, and probably many more, the majority of them English colonists like his master. Joshua routinely hired local men, especially during the busy seasons, putting Adam on a familiar working basis with many English neighbors: Chapmans, Chappells, Harrises, Holts, Lesters, Trumans, and Ways. Working in the field, with the attendant differences in age, origin, and status, formed an undercurrent to mutual work, but the stream flowed in multiple directions.[7]

Over time, the superior knowledge and seniority that Adam earned, and which his master acknowledged, colored his status as a slave. The result was that a long-serving bondsman like Adam might have a working authority over young men called in to mow or hay for the day, no matter who they were. Joshua expressed this effect succinctly in his diary, as when he "hired one Parke a young man to help adm." Late in life, Joshua also hired Ephraim Brown, a youth from a local English family, to be a regular helper for him and Adam in the work of the farm. Of course, any unpropertied English man still remained Adam's superior in stark legal and social terms, a fact that no amount of experience in husbandry could upend. Such everyday incongruities remained ever present, unresolved. Men like Parke, Brown, and Jackson had to work in and around them, maneuvering the untidy civic collision just as they did the rake or the plow.[8]

Of the non-Hempstead men who were Adam's coworkers, less than a quarter who appear in Joshua's diary were fellow slaves. It is easy to imagine that sharing work with another bondsman held particular meaning for Adam, but the limited evidence of Joshua's entries does not allow the inference of any special solidarity. A few fellow slaves did stand out as recurring work companions who could have offered Adam some kind of camaraderie or perhaps friendship. There were at least two Mingos in Adam's life: Mingo Swetland and Mingo Coit, whom Joshua distinguished by their masters' surnames. Mingo was a familiar West African name among enslaved New Englanders, and a sometime indicator of African birth. To a Mingo who came from Africa, the tongue and climate in Connecticut would have remained forever strange.

Working with men from Africa presented a third-generation New Englander like Adam with another daily paradox. Adam might have found more common cultural ground with the English who owned and traded him, but whom he had known all his life, than with men named Mingo who talked with the dropped articles and trilled rs of a distant homeland. Still, the African-born who inhabited Adam's daily life could always make a claim on him from beyond the world he knew, a draw of common history and shared bondage.[9]

Of the two Mingos in Adam's life, one belonged to Benjamin Swetland, a prosperous clothier and shopkeeper who came to New London via Salem and Boston. Mingo lived at Swetland's in the town center, in a home that embodied a comfort and worldliness above the usual New London standard. The bondsman was a regular attendee at Congregational meetings who even owned the covenant in 1742, formally embracing his congregation's promise of fealty with the Lord. During the 1740s and 1750s, he and Adam occasionally worked together hilling corn, butchering hogs, thrashing oats, or stacking barley and hay. Unlike Joshua, the clothier Swetland did not work at Mingo's side, but instead used his slave to perform manual labor he himself would not do.[10]

The second Mingo in Adam's life was Mingo Coit, a slave in the household of Joshua's lifelong neighbor, John Coit, Sr., who operated the nearby Coit shipyard. When John senior died in 1744, Mingo passed to his son John Coit, Jr. Living at the harbor next to the yard, Mingo Coit was accustomed to the commotion and production of shipbuilding. He knew the steady stream of yard labor from local boys, including Joshua Hempstead's own Stephen and outsiders like Jonathan Mawell, a seasoned Boston ship carpenter and longtime

Coit employee. During the evangelical revival of the 1740s, the John Coit, Sr., house became a center for Mr. Adams's conciliatory "Old Lights" (John senior's brother Joseph was the Old Light minister of Plainfield), promoting calm and compromise during turbulent times. Living there, Mingo heard more than his share of evening religious lectures at home. At some point, Mingo did marry, although neither the diarist next door nor the town records identified his wife or any children by name.[11]

Mingo Coit worked occasionally with Joshua and Adam, raking and stacking hay, plowing, and weeding corn. In the close confines of a working neighborhood, servants and slaves like Mingo and Adam played a part in an informal system of exchange that was continuous and often remarkably precise. Sometimes reliant on slave labor, the system in no way revolved around it. When John Hempstead started his own blacksmith shop on his father's house-lot in the 1730s, for example, neighbors naturally turned to him when they needed horses shoed, tools repaired, or wheels rimmed. Joshua's own account with his son was typical. For his father, John set horseshoes, mended the bolt on the well crotch, fixed pot legs, and fire tongs. (Like nearly every early American blacksmith, most of John's trade was repair work.) Occasionally, an account veered from smithy work, as when a loan of "one quart molasses" appeared in Joshua's running tally. A peek at the other side of the ledger showed John clothing his apprentice, Henry, in the neighborhood: rough osnaburg cloth for a coat and breeches from Joshua and a hat from hatter Joseph Truman next door. In return, Henry might have hilled corn.[12]

Mingo's master Coit was one of John Hempstead's biggest customers at his shop, the blacksmith providing a quantity of ironwork for the shipyard, including a titanic supply of boat nails. In return, compensation could come in the form of Mingo, ready to work off Coit's incremental debt. For John Hempstead, Mingo might spend part of a day working at the forge drawing out hot bolts, thinning and elongating the iron with the blunt force of a hammer.[13]

Straightforward two-sided exchange, however, spun quickly out into more elaborate configurations. When Mingo's master Coit needed a log chain to haul lumber out of his sawpit, he borrowed one from his old friend Joshua Hempstead. "Much worn out," the chain broke, wending its way onto John Hempstead's workbench, where it awaited mending for Joshua, with Coit paying the charge. (In the meantime, Coit could offset the borrowing itself to Joshua with time in the field.) Splitting out separate, discernible transactions exposes the system, but it also misses the point. One month after Joshua "got my Logg Chain mended," the diarist was up to his elbows in Coit's sawpit, making repairs (where the chain had failed and lumber fallen), incurring a new credit to his account with his neighbor. And on and on it would go, tallying back and forth until one man died and his estate, or rather his creditors, demanded a final reckoning.[14]

Alongside Mingo, Adam also had considerable contact with another Coit bondsman. Peter Coit was enslaved to John senior's brother Joseph, the Hempstead childhood neighbor who became the minister of Plainfield. Bonded to two brothers, Mingo and Peter Coit were "cousins" in slavery connected through Coit work and kinship. The households they inhabited were quite different, however. While Mingo lived at the epicenter of New London's shipbuilding economy amid the traffic and work of the town's wharves and shipyards, Peter spent much of his time in Plainfield, where his master, Joseph, a graduate of Harvard and Yale, served as that rural settlement's spiritual leader. Mingo resided with a prosperous and prominent artisan, but Peter inhabited the more rarefied atmosphere of a minister's household, a center of communal, spiritual, and intellectual life complete with a considerable "library of books." Like Mingo Swetland, Peter probably did not work alongside his clerical master. When he wasn't plying Mr. Joseph's "husbandry tools" in Plainfield, Peter sometimes worked and stayed in New London, perhaps bedding down there with Mingo at John Coit's.[15]

With Peter's simple European biblical name meaning "rock," rather than a classical or African one more typical of a foreign-born slave, he might have been a native-born New Englander like Adam. Homegrown or not, the name rolled easily off Adam's tongue, since he had a brother of the same name. About eight years Adam's junior, Peter Coit worked with Adam and Joshua during the 1730s and 1740s, helping with a stone wall, raking hay, digging rocks, and mending the highways that Coits and Hempsteads used daily. He shared his master's household with his mistress and their nine children and with at least three other slaves, all women. Of the three, either Rachel or Patience might possibly have been his wife. Old Marme, who had lived there many years before Peter arrived, belonged to an earlier generation.[16]

Joshua Hempstead thought highly of Peter, judging him a "very faithfull Laborious Servt." Like Adam, Peter could be trusted to perform his work with loyalty and industry. There was the time when Joshua struggled to dig stones obstructing a neighborhood artery until "old Mr Coit & his man Peter [arrived] after Sunset & wee finished it bravely." Joshua could also recall the agonizing period when Richard Coit, a beloved grandson of John Coit and grandnephew of Joseph, died of "Longfever [typhus]." The heartrending loss of this only child and new bridegroom cast the neighborhood in grief, expressed in an especially somber and formal funeral. To be expected, perhaps, were the "16 p[ai]r of mournrs [who] followed the Corps"; less so the seventeenth and eighteenth: "Mingo & Peter & their wives brot up ye Rear." Wearing their Sabbath best and walking with the processional, these long-standing Coit slaves were an undeniable part of the family, and also undeniably apart.[17]

ALONG WITH fellow slaves, Adam sometimes worked with free Algonquin and Africans who sold their labor. Especially in Stonington, Adam labored alongside Algonquin who lived closely amid the English of the town. African freedman Thomas Bohan, nicknamed Tommy, had also spent his early years on a North Parish farm, a slave to Jonathan Hill (the same Hill who lost two sons in close succession during the measles epidemic of 1715). After Hill died in 1725, Tommy had continued to serve his master's widow until the Hill heirs granted him freedom. He had worked for Joshua Hempstead at least twice while he was still a slave, but decades later Tommy the freedman became a Hempstead regular. He left no clue why he chose his Irish surname; New Londoners had called him Tommy "Hill" when he was a slave. While still in bondage, he had married Sarah Sales, a free "mulatto" woman. They raised a family of nine children, each born free. Tommy remained poor and propertiless, although he knew relative prosperity in the 1740s, when his taxable estate peaked to twenty-seven pounds. A dip to the nominal eighteen pounds in the decade that followed probably prompted Bohan's need for day labor.[18]

Conversant with the lowly and middling ranks of New London, Adam was also familiar with the uppermost rungs of the town's social ladder through his work. As Joshua's bondsman, Adam labored for no fewer than seventy men (and a few women) other than his master. Because New Londoners relied on the perpetual exchange of farm production, labor, and imported or manufactured goods—in part to address the chronic shortage of currency—a slave like Adam worked for a variety of temporary masters. On occasion, Joshua did let Adam work "all Day for himself," allowing him to earn his own money to make purchases or perhaps even to acquire some capital.[19]

Joshua's diary does not reveal the degree to which he permitted Adam to earn for himself, but Venture Smith, author of the foremost autobiographical narrative of Connecticut slave life in the late eighteenth century, recounted how his own otherwise brutal master allowed that privilege, leading ultimately to Smith purchasing his own freedom with the proceeds. But Smith lived two generations after Adam, at a time when even voluntary manumission by masters was gaining ground. Adam mostly worked on Joshua's account, accumulating a roster of surrogate "employers" that contained some of the town's leading residents: Madam Anne Winthrop, Minister Adams, the ship captain James Braddick, the merchant William Roe, the physician Jeremiah Miller, and even the widow Elizabeth Knight Livingston—his own parents' mistress during some of their darkest hours.[20]

Practiced at navigating New London's social waters, Adam also came into regular contact with its port and principal commerce. Work led him down to the wharves and harbor, where he encountered ships and shipyards, trade goods and sailing men. There Adam performed a range of work. He loaded cider on a sloop bound for Long Island for his master's son John. For "a west India man" he carted three hogsheads. He and Joshua went to Capt. Joseph Coit's nearby warehouse to "unhead a bb[arrel] of [New] York flower" and to David Gardiner's to truck over rum and sugar to the merchant Nicholas Hallam's. At Pickett's wharf, named for John Pickett, who died at sea in 1667, Adam picked up molasses and gravestones with his master's help. Despite the constraints he faced in his daily life and servile status, work at the port may have given Adam some sense of a world outside those bounds.[21]

Work connected Adam to a wider New London, but it also allowed him to spend time alone and to work without supervision. Just seventeen days after Adam first joined his household in 1727, Joshua sent the bondsman off to the salt flats to rake hay alone. Joshua then noted in his diary how Adam completed eight cocks, or stacks, a report that had likely come straight from the bondsman's lips. The speed with which Joshua delegated to Adam displayed his trust in the young man's competence and character. It also illustrated the commonplace of slaves working alone, traveling back and forth as they did. By statute, a slave required his master's written permission to travel—a pass that any English freeman, armed with suspicion or ill will, could demand to see. Even with this rule on the books, a local man like Adam was probably seldom confronted in his movements about town. New Londoners all knew Adam Jackson at a glance, and would have had little interest in impeding Joshua's work. Nevertheless the possibility of being challenged or harassed always remained.[22]

The place where Adam probably knew the most independence was on Joshua's two-hundred-acre Stonington farm. From his earliest years as a Hempstead slave, Adam went to Stonington alone, following Joshua's general directives but routinely using his own judgment about running the farm operations there. In Stonington, Adam plied his considerable animal husbandry skills, maintaining a flock of sheep and looking after animals sent to pasture on the area's rich grasses. He also slaughtered sheep, mowed hay, and held up Joshua's end of local transactions: picking up nine fleeces from the Crouches, taking possession of "2 Little calves that I bot of [neighbor] Stephen Bennit." To get to Stonington—traveling by foot, by horse, and by water, often with animals in tow—could take several hours, eating up most of a morning or afternoon. Once there, Adam might stay several days, probably in the "Cave" Joshua furnished with "a bed & household Stuff," perhaps even a "looking Glass." Adam was so dependable that Joshua could rely on him to carry and deliver valuables beyond the stock and produce of his farm, even a stash of "£49 in bills" and his prized pocket watch which had fallen from his coat one day along a country road.[23]

Adam expected Joshua to oversee his work, but that supervision was anything but systematic. One day when a lame leg prevented Joshua from working, the hobbled yeoman sought some control over the farmwork: "Toward night I Rid out into the Lot & Directed about Stacking 2 Small Stacks." Another time Joshua "went to the Cornfield to See after the Barley adam & Wait Wright is Thrashing," directing his attention to the barley more than the thrashers. (This Wait was the same "mustee" son of William Wright, who had faced prosecution with Adam's father and John Rogers, leading to his banishment.) Similarly, when Adam made cider at the Harrises', Joshua described going out "to See after my Cyder," but not his slave's work per se. When he did check on Adam, Joshua concentrated on the progress of work: "I Rid out to the Cornfield to See how ad[a]m managed the Sowing oats."[24]

One category of work Adam often did on his own was carting and hauling goods from place to place. Within two years of Adam's arrival, Joshua had provided him with a cart and team to operate around town, entrusting him with this significant and indispensable asset at a time when most English farmers owned only one yoke of oxen. (Adam probably also had a set of husbandry tools for his use and, at the very least, an ax to cut wood.) Hired out regularly for specific jobs, Adam was known around town as an able carter of anything. Over the years, he carted an impressive range of items that included agricultural commodities—dung, hay, bark, stones, and dirt; construction materials—timber, slabs or flooring, shingles, and sand—as well as "household stuff" when someone moved house. New London selectmen once entrusted Adam to cart more than one hundred years of town records when a new town clerk took over.[25]

Adam's skills as an animal handler and driver were already well developed when he arrived on Joshua's doorstep; they were probably even a factor in his purchase. Drawing on lifelong knowledge, Adam used his own distinctive pattern of commands and whip strokes to maneuver the beasts, exuding a gentle but firm authority as he did so.[26]

As early as two months after his arrival, he had commanded a team of oxen on his own while performing highway maintenance for his master—an annual duty for able-bodied men. And when his first spring arrived at the Hempsteads', Adam had also taken the lead at the plow, driving Joshua's team with neighbor Ben Truman while his master "held [the plow]." Adam was adept enough to handle notoriously difficult creatures, even those other men avoided. One yoke of oxen was so uncontrollable that no farmer would accept them to pasture ("No one will Keep them they are So unruely"), but Adam was able to drive it alone without mishap. On his own, he could drive a team of six, even while drawing a load of lumber. He also handled small herds of cattle, large flocks of sheep, and teams of horses, sometimes easing the animals in their transport over water. Joshua could count on Adam to find or "look up" stock left out to roam, including the "4 Piggs that have been out in the woods all the fall & winter," the eighty sheep imperiled by "Snow . . . very deep near knee Deep," or the "11 Stray Sheep & 2 lambs" wandering happily through the Stonington backcountry one spring. When the season was right, Joshua could also call on Adam to ride a mare to breed, then to bring her back once nature had taken its course.[27]

Husbanding Joshua's stock required Adam to drive and herd— and also to wield a sharp knife. With his master, Adam gelded colts, spayed sows, and castrated piglets and lambs to make "barrows" and "wethers" that would be fit to eat once grown. At slaughter time, Adam used a firm and deliberate hand to cut throats, guiding streams of blood into a waiting tub so as not to waste a drop. Sticking was the best method. There was a chosen tree at Bream Cove, just like one at the Stonington farm, with a branch the right height and strength where a hog or steer regularly dangled upturned, its throat slit at the breastbone.[28]

By himself Adam readily killed sheep weighing around forty-five pounds. Killing a two-hundred-pound pig was a lot easier with help, although Adam could manage on his own, if necessary. With cattle at the blade, Adam was more likely to have a helper to hold animals that weighed about four hundred pounds. After skinning a carcass and removing the organs, men and boys singed and scraped the skin. Like most New England men, both Adam and Joshua, master and slave, knew slaughter as familiar work, arriving every year with winter's cold.[29]

Once an animal was dressed, Joshua and Adam drew knives and axes to quarter and weigh the remains of the carcass. In quantifying his stock and measuring the yield, Joshua was meticulous. In his mind and accounts, he noted the weight of each part of the slaughter, so that "1 Steer . . . [became 1] hide 54 [pounds;] Tallow 26 [pounds]. Q[ua]r[ter]s[:] 94–109. 95. 94 [pounds each;] all [together] 472 [pounds]. att 14d p[er pound]—£27 10s 8d." Fresh meat, a rarity, might be shared with a neighbor who helped in the slaughter or simply exchanged for other goods or services. Usually Joshua and Adam immediately preserved the kill to serve as protein during the coldest months of the year; most of the meat found its way quickly into large wooden bowls, where the men salted it heavily before barreling. Opening a barrel months or years hence, women had to soak the meat in fresh water, like salt fish, to restore some prior consistency. Still, barreled meat remained exceedingly salty, demanding plenty of cider to wash it down.[30]

Joshua's clipped diurnal references sketched the structural outlines of Adam's work, of what he did and whom he encountered. They also suggested the quality and arduousness of his labors. In the diary, Adam's working hours are faintly apparent; although he began work in the morning and finished in the evening with a midday break for dinner, Adam did not usually begin work long before sunrise or continue to toil well after dark. Finishing farmwork after nine or ten at night and continuing in the dark were unusual enough to deserve special mention in the diary, as when Adam and Joshua hastily fenced the turnip yard to house sheep "Tho Late. almost dark before wee finisht." Neither the slave nor his master was accustomed to performing work, and then returning home "all the way in the night Dark."[31]

Adam worked hard, but he lived in a world where daily manual work for all but a small clerical, mercantile, or professional elite was the norm. He developed specialties and often labored alone, but most of the farmwork he did was indistinguishable from the kind his master performed, although Joshua had a broad range of non-farmwork also available to him. For Adam and Joshua, hard work took place outside a rigid time schedule and with accommodations for weather, local events, and household circumstances—and, of course, simple "going & Com[ing]." Usually Joshua wrote of Adam's work with approval—or more precisely the absence of disapproval. On occasion, he wrote memorably of how much work Adam could carry out in a single day. There was the time Adam carted eleven full loads of stones to and from town without any assistance. Or the day when he and another servant raked an entire field of barley, building seventy cocks. Joshua's sanguine view of Adam's work made reference to any slack performance all the more striking. If Adam saw quiet interference or passive noncompliance as a means of resistance, he seldom tacked such a course.[32]

Only a handful of times in more than thirty years did Adam disappoint his master enough for Joshua to register it in his diary. Aside from his 1739 confinement with the Groton constable after nearly twelve years of service, Adam waited another decade before he "got Staggering Drunk Early," requiring his master to stay home all day and nurse him back to sobriety. Whatever drove Adam to drink pressed hard on him: "By the Midle of the Day [he] was got almost Sober & [then] made a Second Tripp [to drunkenness] & So Ended the day." Another time Joshua's complaint was simple enough: While others dug stones and mended fences, "adam was nothing to day." Yet another diary entry described how Adam simply "gave out" after spending a morning grinding apples. It is not the fact of Adam's small lapses, but their rarity, that stands out.[33]

Joshua acknowledged and even appreciated Adam's long and steadfast service, but the slave would still always straddle a line between valued worker and valuable property in his master's eye. On the surface, Joshua's diary presents Adam's everyday work as largely indistinguishable from that of Hempsteads and hired men, but it also speaks quietly of his commodification. Ever the exacting domestic economist, Joshua took scrupulous accounting of any breakages at Adam's hands, and there were many: axel trees, plow beams, cart wheels, chains, cart tongues, and ladders.[34]

Adam might have been accident prone or even have staged oblique rebellion through conscious sabotage, but more likely he broke no more gear than any other long-term worker, despite the diary's artificial spotlight. Adam's breakages warranted a special accounting for his master, who entered them into a real and imagined ledger, appended to the cost of Adam's purchase and maintenance. Other workers might break things, too, but no other man was so easily reckoned a depreciating asset on the balance sheet in Joshua's accounts and in his mind.

If Adam was forever an elusive asset on a running balance sheet, he was also his master's most consistent companion in his home and his work. No other person stayed longer with Joshua in the house at Bream Cove: no wife, no child. And no other man, not even a son or grandson, worked more years at his side and for his exclusive benefit. Did the moments and hours of "I & adam only" foster a communion of a different sort, resistant to easy naming? Did they never slip into deeper conversation, perhaps on the way to the milky quartz of "the great Hill" in North Stonington "to get up Some Step Stones" that would lie for generations before the house? Was there no time during more than thirty years with "only adm to help me mostly," when the gulf between master and slave narrowed for a moment, pressed against the inescapable force of a task at hand, a beautiful day, or the passage of time?[35]

If such a thing were possible, it could have happened on a long August day spent chasing pigs with two young Hempstead great-grandsons, rain forcing them to hide out in a barn and then walk home, soaked to the bone. On such a day, after more than twenty years together, there could have been a flicker of something other than the state of abject subjugation that bound Adam Jackson and Joshua Hempstead to each other.[36]

JUST SOUTH of Joshua's front door, Long Bridge was a narrow conduit of earth and stones that served as a crossing point before the land dropped into the swamps and marshes of the cove. Though English families like the Hempsteads, Holts, Coits, and Trumans had lived and owned land around the cove for nearly a century, they had left trees in sufficient number to supplement outlying wood-lots. For Joshua, it was an easy place to gather firewood within sight of home. One late autumn in the 1730s the water below Long Bridge was already frigid. Before long it would turn to ice, beating so hard against the bank that frozen blocks sometimes heaved onto the shore.[37]

On this particular November morning, men and boys arrived at Long Bridge in a trickle. Adam got there first. As usual he and Joshua had risen by daybreak to feed horses, oxen, and other stock. Adam had then taken his master's carthorse down to the water, carrying his saw and ax with him, and gotten under way with the morning's work. At first he probably went to the woodpile they had left almost one year before, when snow had prevented them from hauling the wood home. (In their New London, a man could set work aside and leave it for a year or even more, returning to it when the time and weather were right.) Joshua came later, also by horse. He had been writing—legal work and accounts—the kind of work he patched into small chunks of unclaimed time. The diary, too, always beckoned.[38]

The boys arrived last. The Hempstead grandsons, twelve-year-old Josh and nine-year-old Natty, had risen that morning from a shared bed. After breakfast and other chores, they had followed their grandfather's instructions to meet him and Adam at Long Bridge and to bring the ox team with them. Young as they were, Josh and Natty together were competent enough to drive the team without forgetting their axes or the log chain to pull trunks.[39]

Before the boys appeared, the two men had already felled a number of trees. Josh and Natty set to work hacking smaller boughs off the large trunks, while Adam began to load the cart with the uneven logs. Josh balanced himself gamely on the fallen trunks, maneuvering his ax to chop into the joints. Then, with one quick misstroke, the ax caught hard in a jagged shoot and fell.[40]

"Gran[d]father," the boy said matter-of-factly, "I have Cutt of[f] Two of my Toes."[41] From his words and tone Joshua was certain the boy was joking. He looked up from his work to confirm that "he was Jesting," but the child's face was blank and pale.[42]

"I have Really Grandfather," Josh added calmly. With a sharp stroke of awareness, Joshua launched himself toward the boy, picking him up and setting him on the ground. Josh was sturdy, but his grandfather could still lift and envelop him just as he always had. He pulled off the child's shoe, its leather cut through and flooded with blood, and then bound up the cut foot. At some point, a wave of recognition passed over him: This had happened before. Later the diarist would write about it, his memory sharp to the point of producing a description of the wound that bordered on the metaphysical: This latest cut to Josh's "Great Toe" would have measured an inch, "but was Something Shorter by Reason [that the toe] was Cutt off once before about half of the Length of the Nail."[43]

Such accidents were commonplace as men and boys wrangled with the daily rounds of weather, livestock, tools, and raw materials. At twenty, Josh's now-dead father, Nathaniel, had also "cut his knee badly" while out in the woods getting timber for oars. Joshua himself, as a teenage apprentice, had cut his own leg and then written about it with almost grandiose flare: "It being Thursday About 9 or 10 of ye clock in ye morning: I: Joshua Hempstèd Cut My Leg." An ordinary part of life, minor accidents were also very dangerous. With every break of the skin came the risk of infection and, with every infection, the very real risk of death.[44]

Out at Long Bridge, Joshua told Adam to take the cart horse and find physician Miller, while Natty stayed alone to mind the cart and team, and fret over his older brother. In the meantime, Joshua rushed his grandson back to the house as fast as he could, presumably using the horse he had brought with him. By the time they arrived home, Miller was already there, ready with a preparation to stop the bleeding. Having brought the doctor, Adam returned to Long Bridge to keep an eye on Natty and resume the day's work. In fact the slave and the younger boy managed to bring home another two cartloads of wood before evening supper.[45]

Quick treatment and a month of rest allowed Josh's wound to heal completely. A bit of missing toe would not impede the twelve-year-old from later becoming a man of enormous physical stature and the county's best-known sheriff. By the evening following the accident, Josh's grandfather had already turned to other things, even attending a religious gathering next door at the Holts', as he had planned. The day had revealed more than a grandfather's care for his boys; it showed Joshua's easy reliance on Adam to perform ably the work of a servant, but also to help in the breach with Josh and Natty.[46]

Joshua fathered his boys—grandsons and sons before them— through the slow accretion and calm governance of days such as this. At the sides of their beds, in the field, shop, and yard, he gave them his work, his time, his tenderness, and his example. Fatherhood— followed by grandfatherhood—in a sense came quickly. It had summoned him in the wee hours of morning, a shrill cry from the women-filled chamber of birth. It had sounded again, urgently, a low wail in the dim light of a son's fresh grave. But it had also come slowly: keeping an eye at the side of the river, wiping the brow of a feverish child, and gradually, over many years, teaching a boy to hold a tool and use it well.

As Joshua's grandsons grew, the time came to prepare for their future. In Natty's case, Joshua formally apprenticed him at fifteen to the rope maker James Tilley, who operated a rope walk near the harbor. Tilley, a Devonshire native and Anglican who cut a jaunty and prosperous figure in a 1757 portrait by John Singleton Copley, had come to New London from Boston, where he had managed a rope walk on Milk Street. Natty would stay with Tilley until he reached majority. He then set up his own rope walk on the Bream Cove property and later built a stone house there, completed at the time of his grandfather's death.[47]

Joshua's expectations for Josh were self-evident. This eldest son of his eldest son would stay in the house that would be his, perfecting skills at husbandry and preparing himself for a life much like his grandfather's. With Natty at Tilley's, the grandfather's diurnal refrain became "Adm & Josh" or "Josha & adam," revealing the slave as one of the Hempstead heir's most regular companions as he approached adulthood. Josh's nineteenth year was typical: That year he and Adam thrashed oats in January and February, mowed hay in July, and carted it in August. In September, they gathered apples, and they sledded home wood in December.[48]

At first, there had been teacherly, if not paternal, overtones to

Adam's part in preparing his master's grandsons for the work of men. As the boys entered their teens, the rapport between the three probably took on a collaborative, roughly fraternal quality. Working together through many years, they developed a sense of teamwork and cooperation, if not real camaraderie. Then at some point, perhaps almost imperceptibly, the dynamic between Adam and the Hempstead boys started to shift, yielding incrementally to blunt realities. The children Adam once schooled in driving oxen and mowing hay would inevitably become men who could own him. Perpetual servitude relegated the older man, even under the most favorable conception, to remain his master's "ward" for an unending term. If New Englanders regarded their slaves as family, they were "sons and daughters" never permitted to grow up. English boys could daydream of independence and a bright competency. The same reverie became a dark ruse in the minds of their enslaved brethren.[49]

Chapter Fifteen

"THE WONDERFULL
WORK OF GOD"

DURING THE seventeenth and eighteenth centuries New England underwent a series of evangelical revivals that temporarily infused congregations with renewed religious enthusiasm. The celebrated Great Awakening of the 1730s and 1740s was one of many, but it was the first of transatlantic proportions. Although it affected towns across New England and beyond, its manifestations in rambunctious New London, home of the inimitable Rogerenes, were characteristically histrionic. The revival affected local families quite differently depending on their social position. Although African New Englanders did participate broadly in the revival, most servants and slaves in New London fell largely under its radar. They were not the focus of its leaders, nor did they emerge as leaders themselves. Although some servants surely followed their masters' radical leanings, they remained, in local records at least, largely in the background. Those with alternative beliefs like the Jacksons, in particular, had no reason to become involved in an internal Congregational struggle. Elite families like the Winthrops, many of whom had already transferred their allegiance to the Anglican Church, observed the Congregational turmoil with mild detachment, if not derision. For middling yeoman families like the Hempsteads, however, who formed the backbone of the Congregational Church, the movement was a seismic cataclysm, strong enough to tear families apart.[1]

As a Congregationalist, Joshua Hempstead had always been a moderate with a high tolerance for dissent and dissenters. He regarded local Baptists with leniency, and when the Church of England arrived in New London, Joshua showed genuine openness toward the church whose persecutions and intolerance many first New Englanders had fled. In this, he was like other colonists over the course of the eighteenth century who permitted the Church of England to gain a new foothold in their region, as the numbers of high-status imperial (and Anglican) officials increased, and emulation of things English across the North American colonies surged. Joshua was part of this trend, contentedly attending Anglican services on occasion. When Anglicans began to celebrate Christmas in New London, a holiday disapproved of by the Congregational Church as both nonscriptural in origin and secular in practice, Joshua noted the "Great Concourse of people at the Church [of Saint James] to hear Mr Seabury preach a Christmas Sermon & to See fashions" without disparaging any perceived decadence. His assessment was pragmatic and naturally curious: "It being New many went."[2]

Given Joshua's tolerance of non-Congregationalists, he met the changes wrought by the Great Awakening with equanimity. He never wavered in his support of Mr. Adams and the established ministry, but that loyalty did not prevent him from respecting the preaching and activities of the "New Lights," as reforming separatist Congregationalists called themselves. By the time the Awakening touched New London directly in the late 1730s, the townspeople had already heard of revivals in western Massachusetts and in England and had read of the evangelism of George Whitefield, the great English orator who had introduced a new style of evangelical oratory to the English-speaking world.[3]

Drawing on his training in the theater, Whitefield rejected traditional formalistic preaching techniques for enormous, itinerant open-air services at which he spoke loudly and extemporaneously, using ordinary language and producing tremendous displays of exhortative emotion. By the time Whitefield came to preach in

North America in 1739, colonists like Joshua were primed to hear the great evangelical with their own ears. At his first appearance in Philadelphia that November, Whitefield spoke on the courthouse steps to a throng of six thousand, in a city of twelve thousand. When Whitefield was scheduled to speak in Norwich, Connecticut, in October 1740, Joshua made an effort to attend, but "a grt Rain" prevented him. Whitefield failed to appear in any case as "unexpected news . . . turned him towards New York."[4]

Joshua and other Congregationalists participated enthusiastically when the Awakening first struck New London. In March 1741, the shipwright eagerly attended eight sermons over three days given by an itinerant Pennsylvania preacher, Gilbert Tennant, along with "[peo]ple from The farms as well as Town and Groton & many [others]." In Southold in May, Joshua heard the sermons of their brash young minister and Yale graduate, James Davenport. Leading a radical faction of young ministers, Davenport had adopted many of Whitefield's techniques, including open-air services, everyday language, and daily meetings. He was also known for openly and stridently criticizing traditional "Old Light" ministers, criticism Joshua found excessive. Soon after—during the first week of June and with Joshua still on Long Island—"the wonderfull work of God" exploded on the New London scene. That week, evangelicals, Jedediah Mills of Derby and Nathaniel Eells, preached and converted many, leaving Joshua giddy. The "week hath been kept as a Sabbath most of it, & with the greatest Success Imaginable & beyond what is Rational to Conc[ei]ve of it. . . . Never any Such time here & Scarce any where Else."[5]

Though he remained an "Old Light" traditionalist, Mr. Adams, who had long embraced an evangelical preaching style exhorting conversion, initially welcomed the revived religious enthusiasm brought on by the Awakening. From May to November, he took eighty-one new converts into his congregation. Among the converts were Joshua's blacksmith son, John, and his wife, Hannah, who joined the church as full members along with "upwards of 20 grown people" one day in late June. The new converts quickly grew dissatisfied with Mr. Adams's leadership, however. On June 16, the New

Light minister Jonathan "Parsons pr[eached] 3 [Sermons] 2 in the meeting house & 1 att [lawyer and merchant] mr [John] Curtisses in the Evening," where opponents to Mr. Adams had begun to meet.[6]

Having converted in the heat of religious revivalism and reform, John and Hannah Hempstead were sympathetic to a small group of separatists that had formed before they joined the church. During the summer of 1741, that dissenting group continued to meet and hold lectures in the home of their lay leader, the Yale graduate John Curtis, who had been ousted from a ministry in Glastonbury due to his opposition to the clerical establishment. (This was apparently the same John Curtis who had represented Cesar Le Grand, son of the captive Betty, in a successful bid for freedom.)[7]

Initially the dissident meeting attracted a relatively broad audience, with town and church leaders like Joshua attempting to conciliate between factions and avoid an open breach. On June 25, for example, Joshua "went into Town wth Son Robert & wife & John & his wife to mr adams & Madm [Anne] Winthrops & dined there & was at a Lecture at Mr Curtisses." By the time Davenport himself came and preached in New London in July, however, a complete break became certain. Davenport openly criticized Adams as unregenerate, labeling him a "carnal Pharisee." He enthralled and disturbed New Londoners with his unorthodox preaching style, when he "Dismisst the Congregation . . . into the broad ally which was much crowded & there he Screamed out . . . Come to Christ . . . & Come away Come away . . . [then] he went got into ye [pews on the] Mens Side & there he held it Sometime Singing & Sometime paraying; he and his [companions] all took their turns & the women fainting."[8]

Within a few weeks, Joshua again heard Davenport when he "pr[eached] att Groton 4 or 5 days & mighty works followed. near 1000 hearers . . . from all Quarters held ye meeting till 2 Clock at night & Some Stayed all night under the oak tree & in the meeting house." Expressing the religious sensation in martial terms, Joshua saw "about 60 Wounded, many Strong men as well as others." For the rest of the week, Davenport preached daily with "all hands . . . hearing [him]" so that the hay Joshua had arranged for others to mow at the Stonington farm was left undone, and he had to do it himself. The next Sabbath, when Joshua heard Davenport in Stonington "under the Trees," he felt the young minister had gone too far, "He was So Severe in Judging & Condemning Mr Eells [himself an evangelical preacher] that many of the People in the Assembly withdrew into the meetinghouse where Mr Eells preacht to them as he was wont to do."[9]

On the first of November, when Adams baptized John junior, the infant son of John and Hannah Hempstead, they were still members of their father's congregation, even though they had probably continued to participate in the dissident meeting at the Curtis house. That same month, Joshua attended a gathering of ministers and representatives of Connecticut congregations, united to thwart the revivalists by prohibiting ministerial itinerancy, which they accomplished six months later. Meanwhile his son John decided to reject his father's course. On the twenty-ninth, with four other leading members of the dissident faction, John Hempstead separated from the established church and conspicuously absented himself from meeting. His father pointedly noted John's nonappearance in his diary, though he offered no critical commentary.[10]

As the separatists continued to meet at various houses in town, the Yale graduate Timothy Allen arrived in the summer of 1742 (like Curtis, Allen had answered a call to the ministry only to be expelled for excessive revivalist fervor). Allen and Curtis began a center for New Light learning and teaching, the so-called Shepherd's Tent, a seminary for the training of an itinerant evangelical ministry. It operated for about a year in a still-extant house on Truman Street below the Holts', so that Joshua passed it often, especially on his way to the neck. The old shipwright knew the house well: He had helped raise it in 1713 and would one day be its owner, not allowing its radical history to dissuade him from using it as a rental property.[11]

In June 1742 John, Hannah, and the other New London separatists petitioned the county court, receiving legal recognition as "a new society called the Separatists." Their petition expressed more than a desire to split; it was a harsh attack on Adams, whom they argued had been a "direct stop to [their] communion with God." They called him "an unconverted man" and "found his ministry unedify-ing, unsuccessful, [and] unapt for spiritual nourishment and growth in Grace." Joshua did not react in his diary, but John and Hannah's explicit rupture from the congregation, especially from the minister he deeply admired, must have pained him.[12]

In the months that followed, Joshua became increasingly exas-perated with the excesses of the New Lights. Visiting his son Rob-ert in Southold in February 1743, he attended Davenport's meeting but found it "Scarcely worth the hearing." The emotional, confused performance now appalled him: "The praying was without form or Comelyness. it was dificult to distinguish between his pray-ing & preaching for it was all Meer Confused medley . . . then . . . [Davenport said] the hand of the Lord is upon me over & over many times; then Leave of[f] & begin again the Same words verbatim." Leading the congregation in song, Davenport had chanted the same tune thirty or forty times over like a madman "as fast as one word could follow after another." The old diarist found the service so bizarre and outrageous he was unable to "relate the Inconsistance of it."[13]

During that meeting, Davenport also spoke of divine revelations telling him to return to New London and demonstrate the Sepa-ratists' repudiation of the world. On March 6, 1743, minister James Davenport walked New London's main thoroughfare, broadcasting his righteousness while a crowd followed behind him, captivated and dismayed. Old-timers could not help but notice a familiarity to the spectacle. On the very same street nearly fifty years earlier, old John Rogers had declared his self-proclaimed marriage to Mary Ransford, inadvertently paving the way for men like Davenport. Although he had begun as the Congregational minister of Southold, the magnetic Davenport had since become a New Light who sought a radical trans-formation of his church by rejecting "immoral" and "unnecessary" ritual and emphasizing individual communion with God. The day of his march through New London was a Sabbath, and as Joshua and the other congregants recessed from Adams's sermon at the meet-inghouse in their usual fashion, they watched aghast as Davenport and his followers lit a bonfire of heresies, destroying—according to court records—"sundry good and useful treatises books of practical Godliness, the works of able Divines, and whilst said books were consuming in the flames did shout, hollow and scream."[14]

The next day, Davenport presided over another fire, a flaming pile of worldly possessions, including "extravagances" of clothing and jewelry. While his followers viewed the burning with deadly earnestness, others in town were not so taken with Davenport's antics. Jeremiah Miller, Jr., son of the town physician and husband of John Winthrop IV's daughter Margaret amused his Winthrop brother-in-law John Still with a send-up of the bonfire in a personal letter, listing among the items burned: "Christopher Christophers' old wig because he would not burn his new one; Kate Wickwire's under-petticoat; Shapley's old wig that he'd worn these 20 years and worshiped as long; Mr. Adams' sermon upon thunder; and many other books that they didn't like."[15]

As this second fire blazed, a frenzied Davenport tore off his own breeches—"plush breeches," as young Miller jocularly described them—and threw them into the flames. Standing before the crowd in his drawers, the cleric could feel the mood shift irreversibly against him. A now-disgusted young female supporter pulled Davenport's smoldering pants out of the fire and hurled them at him, to the mortification of the assembled. Davenport was chastened and apologetic, but the damage was done. Public opinion had turned, and Davenport became the fanatic who had gone too far. As news of his excesses spread across New England, Davenport left town in disgrace. He publicly recanted his behavior not long after, attributing it to the delirium of the moment, but the minister's rash disrobing augured the end of the Great Awakening in New London. The authorities, including a certain shipwright magistrate, had to choose how to react to Davenport's civil disobedience. They decided not to prosecute the Separatists for the second burning, which had fallen on a Monday. The first, however, had occurred on the Sabbath, and authorities chose to prosecute participants for the petty crime of profanation of the Holy Day. Joshua was the justice who tried the Separatists before a crowd of spectators; his son John was not among the accused. John had refrained from participating in the burnings, perhaps because he had begun to doubt Davenport's leadership.[16]

At this point in his life, Joshua was a leading man of the town, well trusted to mediate conflict among townsmen and apply the law fairly. How he dealt with the Separatists of the Great Awakening was characteristic of that leadership. Although he found all the participants guilty, as they certainly were, Joshua ordered them to pay an insignificant fine of five shillings each, plus costs. Ever the moderate, Joshua had settled on an amount exactly half the statutory maximum. He knew he could make his point without sowing the seeds of further discontent and rebellion. Not long after, the Shepherd's Tent disbanded, and the New London Separatists fell into permanent disarray.[17]

The Awakening tested Joshua's leadership of the town, but it also strained his skills as a patriarch and father at home. Religious dissent had touched his family directly, and it could easily have led to a lasting fissure. Joshua never wrote how he felt about John's rebellion from their congregation, but his behavior around John reveals something of how it impacted their relationship. In the diary, the connection between father and son appeared largely unaffected. Just as he had continued to interact normally with John as the movement gained strength, during the months following the bonfires he "helped John . . . Pry up . . . a very Large Stone 4 or 5 foot high" to make a wall. In haying season, he relied heavily on John who "helpt mow & Sowed [Joshua's] Turnips" in July and a week in August "hclpt mow but 1 day & ½." Despite the religious breach and Joshua's disapproval of the "prevailing disorders & destractions yt are Subsisting in the Country by means of Enthusiasm," father and son appeared to continue as before.[18]

During the heat of the revival, many Old Lights spurned the New Lights as idle, ignorant, and of lesser rank, but Joshua did not indulge in such divisiveness, nor did he seem inclined to personal attack. Perhaps he could understand why John, of all of his children, had been the most receptive to extremism. In 1738, John and Hannah had been especially vulnerable to spiritual consolation and fervor.

First cousins, they watched Hempstead siblings become parents to large healthy families, while they lost three out of their four young children. Joshua was keenly aware in November 1741, when John and Hannah first broke with Mr. Adams's ministry, that their fifth child, John junior, was only four weeks old and still very much at risk.

As the revival movement petered out, many New London Separatists, John and Hannah doubtless among them, asked to return to the fold of the First Congregation within a few years. Adams welcomed them back. The revival had posed difficulties for town leadership both at home and in public life. Despite his disagreements with them and their methods, Joshua remained conciliatory toward the New Lights, his own son in particular. Above all he remained patient, trusting that the movement would ebb and John would come to his senses. He would not permit passing enthusiasms to break up his family. Even important differences in religion would not come between him and the blacksmith son he would ultimately choose to be the executor of his estate.[19]

ON MAY 5, 1750, Southold magistrate and onetime blacksmith Robert Hempstead arrived at his father's house at Bream Cove, distraught and out of breath. Joshua described the reason for his distress: "My Son Robert is Come fro[m] So[ut]hold in Quest of his Daughter Abigail who is Come away privetly with John Ledyard of Groton (her mothers Sisters Son) because her parents Refused to give her to him to wife & he Stayed all day & lodged with me at night." Robert feared that his daughter had eloped with her first cousin, and he immediately looked to his father for help and counsel. Just as New London looked to Joshua Hempstead to smooth out ruffled feathers in town, children and grandchildren turned to their patriarch in times of trouble and conflict.[20]

Joshua's granddaughter Abigail was Robert's eldest daughter and second child, named for her grandmother and aunt. Born in 1727, the year of Adam's arrival at Bream Cove, Abigail had known her grandfather Hempstead from childhood through his frequent visits to her father's house. Not until she was nine years old, however, had she made the trip over the Sound to New London herself, accompanying her parents and elder brother to attend the wedding of her aunt Molly Hempstead—that most happy day in her grandfather's life. On that trip, she and her mother had also stayed at the home of her maternal aunt Deborah, who was married to John Ledyard, a Groton merchant and lawyer. When she reached her teens and entered the marriage market, Abigail returned to New London with her big brother Ben, staying two weeks. Four years later, in 1747, when her aunt Deborah Ledyard died of the measles after giving birth to her tenth child, Abigail again went to Groton to help care for her cousins. Her grandfather next mentioned her in his diary after Robert arrived on his doorstep.[21]

It appeared that Abigail had done more than help around the house during her time in Groton. She and her first cousin John Ledyard, Jr., a fledgling sea captain, had fallen in love. Ledyard, according to family oral history, had asked his uncle Robert Hempstead for Abigail's hand, but he had been soundly rebuffed. The reasons for Robert's refusal were not preserved, but the magistrate may have disapproved of the marriage between cousins, even though such pairings were not universally frowned upon. Robert's own brother John and his wife, Hannah, were an obvious precedent, and several Hempstead grandchildren and great-grandchildren married close cousins with parental approval. Robert took a hard line against the relationship, however, forbidding Abigail from even seeing her cousin. When she disappeared on May 5, it was immediately clear that she had disobeyed his injunction. Following his instincts, Robert ran to the Southold landing place to look for John Ledyard's sailboat.[22]

Finding his nephew's boat missing, Robert fitted out his own and sailed across the Sound to find his wayward girl. Just three months earlier he had received "the malencholy news" that Abigail's twenty-three-year-old brother, Ben, a mariner, had "Sayled f[rom] Barbados . . . & was Lost overbord the night before they arived." He was especially loath to lose another child now, and under these avoidable and unpalatable circumstances. Thoughts of Ben might have fueled his desperation as he looked for Abigail first at New London Harbor and then in town. Finding no clues, he headed to

Bream Cove, where he knew that he would at least find the comfort and counsel of the seventy-one-year-old patriarch. With no sign of Abigail, Robert simply stayed on, unburdening himself to his father. The next day, with nowhere else to look and with travel at a minimum for the Sabbath, father and son attended meeting all day and hoped for news.[23]

With still no word on Monday, Joshua joined in the search for his granddaughter "in Town with my Son Robert till afternoon att Mr Winthrops & Elsewhere." On Tuesday they still had heard nothing. When Wednesday arrived, Robert gave up and headed to the water and home. He scanned the surface of the Sound searching for his runaway child, taking a similar route to the one John Jackson had taken nearly forty years earlier to rescue another daughter, stolen with her mother and brother. For Jackson, his daughter's "running away" with her mother and brother was the only way to get his family back. But to Hempstead a runaway daughter meant the breakup of his family, or so he thought. As he progressed across the Sound, Robert Hempstead concentrated on the skyline until he made out the sails of a familiar boat up ahead. He steered straight for it, recognizing the figures of his Ledyard nephew and another of his daughter's kinsmen, Daniel Youngs Brown. Approaching steadily with a gun now clutched in his hands, Robert bellowed, "Is Miss Hempstead on board there?"[24]

John Ledyard replied unflinchingly, "No, but Mrs. Ledyard is."[25]

The cousins had been married three days earlier at Setaucket, Long Island, having "got a Lycence of Doctor Mawason who had Blanks (to Dispose of) from the Gov[crno]r," as their grandfather rather dubiously made note later. It was a turbulent beginning, but Joshua characteristically took the long view and began quickly the work of helping Hempsteads and Ledyards to reconcile. During the four weeks following their precipitous marriage, Abigail's grandfather went over to Groton twice to call on the young Ledyards and ease the parental breach.[26]

Within two months, Abigail herself ventured to heal the ruptures her elopement had caused. She traveled to Stonington with her grandfather Hempstead to call on friends and relations, belatedly following the custom of a young woman newly wed. She went in particular to see her aunt Abigail Minor, who, since her own mother's death long ago, had likely assumed the role of family matriarch. Aunt Abigail, her niece and namesake probably believed, would hold sway with her father, Robert. In little time he, too, became resigned to the marriage, even calling on his daughter in her new home and allowing the new Mrs. Ledyard to chaperone her younger sisters, Molly and Experience.[27]

The family reconciliation could not avert tragedy for the Ledyards, however. Their sudden marriage ended as abruptly as it began when John Ledyard died at sea at just thirty-five, leaving Abigail and their four children virtually penniless. As a widow, Abigail returned to Southold and to her parents. She remarried, but was widowed a second time and eventually became the proprietess of a well-known tavern in the center of town. Two of her children achieved notoriety. William was a Revolutionary War hero, a martyr killed in the infamous Battle of Groton Heights. John "the Traveler" became a truly extraordinary figure. A handsome, towheaded adventurer, John took part in three of the period's most ambitious expeditions: He explored the North American continent, ventured through the interior of Africa, and joined Captain Cook's third voyage to the Pacific (where he got tattoos in Tahiti that climbed up and down his hands and arms). He counted men like Thomas Jefferson and the Marquis de Lafayette among his friends, and his *Journal of Captain Cook's Last Voyage* (1783) has taken its place in the canon of American travel literature. He died in Eygpt at thirty-eight, having traveled a very long way from his shipwright great-grandfather's house along the banks of the Thames in just a few short decades.[28]

WHETHER IT was helping to mediate in the turmoil of the Great Awakening or in the wake of a granddaughter's elopement, Joshua Hempstead always felt a strong sense of duty toward his family and his town. With Adam's help in his later years, Joshua was able to devote considerable time to answering that powerful call to serve—whether through judicial work, town administration, the care of grandchildren, or visiting the afflicted. His large frame, slightly stooped with age, remained a regular sight in the vicinity, making frequent rounds "avisiting," bringing comfort and company to the ailing and aged, even as his own health weakened and physical prowess waned. Among the varied duties and services he fulfilled was a special obligation to the Winthrops. As a New Londoner and New Englander, Joshua recognized a distinct duty toward this first family of New England. When John Winthrop IV left for England in 1726, he left his family, and particularly his wife, Anne, in a difficult bind. Anne Winthrop was wealthy and privileged, but her husband's assets were tied up in land, leaving her perpetually cash strapped. John IV remained reluctant to sell property out of the estate, so the family was inevitably entangled in ill-managed and uncertain tenancy arrangements that seemed to leave all parties feeling cheated.[29]

As a woman, Anne faced distinct disadvantages managing her husband's affairs. Aside from a lack of experience, she could not confront recalcitrant tenants personally, nor could a Winthrop wife appear in court time after time to represent her husband's interest without diminishing herself. John IV's expensive London lifestyle made matters considerably worse. In spite of her best efforts, Anne could not meet his constant need for cash. That did not prevent John IV from making persistent demands upon her and the estate, demands invariably laced with criticism of her management that greatly added to her anguish.[30]

John IV's success at cutting his sister and brother-in-law Lechmere out of Winthrop lands seemed to have given him little satisfaction. Instead, his dual sense of entitlement and grievance appeared to grow with the years. While he continued to enjoy life in London, relishing his election to the Royal Society, his family wrote him plaintive letters filled with expressions of loyalty and heartbreak. When he bothered to respond, John IV ranted about "all the troubles and abuses I have met with in the world" and liberally sprinkled comments about their lack of duty and appreciation.[31]

After he was gone eight years, his wife, Anne, went to visit relatives and children in Massachusetts, seeking a modest respite from the trials of maintaining the family at home. Upon hearing this,

John IV denounced her disloyalty, even though she had remained the exemplar of steadfast devotion. His letter of reprimand was so cruel, in fact, that their daughter Nanny (Anne junior), whom her father had not written in an age, put pen to paper to defend her heart-sick mother: "My Mother has been a constant observer of her duty always desirous to please you ever feared to offend you and if she has gone contrary to the least of your commands, there has been some circumstance that absolutely required it."[32]

After ten years' absence, it fell again to Nanny to beg her father to come home—not for herself—but now "for my dear brother John [Still] who wants nothing so much as the instruction and direction of a kind father and now laments the loss of it more than ever." John Still, then a teen attending Yale, had been around six when his father left. But calls of fatherly obligation did not move John IV. In the eleventh year of his absence, John IV received another letter from his son-in-law Gurdon Saltonstall, Jr., the venerable minister's son and sometime slave trader who had since married John IV's daughter Rebecca. Gurdon had written several times and received no response; he now told his father-in-law of the grandchildren he had never met: "three hearty children, the eldest christened Gurdon, second Rebecca, and third Katherine, my spouse is in tolerable health awaiting every hour for the birth of another." Rebecca Winthrop Saltonstall had been "not a little weakened by constant child bearing, nursing etc." Gurdon also confirmed the universal good opinion of his mother-in-law, Anne Winthrop, "Madam is daily afflicted with respecting your landed estate & with what wonderful resolution and great good conduct she struggles thru them."[33]

A few weeks after Gurdon wrote this letter, the dutiful Madam Winthrop wrote her "dearest soul" how "no place or company can banish you from my mind." Their newest grandchild had since been born, and she took the opportunity to plead gently for his return. "Your daughter Saltonstall is brought to bed of a son, which I hear is named Winthrop. So your family increased every year . . . if you are not changed from that kind husband and tender father that you once were, I beg that by all the solemn loves and endearments between you and me and by your paternal affection and obligations, that you will no longer keep yourself at distance from us."[34]

John IV's response was to introduce his wife to his new business associate, the London merchant Samuel Sparrow, who would be coming to New England and should be treated well. Sparrow turned out to be just one in a series of commercial connections who inevitably ended up "betraying" and "cheating" him, as John IV would later complain.[35]

By 1738, Rebecca Winthrop Saltonstall had given birth to her sixth child, a son called Dudley. Her husband, Gurdon, wrote his land-rich father-in-law, dropping hints about a desire to enter husbandry to support his large family and a need for real property: Gurdon remained a merchant and trader. By 1741, after fifteen years' absence, John IV had a new scheme. He wanted his son John Still, now a Yale graduate but the same boy who had yearned for a father's care, to come to London and marry "a very agreeable young lady of a noble family . . . [with] a fortune of ten thousand pounds, and a fine woman of sense and ingenuity and an heiress." The match would never take place, but John Still's voyage to England created an opportunity for family and friends to write letters he could deliver by hand to their errant patriarch. Son-in-law Gurdon Saltonstall, Jr., wrote one with sorrowful news. After the birth of seven healthy children and "many wakeful nights and thoughtful days abt her future estate," John IV's daughter Rebecca Saltonstall had lost her senses and descended into madness, in which she remained nearly half a year. Again Gurdon begged for his father-in-law's return.[36]

A second letter came from a most faithful Winthrop retainer. Joshua Hempstead wrote John IV during a driving snowstorm, one of a handful of Hempstead letters to survive. He had watched Madam Winthrop struggle to raise her family and manage her husband's estate, and he probably had a great deal he would have liked to say. In the letter, Joshua shed the stilted diction of his diary, but he would still feel unable to speak his mind to a man of John IV's rank. Joshua's voice was instead fluid, florid—even long-winded—and the tone he struck was deferential, bordering on groveling. He would urge his social superior to do the right thing, but only in a most roundabout way: "I must be so bold as to beg leave to invite you to think a little on your own country; I need not tell you anything concerning your own affairs how your estate has been invaded (all round as I may say) almost in every quarter since you have left . . . nor the fatigues that your prudent consort hath had in preserving it." More than this gentle nudge the old shipwright felt unable to do. It was not his place to reprimand his betters.[37]

By 1745, after he had been nearly thirty years gone, the ramblings of John IV, a man who had always seen betrayal around every corner, seemed to descend nearly into paranoia and delusion. That year he wrote to his wife and children advising them never to sell a certain hill with stone lying in the open that was "really gold ore . . . the richest thing in the known world." It was left to daughter Nanny, who would never marry herself and would stay with her mother through old age and death, to express a last surviving gasp of frustration and disappointment toward John IV, though only indirectly. Writing to her brother John Still, who had joined his father in eating up family resources in London, Nanny again spoke not for herself but for her disconsolate "mother who is now left alone to go through business and troubles too heavy for her especially now in ye evening of her life when everything becomes more burdensome. After so many disappointed hopes and lost endeavors, the vigor, cheerfulness and courage of her mind is much weakened & her heart almost sunk in dispair of all worldly good."[38]

John IV never did return to his homeland, a place of which he once wrote: "O wicked and ungrateful New England to contrive and execute so much mischief to a family that was thy best friends. God will surely return all the evils that you designed to me sevenfold into your bosom but I am tired and quite sick of these follies and will endeavor to forget them." If he really had tried to move past accumulated slights and indignities, however, John IV had done a very poor job. He had been far better at forgetting about the seven children who grew up without him.[39]

This scion of the eminent Winthrop family had chosen to nurse fictitous wounds in the British capital for decades, while other New

England patriarchs overcame real ones much closer to home. In New London, John Jackson, a freedman the Winthrops considered barely human, had fought a marathon battle to bring his family together and had largely succeeded. Joshua Hempstead—a yeoman with whom the extended Winthrops could barely stomach eating a meal—had been bowed down by grief and widowerhood, but had poured enough love into his surviving children that it spilled over into grandchildren. John Winthrop IV, on the other hand, fruit of a once-great family, would never set eyes on any of his many grandchildren, and he would not have recognized his own progeny had he passed them in the street. He was dead by 1747. His long-suffering wife proved much sturdier than their daughter Nanny had feared. Within three years of John IV's death and at age sixty-six, Anne married the town physician and onetime schoolmaster Jeremiah Miller, the very same doctor who had nursed Abigail Hempstead on her deathbed. Madam Anne Winthrop Miller survived her first husband by almost thirty years, dying in the midst of the American Revolution.[40]

UNLIKE JOHN IV, John Jackson surely would have known any one of his children by sight, even though he had often had to live apart from them, in poverty and in servitude. As adults, several of the freed Jackson children chose to remain for life in the New London area. Adam, of course, was bound to Bream Cove, just as Miriam had been bound to Norwich. Jack and Jacob may have been a boat ride away in Newport, where they would have gone for work, but Hannah, who had been free since 1733, lived another twenty years in New London, probably as a local servingwoman. Her life ended quickly in 1753, probably from a massive stroke when she was "taken [during the day] with the Num palsie & Died in the Evening," as Joshua told in his diary. Peter Jackson, who had lost his first wife in 1734, also stayed. He may have remarried to "a negro woman Lois Jackson [who] owned the Covenant [and was B]abtized" in Mr. Adams's congregation in 1741. One of Peter's two daughters, Eunice, did not live to adulthood. Their uncle Adam, perhaps with his master, Joshua, may have attended the funeral of his niece in 1745 when, as Joshua himself wrote, "a Molato Girl buried about 16 yr old Peter Jacksons Daughter. [gan]gerene."[41]

Jerry Jackson, the child who had once been sold in the slave markets of Boston and who had survived alone in Framingham, seems to have managed to hold on to his freedom. He probably stayed in New London, working as a servant or day laborer. A possible trace of him appeared in November 1755, when Jerry would have been around forty-three. A Jeremiah Jackson volunteered to join the Second Connecticut Regiment under Capt. Ben-Adam Gallup in the French and Indian War, the American theater of the Seven Years' War, which embroiled New England in yet another conflict with French Canada. This could have been a different Jeremiah Jackson, but it was likely Adam's brother. The regiment was filled with New Londoners like Jerry, men like "Negro Cato" and "Negro Cesar" and no fewer than seventeen local comrades with Algonquin blood. These were all men with limited opportunities in New London to whom the prospect of pay and perhaps adventure might have been attractive. Jerry may appear old for military service, but his captain, Israel Putnam, was nearly forty during the same campaign. Putnam recruited Jeremiah Jackson personally, and he would later become one of Revolutionary America's leading military figures, a hero and strategist at the Battle of Bunker Hill. As a Connecticut volunteer in the French and Indian War, Jerry would have had to bring "suitable cloaths and a powderhorn and bullet pouch" before he could receive an initial bounty of forty-two shillings. He spent much of his service in the wilds north of Albany at Fort Edward, a primitive supply depot that overflowed with troops and disease, and a place reminiscent of his former master Livingston's Annapolis Royal. Among Jeremiah's regiment were two of Joshua's grandsons, William Roe and Clement, both sons of his daughter Abigail Minor. By 1759, Jeremiah Jackson had risen to the rank of sergeant. With the end of his military service, however, his trail runs cold.[42]

Like Adam at Bream Cove, Jackson brother Abner remained a slave all of his days—living an extraordinary life in its own right. Whether due to his skill as a cooper or another reason, he was never freed, his ownership instead passing from John Rogers, Jr., to his son

James Rogers. It was during James's ownership on a July day in 1753 when an experienced appraiser by the name of Joshua Hempstead came to look over the slave, then nearing fifty, and assessed him at the whopping sum of five hundred pounds. The old appraiser could compare the man to the brother he had owned and lived with for more than a quarter century. Joshua duly noted Abner's mastery of his craft, along with his physical condition, which must have been fine. In fact, the lawsuit that prompted Joshua's coming made evident that the cooper had remained strong and youthful at least into his forties, when he had developed a peculiar ailment: two bad sores, one on an elbow and the other "near his private parts."[43]

When Abner's condition became chronic, his master, James Rogers, had called in the well-respected New London physician and postmaster, Dr. Giles Goddard, to treat him. James Rogers felt that Goddard botched the work, however, and later accused the doctor of what amounted to malpractice—of maiming Abner and rendering him "ruined and spoiled" after lancing an unaffected shoulder made his right arm useless. Whether that was an accurate account is unclear. Goddard himself had a crippling case of gout that left him "decriped [decrepit]." Within a few years he would become bed-ridden, and he was dead by 1757. Perhaps gout made the doctor dangerously inept. But James Rogers's claims were also exaggerated (he had even described Abner as twenty-five at the time, though he had to have been over forty). At best his claims were premature. Given that Joshua appraised Abner at five hundred pounds only two years later, the cooper was anything but useless. Contrived or very real, Dr. Goddard's blunderings had illuminated a brief moment in Abner Jackson's life in slavery. Afterward the Jackson brother would again blend into the background of recorded, quotidian New London.[44]

Abner lived on, however. After serving John junior's son James, he then served John junior's grandson, another James—an entire lifetime at Mamacock. His brother Adam never lived to mouth the word "revolution," but Abner lived to see it with his own eyes. He greeted a new nation and even a new century, witnessing a time when the gradual emancipation of slaves became widespread across New England.[45]

By the 1770s slavery in New England and the Middle Atlantic was beginning to end incrementally through a combination of legislation, judicial decisions, constitutional measures, and individual manumissions, but the process would be long and painful for enslaved men and women. Before and during the War of Independence, Revolutionary ideologies of liberty and natural rights inspired some individual masters to manumit their slaves as John Rogers had done a century earlier. Others conditioned freedom on bondsmen taking part in the battle against Britain. In 1774, Connecticut passed a Nonimportation Act that prohibited the importation and sale of enslaved people within its borders, although exceptions were made and the law was sometimes evaded. After statehood, Connecticut joined with Pennsylvania, New York, New Jersey, and Rhode Island in passing gradual emancipation legislation that eked out slavery's end over another half century. Connecticut's Act Concerning Indian, Mulatto, and Negro Servants and Slaves of 1784 promised freedom to the children of slaves born after March of that year, but only once they reached the age of twenty-five and had spent half a lifetime in servitude. This abolition legislation was an attempt to balance property rights with a graduated end to slavery. Still, under its rules, no Connecticut slave would be freed before 1809. Massachusetts, New Hampshire, and Vermont, by contrast, embraced immediate abolition, although implementation was also variable there. It was not until 1848 that the Connecticut legislature finally enacted emancipation legislation and any Jackson descendants could be sure of freedom.[46]

Like slavery, the Rogerene movement that had gripped the Jackson family also lost ground toward the end of the eighteenth century. After the deaths of old John Rogers and John junior, the movement continued but would never regain its early momentum. Several branches had moved to New Jersey in the first half of the eighteenth century and continued there. It carried on among a few families in its native town, but by the early twentieth century the sect in New London was largely a historical artifact. Abner, too, the last living child of John and Joan Jackson, would become a relic of a disappearing world, an already distancing past. He would live until 1801, closing in on his one hundreth year. An aging bondsman, he would never be free, but he would have seen what the future held.

As Joshua Hempstead reached old age, he needed more and more help at home. While he could entrust Adam to do the work of the field with help from sons and hirelings, he relied on elderly women, respectable widows above sexual reproach, to live with him and keep house. Mary Hobbs was one such local widow, though in fact a mother of three who had divorced on the grounds of abandonment after her husband was presumed dead. Hobbs and Joshua had exchanged work from time to time over the years, she combing wool and Adam bringing her firewood in return. Then, when he was in his seventies, Joshua asked Hobbs to "come to live with me a while to do my house work for her houseroom & fire." The day after she arrived, in April 1750, Joshua helped her with her room, setting up her things. Both widow and widower had suffered terrible losses, and perhaps as Joshua worked, "helping Ms Hobbs Cord up her bed in the new chamber," they could offer each other comfort. There was at least a family feeling between them, as when Mary Hobbs had her eighteen-year-old son, John, join them to sup on a day of "publick Thanksgiving."[47]

Mary Hobbs left Bream Cove abruptly in 1752, "prest [by the Selectmen] to Nurse" a smallpox victim; she later buried the body in a pasture, bravely and alone, to avoid contaminating others, drawing "the Coffin with long Ropes on the ground." Older widows were a logical choice for such dangerous work. They were experienced healers and had no husband or child to care for at home. Hobbs was a particularly fitting choice. She had grown up at Mamacock alongside Adam Jackson's siblings. Perhaps in 1721, when she was just nineteen, she had acquired a hard-earned immunity when old John Rogers had come home from Boston during the epidemic and infected the compound. Hobbs had survived that terrible outbreak, which killed her father, aunt, and first cousin.

The widow Mary Hobbs was the daughter of old John Rogers and

Mary Ransford, the volatile English servant girl he had "married" long after his first divorce. Ransford had borne him two children: a son and a daughter. Mary was this girl. When Ransford fled to Block Island, John Rogers had kept Mary and her older brother and raised them at Mamacock. When, as a widow, Mary came to live at Bream Cove, she shared more than basic rooms and a fire. A common history connected her to Joshua's slave, a shared story that no one at Bream Cove, no family in New England, could escape.[48]

EPILOGUE

TOWARD THE end of the 1750s, a walk up the stairs on the "old" side of Joshua's house led to the shipwright's own chamber. In this simple, large room above the hall, the old shipwright slept and stored most of his personal belongings. A cupboard held two silver spoons, one of them an "old [one] markt I. A H.," back in its place after grandsons had sneaked in to "kindle . . . a fire up & Roast . . . Potatoes & play . . . a while in [his] Room" and [then] hidden it "or Else worse." Locked away in a trunk were some of Joshua's treasures. There were the precious turtle-shell spectacles in a fish-skin case that had once belonged to John Winthrop IV and a collection, carefully preserved, of black and purple gloves of the sort given to principal mourners at a funeral. In another locked trunk were a gold locket, a gold ring, and an amber necklace, along with a stash of silver coinage. What pieces of his relatively modest wardrobe that were not on his back or in the wash lay folded in another chest. Alongside the better items were osnaburg breeches, staple working pants of the kind worn by slaves in the Southern colonies. In yet another chest he stored his well-used surveying instruments.[1]

Near the light of a window stood Joshua's desk. In some of its locked drawers he kept important documents: deeds, surveys, court records, bonds, and even currency. The loose papers, following the custom of the law clerk, he folded into small rectangles, labeled with a careful hand and filed according to a method that rarely failed him. At this desk, Joshua was accustomed to write nearly every day and sometimes "all day," next to a small selection of books that included a Bible, some legal reference works, and a few printed sermons, those of Mr. Adams, in particular. He had a great deal to write—accounts, deeds, surveys, wills, bonds, summonses, and letters—and often he wrote for others and received a fee, but writing was hardly unpleasant to him. In words, at times, he could erase the awareness of the day as he memorialized it, reminding himself of a broader, divine plan.[2]

In the early winter of 1758, Joshua lay in his bed, its curtains pulled around for warmth, allowing only partial views of the chamber he had occupied most of his life. He had turned eighty the first of September but that had not prevented him from "mow[ing] . . . at Cros[s]m[an] lot" and going "down to the medows to carry Dinner for [freedman] Tomy [Bohan] & Ad[am] & 1 more Rakers of the Salt Hay att the gutt [a bay in Niantic]" that same month. In October he had gathered apples and helped to divide an estate, but many days he had spent quietly at home. On the twenty-eighth, while he was stacking corn tops "handl[ing] Every She[ave]" himself, the old shipwright felt "a pain in my Bowels." The next day was a Sabbath, but he felt too unwell to attend meeting. Two days later he managed to go out and lend Adam and Tommy Bohan a hand unloading salt hay, but the effort landed him back in bed. He would never leave the house again. For three days, he still managed to make short accounts in his diary. On the fourth he could write no more.[3]

Joshua's middle daughter, Betty Starr, "[Stood] by [him]." Though she was a wife and mother, to her dying father Betty was still the same little girl he had watched painfully float away to Long Island after her mother was taken from them. Betty now cared for her father, leaning over and wiping the perspiration from his brow with a damp cloth. She tried to spoon cornmeal sweetened with milk and honey into his mouth, to help him wash it down with a sip of rum, but the old man, "Exceeding Sore in [his] Bowels," had little stomach for it. After lying in bed more than two months, Joshua Hempstead died on December 22, 1758. His children and grandchildren buried him the next day.[4]

New London's first newspaper had been in operation just three months when Joshua died; it was the latest attempt to bring the outside world to the scruffy little port that had remained so stubbornly provincial. The paper took pains to celebrate Joshua's life, giving the beloved local leader a formal obituary: "a useful Friend, a promoter of Peace, and a valuable Member of Society. In all the publick Offices he sustained, his Conduct was unexceptionable; he acted with uniform Integrity, and preserved an unblemished Character." The words would have pleased their subject not a little. A few weeks earlier Joshua had given himself an inadvertent epitaph in the last entry of his diary: "I keep house Still."[5]

Joshua's will made no mention of his slave of more than thirty years: the "old Negro man named Adam," as the estate inventory described him. Joshua had written scores of testamentary instruments, so the omission was surely intentional. Less deliberate was the final, fitting enigma it also created—another blank space between these lives intertwined and forever beyond reach. Manumitting a slave was still uncommon in midcentury New England—uncommon enough that Joshua might not have even considered freeing Adam. Nor was emancipation, especially for a long-serving man on the verge of old age, an unambiguous good. Elderly freedmen faced lives of singular struggle and privation, as Adam well knew, and freedom could throw moral and legal entitlement to care by a master into question.[6]

Joshua probably shared his intentions toward Adam with his son and neighbor John, the blacksmith he chose as his executor. It is with John that Adam apparently remained, at least in part, perhaps splitting his time between John's household and the one he knew better than any other. There sailor-turned-husbandman Stephen Hempstead continued to live for a few years after his father's death while he finished his own house nearby. Only then did Joshua's grandson Josh—the new owner of the old Hempstead house at Bream Cove and the same boy once schooled in husbandry and companionship by Adam—move in with his family.[7]

When Joshua's diary fell silent, the window onto Adam's life, never more than ajar, now closed tightly. Then, in 1760, a new name appeared on the New London tax rolls: Adam Jackson, free man, with a minimal estate of eighteen pounds. Within four years, his name had disappeared. When Adam died, as he probably did in 1764, he left neither estate nor children, probably not even a stone to mark his grave. Had John Hempstead decided to free him after his father was gone? Or had Joshua, the meticulous chronicler, arranged this ending before he died—if not how the ending might be read? Was Joshua the "fatherly" master who freed a dutiful slave while still providing for his care? Or was he the callous owner trying to spare his heirs the expense of an old and worthless bondsman? Or somewhere in between. Or perhaps it had been Adam Jackson, the proud and manifest son of John and Joan Jackson, who had seized the means of his own liberation and would not let go.

ACKNOWLEDGMENTS

THE DEBTS I have incurred in realizing this book are great. Chief among these is the inestimable one I owe to family and friends, who have given me their unflagging support and encouragement.

This book, and the dissertation that preceded it, received generous and invaluable institutional support from Connecticut Landmarks, the Gilder Lehrmann Foundation, the Mellon Foundation, New York University School of Law, the Pew Foundation, the William Nelson Cromwell Foundation, Yale Law School, and Yale University. It drew on the vital work and resources of archivists, librarians, and record keepers in the Connecticut State Library, the Gilder Lehrmann Collection, the Hempsted House Archives, the New London County Historical Society, the New London City Clerk's Office, the New London Probate Office, the Connecticut Historical Society, and the Massachusetts Historical Society. It also stands on the broad shoulders of nineteenth-century antiquarians and twentieth-century geneaologists who make this sort of family history possible.

For their professional support and friendship, I give special thanks to Ellen Cohn, Bob Gordon, Paul Grant-Costa, Bill Keegan, William McFeely, George Priest, Alice Prochaska, Patricia Schaefer, Bruce Stark, Mark Weiner, Jim Whitman, and Lisa Wilson. No one spurs me on more in a mutual love of history than Rob Campbell. From Mary Elizabeth Baker and Sally Ryan, I learned things about Joshua and New London that I could never have discovered on my own. Since the book's very academic beginnings, Elyse Cheney saw its promise and gave it entrée to a world I never thought possible. Because of her I had the great good fortune of having my editor, Bob Weil, choose me—and then of being able to choose him in return. The book and I have benefited from his guidance, vision, and patience every step of the way. When Katie Adams joined the project, she gave indispensable advice and insight—I owe chapter 13 to her. Working with Alice Truax has been my own little "great awakening."

I have a particular obligation to two scholars who privileged me with their mentorship as members of my Ph.D. committee. Jon Butler took a risk, taking me on without knowing me, and has always been one step ahead in appreciating the potential lurking in Joshua's diary. Learning about material culture from Ned Cooke changed my life.

John Demos—adviser, teacher, mentor, friend—he believed in this project, and in me, when there was every reason to doubt. I hope that what we made, for Adam's sake, pleases him.

❧ FAMILY TREES ❧

HEMPSTEAD FAMILY

Robert Hempstead (ca.1613–1655), born in Steeple Bumpstead, Essex, England, m. Joane?

Children of Robert Hempstead and Joane? (grandparents of diarist):
Mary (1647–1711), m. Robert Douglas (1639–1716).
Joshua (1649–89), m. Elizabeth Larrabee (1652–1727) [Elizabeth married (2) John Edgecombe (d. 1721)]. John Edgecombe's daughter Sarah married John Bolles, the lone survivor of the Bolles family massacre of 1675.
Hannah (1652–1720), m. (1) Abel Moore; (2) Samuel Waller.

Children of Joshua Hempstead, Sr., and Elizabeth Larrabee (parents of diarist):
Phoebe (1670–died in infancy).
Elizabeth (1670–70).
Elizabeth (1672–1733), m. John Plumb.
Mary (1675–1751), m. Green Plumb (divorced).
Phoebe (1676–1725), mentally disabled from birth.
Joshua junior (diarist) (1678–1758), m. Abigail Bailey (1677–1716), daughter of Stephen Bailey (ca. 1652–1715) and Abigail Cooper (ca. 1655–1712) of Southold, New York. Joshua owned Adam Jackson from 1727 to 1758.
Hannah (1681–99), m. John Edgecombe, Jr. (her stepbrother).
Patience (168?–1725), m. (1) Thomas Ross; (2) James Hodsell.
Lucy (1682–1749), m. Jonathan Hartshorn.

Child of Elizabeth Larrabee Hempstead (mother of diarist)
and John Edgecombe, Sr.:
Thomas Edgecombe (1694–1745), m. Katherine Copp (1692–1742). They
lived in Norwich, Connecticut.

Children of Joshua Hempstead (diarist) and Abigail Bailey:
Joshua (1699–1716).
Nathaniel (1701–29), m. Mary (Molly) Hallam, daughter of Nicholas
Hallam and Sarah Pygan [Molly married (2) Joseph Truman
(Hempstead next-door neighbor)].
Robert (1702–79), m. Mary Youngs of Southold, New York. They had
nine children, including Abigail (1727–?), m. (1) John Ledyard of
Groton, Connecticut (her first cousin).
Stephen (1705–74), m. Sarah Holt (daughter of Hempstead neighbor
William Holt). They had nine children.
Thomas (1708–29).
John (1709–78), m. Hannah Salmon (his first cousin), daughter of
William Salmon and Hannah Bailey (sister of Abigail Bailey
Hempstead) of Southold, New York. They had six children; only three
survived childhood.
Abigail (1712–?), m. Clement Minor of Stonington, Connecticut. They
had ten children.
Elizabeth (Betty) (1714–1776), m. Daniel Starr (son of Hempstead
neighbor Benjamin Starr). They had eight (?) children.
Mary (Molly) (1716–?), m. Thomas Pierpont of Stonington, Connecticut,
and Boston, Massachusetts. They had ten children.

Children of Nathaniel Hempstead and Mary (Molly) Hallam:
Joshua (Josh) (1724–1806), m. Lydia Burch. They had eight children.
Nathaniel (Natty) (1727–91), m. Hannah Booth. They had six children.
Mary (Molly) (1729–1811), m. Christopher Eldridge of Stonington,
Connecticut. They had three children.

JACKSON FAMILY

Maria (1650s?–90s?), born in the West Indies or perhaps Africa.

Child of Maria and an unknown English colonist:
Joan (ca. 1679/80–1730), m. John Jackson (ca. 1668–1737), born in the
West Indies or perhaps Africa.

Children of John Jackson and Joan, daughter of Maria:
Adam (ca. 1700–64).
Miriam (ca. 1702/3–after 1732), m. Cuff (enslaved to [1] Samuel and
Bathshua Fox; [2] Nathaniel Lathrop). They had two children.
Abner (ca. 1703/10–1801).
Hannah (ca. 1703/10–53).
Peter (ca. 1703/10–after 1735), m. (1) Hagar (enslaved to Elizabeth Tongue
"Winthrop"), (2) Lois? Peter and Hagar had two daughters, Eunice
and Rose.
John junior (Jack) (ca. 1708–?).
Rachel (ca. 1711–12).
Jeremiah (Jerry) (ca. 1712/13–?).
Jacob (ca. 1717–?).

LIVINGSTON FAMILY

Robert Livingston (1654–1728), son of the Rev. John Livingstone (1603–72)
and Janet Fleming (1613–94), born in Ancram, Scotland,
m. Alida Schuyler (1656–1729), widow of Nicholas Van Rensselaer.

Children of Robert Livingston and Alida Schuyler Van Rensselaer:
John/Johannes (1680–1720), m. (1) Mary Winthrop (ca. 1676–1713);
(2) Elizabeth Knight (d. 1736), daughter of Richard Knight and Sarah
Kemble (1666–1727).
Margaret (1681–1758), m. Samuel Vetch (1668–1732), son of the Rev.
William Veitch and Marion Fairly. Only their daughter Alida survived;
she married Stephen Bayard and had seven children.
Johanna Philippina (1684–90).
Philip (1686–1749), Second Lord of Livingston Manor, m. Catherine/
Catrina Van Brugh.
Robert (1688–1775), m. Margaret Howarden.
Gilbert/Hubertus (1690–1746), m. Cornelia Beekman (1693–1742).
William (1692–92).
Johanna (1694–1734), m. Cornelius Van Horne (1694–1752).
Catherine/Catrina (1698–99).

ROGERS FAMILY

James Rogers, Sr. (ca. 1615–87), born in England,
m. Elizabeth Rowland (ca. 1621–ca. 1709).

Children of James Rogers, Sr., and Elizabeth Rowland:
Samuel (ca. 1640–1713), m. (1) Mary Stanton; (2) Joanna Williams.
First English settler in the North Parish.
Joseph (1646–1728), m. Sarah ____.
Lived on the General Neck.
John (1648–1721), m. Elizabeth Griswold (ca. 1652–1727), daughter of
Matthew Griswold and Ann Wolcott of Lyme, Connecticut (divorced);
(2) Mary Ransford ("married" in county court) (separated) [Ransford
married (2) Robert Jones of Block Island, Rhode Island]; (3) Sarah
Coles, widow, of Oyster Bay, New York. [Elizabeth Griswold
Rogers married (2) Peter Pratt (d. 1688), with whom she had a son,
Peter; (3) Matthew Beckwith, Jr. (1637–1727), widower, of Lyme,
Connecticut.] Founder of the Rogerenes.
Bathshua/Bathsheba (1650–1711); m. (1) Richard Smith (ca. 1640?–ca.
1682); (2) Samuel Fox (1651–1727).
James (1652–ca. 1713), m. Mary Jordan.
Jonathan (1656–97), m. Naomi Burdick.
Elizabeth (1658–1716), m. Samuel Beebe of New London and Southold,
New York.

Children of John Rogers, Sr., and Elizabeth Griswold:
Elizabeth (1671–1737); m. Stephen Prentice (1666–1758), son of John and
Hester Prentice. Elizabeth joined the Congregational Church in 1693.
John junior (1674–1753); m. Bathshua (his first cousin) (16??–1721),
daughter of Bathshua Rogers Smith Fox and Richard Smith;
(2) Elizabeth Dodge.

Children of John Rogers, Sr., and Mary Ransford:
Gershom (1700–?), m. Sarah Wheeler of Groton, Connecticut. Gershom
was a shipbuilder.
Mary (1702–81), m. John Hobbs (1704–51), son of John Hobbs of Boston,
Massachusetts.

WINTHROP FAMILY

John Winthrop, Sr. (1587–1649), born in Edwardstone, Suffolk, England,
m. (1) Mary Forth (1583–1615), (2) Thomasine Clopton,
(3) Margaret Tyndale, (4) Martha Rainsborough, widow.
First governor of Massachusetts Bay Colony.

Children of John Winthrop, Sr., and Mary Forth:
John junior (1606–1676), born in Groton, Suffolk, England, m. (1) Martha
Fones (16??–1634), (2) Elizabeth Reade, daughter of Edmund Reade
of Wickford, Essex, England (16??–1672). Founder of New London;
governor of Connecticut.
Henry (1607–30), born in Groton, England, drowned in Massachusetts,
m. Elizabeth Fones.
Forth (1609–30).
Mary (ca. 1612), died young?
Anne (1614–14).
Anne (1615–15).

Children of John Winthrop, Jr., and Elizabeth Reade:
Fitz-John (Fitz) (1638–1707), born in Ipswich, Massachusetts, common-
law marriage with Elizabeth Tongue (1653–1731), daughter of George
Tongue of New London, Connecticut. Governor of Connecticut
(1697–1707).
Wait Still (1642–1717), m. (1) Mary Browne (1656–1690), daughter of
William Browne of Salem, Massachusetts, (2) widow of John Eyre?
Chief justice of Massachusetts; judge of the Court of Admiralty; major
general of the Colonial Militia.
Martha (b. 1646).
Margaret (b. 1648).
Anne (b. 1650).

Child of Fitz Winthrop and Elizabeth Tongue:
Mary (ca. 1676–1713), m. John Livingston (1680–1720), son of Robert Livingston and Alida Schuyler. Mary and John had no children.

Children of Wait Winthrop and Mary Browne:
John IV (1681–1747), m. Anne Dudley (1684–1776), daughter of Joseph
Dudley (1647–1720), governor of Massachusetts, and Rebecca Tyng
[Anne m. (2) Jeremiah Miller, Sr., of New London], died in Sydenham,
Kent, England.

Ann (1686–1746), m. Thomas Lechmere (1683–1765), son of Edmund
Lechmere (1648–1703) of Hanley Castle, Worcester, England, and Lucy
Hungerford (1649–1729), daughter of Anthony Hungerford of Farley
Castle, Somerset, England. Thomas was the brother of Nicholas, Lord
Lechmere, who married Lady Elizabeth Howard (1701–39), daughter
of Charles Howard, Earl of Carlisle. Ann and Thomas had eight
children, four of whom survived to adulthood. Richard (1727–ca. 1814)
and Nicholas (1722–bef. 1809) (customs official at New London and
Newport, Rhode Island). Nicholas married Elizabeth Gardiner (1722–
89), whom he left in Newport when he fled to England as a Loyalist
in the Revolution, along with his brother Richard. Both brothers were
banished and their estates confiscated. They died in England.
John, died in infancy.
Elizabeth, died in infancy.
William, died in childhood.
Joseph, died in childhood.

Children of John Winthrop IV and Anne Dudley:
Mary (1708–67), m. Joseph Wanton, Governor of Rhode Island.
Ann (Nanny) (1709–94), never married.
Katherine (1711–81), m. (1) Samuel Browne of Salem, Massachusetts,
(2) Epes Sargeant of Gloucester, Massachusetts.
Rebecca (1713–76), m. Gurdon Saltonstall, Jr. (1708–85), son of the
Rev. Gurdon Saltonstall (1666–1724), minister of New London and
governor of Connecticut (1708–1724) and Elizabeth Rosewell (1679–
1710). They had fourteen children.
Elizabeth (ca. 1714/15), died in infancy.
John (1716–16), died in infancy.
Margaret (1719–1803), m. Jeremiah Miller, Jr. (1719–97), of New London,
Connecticut.
John Still (1720–76), m. (1) Jane Borland (ca. 1732–60), daughter of
Francis Borland, (2) Elizabeth Shirreffe, widow of Capt. John Hay.
Basil (1722–76), never married.

SOURCES: Frances M. Caulkins, *History of New London, Connecticut, from
the First Survey of the Coast in 1612, to 1860* (New London, CT: H. D. Utley,
1895; reprint 1985), pp. 201–21; William Freeman Fox, *Thomas Fox of Concord and His Descendants* (Albany, NY: J. B. Lyon Co., 1909), pp. 18–22;
"Gleanings (No. 22)," *New England Historical and Genealogoical Register*
13 (1859), pp. 302–303; Joshua Hempstead, *The Diary of Joshua Hempstead:
A Daily Record of Life in New London, Connecticut, 1711–1758* (New London, CT: New London County Historical Society, 1999), pp. vi–vii; Edwin

Brockholst Livingston, *The Livingstons of Livingston Manor* (New York: Knickerbocker Press, 1910), pp. 539–43; Joseph James Muskett and Robert Charles Winthrop, *Evidences of the Winthrops of Groton, County Suffolk* (privately printed, 1894–96); James Swift Rogers, *James Rogers of New London, Ct.: And His Descendants* (Boston: James Swift Rogers, 1902), pp. 38–68; James M. Rose and Barbara W. Brown, *Tapestry: A Living History of the Black Family in Southeastern Connecticut* (New London, CT: New London County Historical Society, 1979), pp. 75–77; James H. Stark, *The Loyalists of Massachusetts* (Boston: James H. Stark, 1910), pp. 413–414; G. M. Waller, *Samuel Vetch: Colonial Enterpriser* (Chapel Hill: University of North Carolina Press, 1960), pp. 4–5, 284; Elizabeth P. Whitten, comp., "Hempsteads of New London" (typescript, 1984), New London County Historical Society; author's research.

NOTES

Introduction

1. Samuel Sewall, *Diary of Samuel Sewall*, vol. 3, in Collections of the Massachusetts Historical Society (hereafter MHS), 5th series, vols. 5–7 (Boston: MHS, 1878–1882); Francis G. Walett, ed., *The Diary of Ebenezer Parkman, 1703–1782: First Part, Three Volumes in One, 1719–1755* (Worcester, MA: American Antiquarian Society, 1974). The diary of John May is similar to Joshua's: John May, *Diary, 1708–1766*, American Antiquarian Society. A similar almanac-style diary from a later period is that of New Hampshire tanner Samuel Lane: Jerald E. Brown, ed., *The Years of the Life of Samuel Lane, 1718–1806: A New Hampshire Man and His World* (Hanover, NH: University Press of New England, 2000).

2. The New London County Historical Society (hereafter NLCHS) published a new edition of the diary in 1999 and Patricia Schaefer's *A Useful Friend: A Companion to the Joshua Hempstead Diary, 1711–1758* in 2008. Of the three sections transcribed and published by the NLCHS in 1901, one subsequently went missing. It resurfaced in 2011, at which time it was purchased by the NLCHS. A number of scholars have used the Hempstead diary for topical case studies, e.g., Judith M. Adkins, "Bodies and Boundaries: Animals in the Early American Experience" (Ph.D. diss., Yale University, 1998); Richard D. Brown, *Knowledge Is Power: The Diffusion of Information in Early America, 1700–1865* (New York: Oxford University Press, 1989); Ernest Caufield, "Connecticut Gravestones XII: John Hartshorn (1650–ca. 1738) vs. Joshua Hempstead (1678–1758)," *Connecticut Historical Society Bulletin* 32 (1967): 65–79; Allen I. Ludwig, *Graven Images: New England Stonecarving and Its Symbols, 1650–1815* (Middletown, CT: Wesleyan University Press, 1966); Joanne P. Melish, *Disowning Slavery: Gradual Emancipation and "Race" in New England, 1780–1860* (Ithaca: Cornell University Press, 1998).

3. Laurel Thatcher Ulrich's *A Midwife's Tale: The Life of Martha Ballard, Based on Her Diary, 1785–1812* (New York: Vintage Books, 1990) was an inspiration for this book. Before *A Midwife's Tale*, Kenneth A. Lockridge and David D. Hall also produced two extraordinary examples of diurnal interpretation from colonial America: Kenneth A. Lockridge, *The Diary, and Life, of William Byrd II of Virginia, 1674–1744* (Chapel Hill: University of North Carolina Press, 1987); David D. Hall, "The Mental World of Samuel Sewall," in *Saints & Revolutionaries: Essays on Early American History*, ed. David D. Hall, John M. Murrin, and Thad W. Tate (New York: W. W. Norton, 1984), pp. 213–46. See also Alan Macfarlane, *The Family Life of Ralph Josselin: A Seventeenth-Century Clergyman* (New York: W. W. Norton, 1977).

4. Ira Berlin, *Many Thousands Gone: The First Two Centuries of Slavery in North America* (Cambridge, MA: Harvard University Press, 1998), p. 58. See Melish, *Disowning Slavery*.

5. Berlin, *Many Thousands Gone*, pp. 17–28.

6. There is a small number of autobiographical accounts of Connecticut slaves, including those of Venture Smith and James Mars: Arna Bontemps, ed., *Five Black Lives: The Autobiographies of Venture Smith, James Mars, William Grimes, G. W. Offley and James L. Smith* (Middletown, CT: Wesleyan University Press, 1958).

7. Historians have not ignored the Jacksons. See, e.g., Catherine Adams and Elizabeth H. Pleck, *Love of Freedom: Black Women in Colonial and Revolutionary New England* (New York: Oxford University Press, 2010), pp. 127, 131–35, 241; James M. Rose and Barbara W. Brown, *Tapestry: A Living History of the Black Family in Southeastern Connecticut* (New London, CT: NLCHS, 1979), pp. 6–8.

Chapter One: "As in the Beginning of the World"

1. Joshua Hempstead, *The Diary of Joshua Hempstead: A Daily Record of Life in New London, Connecticut, 1711–1758* (New London, CT: NLCHS, 1999) (hereafter *DJH*), vi, 343 (21 February 1739), 448 (5 February 1746), 593 (15 May 1753); Frances M. Caulkins, *History of New London, Connecticut, from the First Survey of the Coast in 1612, to 1860* (New London, CT: H. D. Utley, 1895; reprint, 1985), p. 72.

2. Inventory of the Goods of Robert Hempstead, November 17, 1654, Hempsted House Archives (hereafter HHA); Aldren A. Watson, *The Blacksmith: Ironworker and Farrier*, paperback ed. (New York: W. W. Norton, 2000), pp. 10–11, 93.

3. Charles Molyneux Holloway, "Historic New London," *New England Magazine* 5 (1886): 119–40, 122–23; Caulkins, *History of New London*, pp. 47, 51; Eva L. Butler (hereater ELB) Transcripts, Box 1, Miscellaneous New London Land Records, New London Land Records, vol. 3, pp. 9–10; John Winthrop, Jr., to John Winthrop, Sr., January 17, 1649, in *The Winthrop Papers*, MHS, 5th series, vol. 8 (Boston: MHS, 1882), p. 40.

4. Although Robert's movements prior to arriving in New London are uncertain, most genealogists consider this is the most likely scenario. See, for example,

Charles Edward Banks, "Notes from Genealogical Gleanings," MSS H–M, folio 689, Hempstead, Library of Congress.

5. Caulkins, *History of New London*, pp. 92, 108–11. This cluster included the house of the minister, Mr. Simon Bradstreet: Frances M. Caulkins, *Ye Antient Buriall Place of New London, Connecticut* (New London, CT: Day Publishing, 1899), p. 29. For the centripetal orbit of New England towns, see John R. Silgoe, *Common Landscape of America, 1580–1845* (New Haven, CT: Yale University Press, 1982), p. 53.

6. Caulkins, *History of New London*, pp. 59–60, 86; George Chandler, *The Chandler Family: The Descendants of William and Annis Chandler* . . . (Worcester, MA: Press of Charles Hamilton, 1883), p. 53.

7. David Grayson Allen, *In English Ways: The Movement of Societies and the Transferal of English Local Law and Custom to Massachusetts Bay in the Seventeenth Century* (Chapel Hill: University of North Carolina Press, 1981), pp. 9–11; Robert did not baptize his son, Joshua, until February 12, 1670, when Robert had his infant daughter baptized with himself and his wife: S. Leroy Blake, *The Later History of the First Church of Christ, New London, Connecticut* (New London, CT: Press of the Day Publishing, 1900), p. 445; Inventory of the Goods of Robert Hempstead, November 17, 1654, HHA.

8. Don A. Sanford, *A Choosing People: The History of Seventh Day Baptists* (Nashville: Boardman Press, 1992), pp. 37–38; Samuel Danforth, *A Brief Recognition of New Englands [sic] Errand into the Wilderness* (Cambridge, MA: Printed by S. G. and M. F., 1671).

9. Sanford, *A Choosing People*, pp. 37–38.

10. Morris Aaron Gutstein, *To Bigotry No Sanction: A Jewish Shrine in America, 1658–1958* (New York: Bloch Publishing Company, 1958), pp. 24–26.

11. Robert C. Black, *The Younger John Winthrop*, 2nd ed. (New York: Columbia University Press, 1968), pp. 1–138; Margaret Mather Byard, *Books in the Wilderness*, the Winthrop Collection at the New York Society Library, www.nysoclib .org/winthrop.html (accessed January 27, 2006), p. 2.

12. Walter Woodward, *Prospero's America: John Winthrop, Jr., Alchemy, and the Creation of New England Culture, 1606–1676* (Chapel Hill: University of North Carolina Press, 2010), pp. 14–74, 161–62; Byard, *Books in the Wilderness*, pp. 3–4.

13. Richard S. Dunn, *Puritans and Yankees: The Winthrop Dynasty of New England, 1630–1717* (New York: W. W. Norton, 1971), pp. 64–65; Craig Yirush, *Settlers, Liberty, and Empire: The Roots of Early American Political Theory, 1675–1775* (New York: Cambridge University Press, 2011), p. 114; Paul J. Grant-Costa, "The Last Indian War in New England: The Mohegan Tribe of Indians vs. the Governour Company of Connecticut, 1703–1774," (Ph.D. diss., Yale University, 2008), pp. 23–24.

14. Jackson Turner Main, *Society and Economy in Colonial Connecticut* (Princeton, NJ: Princeton University Press, 1985), pp. 4–6.

15. Caulkins, *History of New London*, pp. 189–90; Holloway, "Historic New London," 122.

16. Kevin A. McBride, "'Ancient and Crazie': Pequot Lifeways during the

Historic Period," in *Algonkians of New England: Past and Present*, Dublin Seminar for New England Folklife, ed. Peter Benes (Boston: Boston University, 1991), pp. 63–75, 64; Thomas Franklin Waters and Robert Charles Winthrop, Jr., *A Sketch of the Life of John Winthrop the Younger . . .* , Publications of the Ipswich Historical Society, vol. 7 (Cambridge, MA: University Press, 1899), pp. 34, 41.

17. John Winthrop, Jr., to Henry Oldenburg, November 12, 1668, *Winthrop Papers*, vol. 8, p. 133.

18. Holloway, "Historic New London," pp. 123, 125–26.

19. Woodward, *Prospero's America*, pp. 113–14; Caulkins, *History of New London*, p. 70; *Winthrop Papers*, vol. 8, pp. 10, 46, 67, 408, 532; *Winthrop Papers*, MHS, 6th series, vol. 3 (Boston: MHS, 1888), pp. 6, 25, 32, 46, 415, 503; C. S. Manegold, *Ten Hills Farm: The Forgotten History of Slavery in the North* (Princeton, NJ: Princeton University Press, 2010), pp. 75–76.

20. Woodward, *Prospero's America*, pp. 113–14, 189–90; Rebecca Tannenbaum, *The Healer's Calling: Women and Medicine in Early New England* (Ithaca, NY: Cornell University Press, 2002), pp. 10–11, 77–84. For later generations still producing and supplying rubila, see John Winthrop IV to Wait Winthrop, January 23 or 30, 1712, *Winthrop Papers* microfilm, Reel 18; Wait Winthrop to John Winthrop IV, May 6, 1717, *Winthrop Papers* microfilm, Reel 18.

21. Byard, *Books in the Wilderness*, p. 2; Woodward, *Prospero's America*, p. 70; Dunn, *Puritans and Yankees*, pp. 75–76.

22. Lawrence H. Leder, *Robert Livingston, 1654–1728, and the Politics of Colonial New York* (Chapel Hill: University of North Carolina Press, 1961), pp. 3–7; John Livingstone, "The Life of Mr. John Livingstone . . . ," in *Select Biographies Edited for the Wodrow Society*, ed. Rev. W. K. Tweedie, vol. 1 (Edinburgh: Wodrow Society, 1845), pp. 127–98, pp. 190–92.

23. Livingstone, "Life of Mr. John Livingstone," p. 192.

24. Ibid., p. 193.

25. Ibid., p. 197; Leder, *Robert Livingston*, pp. 7–11.

26. Leder, *Robert Livingston*, pp. 3–21; Cynthia A. Kierner, *Traders and Gentlefolk: The Livingstons of New York, 1675–1790* (Ithaca, NY: Cornell University Press, 1992), pp. 39–41; Bruce E. Naramore, "Introduction," in *The Livingston Legacy: Three Centuries of American History*, ed. Richard T. Wiles (Annandale-on-Hudson, NY: Bard College, 1987), p. 6. See Daniel K. Richter, *Facing East from Indian Country: A Native History of Early America* (Cambridge, MA: Harvard University Press, 2001), pp. 129–49.

27. James Swift Rogers, *James Rogers of New London, Ct.: And His Descendants* (Boston: James Swift Rogers, 1902), pp. 28–29; Caulkins, *History of New London*, p. 152; Holloway, "Historic New London," 129.

28. Robert Blair St. George, "Set Thine House in Order: The Domestication of the Yeomanry in Seventeenth-Century New England," in *New England Begins: The Seventeenth Century*, ed. Robert F. Trent et al., vol. 2 (Boston: Museum of Fine Arts, 1982), pp. 159–86, p. 166; Holloway, "Historic New London," 129; Dunn, *Puritans and Yankees*, p. 105; Anna B. Williams, "A History of the Rogerenes," in *The Rogerenes: Some Hitherto Unpublished Annals belonging to the Colonial His-*

tory of Connecticut (Boston: Stanhope Press, 1904), pp. 121–341, 121–23; Caulkins, *History of New London*, pp. 201–2; Susan C. Kim, "Mr. Rogers's Neighborhood: Religious Dissent in New London, 1674–1721" (Ph.D. diss., University of California, 2006), pp. 33–35; Lila Parrish Lyman, *The New London Homestead of the Winthrop Family* (Stonington, CT: Pequot Press, 1957), p. 3. The Winthrop mansion built by the Newport architect Peter Harrison in 1752–54 (since demolished) was located on the site of the original Rogers house.

29. Caulkins, *History of New London*, pp. 316, 328, 337.

30. Dunn, *Puritans and Yankees*, pp. 192–99.

31. Ibid., pp. 195–205, 201–2; Caulkins, *History of New London*, pp. 189–90, 199–206.

32. Caulkins, *History of New London*, pp. 91–92; Denise Schenk Grosskopf, "The Limits of Religious Dissent in Seventeenth-Century Connecticut" (Ph.D. diss., University of Connecticut, 1999), pp. 9, 35–41; Holloway, "Historic New London," 129; R. B. Wall, "Stories of Waterford: Echoes of Stormy Days," *New London Day* (hereafter *NLD*), June 9, 1915; Williams, "History of the Rogerenes," pp. 124, 153. Present-day Waterford is the only locality in colonial Connecticut that did not have its own Congregational parish.

33. Kim, "Mr. Rogers's Neighborhood," pp. 35–37; Ellen Starr Brinton, "The Rogerenes," *New England Quarterly* (hereafter *NEQ*) 16 (1943): 2–19; *Samuel Rogers v. John Rogers*, New London County Superior Court Records (hereafter NLCSCR), Files, Box 7, File of March 1737; Attachment (of the estates of Samuel Beebe, John Rogers, Jr., and Samuel Fox, Sr.) in *James Rogers, Jr. v. Beebe et al.*, New London County County Court records (hereafter NLCCCR), Files, Box 156, File of November 1711. Much of the old Rogers property is now the Harkness Memorial State Park.

34. Caulkins, *History of New London*, pp. 175–77; Harriet C. Chesebrough, *Glimpses of Saybrook in Colonial Days* (Saybrook, CT: Celebration 3 1/2, 1984), p. 25; Sophia Fidelia Hall Coe, *Memoranda relating to the Ancestry and Family of Sophia Fidelia Hall* (Meriden, CT: Curtiss-Way, 1902), pp. 151–53.

35. Rogers, *James Rogers*, pp. 33–34.

36. Ibid.

37. John A. Sainsbury, "Indian Labor in Early Rhode Island," *NEQ* 48 (1975): 378–93, 380–81.

38. ELB Transcripts, Box 2, New London Land Records, vol. 8, p. 6.

39. Annette Gordon-Reed, *The Hemingses of Monticello: An American Family* (New York: W. W. Norton, 2008), p. 45.

40. Winthrop Jordan, "American Chiaroscuro: The Status and Definition of Mulattoes in the British Colonies," in *Slavery in the New World*, ed. Laura Foner and Eugene D. Genovese (Englewood Cliffs, NJ: Prentice-Hall, 1969), pp. 189–201, 191.

41. Rogers, *James Rogers*, pp. 31–34.

42. Christian M. McBurney, "The Rise and Decline of the South Kingston Planters, 1660–1783" (B.A. thesis, Brown University, 1981 [on file at Newport Historical Society (hereafter NHS)]), p. 94. See a similar use of the term "Span-

ish" in a case against alleged runaways: "Cesar a mulatto man and Ann an Indian Spanish Squaw and Ann an Indian girl and Phyllis an Indian girl, all servants and slaves to Stephen Gardiner": *Gardiner v. Cesar*, NLCCCR, Files, Box 189, File of November 1743, part 1; Lorenzo Greene, *The Negro in Colonial New England* (New York: Atheneum, 1971), pp. 31–36; Berlin, *Many Thousands Gone*, pp. 47–49. See also Winthrop D. Jordan, "The Influence of the West Indies on the Origins of New England Slavery," *William and Mary Quarterly* (hereafter *WMQ*) 18 (1961): 243–65, 250.

43. Oscar Reiss, *Blacks in Colonial America* (Jefferson, NC: McFarland & Co., 1997), p. 72; *Boston Gazette*, August 1–8, 1726, p. 2.

44. See *Samuel Richards v. Cesar ye Great*, NLCSCR, Files, Box 9, File of September 1741; Eric B. Schultz and Michael J. Tougias, *King Philip's War: The History and Legacy of America's Forgotten Conflict* (New York: W. W. Norton, 2000), p. 5; Henry Sheres to the Board of Admiralty, February 20, 1677, and Entry in the Admiralty Journal Regarding Indian Slaves, April 29, 1767, Indian Papers Project; Betty Wood, *The Origins of American Slavery: Freedom and Bondage in the English Colonies* (New York: Hill & Wang, 1997), p. 11; Bernard C. Steiner, *History of Slavery in Connecticut*, Johns Hopkins University Studies in Historical and Political Science, ed. Herbert B. Adams (Baltimore: Johns Hopkins University Press, 1893); Dunn, *Puritans and Yankees*, pp. 208–9.

45. William D. Johnston, "Slavery in Rhode Island, 1755–1776," *Proceedings of the Rhode Island Historical Society* 2 (1894): 113–64, 126–28, 137; Edward Channing, *The Narragansett Planters: A Study of Causes*, Johns Hopkins University Studies in Historical and Political Science, ed. Herbert B. Adams (Baltimore: Johns Hopkins University Press, 1886), pp. 8–11; Howard S. Russell, *A Long, Deep Furrow: Three Centuries of Farming in New England* (Hanover, NH: University Press of New England, 1982), p. 111; William B. Weeden, *Early Rhode Island: A Social History of Its People* (New York: Grafton Press, 1910), pp. 143–44, 152, 156. The Narragansett is the west shore of Narragansett Bay from Wickford to Point Judith.

Chapter Two: The Rogerenes

1. John Rogers, Jr., *An Answer to a Book Lately Put Forth by Peter Pratt* (New York: privately printed, 1726), pp. 32–33.

2. I am grateful to Sally Ryan, New London's municipal historian, and Mary Elizabeth Baker, director of the Stonington Historical Society, for taking me to visit Mamacock and many other sites in and around New London. Roger Williams, *A Key into the Language of America* (London: Gregory Dexter, 1643; reprint, 1926), p. 116; *DJH*, 263 (27 October 1733); Brinton, "The Rogerenes," 6; Williams, "History of the Rogerenes," pp. 125–27; Rogers, *James Rogers*, p. 43.

3. Caulkins, *History of New London*, pp. 143–44, 669.

4. George Francis Dow, John Henry Edmonds, *The Pirates of the New England Coast, 1630–1730* (Salem, MA: Marine Research Society, 1923), p. 9; Elaine Forman Crane, *A Dependent People: Newport, Rhode Island in the Revolutionary*

Era (New York: Fordham University Press, 1985), pp. 36–37; Weeden, *Early Rhode Island*, p. 189; Kevin Gaines and Beth Parkhurst, "African-Americans in Newport, 1660–1960," *Report to the Rhode Island Black Heritage Society* (Providence: NHS, 1992), p. 10.

5. Cotton Mather, *Magnalia Christi Americana*, vol. 2 (Hartford, CT: Silus Andrus & Son, 1853), p. 520; Gutstein, *To Bigotry No Sanction*, pp. 24–26.

6. Robert G. Gardener, *Baptists of Early America: A Statistical History* (Atlanta: Georgia Baptist Historical Society, 1983), p. 14; Roll of Members of the First Baptist Church, 1644–1884, NHS.

7. C. Edwin Barrows, ed., "The Diary of John Comer," in *Collections of the Rhode Island Historical Society*, vol. 8 (Newport: Rhode Island Historical Society, 1893), p. 7; Sanford, *A Choosing People*, pp. 40–41; Gardener, *Baptists of Early America*, pp. 36, 50–51.

8. Roll of Members of the First Baptist Church, 1644–1884, #44, November 3, 1652, NHS. See also Gardener, *Baptists of Early America*, pp. 39, 46; Cotton Mather, *The Negro Christianized: An Essay to Excite and Assist That Good Work, the Instruction of Negro-Servants in Christianity* (Boston: 1706). Anglican minister Dr. James MacSparren wrote in his *Letter Book* of baptizing and catechizing slaves and local Narragansetts in South Kingston, Rhode Island: see James Mac-Sparren, *Letter Book & Abstract of Our Services*, ed. Daniel Goodwin (Boston: Merrymount Press, 1899), pp. 4, 9, 85n.

9. Gardener, *Baptists of Early America*, pp. 36, 44, 50; Sanford, *A Choosing People*, pp. 97–98, 100; Edwin S. Gaustad, ed., *Baptist Piety: The Last Will and Testimony of Obadiah Holmes* (Grand Rapids, MI: Christian University Press, 1978), pp. 52–60; James Gregory Mumford, *Mumford Memoirs, Being the Story of the New England Mumfords from the Year 1655 to the Present Time* (Boston: B. D. Updike, 1900), pp. 16–18; Ilou M. Sanford and Don A. Sanford, *Newport Seventh Day Baptist Trilogy* (Bowie, MD: Heritage, 1998), pp. 10, 14–15; Sydney V. James, *The Colonial Metamorphoses in Rhode Island: A Study of Institutions in Change*, ed. Bruce C. Daniels and Sheila L. Skemp (Hanover, NH: University Press of New England, 2000), pp. 102–3; see also entry for 1665: Roll of Members of the First Baptist Church, 1644–1884, NHS. The Mumford schism was the second among Newport's Baptists. In 1656, the First Baptist Church split over the issue of the "Sixth Principal" when a minority formed the Second Baptist Church, following the General Sixth Principle (based on Hebrews 6:1–2) and making the laying on of hands a requirement for church membership. Stephen Mumford's house is the Wanton-Lyman-Hazard House, the oldest surviving house in Newport.

10. John Rogers Bolles, "A Vindication," in *The Rogerenes: Some Hitherto Unpublished Annals Belonging to the Colonial History of Connecticut* (Boston: Stanhope Press, 1904), pp. 19–117, 22–23; see also Grosskopf, "The Limits of Religious Dissent," p. 6.

11. Roll of Members of the First Baptist Church, 1644–1884, NHS. James Rogers may have led his son into the Baptist Church, as James Rogers is listed as member #44, having been baptized on November 16, 1652, in Newport by Joseph Torrey along with four others, including "Jack, a colored man." John Rogers appears as

member #56, although the date of his baptism is not recorded. The roll describes him as having "[drawn] off with Daniel White in 1720," so he may have retained some affiliation or membership with the First Baptists well into the eighteenth century. Members of the Rogers family (including Samuel, Joseph, Sarah, Lydia, and John junior [?]) continued to be at least nominal members of the First Baptist Church after 1725: Record Book of the First Baptist Church of Newport, 1725, p. 6, NHS.

12. Sanford, *A Choosing People*, p. 100; Gardener, *Baptists of Early America*, p. 48; Kim, "Mr. Rogers's Neighborhood," pp. 52–54; Carla Gardina Pestana, *Liberty of Conscience and the Growth of Religious Diversity in Early America, 1636–1786* (Providence: John Carter Brown Library, 1986), exhibition catalog, p. 57. The Westerly faction separated into its own church in 1708: George B. Utter, *Old "Westerlie," Rhode Island* (Westerly: Westerly Chamber of Commerce, 1936), p. 17. Stephen Mumford's voyage to England in 1675 might have been a factor in the splintering of the Sabbatarians and the emergence of the Rogerenes: Mumford, *Mumford Memoirs*, pp. 17–18. For retained associations between Sabbatarians in Newport, Westerly, and New London (including Rogerenes), see Sanford, *A Choosing People*, pp. 115–17.

13. "The land of steady habits" is a nickname for Connecticut coined in the nineteenth century. *DJH*, 54 (22 April 1716); Bolles, "A Vindication," p. 13.

14. Kim, "Mr. Rogers's Neighborhood," pp. 126–28; *Acts and Laws of His Majestie's Colony of Connecticut in New-England* (New London, CT: Timothy Green, 1715), p. 105; Gardener, *Baptists of Early America*, pp. 36, 39, 41, 46.

15. Gardener, *Baptists of Early America*, p. 50; Brinton, "The Rogerenes," pp. 8–9; Sanford, *A Choosing People*, p. 117; Williams, "History of the Rogerenes," pp. 140–41. The Rogerenes were also pacifists: Bolles, "A Vindication," p. 48.

16. Brinton, "The Rogerenes," p. 11; Kim, "Mr. Rogers's Neighborhood," pp. 205–6. For Rogerene involvement in the manumission movement in the late eighteenth century, see Augustus Griffin, *Griffin's Journal, First Settlers of Southold* (Orient, NY: Augustus Griffin, 1857; reprint, 1983), p. 105.

17. William Edmundson and John Stoddart, *A Journal of the Life, Travels, Sufferings, and Labour of Love in the Work of the Ministry* (London: Harvey and Darton, 1829), p. 87.

18. Ibid., pp. 87–89.

19. Ibid., p. 87.

20. Ibid.

21. Joan's birth is based on the following: Joan married and had her first child around 1700; she was described in a document of dubious authenticity in 1693 as a girl (although there is no reason to think its description of Joan would be false): *Beebe v. Rogers*, NLCCCR, Files, Box 156, File of September 1710. Presumably she was around ten when given to Bathshua to help her during her widowhood (which ended in 1690 when she married Samuel Fox): Deposition of John Rogers, Massachusetts Archives, Suffolk Files, vol. 110, #11708, pp. 71–74.

22. *DJH*, 197 (18 June 1728), 650 (17 April 1756); MacSparren, *Letter Book*, e.g. pp. xxxix, 18, 21, 121; *Boston Gazette*, October 8–15, 1722, p. 4. My understanding

of the early vocabulary of race comes from Jack D. Forbes, *Africans and Native Americans: The Language of Race and the Evolution of Red-Black Peoples* (Chicago: University of Illinois Press, 1993).

23. Jeremiah Bumstead, "Diary of Jeremiah Bumstead of Boston, 1722–1727," *New England Historical and Genealogical Register* (hereafter *NEHGR*) 15 (1861): pp. 193–204, 203. Sarah Kemble Knight, "The Journal of Madam Knight (1704)," in *Colonial Travel Narratives*, ed. Wendy Marton (New York: Penguin, 1994), pp. 49–75. (The accuracy of Knight's journal—which may have passed through overzealous or perhaps malicious nineteenth-century editing—has since been called into question: Peter Benes, "Another Look at Madam Knight," in *In Our Own Words: New England Diaries 1600 to the Present*, Dublin Seminar for New England Folklife (Boston: Boston University, 2009), pp. 13–23); Sarah Kemble Knight to Capt. Thomas Tilestone, November 15, 1717, in *Stone v. Livingston*, NLCCCR, Files, Box 174, File of September 1720. New Londoner Abigail Camp also describes Joan as mulatto in 1717: *John Jackson v. John Stone*, Massachusetts Archives, Suffolk Files, vol. 110, #11708, pp. 71–74. In the same case file, John Rogers, Sr., also describes Joan as mulatto. In his diary, Joshua Hempstead refers to Joan's daughter, Hannah, with "Negro" John Jackson, as "molato": *DJH*, 591 (14 April 1753). Joan's son Jack or John junior (also by John Jackson) is also described as "mulatto" in court records: *Samuel Beebe v. John Jackson, Jr.*, NLCCCR, Trials, vol. 17, November 1731.

24. Caulkins, *History of New London*, pp. 144, 203; see Gordon-Reed, *The Hemingses*, pp. 81–82.

25. Rogers, *An Answer*, pp. 35–36.

26. Ibid., pp. 4–5, 33–41; Caulkins, *History of New London*, p. 251; Williams, "History of the Rogerenes," pp. 126–32; Kim, "Mr. Rogers's Neighborhood," pp. 100–101; *Public Records of the Colony of the Connecticut*, vol. 2 (Hartford, CT: Case, Lockwood and Brainard, 1850), p. 326.

27. Cornelia Hughes Dayton, *Women Before the Bar: Gender, Law, and Society in Connecticut, 1639–1789* (Chapel Hill: University of North Carolina Press, 1995), pp. 105–12; Linda K. Kerber, *Women of the Republic: Intellect and Ideology in Revolutionary America* (Chapel Hill: University of North Carolina Press, 1980), pp. 109–11, 159–61; Rogers, *An Answer*, p. 31.

28. *Crimes and Misdemeanors*, vol. 1, pp. 73–79, Connecticut Archives; Simon Bradstreet, "Memoires," manuscript reproduced in *First Impressions: Printing in Cambridge, 1639–1989*, ed. Hugh Armory (Cambridge, MA: Harvard University Press, 1989), exhibition catalog, p. 57; see William McLoughlin, *Soul Liberty: The Baptists' Struggle in New England, 1630–1833* (Hanover, NH: University Press of New England, 1991), pp. 20–21.

29. Bradstreet, "Memoires," p. 57; Simon Bradstreet, "Bradstreet's Journal," *NEHGR* 8 (1854), pp. 325–33; Sharswood died on May 1, 1674: [Grace Shaw Woldf], New London Vital Statistics from the Collated Copy from the Original Records, vol. 1, (S.l.: s. n., ca. 1900?), rebound copy in custody of the Memphis Public Library, Memphis, TN, *New London Vital Statistics Copy, Vol. 1*, p. 75, trans. Susan G. Taylor, as part of the USGenWeb New London, CT, project http://

www.rootsweb.com/~ctcnewlo/ (accessed November 16, 2006); Caulkins, *History of New London*, pp. 146, 207–8; see Rogers, *An Answer*, p. 42.

30. Bradstreet, "Memoires," p. 57; Edmundson and Stoddart, *Journal*, pp. 94–95.

31. Rogers, *An Answer*, pp. 36–37; Bradstreet, "Memoires," p. 57; *Beebe v. Rogers*, NLCSCR, Files, Box 1, File of September 1712; *Rogers v. Williams*, NLCCCR, Files, File of June 1720; see, e.g., Harry MacSparren, baptized with his master Rev. James's surname: MacSparren, *Letter Book*, p. 81n; see also George Waller-Frye, *Adam and Katherine Rogers of New London, Connecticut, James and Katherine Merritt of Killingworth, Connecticut* (Storrs, CT: Spring Hill Press, 1977).

32. *Public Records of the Colony of Connecticut, 1636–1776*, vol. 2, p. 292; Rogers, *An Answer*, pp. 36, 44, 47; Caulkins, *History of New London*, p. 208; Dayton, *Women Before the Bar*, pp. 122–23. This was the reported opinion of Elizabeth Rogers's second husband, Peter Pratt.

33. Rogers, *An Answer*, pp. 42–44.

34. Bolles, "A Vindication," pp. 40–44; Main, *Society and Economy*, p. 113.

35. Jackson most likely arrived in New England via the West Indies: Jordan, "The Influence of the West Indies," p. 247; Winthrop D. Jordan, "Enslavement of Negroes in America to 1700," in *Colonial America: Essays in Politics and Social Development*, ed. Stanley N. Katz and John M. Murrin (New York: Alfred A. Knopf, 1983), pp. 250–89, 267; *Stewart v. Rogers*, NLCSCR, Files, Box 9, File of September 1742.

36. Caulkins, *History of New London*, p. 306; *Stewart v. Rogers*, NLCSCR, Files, Box 9, File of September 1742; by contrast, twenty-year-old Nero, who fled his Norwich master in 1759, spoke only "broken English": *New London Summary*, August 31, 1759, p. 4.

37. *Stewart v. Rogers*, NLCSCR, Files, Box 9, File of September 1742.

38. According to Joshua Hempstead, a "Brigg with Negros" bound for New York sought harbor in 1715 in New London: *DJH*, 45 (30 May 1715), 46 (15 June 1715); see also Berlin, *Many Thousands Gone*, p. 46. As the century went on, the number of ships sailing directly to Africa did increase, though it remained small; see the New London Custom House entries of sailings to and from the harbor in New London's first newspaper, *New London Summary*, September 29, 1758, p. 4; compare with records of sailings from New London Harbor in Joshua's diary in early parts of the century, when such voyages were very infrequent. See, for example, the *Africa*, commanded by John Easton, which sailed from New London to the African coast in 1757, obtaining a cargo of eight slaves (four men, two girls, two boys): "The *Africa*, John Easton," Log Books of Slave Traders between New London and Africa, January–April 1757, Nantucket Whaling and Marine Manuscript Archives.

39. Berlin, *Many Thousands Gone*, p. 49; *Job v. Graves*, NLCCCR, Files, Box 173, File of June 1734, part 1; *Winthrop v. Walsworth*, NLCSCR, Files, Box 4, File of September 1721; *Willoughby v. Wolfe*, NLCCCR, Files, Box 161, File of November 1718, part 2.

40. *DJH*, 276 (15 September 1734), 287 (10 July 1735).

41. William Greer to Ebenezer Dennis, ELB Transcripts, Box 2, New London

Land Records, vol. 8, p. 76; *Buor v. Ellard*, NLCSCR, Files, Box 7, File of March 1738; John Merritt to James Harris, ELB Transcripts, Box 2, New London Land Records, vol. 8, p. 330; Joseph Coit to Elisha Hide, October 29, 1743, Slavery Documents (1732–1861), Connecticut Historical Society (hereafter CHS).

42. Caulkins, *History of New London*, p. 190–93, 197–98; New London, First Congregational Church, vol. 1, Reel 307, p. 5, Connecticut State Library (hereafter CSL).

43. Robert E. Moody, ed., *The Saltonstall Papers, 1607–1815*, vol. 1 (Boston: MHS, 1972), pp. 27, 58–59; Bolles, "A Vindication," p 37; J. M. Poteet, "The Lordly Prelate: Gurdon Saltonstall Against His Times," *NEQ* 53 (1980): 483–507, esp. 483.

44. Geoffrey Plank, *An Unsettled Conquest: The British Campaign Against the Peoples of Acadia* (Philadelphia: University of Pennsylvania Press, 2001), p. 11.

45. Documents related to the delay in processing the estate are located in Documents of James, John, Samuel Rogers, et al., CHS. Descriptions of the Rogers estate litigation appear in Williams, "History of the Rogerenes," p. 163; Caulkins, *History of New London*, p. 207. Both authors exaggerate their respective, and conflicting, accounts of events; testimony by Elizabeth Rogers's grandson John Smith (Bathshua's son from her first marriage) in *Samuel Rogers v. John Rogers*, NLCSCR, Files, Box 7, File of March 1737; attachment (of the estates of Samuel Beebe, John Rogers, Jr., and Samuel Fox, Sr.) in *James Rogers, Jr. v. Beebe et al.*, NLCCCR, Files, Box 156, File of November 1711; Rogers, *James Rogers*, pp. 33, 44; William F. Fox, *Thomas Fox of Concord and His Descendants* (Albany, NY: J. B. Lyon Co., 1909), p. 19.

46. *Samuel Rogers v. John Rogers*, NLCSCR, Files, Box 7, File of March 1737; Rogers, *James Rogers*, pp. 33, 44; Fox, *Thomas Fox of Concord*, pp. 19–21. Bathshua's first husband, Richard Smith, died in 1682; the children Bathshua brought into her marriage to Samuel Fox were John and Bathshua Smith. Samuel's four children by Mary Lester were Abigail, Elizabeth, Anna, and Samuel; Samuel's two children by his second wife, Joanna, were Isaac and Benjamin; Deposition of John Rogers, Massachusetts Archives, Suffolk Files, vol. 110, #11708, pp. 71–74.

47. Another reference to Maria and her status occurs in *Samuel Rogers v. John Rogers*, NLCSCR, Files, Box 7, File of March 1737. For testimony declaring Joan to be Maria's daughter, see *Beebe v. Rogers*, NLCCCR, Files, Box 156, File of September 1710. See also L. H. Sigourney, *Sketch of Connecticut Forty Years Since* (Hartford, CT: Oliver D. Cooke & Sons, 1824), p. 19.

48. Fox, *Thomas Fox of Concord*, pp. 20–21. Bathshua's ownership of Joan comes from her brother John's memory: Deposition of John Rogers, Massachusetts Archives, Suffolk Files, vol. 110, #11708, pp. 71–74. For Bathshua's activities in this period, see *Samuel Rogers v. John Rogers*, NLCSCR, Files, Box 7, File of March 1737. For an example of "familial" kindnesses and affection between the child of an Indian servant and the children of his master, see the 1678 testimony of "Jared, an Indian": J. Wickham Case, ed., *Southold Town Records*, vol. 1 (Southold and Riverhead, NY: Towns of Southold and Riverhead, 1882), p. 154. Both John Rogers and Bathshua Fox later testified that Joan was not in their father's possession at the time of his death: *Beebe v. Rogers*, NLCCCR, Files, Box 156, File of

June 1710. Bathshua's son, John Smith, testified in 1736 that Joan was already in his mother's possession well before his grandfather's death: *Samuel Rogers v. John Rogers*, NLCSCR, Files, Box 7, File of March 1736.

49. [Woldf], New London Vital Statistics, vol. 1, pp. 63–64; Fox, *Thomas Fox of Concord*, p. 19. Several baptisms of Fox children can be found in Baptisms of the First Congregational Church of New London, vol. 1 (1670–1756), June 3, 1677, December ?, 1679, April 9, 1682, FMC Papers; *Beebe v. Rogers*, NLCCCR, Files, Box 156, File of November 1711; Bernard Bailyn, *The New England Merchants in the Seventeenth Century* (Cambridge, MA: Harvard University Press, 1955), pp. 56–62; Henry A. Baker, *History of Montville, Connecticut, formerly the North Parish of New London, from 1640 to 1896* (Hartford, CT: Case, Lockwood and Brainard, 1896; reprint, 2005), pp. 365–67; Descendants of Samuel Fox of New London, Connecticut (typescript, 1934), p. 4; Jill Lepore, *The Name of War: King Philip's War and the Origins of American Identity* (New York: Alfred A. Knopf, 1998), pp. 85–89, 173–90. Samuel Fox died with an estate of more than £2,200 in 1727: District of New London Probate Records, vol. C, Samuel Fox, 390, Office of the Judge of Probate, New London; Sylvester Judd, "The Fur Trade on Connecticut River in the Seventeenth Century," *NEHGR* 11 (1857): 217–19.

50. For a local Mohegan bringing beaver skins to market, see *Chaw-Chaw v. Benone Philip*, NLCCCR, Files, Box 157, File of November 1712. For evidence as to how Algonquin used skins to trade for English goods, see the case of *John Chandler, Jr., of Woodstock v. Simon, alias Mautshinamaug, Indian of Lyme*, NLCCCR, Files, Box 164, File of November 1723.

51. New London, First Congregational Church, vols. 1–5, Reel 307, p. 8, CSL; Fox may have been influenced by Bathshua who, based on her signature, appears to have been better educated: *Private Controversies*, 1st Series, vol. 5, Reel 104, Roll 101–75, p. 95, Connecticut Archives; Williams, "History of the Rogerenes," p. 179; R. B. Wall, "Old Waterford Fishermen worked hard for a living . . . ," *NLD*, March 14, 1923.

52. For testimony regarding the inferiority of New London's jail, see that of John Coit, Jr., in which he describes, among other things, a woman cutting a hole in the wooden boards of the jail yard wall: *Rex v. Rogers*, NLCCCR, Files, Box 162, File of November 1719. Another reference (in Joshua Hempstead's handwriting) to the defectiveness of the prison and the resulting escape of a prisoner can be found in *Crimes and Misdemeanors*, vol. 1, p. 260, Connecticut Archives; Williams, "History of the Rogerenes," pp. 179–81; Kim, "Mr. Rogers's Neighborhood," pp. 1, 51. There were two Congregational meetings nearly every Sunday, one in the morning and one in the afternoon, with a break for "dinner" in between. For the association of shoemaking with spiritual nourishment, i.e. "sole mending," in early modern England, see Alison A. Chapman, "Whose Saint Crispin's Day Is It?: Holiday Making and the Politics of Memory in Early Modern England," *Renaissance Quarterly* 54 (2001): 1467–94.

53. John Rogers, *A Mid-Night-Cry from the Temple of God to the Ten Virgins* (New London, CT: ca. 1694), p. 8; Rogers, *An Answer*, pp. 54–55.

54. Williams, "History of the Rogerenes," pp. 184–85; Kim, "Mr. Rogers's

Neighborhood," pp. 162–63; Norbert B. Lacey, "The Records of the Court of Assistants of Connecticut, 1665–1701," 2 vols. (unpub. M.A. thesis, Yale University, 1937) (hereafter CAC), vol. 1, May 18, 1694, p. 209; Bolles, "A Vindication," pp. 28–29, 37.

55. CAC, vol. 1, October 4, 1694, pp. 214–15. See also Williams, "History of the Rogerenes," pp. 185–89. For "image magic," practitioners of which used "poppets," see Robert Blair St. George, *Conversing by Signs: Poetics of Implication in Colonial New England Culture* (Chapel Hill: University of North Carolina Press, 1998). Ideas for this paragraph come from David D. Hall, *Worlds of Wonder, Days of Judgment: Popular Religious Belief in Early New England* (Cambridge, MA: Harvard University Press, 1989).

56. CAC, vol. 1, October 4, 1694, pp. 214–15.

57. Ibid.

58. The date of the Foxes' removal to the North Parish is uncertain. Williams dates it in 1698: Williams, "History of the Rogerenes," p. 189; Baker, *History of Montville*, p. 32.

59. *Beebe v. Rogers*, NLCCCR, Files, Box 156, File of September 1710.

Chapter Three: "Fore-runners of Evil"

1. Edmund S. Morgan, *Visible Saints: The History of a Puritan Idea* (New York: Cornell University Press, 1963), pp. 113, 126–32.

2. Barbara E. Lacey, "Gender, Piety, and Secularization in Connecticut Religion, 1720–1775," *Journal of Social History* 24 (1991): 799–821, 799; Gerald Moran, "The Puritan Saint: Religious Experience, Church Membership, and Piety in Connecticut, 1636–1776" (Ph.D. diss., Rutgers University, 1974), pp. 131–32; Harry S. Stout and Peter Onuf, "James Davenport and the Great Awakening in New London," *Journal of American History* 71 (1983): 556–78, 560. For the "tenuous" competitive position of the New London Congregation, see Peter S. Onuf, "New Lights in New London: A Group Portrait of the Separatists," *WMQ* 37 (1980): 627–43, 632. Groton's Baptist church, established in 1705, was Connecticut's first: Lacey, "Gender, Piety, and Secularization," 801.

3. Journal record of King Philip's War: Samuel Sewall, "New England Chronology," *NEHGR* 7 (1853): 341–43.

4. John Augustus Bolles, *Genealogy of the Bolles Family in America* (Boston: Henry W. Dutton, 1895), pp. 5–7.

5. Nancy H. Steenburg, *Children and the Criminal Law in Connecticut, 1635–1855* (New York: Routledge, 2005), pp. 64–68; Bradstreet, "Bradstreet's Journal," pp. 331–32; Bolles, *Genealogy of the Bolles Family*, pp. 5–7.

6. Bradstreet, "Bradstreet's Journal," pp. 331–32; Sewall, "Chronology," p. 344.

7. Caulkins, *History of New London*, p. 190; Main, *Society and Economy*, pp. 96–97.

8. Joanna's death occurred within five years of her marriage to Lester; Joshua senior's occupation is referred to in 1671 in New London Land Records, vol. 5,

p. 15, Marriages, Births, and Deaths in New London (hereafter NLCCO); Aldren A. Watson, *The Blacksmith: Iron Worker and Farrier*, paperback ed. (New York: W. W. Norton, 2000), pp. 53, 80–91.

9. *Public Records of the Colony of Connecticut*, vol. 2, pp. 115–16; FMC Papers, Town Officers: New London, December 20, 1679, February 22, 1683, December 25, 1684, May 21, 1688; NLCCCR, Trials, vols. 4, 5, and 6 in 1 vol., 1681–1701, p. 25; ELB Transcripts, Box 1, Indians: The Beginnings of Pequot Plantation, p. 15; New London, First Congregational Church, Reel 307, vol. 1, April 3, 1681, December 29, 1672, March 28, 1675, July 16, 1676, June 30, 1680, pp. 4, 87, 89, 94, CSL; Moran, "The Puritan Saint," pp. 187–88; Frances M. Caulkins, ed., *Memoir of the Rev. William Adams of Dedham, Massachusetts, and of the Rev. Eliphalet Adams of New London, Connecticut* (Cambridge, MA: Metcalfe & Co., 1849), p. 27.

10. CAC, vol. 2, October 12, 1709, pp. 678–82; CAC, vol. 1, May 1, 1707, p. 520. See Baptist minister John Comer, who bemoaned the "abuses" he suffered after losing his father and assuaged them with the prevailing belief that "God has promised to avenge ye wrongs of ye fatherless": Barrows, ed., "Diary of John Comer," p. 17.

11. John Reynolds Totten, *Christophers Genealogy: Jeffreys and Christophers, Christophers of New London, Connecticut* (New York: New York Genealogical and Biographical Society, 1921), p. 43; Caulkins, *History of New London*, p. 666; *Acts and Laws* (1715), p. 29; CAC, vol. 2, October 12, 1709, pp. 678–82.

12. CAC, vol. 2, October 12, 1709, pp. 678–82.

13. Sewall, "Chronology," p. 343; ELB Transcripts, New London Land Records, vol. 4, 1668–1707 (reference immediately after index); Thomas L. Purvis, ed., *Colonial America to 1763, Almanacs of American Life* (New York: Facts on File, 1999), p. 173; New London, First Congregational Church 1670–1888, Reel 307, vols. 1, and 5, November 29, 1691, January 24, 1692, pp. 5, 6.

14. Rogers and Jackson, NLCCCR, Trials, Box 7, June 1693 (John Rogers, Jr., was a codefendant), p. 97.

15. *Jackson v. Stone*, Suffolk Files, vol. 110, #11708, pp. 71–74, Massachusetts Archives; *Stone v. Livingston*, NLCCCR, Files, Box 174, File of September 1720; *Jackson v. Stone*, Middlesex County, Court of Common Pleas, Record Book, vol. 16-99-1722, December 1716, p. 234, Massachusetts Archives; Main, *Society and Economy*, pp. 28–29.

16. *Jonathan Rogers v. James Rogers*, NLCSCR, Files, Box 2, File of September 1716; ELB Transcripts, Box 2, New London Land Records, vol. 6, part 2, book reversed, p. 6.

17. Wendy Warren, "Enslaved Africans in New England, 1638–1700" (Ph.D. diss., Yale University, 2008), pp. 228–42.

18. Ibid.; Johnston, "Slavery in Rhode Island," p. 144.

19. W. Jeffrey Bolster, *Black Jacks: African American Seamen in the Age of Sail* (Cambridge, MA: Harvard University Press, 1997). For the Irish and Scots as "un-English," see Jordan, "Enslavement of Negroes," pp. 280–82; see also Noel Ignatiev, *How the Irish Became White* (New York: Routledge, 1996). For the New London marriage between a Native American man and an Irish woman (performed

by Joshua Hempstead), see that of Samuel Wangs and Barbara Ryan: *Joshua Hempsted His Book, 1727 (Record of Marriages)*, December 6, 1741, NLCHS; [Woldf], New London Vital Statistics, vol. 1, p. 65.

20. There was an English family in New London County by the name of Jackson who may or may not have had any association with John Jackson; Newbell Niles Puckett, *Black Names in America: Origins and Usage*, ed. Murray Heller (Boston: G. K. Hall, 1975), pp. 6–13; *Stewart v. Rogers*, NLCSCR, Files, Box 9, File of September 1742.

21. Gaines and Parkhurst, "African-Americans in Newport," p. 9.

22. New London opposed freedman Robert Jacklin's right to purchase land: Rose and Brown, *Tapestry*, pp. 71–72.

23. *Jackson v. Stone*, Suffolk Files, vol. 110, #11708, pp. 71–74, Massachusetts Archives; Rogers and Jackson, NLCCCR, Trials, Box 7, June 1693, p. 97; slaves sometimes accompanied their masters when they traveled, as did the "negro man" of Patrick Grant of Newport: *DJH*, 615 (11 June 1754); John Rogers himself describes Jackson's house as near his own dwelling: *Beebe v. Rogers*, NLCSCR, Files, Box 1, File of September 1711.

Chapter Four: "Brought Up in Learning"

1. While there is no direct evidence to support Elizabeth's staying at the house and hiring laborers, she is likely to have done so, based on her dower rights to the use of one-third of the house. I infer the dating of Elizabeth's remarriage as between December 1691 and December 1692. In a 1691 petition and land sale in ELB Transcripts, Box 2, New London Land Records, vol. 5, pp. 135, 137, Elizabeth is still referred to as Elizabeth Hempstead, widow of Joshua Hempstead deceased. Looking ahead to ELB Transcripts, Box 2, New London Land Records, vols. 2–4, Grants and Deeds, vol. 2, p. 72, Elizabeth *Hempstead* receives a payment on the previously mentioned sale on December 19, 1692. Twelve months later it is her new husband, John Edgecombe, who accepts payment in right of his wife, Elizabeth Hempstead Edgecombe. For her 1691 petition to make sales from the Hempstead estate, see ELB Transcripts, Box 1, New London Land Records, vol. 5, p. 135. For Elizabeth's literacy skills, see her "marks" on the following documents: New London Land Records, vol. 2, December 19, 1691, p. 72; New London Land Records, vol. 5, September 25, 1671, December 19, 1691, pp. 15, 137, New London Land Records, vol. 8, October 25, 1721, p. 84, NLCCO; Elizabeth Edgecombe, Certification, April 1707, HHA. Elizabeth's poor literacy skills were not unusual, see Kenneth Lockridge, *Literacy in Colonial New England* (New York: W. W. Norton, 1974). *DJH*, 160 (11 September 1725); Richard Burn, *The Justice of the Peace and Parish Officer*, vol. 2, 2nd ed. (London: Hanery Lintot for A. Millar, 1756), p. 141; Margaret McGlynn, "Idiots, Lunatics and the Royal Prerogative in Early Tudor England," *Journal of Legal History* 26 (2005): 1–20, 2.

2. Caulkins, *History of New London*, pp. 84, 183, 365; R. B. Wall, "History of the St. James Church Since Foundation in 1725: In Step with Progress of Age,"

NLD, September 21, 1925; Marriages, Births and Deaths in New London, p. 319, NLCCO; See also [Woldf], New London Vital Statistics, vol. 1, p. 12; Edgecombe Family, Camp Collection, CHS.

3. Inventory of John Edgecombe, April 21, 1721, Misc. Financial, Box 37, Photocopies, Misc.: Hempstead Family Probate Documents (1600–1700), HHA; see David Hackett Fischer, *Albion's Seed: Four British Folkways in America* (Oxford: Oxford University Press, 1989); Allen, *In English Ways*.

4. See ELB Transcripts, Box 2, New London Land Records, vol. 5, p. 126; *Fish v. Edgecombe*, NLCCCR, Files, Box 156, File of September 1710; for another grandson who saw his grandfather in his family home/home-lot, see Walter Rose, *The Village Carpenter* (Hertford, UK: Stobart Davies Limited, 1995), p. 23.

5. *DJH*, 578 (25 July 1752); the "art and mystery" is legal boilerplate in apprenticeship contracts; Rose, *The Village Carpenter*, p. 24; *Johnson v. Edgecombe*, NLCCCR, Files, Box 159, File of November 1715, part 1; J. Wickham Case, ed., *Southold Town Records*, vol. 2 (Southold and Riverhead, NY: Towns of Southold and Riverhead, 1884), p. 308. Although this indenture arrangement fell apart, Samuel did become a master shipwright: ELB Transcripts, Box 1, New London Land Records, vol. 7, p. 308. For general requirements regarding indenture, see *Acts and Laws* (1715), p. 16.

6. *DJH*, 25 (7 August 1713), 48 (25 August 1715), 578 (25 July 1752); Manwaring, NLCCCR, Files, Box 155, File of September 1706; Joseph F. Cullon, "Colonial Shipwrights and their World: Men, Women, and Markets in Early New England" (Ph.D. diss., University of Wisconsin, 2003), p. 186; FMC Papers, Baptisms of the First Congregational Church of New London, vol. 1, June 9, 1700; D. Hamilton Hurd, *History of New London County, Connecticut* (Philadelphia: J. W. Lewis & Co., 1882), p. 150. Thomas Mitchell's origins are elusive, but he may have been related to the still-extant Mitchells of Block Island; see the gravestone of a Capt. Thomas Mitchell, Jr. (1682–1741) in Edward Doubleday Harris, ed., *A Copy of the Old Epitaphs in the Burying Ground of Block Island, Rhode Island* (Cambridge, MA: John Wilson & Son, 1883), p. 21; Helen Winslow Mansfield, comp., *Old Cemetery at Block Island . . .* (Salem, MA: Higginson Book Co., 1950; reprint, 1997), p. 56. Moriarty rejects Thomas Mitchell's connection to the Block Island Mitchells: G. Andrew Moriarty, "Early Block Island Families," *NEHGR* 82 (1928): 457–59.

7. Edmund S. Morgan, *The Puritan Family: Religion and Domestic Relations in Seventeenth-Century New England*, new ed. (New York: Harper & Row, 1966), pp. 68–78; *Acts and Laws* (1715), p. 16.

8. Morgan, *The Puritan Family*, pp. 68–78.

9. Ibid.

10. Cullon, "Colonial Shipwrights," p. 186.

11. Ibid., pp. 134, 233; felling trees and shaping ladder spokes was also boy's work: Rose, *The Village Carpenter*, pp. 20, 24–25.

12. Robert Tarule, *The Artisan of Ipswich: Craftsmanship and Community in Colonial New England* (Baltimore: Johns Hopkins University Press, 2004), p. 23; Cullon, "Colonial Shipwrights," pp. 4–5, 28, 44, 99–100.

13. Tarule, *Artisan of Ipswich*, pp. 20, 48; Russell, *A Long, Deep Furrow*, pp. 93–96.

14. Tarule, *Artisan of Ipswich*, pp. 16–17, 48–51, 77–79; Rose, *The Village Carpenter*, p. 30; George Sturt, *The Wheelwright's Shop* (Cambridge, UK: Cambridge University Press, 1923; reprint, 1993), pp. 19–20. This characterization of Joshua's relationship with his father is based on colonial English child-rearing practices in general and especially on Joshua's own example of fatherhood. For family life and education generally, see John Demos, *A Little Commonwealth: Family Life in Plymouth Colony* (New York: Oxford University Press, 1970); Morgan, *The Puritan Family*; James Axtell, *The School upon the Hill: Education and Society in Colonial New England* (New Haven, CT: Yale University Press, 1974).

15. Lockridge, *Literacy*, p. 13. A high number of New Englanders possessed what David D. Hall has termed "traditional literacy." Simply stated, Hall's characteristics of traditional literacy include an emphasis on reading over writing; the teaching of reading through the memorization of certain, especially religious, texts; and access to a very limited number of widely circulated books. In addition, premodern literacy did not signify one particular set of skills as it does today, but rather a broad range of abilities from reading print and signing one's name to reading and writing complex or even erudite manuscripts. Premodern literacy of this kind did not imply any connection to a cosmopolitan book or learned culture: David D. Hall, "The Uses of Literacy in New England, 1600–1850," in *Cultures of Print: Essays in the History of the Book* (Amherst: University of Massachusetts Press, 1996), pp. 36–78, esp. 57.

16. For a fictionalized oral-history account of a late eighteenth-century local African man's religious education and faith, see Sigourney, *Sketch of Connecticut*, pp. 89–90. Sigourney is a highly mediated and undocumented source; nevertheless she gives voice to a nearly contemporary local perspective. For "Negro" religious instruction, see also MacSparren, *Letter Book*, p. 6. *Beebe v. Rogers*, NLCCCR, Files, Box 156, File of June 1711; *Edward Robinson v. Samuel Richards*, NLCSCR, Files, Box 7, File of September 1736. African freedman Robert Jacklin's mark (his initials written in shaky capitals) showed a rudimentary knowledge of writing (greater than Jackson's, but less than Adam Rogers's): *Fox v. Jacklin*, NLCCCR, Files, Box 167, File of August 1726. The methodology of using signatures to represent literacy is problematic at best. Still, it is the best available evidence. New London Land Records, vol. 2, December 19, 1691, p. 72 ; vol. 5, September 25, 1671, pp. 15, 19, December 19, 1691, p. 137; vol. 8, October 25, 1721, p. 84; Elizabeth Edgecombe, Certification, April 1707, HHA; *Adam Rogers v. Thomas Jones*, NLCCCR, Files, Box 163, File of November 1720, part 1. See also Ishmael Mux, "mulatto" servant to Pygan Adams (son of minister Eliphalet), who could "read, write, and cipher well" in 1761: *New London Summary*, January 9, 1761, p. 2.

17. *Joshua Hempsted His Book, 1695*, NLCHS. For similar examples of math problems: Jonathan Burnham, *A Small Tract of Arithmetick for the Use of Farmers and Country-People* (New London, CT: Timothy Green, 1747).

18. *Joshua Hempsted His Book, 1695*, NLCHS.

19. Kierner, *Traders and Gentlefolk*, pp. 39–41.

20. Ivor Noël Hume, *A Guide to Artifacts of Colonial America* (New York: Alfred A. Knopf, 1969), pp. 177–84; Jack Larkin, *The Reshaping of Everyday Life, 1790–1840* (New York: Harper & Row, 1988), pp. 180–81. John's Dutch ethnic-

ity came out in other ways, as in a bill of exchange due in "eight days' sight" or one week in the Dutch fashion: John Livingston, autograph note signed to John Borland, February 2, 1708, Gilder Lehrman Collection (hereafter GLC) 856; see also his Germanic spelling of "Doktor" in John Livingston to Robert Livingston, March 21, 1711, GLC 861. John Livingston to Robert Livingston, October 15, 1701, GLC 645; Kierner, *Traders and Gentlefolk*, pp. 51–52. John had some legal knowledge typical of a man of his status, sufficient to have served as an "attorney" for Samuel Beebe. His brother Robert trained at the Middle Temple and had an ample law library even in 1711: A Catalogue of Books belonging to Robert Livingston, Jr., in the custody of Archibald Johnson of the Middle Temple, New York, September 9, 1711, GLC 890; books purchased by Robert Livingston, London, ca. September 7, 1696, GLC 332.

21. Gary B. Nash, *The Urban Crucible: The Northern Seaports and the Origins of the American Revolution* (Cambridge, MA: Harvard University Press, 1979), pp. 21–23; Dunn, *Puritans and Yankees*, pp. 251–56; Nathaniel Byfield, "An Account of the Late Revolution in New-England," in *The Andros Tracts . . .* , ed. William Henry Whitmore (New York: Burt Franklin, 1868), pp. 3–8; Everett Kimball, *The Public Life of Joseph Dudley* (New York: Longmans, Green, and Co., 1911), pp. 50–56.

22. Nash, *The Urban Crucible*, pp. 23–28; Leder, *Robert Livingston*, pp. 57–64.

23. Leder, *Robert Livingston*, pp. 65–69; Clare Brandt, *An American Aristocracy: The Livingstons* (New York: Doubleday, 1986), p. 33.

24. Leder, *Robert Livingston*, pp. 70–73; Lawrence Shaw Mayo, *The Winthrop Family in America* (Boston: MHS, 1948), pp. 89–90.

25. Caulkins, *History of New London*, pp. 256–57; Leder, *Robert Livingston*, pp. 74–76.

26. Leder, *Robert Livingston*, pp. 3–5.

27. Fitz Winthrop to Robert Livingston, [December 1691], *Winthrop Papers*, 6th series, vol. 3, p. 512; Edwin Brockholst Livingston, *The Livingstons of Livingston Manor* (New York: Knickerbocker Press, 1910), p. 133.

28. Brandt, *American Aristocracy*, p. 53.

29. Books at the Manor included a book of reels and Richard Allestree's popular conduct manual, *A Gentleman's Calling*: Books purchased by Robert Livingston, London, ca. September 7, 1696, GLC 332; Samuel Vetch to John Livingston, March 8, 1714, GLC 1053.

30. English Translation of Robert Livingston's Journal . . . During His Voyage to England, December 9, 1694–October 3, 1695, trans. A. J. F. van Laer, Box 3, Folder 30, GLC 3107, pp. 2–3, 16, 25–26, 29, 35–36, 38, 44.

31. Ibid., pp. 16, 44–69, 77; Leder, *Robert Livingston*, pp. 96–116; Account of Robert Livingston, Bought of Joseph Collins in Mumford's Court in Milk Street, February 8, 1695, GLC 283.

32. Berlin, *Many Thousands Gone*, pp. 48–55; Richard Shannon, "Slavery on Long Island: Its Rise and Decline during the Seventeenth through Nineteenth Centuries" (Ph.D. diss., St. John's University, 1985), pp. 1, 22–23; William P. McDermott, "The Livingstons' Colonial Land Policy: Personal Gain over Public

Need," in *The Livingston Legacy: Three Centuries of American History*, ed. Richard T. Wiles (Annandale-on-Hudson, NY: Bard College, 1987), pp. 10–37, 12–13.

33. Kierner, *Traders and Gentlefolk*, pp. 89–90, 92–98; McDermott, "The Livingstons' Colonial Land Policy," pp. 11–12, 16–30; Sung Bok Kim, "Introduction: The Livingstons as Land Developers," in *A Portrait of Livingston Manor, 1686–1850*, ed. Ruth Piwonka (Clermont, NY: Friends of Clermont, 1986), pp. 11–15, 12–14; Kierner points out that tenants' indebtedness was not necessarily an indication of failure, as some of the manor's most prosperous tenants maintained relatively high levels of debt.

34. Philip Livingston to Robert Livingston, May 3, 1717, GLC 1139; Roberta Singer, "The Livingstons as Slave Owners: The 'Peculiar Institution' of Livingston Manor and Clermont," in *The Livingston Legacy: Three Centuries of American History*, ed. Richard T. Wiles (Annandale-on-Hudson, NY: Bard College, 1987), pp. 12–13, 69, 73, 81–83; Robert Livingston to Alida Livingston, April 28, 1714 (trans. from the Dutch), GLC 2251; Robert Livingston, Justice of the Peace Minutes, February 2, 1715, GLC 1103; Kierner, *Traders and Gentlefolk*, pp. 58–64.

35. Singer, "Livingstons as Slave Owners," pp. 73–76, 79. In a number of places in colonial America like the Chesapeake iron works, slaves were industrial workers: John Bezís-Selfa, *Forging America: Ironworkers, Adventurers, and the Industrious Revolution* (Ithaca, NY: Cornell University Press, 2004), pp. 91–99. Kierner, *Traders and Gentlefolk*, pp. 41, 91.

36. Kierner, *Traders and Gentlefolk*, pp. 51–52; John Livingston to Robert Livingston, October 15, 1701, GLC 645.

Chapter Five: "Fornication Among You"

1. Dayton, *Women Before the Bar*, pp. 157–230.

2. *Joshua Hempstead His Book, 1695*, NLCHS.

3. Bertha Lee Benn, "Six Generations of the Hempstead Family: Descendants of Robert the Emigrant of New London" (typescript, 1944), CSL, p. 10; Elizabeth P. Whitten, comp., "Hempsteads of New London, CT and Vicinity" (typescript, 1984), NLCHS; Case, ed., *Southold Town Records*, vol. 1, pp. 45–47, 55, 59, 428–29; Gaynell S. Levine, "Colonial Long Island Grave Stones: Trade Network Indicators, 1670–1799," in *Puritan Gravestone Art II*, ed. Peter Benes, Dublin Seminar for New England Folklife (Boston: Boston University, 1978), pp. 46–57, esp. 47; John Murrin, "East Hampton in the 17th Century," lecture delivered May 30, 1998, http://www.easthamptonlibrary.org/lic/lectures/lecture.htm (accessed January 18, 2006); Joshua Hempstead, New London, 1759, New London Probate Packet 1675–1850, Reel 983, no. 2573, CSL.

4. Case, ed., *Southold Town Records*, vol. 1, pp. 89, 129–30, 248, 341, 432; "Diagram of the Village of Southold Showing the Lots of the First Settlers," in Case, ed., *Southold Town Records*, vol. 2; *DJH*, 240 (15 November 1731); Jane C. Nylander, *Our Own Snug Fireside: Images of the New England Home, 1760–1860* (New Haven, CT: Yale University Press, 1994), pp. 46–50.

5. Whitten, "Hempsteads of New London"; Joshua and Abigail were married sometime around October 1698, when they conceived their first child. The actual date when Joshua and Abigail moved into the Hempstead house is unknown. See Nylander, *Our Own Snug Fireside*, pp. 54–66. Joshua refers to Abigail's sisters' marriages in a conveyance to his grandson, Nathaniel (Natty) Hempstead, March 12, 1723, HHA. Charles D. Parkhurst identifies Abigail's four sisters as Temperance, who married Henry Conkling; Mary, who married Thomas Tallmadge; Hannah, who married William Salmon; and Christian who married (1) James Patty and (2) Josiah Smith: Charles D. Parkhurst, "Comments On, and Corrections of, Some Curious Errors, which are to be found recorded in the Introduction to Hempstead's Diary," *New York Genealogical and Biographical Record* 51 (1920): 259–65, esp. 263.

6. "Proposal of Marriage by Daniel Hubbard for the Hand of Miss Coit," *NEHGR* 48 (1894): 465.

7. Samuel Fosdick, NLCCCR, Files, Box 155, File of September 1706.

8. Division of the estate of Joseph Truman to his sons Thomas and Joseph, April 20, 1728; Will of Joseph Truman (1696); Joseph Truman, Jr., Inventory, November 22, 1745, Misc. Financial, Box 37, Photocopies: Hempstead Family Probate Documents, HHA; Truman, NLCCCR, Files, Box 154, File of June 1705; Truman, NLCCCR, Files, Box 155, File of September 1706. As fornication became increasingly prevalent over the course of the eighteenth century, community attitudes relaxed and punishments were reduced commensurably. Church confessions of fornication also became more common, perhaps obviating the need to prosecute fornication criminally: Dayton, *Women Before the Bar*, pp. 157–230.

9. Truman, NLCCCR, Files, Box 155, File of September 1706.

10. Ibid.

11. Ibid.

12. Ibid. Susanna was not the only woman who refused, for whatever reason, to reveal the identity of her baby's father. On February 16, 1730, Joshua's servant Mary Dart appeared before her master in his capacity as magistrate and pleaded guilty to fornication, refusing to identify her illegitimate baby's father: Dart, NLCCCR, Files, Box 170, File of June 1730.

13. See, e.g., the division of the Truman house more than twenty years later: Division of the Estate of Joseph Truman, Sr., April 20, 1728, Miscellaneous Financial, Box 37, File: Photocopies, Misc., Hempstead Family Probate Documents, HHA. There is ample evidence in the legal record of the expectations regarding "close neighbors"; see, for example, the adultery case of Bradford, NLCCCR, Files, Box 157, File of November 1713.

14. Women, of course, were not the only ones who could not vote or hold office in Connecticut. To do either, one had to be "an admitted inhabitant, householder and a man of sober conversation" and have an estate rated at fifty shillings in the common tax list: *Acts and Laws* (1715), p. 113. For more on the limits of patriarchy in defining and understanding the roles of early modern English men and women, see Alexandra Shepard, *Meanings of Manhood in Early Modern England* (Oxford:

Oxford University Press, 2003). For women's vulnerability to charges of witchcraft: Carol F. Karlsen, *The Devil in the Shape of a Woman: Witchcraft in Colonial New England* (New York: Vintage, 1987), pp. 46–76, esp. 74–75.

15. The active roles early American women played in court were as the accused, as litigants, or as witnesses (or infrequently as jurors on a jury of matrons). The only woman with any real authority in the colonial courtroom was the midwife, who was regularly called on to testify as an expert witness in fornication and bastardy cases. Truman, NLCCCR, Files, Box 155, File of September 1706.

16. Alida Livingston to Robert Livingston, June 6, 1698, GLC 34; Alida Livingston to Robert Livingston, June 24, 1698, GLC 40.

17. Kierner, *Traders and Gentlefolk*, p. 52.

18. Caulkins, *History of New London*, p. 252; John Livingston to Robert and Alida Livingston, December 10, 1700, GLC 587; Fitz Winthrop to Robert Livingston, December 9, 1700, GLC 591; Leder, *Robert Livingston*, pp. 158–59.

19. John Livingston to Robert and Alida Livingston, December 10, 1700, GLC 587.

20. Ibid.; Daniel Wetherell to Fitz-John Winthrop, December 20, 1697, *Winthrop Papers*, vol. 3, p. 253; *Saltonstall v. Rogers*, NLCCCR, Files, Box 153, File of January/September 1698.

21. Hugh Armory and David D. Hall, *A History of the Book in America*, vol. 1: *The Colonial Book in the Atlantic World* (Cambridge, UK: Cambridge University Press, 1999), p. 97; Duncan Campbell to Robert Livingston, November 2, 1700, GLC 585.

22. John Livingston to Robert and Alida Livingston, December 10, 1700, GLC 587.

23. Duncan Campbell to Robert Livingston, November 2, 1700, GLC 585; James Graham to Robert Livingston, December 3, 1700, GLC 586.

24. Mayo, *Winthrop Family*, p. 93.

25. G. M. Waller, *Samuel Vetch: Colonial Enterpriser* (Chapel Hill: University of North Carolina Press, 1960), pp. 3–45.

26. Livingston, *Livingstons of Livingston Manor*, p. 52; Waller, *Samuel Vetch*, pp. 3–45; Plank, *An Unsettled Conquest*, p. 42.

27. Waller, *Samuel Vetch*, pp. 47–56.

28. Fitz Winthrop to Robert Livingston, September 3, 1701, GLC 635; John Livingston to Robert Livingston, September 16, 1701, GLC 639.

29. Caulkins, *History of New London*, pp. 428–32; John Livingston to Robert Livingston, May 20, 1713, GLC 961.

30. Robert Livingston, Jr., to Robert Livingston, July 3, 1717, GLC 1151; John Livingston to Robert Livingston, November 20, 1717, GLC 1199. Johanna Livingston and Mary Winthrop Livingston each had personal slave girls: Johanna Livingston to Robert Livingston, March 17, 1713, GLC 984; Johanna Livingston to Robert Livingston, July 6, 1713, GLC 1018.

31. See [Woldf], New London Vital Statistics, vol. 1, p. 19; Grosskopf indicates that John and Joan were married in 1705: Grosskopf, "The Limits of Religious Dis-

sent," p. 173; Jackson, NLCCCR, Trials, Box 7, September 1701, p. 317; Jackson, NLCCCR, Files, Box 153, File of February 1702; Dayton, *Women Before the Bar*, p. 157.

32. Jackson, NLCCCR, Files, Box 153, File of February 1702.

33. John Rogers, *An Impartial Relation of an Open and Publick Dispute Agreed Between Gurdon Saltonstall, Minister of the Town of New London, and John Rogers of the Same Place* ([New York or Philadelphia]: John Rogers, 1701).

34. Nicholas Noyes, "An Essay Against Periwigs," in *The English Literatures of America, 1500–1800*, ed. Myra Jehlen and Michael Warner (New York: Routledge, 1997), pp. 408–14; Bolles, "Vindication," pp. 26–27; Kim, "Mr. Rogers's Neighborhood," pp. 66–67, 87–88.

35. See Rose and Brown, *Tapestry*, p. 65; Waller-Frye, *Adam and Katherine Rogers*.

36. For a case that implies a consensual relationship between an Englishwoman and a man of African origin, see that of Hannah Welch Gold, who married John Gold, an Englishman, while already pregnant with a "mulatto" child by another man. John claimed that Hannah entered the marriage under fraudulent contract: *Gold v. Gold*, NLCSCR, Files, Box 13, File of March 1756. See also the case of (English) Hannah Taylor who "lives and cohorts with one Joseph Allyn, a [N]egro servant . . . " in Ross, "Slavery on Long Island," p. 39.

37. Waller-Frye, *Adam and Katherine Rogers*.

38. Grosskopf, "The Limits of Religious Dissent," p. 173; Jackson marriage mentioned by John Rogers: *Jackson v. Stone*, Suffolk Files, vol. 110, #11708, pp. 71–74, Massachusetts Archives. For romantic love between an enslaved man and woman, see John Winthrop IV to Wait Winthrop, ca. July 23, 1711, *Winthrop Papers* microfilm, Reel 18; Thomas Lechmere to Wait Winthrop, August 27, 1711, *Winthrop Papers* microfilm, Reel 18.

39. Gardener, *Baptists of Early America*, p. 50.

40. Gaines and Parkhurst, "African-Americans in Newport," pp. 9, 11; Edmund Morgan, *American Slavery, American Freedom: The Ordeal of Colonial Virginia* (New York: W. W. Norton, 2003), pp. 297–307; Wood, *Origins of American Slavery*, p. 82; William Piersen, *Black Yankees: The Development of an Afro-American Subculture* (Amherst: University of Massachusetts Press, 1988), pp. 14–16.

41. Were it not for a summons to Samuel Fox dated May 23, 1710, we could not be at all certain of Adam's age: *James Rogers, Jr. v. Samuel Fox*, NLCCCR, Files, Box 156, File of September 1710. Rose and Brown refer to Adam as being born sometime between 1693 and 1713: *Tapestry*, p. 6. Puckett, *Black Names*, p. 8.

42. My thanks to John Geary and John Chase for information about the Fox property. The brook to which I refer is Fox Brook. The Fox house was located along the upper part of Fox Road.

43. Ecclesiastical Affairs, Reel 27; Roll 75-75, vol. 1, part 1, Connecticut Archives, p. 81; *Public Records of the Colony of Connecticut*, vol. 3 (Hartford, CT: Case, Lockwood and Brainard, 1859), p. 144.

44. Rogers, *An Answer*, p. 61.

45. Ibid., pp. 48–50; Coe, *Memoranda relating to the Ancestry and Family of Sophia Fidelia Hall*, p. 146.

46. Rogers, *An Answer*, pp. vii, 44–46; Coe, *Memoranda relating to the Ancestry and Family of Sophia Fidelia Hall*, p. 146; *Jonathan Rogers v. James Rogers*, NLCSCR, Files, Box 2, File of September 1716; Williams, "History of the Rogerenes," pp. 179–95.

47. CAC, vol. 1, p. 264.

48. Rogers, *James Rogers*, p. 21.

49. Caulkins, *History of New London*, pp. 216–17; Williams, "History of the Rogerenes," pp. 196–206; Mary Rogers, Ecclesiastical Affairs, vol. 4, p. 111, Connecticut Archives; Mary Ransford, NLCCCR, Trials, Box 7, June 1699; Mary Ransford, NLCCCR, Trials, Box 7, June 1703, p. 365; John Rogers, Jr., and Mary Ransford, NLCCCR, Files, Box 153, File of June 1700.

50. Rogers, *An Answer*, pp. 61–63, 174–75; Kim, "Mr. Rogers's Neighborhood," pp. 104–5.

51. John Rogers, Jr., and Mary Ransford, NLCCCR, Files, Box 153, File of June 1700.

52. Ransford, NLCCCR, Trials, vol. 7, June 4, 1700, p. 282; Williams, "History of the Rogerenes," pp. 198–202. It was after this first Ransford prosecution that Katherine Jones accused Jackson of fathering her baby, the timing perhaps lending credence to the idea that Jackson's trial was part of a broader legal attack against the Rogerenes. Ransford, NLCCCR, Trials, vol. 7, September 15, 1702, p. 351; Williams, "History of the Rogerenes," pp. 202–6.

53. *Crimes and Misdemeanors*, vol. 1, p. 283, Connecticut Archives; Williams, "History of the Rogerenes," pp. 204–5; *Beckwith v. Rogers*, NLCCCR, Files, Box 154, File of June 1703; Beckwith, NLCCCR, Files, Box 154, File of September 1703.

54. Bathshua's son, John Smith, remembered Joan's grant of freedom: *Rogers v. Rogers*, NLCSCR, Files, Box 7, File of March 1737.

Chapter Six: "One Flesh"

1. Caulkins, *History of New London*, pp. 190, 259–60, 263–66, 319–20, 358–60.

2. Ibid., pp. 230, 234–35, 263; ELB Transcripts, Box 1, New London Land Records, vol. 4, pp. 1, 29, 51; Cullon, "Colonial Shipwrights," pp. 12–13; Russell, *A Long, Deep Furrow*, pp. 34–37; Hurd, *New London County*, pp. 206–7; Main, *Society and Economy*, p. 305.

3. Caulkins, *History of New London*, pp. 401, 414–15, 417.

4. Tarule, *Artisan of Ipswich*, pp. 60–61; Caulkins, *History of New London*, pp. 253, 263.

5. Alexander Hamilton, "The Itinerarium of Dr. Alexander Hamilton," in *Colonial American Travel Narratives*, ed. Wendy Marton (New York: Penguin, 1994), pp. 173–327, 248; Caulkins, *History of New London*, pp. 14–15, see also p. 268; Robert Watts to Robert Livingston, November 26, 1701, GLC 657;

Knight, "Journal of Madam Knight," pp. 56–57, 73–74; John Winthrop IV to Wait Winthrop, January 23 or 30, 1712, *Winthrop Papers* microfilm, Reel 18; Thomas Lechmere to John Winthrop IV, April 29, 1723, *Winthrop Papers* microfilm, Reel 19.

6. Tarule, *Artisan of Ipswich*, pp. 60–61, 89; Caulkins, *History of New London*, pp. 283, 314–15. Joshua's sisters Patience and Lucy helped him to shore up assets in 1709, when they transferred their portions of land contiguous to his house-lot to him: ELB Transcripts, Box 2, New London Land Records, vol. 6, p. 181.

7. See John M. Murrin, "Anglicizing an American Colony: The Transformation of Provincial Massachusetts" (Ph.D. diss., Yale University, 1966).

8. Joshua's descendant Mary L. B. Branch discusses the rifle's place on the summer beam of the hall (where it remains): Mary L. B. Branch, *The Old Hempstead House: The Home of Eight Generations* (New London, CT: Local History Publishing Co., 1931), p. 15.

9. Nylander, *Our Own Snug Fireside*, pp. 20–22, 51, 88, 103–6; Larkin, *The Reshaping of Everyday Life*, pp. 57–66, 127–32.

10. Ibid. Sons Thomas (b. April 14, 1708) and John (b. December 26, 1709) were only twenty-one months apart. An English visitor to Connecticut in the 1790s complained that houses there were untidy, "cold, comfortless and dirty": S. H. Jeyes, *The Russells of Birmingham in the French Revolution and in America, 1791–1814* (London: George Allen, 1911), p. 233.

11. *Williams v. Rogers*, NLCCCR, Files, Box 157, File of November 1713.

12. *DJH*, 1 (15 September 1711), 17–18 (17, 22–24, 27 December 1712), 20 (7 February 1713), 24 (19 June 1713), 34 (1 May 1714); Caulkins, *History of New London*, pp. 240–41.

13. Edward Johnson, *Wonder-Working Providence of Sion's Saviour in New England* (London: 1654), pp. 247–48; Edward M. Cooke, *The Fathers of the Towns: Leadership and Community Structure in Eighteenth-Century New England* (Baltimore: Johns Hopkins University Press, 1976).

14. Elizabeth Edgecombe certified the rejection of Joshua senior's first will in Elizabeth Edgecombe, Certification, April 1707, HHA. Her petition appears in New London Land Records, vol. 5, 1691, pp. 135, 137, NLCCO. The farm, with Fish as neighbor: Daboll and Crandall, "Map of the Edmund Fanning Farm at Stonington, Connecticut 1683" (Worcester: Walter F. Brooks, 1902). For Fish's payments, see New London Land Records, vol. 2, December 19, 1691, December 22, 1693, February 26, 1695, p. 72, NLCCO. Elizabeth Hempstead also sold a different tract in Norwich to Joseph Avery: *Edgecombe v. Avery*, NLCSCR, Files, Box 4, File of September 1724. CAC, vol. 2, pp. 671–73, 675–76, 678–82.

15. *DJH*, 593 (15 May 1753); CAC, vol. 2, p. 520; Caulkins, *History of New London*, pp. 273, 300–301. A copy of the will is at NLCHS.

16. CAC, vol. 2, pp. 671–73, 675–76, 678–82. When the court named Joshua administrator of his father's estate, it also added his sisters Patience and Lucy, who were unborn at the writing of the will, as heirs. Joshua came to court prepared, offering a signed release from Patience and Lucy certifying that they had already received their portions from their brother: New London Land Records, vol. 5,

p. 181, NLCCO. *Public Records of the Colony of Connecticut*, vol. 4 (Hartford, CT: Case, Lockwood and Brainard, 1870), p. 150.

17. It is likely that Joshua did write down his pleas (as he did most everything of importance). For an example of him writing down pleas, see Connecticut Archives, Series 1, vol. 6, Roll 102-75, May 13, 1714, p. 349; FMC Papers, Town Officers: New London, Subscription committee for Eliphalet Adams's settlement, November 11, 1708, committee to represent New London in the "Liveen money" case, December 13, 1709.

18. Cooke, *Fathers of the Towns*, esp. p. 22; Kenneth A. Lockridge, *The New England Town: The First Hundred Years*, expanded ed. (New York: W. W. Norton, 1985), esp. pp. 42–46; FMC Papers, Town Officers: New London, December 14, 1709.

19. Deposition of Widow Abigail Camp, *Jackson v. Stone*, Suffolk Files, vol. 110, #11708, pp. 71–74, Massachusetts Archives.

20. *Jackson v. Tracy*, NLCCCR, Files, File of November 1719; Deposition of Widow Abigail Camp, *Jackson v. Stone*, Suffolk Files, vol. 110, #11708, pp. 71–74, Massachusetts Archives.

21. *Encyclopedia of African American History, 1619–1895*, vol. 1 (New York: Oxford University Press, 2006), p. 493; Piersen, *Black Yankees*, p. 14; *DJH*, 340 (30 December 1738).

22. See MacSparren, *Letter Book*, p. 57; Daniel Langon Tappan, *Tappan-Toppan Genealogy . . .* (Arlington, MA: Daniel Langdon Tappan, 1915), p. 7; New London Land Records, vol. 4, p. 263, NLCCO.

23. *Samuel Beebe v. John Jackson, Jr.*, NLCCCR, Trials, vol. 17, November 1731; *Samuel Beebe v. John Rogers, Jr.*, NLCCCR, Files, Box 171, File of February 1732; New London Land Records, vol. 7, 1711, p. 119; *James Rogers, Jr. v. Beebe*, NLCCCR, Files, Box 156, File of November 1711; *Jackson v. Stone*, Suffolk Files, vol. 110, #11708, pp. 71–74, Massachusetts Archives.

24. Richard Anson Wheeler, *History of the Town of Stonington . . .* (New London, CT: Press of the Day, 1900), p. 637; Depositions of Widow Abigail Camp and John Rogers, *Jackson v. Stone*, Suffolk Files, vol. 110, #11708, pp. 71–74, Massachusetts Archives; *Jackson v. Tracy*, NLCCCR, Files, File of November 1719.

25. *Samuel Beebe v. Joshua Hempstead*, NLCCCR, Files, Box 167, File of November 1728. The age of weaning was around two: Demos, *A Little Commonwealth*, p. 133.

26. Fox, *Thomas Fox of Concord*, p. 28.

27. In Samuel Fox's 1727 inventory, there is equipment Adam may have used to tan hides, "4 old knives for tanning & a bark shave," along with tools of Adam's own trade of husbandry: District of New London Probate Records, vol. C, pp. 390–92, esp. 391, Office of the Judge of Probate; *Rex v. Thomas Stanton*, NLCSCR, Files, Box 5, File of March 1726.

28. Inventory of Estate of Samuel Fox, District of New London Probate Records, vol. C, pp. 390–92, esp. 391, Office of the Judge of Probate.

29. For a biased local perspective, see Sigourney, *Sketch of Connecticut*, pp. 89–90; MacSparren, *Letter Book*, p. 6.

30. *Acts and Laws* (1715), p. 76.

31. *Bump v. Rood*, NLCCCR, Files, Box 163, File of November 1720, part 2; for the trial itself, see *Bump v. Rood*, NLCCCR, Trials, vol. 17, Court of November 22, 1720.

32. Ibid.

33. Ibid. The characterization of the role of near neighbors draws on *Bethia Taylor v. Thomas Willey*, NLCCCR, Files, Box 164, File of June 1723.

34. "Gleanings (No. 22)," *NEHGR* 13 (1859): 302–3. This assessment of Thomas Lechmere is based on a reading of his letters in the *Winthrop Papers* at MHS. Case files related to Zeno's death are located in Nicholas Lechmere, NLCSCR, Files, Box 12, File of September 1751. The outcome is in Superior Court, New London County Dockets, 1713–1835, Box 35, September 1751.

35. Lechmere, NLCSCR, Files, Box 12, File of September 1751; *DJH*, 550 (25 January 1751).

36. Chatfield, NLCCCR, Files, Box 156, File of June 1711.

37. Ibid.

38. MacSparren, *Letter Book*, e.g., p. xxxix; Knight, "Journal of Madam Knight," p. 64; Fitts determined Narragansett slavery to be a harsh regime, though most of his examples date from a later period: Robert K. Fitts, *Inventing New England's Slave Paradise: Master/Slave Relations in Eighteenth-Century Narragansett, Rhode Island* (New York: Garland, 1998).

39. MacSparren, *Letter Book*, p. 52.

40. Ibid., p. 159n.

41. Marriages, Births, and Deaths in New London, p. 263, NLCCO.

42. *DJH*, 458 (21 August 1746), 506 (13 March 1749), 573 (18 April 1752), 680 (19 February 1758).

43. MacSparren, *Letter Book*, pp. 26–27, 58, 78n.

44. *Acts and Laws* (1715), pp. 138, 291; for a case involving a Norwich slave who was accused of "disturbing the peace and striking a white man," see Norwich Justice Courts, Box 574, Isaac Huntington (1744–1760), File of Complaints and Warrants, August 30, 1744.

45. *Acts and Laws* (1715), pp. 87, 136; for an actual pass, see Robert Jacklin's in Marriages, Births, and Deaths in New London, p. 263, NLCCO.

46. Knight, "Journal of Madam Knight," p. 64.

47. Cathy Matson, *Merchants and Empire: Trading in Colonial New York* (Baltimore: Johns Hopkins University Press, 1998), p. 143; Plank, *An Unsettled Conquest*, p. 44; Leder, *Robert Livingston*, pp. 175–77.

48. Robert Watts to Robert Livingston, November 26, 1701, GLC 657; Waller, *Samuel Vetch*, pp. 5–7; Duncan Campbell to Robert Livingston, November 27, 1701, GLC 658; John Livingston to Robert Livingston, July 16, 1717, GLC 1156; John Livingston to Robert Livingston, September 9, 1717, GLC 1182.

49. Lord Cornbury to Fitz Winthrop, September 25, 1704, *Winthrop Papers*, vol. 3, pp. 267–68.

50. Grant-Costa, "The Last Indian War," pp. 34–35.

51. William Whiting to Fitz Winthrop, July 1704, *Winthrop Papers*, vol. 3,

pp. 241–42; Fitz Winthrop to Peter Schuyler, September 10, 1704, *Winthrop Papers*, vol. 3, p. 263.

52. Rev. John Williams to Mary Livingston, April 21, 1705, *Winthrop Papers*, vol. 3, p. 296; Richard Lord to Mary Livingston, May 31, 1705, *Winthrop Papers*, vol. 3, p. 296.

53. Ibid.; Joseph Dudley to Fitz Winthrop, June 4, 1705, *Winthrop Papers*, vol. 3, p. 295; John Livingston to Fitz Winthrop, June 20, 1705, *Winthrop Papers*, vol. 3, p. 297.

54. Plank, *An Unsettled Conquest*, pp. 36–37, 44; Waller, *Samuel Vetch*, pp. 83–106.

55. Plank, *An Unsettled Conquest*, pp. 41–42, 47–51; Waller, *Samuel Vetch*, pp. 83–106.

56. Wait Winthrop to Samuel Reade, March 5, 1708, *Winthrop Papers*, 6th series, vol. 5 (Boston: MHS, 1892), p. 164n.

57. D. P. Wight, "Graduates of Harvard College Born in Dedham," *NEHGR* 4 (1850): 354; Caulkins, ed., *Memoir of the . . . Rev. Eliphalet Adams*, pp. 27, 34; Waller, *Samuel Vetch*, pp. 83–106.

58. Wait Winthrop to Fitz Winthrop, July 14, 1701, *Winthrop Papers*, vol. 5, p. 93.

59. Joseph Dudley to Wait Winthrop, May 24, 1708, *Winthrop Papers*. vol. 5, p. 167; Holloway, "Historic New London," p. 128.

60. William Williams to John Winthrop IV, April 7, 1709, *Winthrop Papers*, vol. 5, pp. 182–83; William Williams to John Winthrop IV, April 25, 1709, *Winthrop Papers*, vol. 5, pp. 184–85; Wait Winthrop to Gurdon Saltonstall, January 23, 1710, *Winthrop Papers*, vol. 5, pp. 202–3.

61. Wait Winthrop to John Winthrop IV, October 26, 1710, *Winthrop Papers*, vol. 5, pp. 224–25; Wait Winthrop to John Winthrop IV, July 26, 1711, *Winthrop Papers*, vol. 5, pp. 236–38.

62. Plank, *An Unsettled Conquest*, pp. 45–51.

63. John Winthrop IV to Wait Winthrop, May, 1709, *Winthrop Papers*, vol. 5, pp. 186–88; John Winthrop IV to Wait Winthrop, May 18, 1709, *Winthrop Papers*, vol. 5, pp. 189–90.

64. Gurdon Saltonstall to Henry Ashurst, January 30, 1710, *Winthrop Papers*, vol. 5, pp. 208–12; Waller, *Samuel Vetch*, pp. 107–55.

65. Waller, *Samuel Vetch*, pp. 155–57; Gurdon Saltonstall to Henry Ashurst, January 30, 1710, *Winthrop Papers*, vol. 5, pp. 208–12.

66. Gurdon Saltonstall to Henry Ashurst, January 30, 1710, *Winthrop Papers*, vol. 5, pp. 208–12; Waller, *Samuel Vetch*, pp. 171–75.

67. Plank, *An Unsettled Conquest*, pp. 40–41.

68. Ibid., pp. 40–41, 74.

69. Ibid., p. 44.

70. Livingston, *Livingstons of Livingston Manor*, pp. 135–36.

71. *DJH*, 1 (8 September 1711).

72. David Shields calls "spiritual" diaries, written primarily by clergymen, journals of spiritual self-examination: David Shields, "A History of Personal

Diary Writing in New England, 1620–1745" (Ph.D. diss., University of Chicago, 1982), pp. 79–81.

73. Lockridge, *Literacy*; Charles W. Wootton and Mary Virginia Moore, "The Legal Status of Account Books in Colonial America," *Accounting History* 5 (2000): 33–58.

74. Shields credits the use of the public serial entry format for private writing to a new sense of individuality brought on by the Reformation that oriented toward privacy. Rather than indicating a new orientation toward privacy, however, diaries like Joshua's show the very public nature of "private life" in early New England. (A major example of early individuality in diurnal form is the diary of English naval administrator Samuel Pepys [1633–1703].) Shields, "Personal Diary Writing."

75. St. George, "Set Thine House in Order," p. 180; See Patricia Cline Cohen, *A Calculating People: The Spread of Numeracy in Early America* (Chicago: University of Chicago Press, 1982); Alfred Crosby, *The Measure of Reality: Quantification in Western Europe, 1250–1600* (New York: Cambridge University Press, 1997).

76. Jeremiah Bumstead, born in the same year as Joshua, wrote diary entries in almanac marginalia: Bumstead, "Diary of Jeremiah Bumstead," 193–204; Shields, "Personal Diary Writing," esp. pp. 197–98. The preeminent interpretation of a New England almanac-style diary is Laurel Thatcher Ulrich's *A Midwife's Tale*.

77. *DJH*, 1–3 (8 September–31 October 1711).

Chapter Seven: "She Was Taken Away from Me Wrongfully"

1. Rose and Brown, *Tapestry*, pp. 71–72.

2. Beebe, NLCCCR, Trials, vol. 7, Court of January 24, 1695, pp. 134–35; Beebe, NLCCCR, Trials, vol. 7, Court of June 2, 1702, p. 339; Beebe, NLCCCR, Trials, vol. 7, Court of August 25, 1702, p. 349. Elizabeth and Samuel Beebe were not the only heirs who objected to John and Bathshua's administration of their father's estate. Their quarrelsome brother Jonathan Rogers also posted his objections to his siblings' care of their mother, complaining that they did not adequately feed or clothe her. Eventually John and Bathshua's opponents succeeded in obtaining a revocation of their administration of the estate. For Jonathan's objections, see Petition of Jonathan Rogers, NLCCCR, Files, Box 153, File of 1692–96. For references to the revocation of their administration, see *Samuel Rogers v. John Rogers*, NLCSCR, Files, Box 7, File of March 1737. The administration was eventually transferred to James Rogers, Jr., grandson of the testator: Rogers, *James Rogers*, pp. 31–32. *Beebe v. Rogers*, NLCSCR, Files, Box 1, File of March 1712; *Beebe v. Rogers*, NLCCCR, Files, Box 156, File of June 1710.

3. Clarence Beebe, *A Monograph of the Family of Beebe* (New York: Clarence Beebe, 1904), pp. 11, 17; Case, ed., *Southold Town Records*, vol. 2, pp. 197–98; "Marriages by John Hempstead," *NEGHR* 128 (1974): 18–21, p. 18; Wait Winthrop to John Winthrop IV, July 12, 1711, *Winthrop Papers* microfilm, Reel 18; Wait Winthrop to John Winthrop IV, July 19, 1711, *Winthrop Papers* microfilm, Reel 18.

4. *Beebe v. Rogers*, NLCCCR, Files, Box 156, File of June 1710; the Widow Rogers's signature is nothing but a *C*-shaped scratch, and the witnesses to this suspect document (her son Jonathan and his wife, Naomi, opposed John and Bathshua. John and Bathshua appear to have little access to their mother at this point, Bathshua having been thrown out of her father's house in May 1690, according to her own testimony): Private Controversies, First series, vol. 5, Reel 104, Roll 101-75, p. 96, Connecticut Archives.

5. Jack is described as two and one-half in *Jackson v. Tracy*, NLCCCR, Files, File of November 1719; *Beebe v. Rogers*, NLCCCR, Files, Box 156, File of June 1710; Griffin, *Griffin's Journal*, pp. 30, 35. Elizabeth Rogers Beebe was buried near her house at the time of her death: Griffin, *Griffin's Journal*, p. 189.

6. Brinton, "The Rogerenes," p. 11; Kim, "Mr. Rogers's Neighborhood," pp. 205–6. For Rogerene involvement in the manumission movement in the late eighteenth century, see Griffin, *Griffin's Journal*, p. 105.

7. *James Rogers, Jr. v. Beebe*, NLCCCR, Files, Box 156, File of November 1711. Based on the recorded ages of John junior and Rachel, Rachel was probably born at the Beebes in January 1711 (and John junior in the summer of 1708): New London Land Records, vol. 7, 1711, p. 119; *Jackson v. Stone*, Suffolk Files, vol. 110, #11708, Massachusetts Archives, pp. 71–74. The story of John and Joan Jackson is also told at length in Grosskopf, "The Limits of Religious Dissent," pp. 166–77.

8. Rogers, NLCSCR, Files, Box 1, File of September 1711.

9. *Public Records of the Colony of Connecticut*, vol. 2, p. 326. On the night of May 29, the moon appeared waxing gibbous with 92 percent illumination: "Sun and Moon Data for 29 May 1711," U.S. Naval Observatory Astronomical Applications Department, http://aa.usno.navy.mil/cgi-bin/aa_pap.pl (accessed January 11, 2007). Ninety-two percent lunar illumination appears full to the naked eye: "Phases of the Moon and Percent of the Illuminated," U.S. Naval Observatory Astronomical Applications Department, http://aa.usno.navy.mil/faq/docs/moon_phases.html, p. 2 (accessed January 11, 2007); Rogers, NLCSCR, Files, Box 1, File of September 1711; *Beebe v. Jackson*, NLCSCR, Files, Box 1, File of September 1711. The garret and the back lean-to are two likely places where Joan and the children would have slept.

10. John Jackson testified that he went to bed with his wife at the Beebe house: *Beebe v. Jackson*, NLCSCR, Files, Box 1, File of September 1711; Rogers, NLCSCR, Files, Box 1, File of September 1711; sunrise was at 4:18 a.m.: "Sun and Moon Data for 30 May 1711."

11. Rose and Brown, *Tapestry*, pp. 6–7. Between the time that Joan went to live with the Beebes and her husband took her away, there was also an attempt on the part of the new administrator of James Rogers, Sr.'s estate, James Rogers, Jr. (the testator's grandson), to recover Joan from Samuel Beebe and also Adam and Miriam from Samuel Fox: see *Rogers v. Rogers*, NLCCCR, Files, Box 156, File of September 1710. In that litigation there is also an enticing reference to Joan being personally served a summons on June 22, 1710. At trial, Beebe won. James Rogers, Jr., tried a second time to reassert his claim to Joan via an action of fraud (the first trial was initiated by a writ of detainer), but was unsuccessful at getting the court

to rehear the case: *James Rogers, Jr. v. Beebe*, NLCCCR, Files, Box 156, File of November 1711. *Beebe v. Rogers*, NLCSCR, Files, Box 1, File of September 1711.

12. *Beebe v. Rogers*, NLCSCR, Files, Box 1, File of September 1711.

13. Ibid.

14. Ibid.

15. Ibid.

16. Ibid.

17. Ibid.

18. Ibid.

19. Ibid.

20. Ibid.; in the information of John Read, Crown attorney in the defamation case against Rogers, Read claimed that Jackson, too, had slandered the magistrates. The court files are unclear as to whether this charge was prosecuted against Jackson.

21. Ibid.

22. Ibid.

23. *Beebe v. Rogers*, NLCCCR, Files, Box 156, File of June 1711.

24. Samuel Beebe to John Livingston, New London Land Records, vol. 8, June 13, 1711, p. 119, NLCCO.

25. Plank, *An Unsettled Conquest*, pp. 75–77.

26. John Livingston to Robert Livingston, March 21, 1711, GLC 861.

27. See John Livingston to Robert Livingston, [February] 24, 1712, GLC 900.

28. Waller, *Samuel Vetch*, pp. 210–11.

29. *Jackson v. Livingston*, NLCCCR, Files, Box 159, File of June 1716.

30. Johanna Livingston and Mary Winthrop Livingston each had a maidservant: Johanna Livingston to Robert Livingston, March 17, 1713, GLC 984; Johanna Livingston to Robert Livingston, July 6, 1713, GLC 1018.

31. Waller, *Samuel Vetch*, pp. 210–11.

32. Wait Winthrop to John Winthrop IV, July 26, 1711, *Winthrop Papers*, vol. 5, pp. 236–38; *Winthrop Papers*, vol. 5, pp. 201–2; Kierner, *Traders and Gentlefolk*, p. 133; John Livingston to Robert Livingston, March 21, 1711, GLC 861; Daniel De Moulin, *A History of Surgery with Emphasis on the Netherlands* (Boston: Martinus Nijhoff Publishers, 1988), p. 228.

33. John Livingston to Robert Livingston, June 21, 1712, GLC 920; Robert Livingston to Alida Livingston, trans. Jos. Van der Linde, September 8, 1711, GLC 2202; Robert Livingston to Alida Livingston, trans. Jos Van der Linde, September 7, 1711, GLC; Gerald M. Mager, "Zabdiel Boylston: Medical Pioneer of Colonial Boston" (Ph.D. diss., University of Illinois, 1975), pp. 11–12; advertisement concerning breast cancer operation by Dr. Boylston on the wife of Edward Winslow, *Boston Gazette*, November 28, 1720, p. 4; see also advertisement of Dr. Sharp of London, *Boston Gazette*, October 10–17, 1720, p. 4.

34. Robert Livingston to Alida Livingston, trans. Jos. Van der Linde, September 8, 1711, GLC 2202; see also Samuel Vetch to Robert Livingston, April 24, 1713, GLC 1007; Robert Livingston to Alida Livingston, trans. Jos. Van der Linde, September 26, 1711, GLC 2209.

35. Thomas Lechmere to Wait Winthrop, August 27, 1711, *Winthrop Papers* microfilm, Reel 18.

36. John Livingston to Robert Livingston, July 1, 1713, GLC 1017; *DJH*, 4 (24 November 1711).

37. John G. Reid, "The 'Conquest' of Acadia: Narratives," in John G. Reid et al., *The "Conquest" of Acadia, 1710: Imperial, Colonial, and Aboriginal Constructions* (Toronto: University of Toronto Press, 2004), pp. 3–24, 16–17; Thomas Lechmere to Wait Winthrop, October 8, 1711, *Winthrop Papers*, vol. 5, pp. 248–49.

38. Thomas Lechmere to Wait Winthrop, October 15, 1711, *Winthrop Papers*, vol. 5, p. 250; Waller, *Samuel Vetch*, pp. 237–38; John Livingston to Robert Livingston, December 24, 1712, GLC 3107; John Livingston to Robert Livingston, May 27, 1712, GLC 909; Samuel Vetch to Robert Livingston, November 19, 1712, GLC 995.

39. Margaret Vetch to Robert Livingston, August 25, 1712, GLC 2236; Johanna Livingston to Robert Livingston, November 19, 1712, GLC 944.

40. Gurdon Saltonstall to Robert Livingston, September 3, 1712, GLC 939; Johanna Livingston to Robert Livingston, November 19, 1712, GLC 968.

41. *Stone v. Livingston*, NLCCCR, Files, Box 174, File of September 1720; Samuel Vetch to Robert Livingston, January 25, 1713, GLC 995.

42. Johanna Livingston to Robert Livingston, January 18, 1713, GLC 999; Frances M. Caulkins, "Ancient Burial Ground at New London, Connecticut," *NEGHR* 11 (1857): 21–30, 25.

43. *Dr. Daniel Hooker v. John Livingston*, NLCCCR, Files, Box 158, File of November 1714; *Encyclopædia Britannica* (1911), s.v. "Pharmacy"; Brandt, *American Aristocracy*, p. 64.

44. John Livingston to Robert Livingston, May 20, 1713, GLC 961; for John's poor financial straits, see Joseph Dudley to John Winthrop IV, February 5, 1713, *Winthrop Papers* microfilm, Reel 18; John Livingston to Robert Livingston, April 16, 1713, GLC 967; John Livingston to Robert Livingston, May 20, 1713, GLC 961; see also Margaret Vetch to Johanna Livingston, January 24, 1713, GLC 996.

45. Samuel Beebe to John Winthrop IV, house on Mill Cove now occupied by Madam Elizabeth Winthrop, New London Land Records, 1714, vol. 7, p. 235, NLCCO; Elizabeth Tongue "Winthrop" eventually moved into a Tongue family property and lived until 1731: Holloway, "Historic New London," p. 128.

46. John Livingston to Robert Livingston, June 15, 1713, GLC 1009; Johanna Livingston to Robert Livingston, June 29, 1713, GLC 1014; "Obituary of Mrs. Elizabeth Levingston [sic]," *New England Weekly Journal*, March 30, 1736, p. 2.

47. Johanna Livingston to Robert Livingston, June 22, 1713, GLC 1013.

48. Margaret Vetch to Robert Livingston, June 19, 1713, GLC 1015; Johanna Livingston to Robert Livingston, June 22, 1713, GLC 1013.

49. John Livingston to Robert Livingston, June 15, 1713, GLC 1009; John Livingston to Robert Livingston, July 9, 1713, GLC 1019; Johanna Livingston to Robert Livingston, June 29, 1713, GLC 1014; Samuel Vetch to Robert Livingston, January 25, 1714, GLC 1043; John Livingston to Robert Livingston, April 21, 1714, GLC 1066.

50. John Livingston to Robert Livingston, April 27, 1714, GLC 1070.

51. John Livingston to Robert Livingston, February 15, 1714, GLC 1049; John Livingston to Robert Livingston, April 21, 1714, GLC 1066; John Livingston to Robert Livingston, April 21, 1714, GLC 1066; John Livingston to Robert Livingston, March 21, 1711, GLC 861.

52. John Livingston to Robert Livingston, February 24, 1712, GLC 900.

53. John Livingston to Robert Livingston, April 21, 1714, GLC 1066; John Livingston to Robert Livingston, May 20, 1713, GLC 961.

54. John Livingston to Robert Livingston, July 1, 1713, GLC 1017.

55. John Livingston to Robert Livingston, February 15, 1714, GLC 1049; Jack was born around 1708: *Samuel Beebe v. John Jackson, Jr.*, NLCCCR, Files, Box 170, File of November 1731; Jerry was born in late 1712 or early 1713: *John Stone v. John Livingston*, NLCCCR, Files, Box 160, File of November 1717.

56. *Stone v. Livingston*, NLCCCR, Files, Box 174, File of September 1720; Livingston in Boston at time of the sale: John Livingston to Robert Livingston, February 15, 1714, GLC 1049; see "Sun Tavern on Dock Square," *Boston Gazette*, March 7–14, 1726, p. 2; "Crown Coffee-House in King Street," *Boston Gazette*, July 23–30, 1722, p. 4; "Mrs. Bulfinch's near the Mill Creek," *Boston Gazette*, September 26–October 3, 1726, p. 2; "Widow Ann Leblond's in Tree Mont Street," *Boston Gazette*, May 30–June 6, 1726, p. 2; classified ad, *Boston Gazette*, March 25–April 1, 1723, p. 2; see a similar advertisement in the *Boston Gazette*, August 29–September 5, 1720, p. 4; George E. Stone, *The Oxford Descendants of Gregory Stone of Cambridge, Massachusetts* (Amherst, MA: Carpenter & Morehouse, 1904), pp. 2–3.

57. Penny Bradford, comp., "Winslow Tracy," in Bradford/Robinson Families 2002, www.gencircles.com/users/pennybradford85/1/data/1089 (accessed September 12, 2007); *Tracy v. Hartshorn*, NLCCCR, Files, Box 162, File of June 1720; Lucius Barnes Barbour, "Genealogical Data from Connecticut Cemeteries," *NEHGR* 86 (1932): 372–90, 382.

Chapter Eight: "The Ways of Providence"

1. *DJH*, 12 (29 July 1712), 15 (2 October 1712), 16 (12 November 1712), 19 (26 January 1713), 21 (23 March 1713), 24 (24 June 1713), 34 (11 May 1714), 57 (11 July 1716), 62 (31 December 1716); Hurd, *New London County*, p. 159; New London Land Records, vol. 7, p. 267, NLCCO; Caulkins, *History of New London*, p. 338.

2. *DJH*, 46 (22 June 1715), 64 (30 January 1717).

3. Marcie Cohen, "The Journals of Joshua Whitman, Turner, Maine, 1809–1846," in *The Farm*, ed. Peter Benes, Dublin Seminar for New England Folklife (Boston: Boston University, 1986), pp. 49–59, 54; Cullon, "Colonial Shipwrights," pp. 29–36; *DJH*, 11 (27 June 1712), 23 (10 June 1713), 26 (24 August 1713), 28 (8–9 November 1713), 40 (28 December 1714), 63 (18 January 1717).

4. *Plumb v. Hayden*, NLCCCR, Files, Box 164, File of February 1723; Mary

Plumb, NLCSCR, Papers by Subject: Divorce, 1719–1875, Box 124; *DJH*, 29 (4 December 1713); see also *DJH*, 44 (18 April 1715), 69 (8 October 1717).

5. *DJH*, 32 (26 February, 4 March 1714).

6. *DJH*, 32 (26 February 1714), 35 (18 June 1714), 44 (12, 22, 30 April, 5 May 1715), 49 (1 November 1715), 55 (2, 3 May 1716), 56 (18 June 1716), 58 (1, 3, 8 September 1716), 60 (13 October 1716); Caulkins, *History of New London*, p. 320.

7. Wait Winthrop to John Winthrop IV, August 20, 1716, *Winthrop Papers*, vol. 5, p. 323.

8. *DJH*, 42 (12 February 1715); Larkin, *The Reshaping of Everyday Life*, p. 99.

9. *DJH*, 42 (12–15 February 1715).

10. Ibid.

11. *DJH*, 42–43 (2 February–10 April 1715).

12. *DJH*, 43 (23 March–10 April 1715).

13. *DJH*, 43–44 (11 March–2 May 1715).

14. *DJH*, 43 (9 April 1715), 44 (28 April 1715), 45 (17 May 1715).

15. *DJH*, 46 (22 June 1715), 64 (6 February 1717).

16. *DJH*, 57 (28, 30 July 1716), 564 (6 November 1751); see also *DJH*, 459 (12 September 1746), 687 (26 July 1758); *The Compact Edition of the Oxford English Dictionary*, vol. 1 (Oxford: Oxford University Press, 1971), p. 1195; Laurel Thatcher Ulrich, *Goodwives: Image and Reality in the Lives of Women in Northern New England, 1650–1750* (New York: Alfred A. Knopf, 1982), pp. 126–32.

17. *DJH*, 57 (30 July 1716); even soft-spoken conversations emanating from the hall are clearly audible in the chamber above; Betty's is the only other Hempstead sibling birth that occurs during the span of the diary: *DJH*, 34 (27 April 1714).

18. Ulrich, *A Midwife's Tale*, p. 190; Rebecca J. Tannenbaum, *Health and Wellness in Colonial America* (Denver, CO: Greenwood, 2012), p. 73; Ulrich, *Goodwives*, p. 129.

19. *DJH*, 57 (31 July, 1–4 August 1716).

20. *DJH*, 57 (4 August 1716); Tannenbaum, *The Healer's Calling*, pp. 10–11, 77–84; John Winthrop IV to Wait Winthrop, May 6, 1717, *Winthrop Papers* microfilm, Reel 19.

21. *DJH*, 6 (5 January 1712).

22. Caulkins, *History of New London*, pp. 398–99, 670; Franklin Bowditch Dexter, *Biographical Sketches of the Graduates of Yale College* (New York: Henry Holt, 1885), pp. 83–84; Tannenbaum, *The Healer's Calling*, pp. 8–9; see also Mac-Sparren, *Letter Book*, p. 5; *DJH*, 46 (11 July 1715), 57 (4 August 1716).

23. See Tannenbaum, *The Healer's Calling*, esp. p. 8.

24. *DJH*, 57 (5 August 1716); Ulrich, *A Midwife's Tale*, pp. 192–93; see also John Rushton Pagan, *Anne Orthwood's Bastard: Sex and Law in Early Virginia* (New York: Oxford University Press, 2003), p. 88.

25. Joseph Coit, "Personal History of New London and Norwich," p. 18, CHS; Mary L. B. Branch, *Misc. (1840–1922), Notebook: Family History*, diary, Aunt Patty, late nineteenth or early twentieth century, Box 6A, no. 29, pp. 6–7, HHA.

26. Branch, Notebook, pp. 6–7; Abigail's thoughts are similar to those expressed

by Anne Bradstreet in "To My Dear Children," in *Early American Writing*, ed. Giles Gunn (New York: Penguin, 1994), pp. 188–92.

27. *DJH*, 57 (4, 5 August 1716); Larkin, *The Reshaping of Everyday Life*, pp. 98–102; Joshua mentions visiting, sitting up with, or "watching" corpses: *DJH*, 41 (29 January 1715), 47 (? August 1715), 645 (15 January 1756).

28. *DJH*, 47 (6 August 1716); Larkin, *The Reshaping of Everyday Life*, pp. 100–101; See *DJH*, 601 (26 September 1753), 604 (27 November 1753), 620 (21 September 1754), 629 (8 March 1755), 653 (24 June 1756), 663 (24 February 1757).

29. Branch, Notebook, p. 6; *DJH*, 57 (9 August 1716).

30. *DJH*, 57 (6, 7 August 1716), 448 (5 February 1746).

31. *DJH*, 57–58 (9–11 August 1716).

32. *DJH*, 58 (12 August 1716); Joshua Hempstead, Diary (manuscript), NLCHS.

33. *DJH*, 58 (esp. 30–31 August 1716).

34. *DJH*, 58 (24 August 1716); for the Bailey sisters, see Joshua Hempstead conveyance to his grandson Nathaniel Hempstead, March 12, 1723, HHA.

35. Case, ed., *Southold Town Records*, vol. 2, p. 196; William Salmon, *The Salmon Records: A Private Register of Marriages and Deaths of the Residents of the Town of Southold, Suffolk County, New York, 1696–1811*, ed. William A. Robbins (New York: New York Genealogical and Biographical Society, 1918), p. 11.

36. *DJH*, 59 (12–18 September 1716).

37. *DJH*, 59 (18 September 1716); Williams, "History of the Rogerenes," p. 140; my appreciation to Sally Ryan and Mary Elizabeth Baker for taking me to this site.

38. *DJH*, 60 (17 October 1716).

39. *DJH*, 60–61 (6–16 November 1716); for weekly rates for infant care, see three shillings in Walter Palmer, NLCCCR, Trials, vol. 8, November 1712; two shillings six pence in Joseph Elderkin, NLCCCR, Trials, vol. 11, June 1719; two shillings six pence in Richard Smith, NLCCCR, Trials, vol. 14, November 1724.

40. *Fitch v. Huntington*, NLCSCR, Files, Box 7, File of March 1736; *Minor v. Denison*, NLCSCR, Files, Box 8, File of March 1739; Joshua also writes of a grandchild Irene Crettington being raised by her maternal grandparents "from a Sucking Child": *DJH*, 487 (18 February 1748).

41. *DJH*, 75 (21 April 1718); *Minor v. Denison*, NLCSCR, Files, Box 8, File of March 1739.

42. Larkin, *The Reshaping of Everyday Life*, p. 102; for mourning practices among the New London Winthrops, see Wait Winthrop to John Winthrop IV, March 12, 1717, *Winthrop Papers* microfilm, Reel 18; see also Lisa Wilson, *Ye Heart of a Man: The Domestic Life of Men in Colonial New England* (New Haven, CT: Yale University Press, 1999), pp. 144–54.

43. *DJH*, 297 (8 March 1736), 488 (7 March 1748); this Sarah married the lone survivor of the Bolles family massacre.

44. Demos, *A Little Commonwealth*, pp. 66–67; Wilson, *Ye Heart of a Man*, p. 144; [Woldf], New London Vital Statistics, vol. 1, p. 48; *DJH*, 43 (25 March 1715).

45. Wilson, *Ye Heart of a Man*, pp. 154–57; Ann Bradstreet wrote of her concern about relinquishing her children to a stepmother in the event of her death: Anne Bradstreet, "Before the Birth of One of Her Children (1678)," in *Early Ameri-*

can Writing, ed. Giles Gunn (New York: Penguin, 1994), pp. 178–79; see John L. Watson, "Passages in the Life of Priscilla (Thomas) Hobart," *NEHGR* 27 (1873): 24–26, 25.

46. *DJH*, 230 (22 February 1731), 425–26 (26 September 1744), 639 (26 September 1755).

47. *DJH*, 166 (28 March 1726), 220 (22 May 1730), 285 (18 May 1735), 476 (26 July 1747).

48. Dayton, *Women Before the Bar*, pp. 157–230.

49. *Acts and Laws* (1715), p. 4; *DJH*, 92 (27–28 November 1719), 93 (2 December 1719); William Bloggett, NLCCCR, Records of Trials, vol. 11, November 1719, p. 216; for difficulties getting away with adultery, see *Murrow v. Bradford*, NLCCCR, Files, Box 157, File of November 1713.

50. Sewall, *Diary of Samuel Sewall*, vol. 3, MHS, 5th series, vol. 7 (Boston: MHS, 1882), October 19, 1728, p. 392; *DJH*, 63 (23 January 1717).

51. *DJH*, 65 (23 March, 21 April 1717), 67 (9 July 1717), 68 (24 July 1717), 69 (13–14 October 1717), 70 (21 November 1717).

52. *DJH*, 52 (18 January 1716), 263 (6 October 1733), 382 (13 January 1742).

53. See *DJH*, 49 (24 October 1715); Cullon, "Colonial Shipwrights," pp. 155–72, 230–34.

Chapter Nine: A Higher Court

1. Paul Dudley to John Winthrop IV, October 30, 1721, *Winthrop Papers* microfilm, Reel 19.

2. Thomas Lechmere to John Winthrop IV, March 22, 1720, *Winthrop Papers* microfilm, Reel 19; Thomas Lechmere to John Winthrop IV, March 17, 1720, *Winthrop Papers* microfilm, Reel 19; Matson, *Merchants and Empire*, pp. 131–32; St. George, *Conversing by Signs*, p. 308; Cullon, "Colonial Shipwrights," pp. 173, 175–76.

3. *John Jackson v. John Stone*, Middlesex County, Court of Common Pleas, Record Book, vol. 1699–1722, December Term 1716, p. 234, Massachusetts Archives; *Samuel Beebe v. John Rogers, Jr.*, NLCSCR, Files, File of September 1732; *John Stone v. John Livingston*, NLCCCR, Files, File of September 1720.

4. *John Jackson v. John Stone*, Middlesex County, Court of Common Pleas, Record Book, vol. 1699–1722, December Term 1716, p. 234, Massachusetts Archives; *John Stone v. John Livingston*, NLCCCR, Files, File of September 1720.

5. Sarah Knight to Thomas Tilestone (John Stone's brother-in-law), November 15, 1717, in *John Stone v. John Livingston*, NLCCCR, Files, File of September 1720.

6. John Livingston to John Stone, July 23, 1717, in *John Stone v. John Livingston*, NLCCCR, Files, File of September 1720.

7. John M. Murrin, "The Bench and Bar of Eighteenth-Century Massachusetts," in *Colonial America: Essays in Politics and Social Development*, ed. Stanley N. Katz (Boston: Little, Brown, 1976), pp. 415–49, pp. 422–23; Andrew M. Davis, ed., "Reflections upon Reflections: Or, More News from Robinson Cruso's

Island . . . ," July 12, 1720, reprinted in *Colonial Currency Reprints*, Prince Society Publications, vol. 2 (Boston: John Wilson & Son, 1911), pp. 115–16, 123–24.

8. John Livingston to John Stone, July 23, 1717, in *Stone v. Livingston*, NLCCCR, Files, File of September 1720; *John Jackson v. John Stone*, Suffolk Files, vol. 110, #11708, Massachusetts Archives, pp. 71–74.

9. *Jackson v. Livingston*, NLCCCR, Files, Box 159, File of June 1716.

10. *Stone v. Livingston*, NLCCCR, Files, File of September 1720.

11. Jacob was born around 1717: *Samuel Rogers v. John Rogers*, NLCCCR, Files, Box 175, File of June 1736, part 1.

12. *Stone v. Livingston*, NLCCCR, Files, File of September 1720.

13. *Samuel Beebe v. John Jackson, Jr.*, NLCCCR, Records of Trials, vol. 17, November 1731; *Jackson v. Tracy*, NLCCCR, Files, Files of November 1718, November 1719. *Jackson v. Tracy*, NLCCCR, Records of Trials, vol. 11, June 1718, p. 10, November 1718, p. 47; *Jackson v. Tracy*, NLCCCR, Records of Trials, vol. 11, November 1719, p. 178; *Jackson v. Tracy*, NLCCCR, Records of Trials, vol. 11, June 1719, p. 154.

14. Ibid.; *DJH*, 90 (6 September 1719); John Bolles, NLCCCR, Records of Trials, vol. 13, June 1721; John Rogers, NLCCCR, Records of Trials, vol. 11, November 1719, pp. 212–17; John Waterouse, NLCCCR, Records of Trials, vol. 12, June 1720; John Bolles, John Rogers, Sr., and Sarah Bolles: John Bolles, NLCCCR, Records of Trials, vol. 13, June 1721.

15. Bumstead, "Diary of Jeremiah Bumstead," p. 200; Henry W. Foote, *Annals of King's Chapel from the Puritan Age . . .* , vol. 1 (Boston: Little, Brown and Co., 1882), pp. 247–48.

16. John Livingston to Robert Livingston, June 15, 1713, GLC 1009.

17. John Livingston to Robert Livingston, March 27, 1712, GLC 909; John Livingston to Robert Livingston, June 21, 1712, GLC 920; John Livingston to Alida Livingston, June ?, 1712, GLC 928; Alida Livingston to Robert Livingston, August 31, 1712, GLC 187; Writ of Attachment against Samuel Vetch, February 24, 1713, GLC 988; Samuel Vetch to Robert Livingston, April 6, 1714, GLC 1060; John Borland to Robert Livingston, April 19, 1714, GLC 1063; John Livingston to Robert Livingston, April 21, 1714, GLC 1066; John Livingston to Robert Livingston, April 27, 1714, GLC 1070; Waller, *Samuel Vetch*, pp. 253–59; Samuel Sewall to John Winthrop IV, July 17, 1714, *Winthrop Papers*, vol. 5, p. 296.

18. Samuel Vetch to Robert Livingston, August 25, 1716, GLC 1112.

19. John Winthrop IV to Wait Winthrop, November [after 5] 1711, *Winthrop Papers* microfilm, Reel 18; Joseph Dudley to John Winthrop IV, February 5, 1714, *Winthrop Papers*, vol. 5, p. 283; Paul Dudley to Anne Winthrop, February 8, 1714, *Winthrop Papers*, vol. 5, p. 284; Wait Winthrop to Gurdon Saltonstall, *Winthrop Papers*, vol. 5, April 5, 1714, p. 288.

20. E. B. Livingston, "Colonel John Livingston of New London . . . ," *New York Genealogical and Biographical Record* 46 (1915): 230–31, 231; Samuel Vetch to Robert Livingston, August 25, 1716, GLC 1112; Waller, *Samuel Vetch*, pp. 284–85; Will of John Livingston, Public Record Office, National Archives, London, United Kingdom, Probate 11/574.

21. Caulkins, *History of New London*, p. 365.

22. Brandt, *American Aristocracy*, p. 70; "Obituary of Mrs. Elizabeth Levingston [*sic*]."

23. Waller, *Samuel Vetch*, p. 284; Kierner, *Traders and Gentlefolk*, pp. 50–53, 61–63.

24. Paul Dudley to Anne Winthrop, February 8, 1714, *Winthrop Papers*, vol. 5, p. 284; Joseph Dudley to John Winthrop IV, March 8, 1714, *Winthrop Papers*, vol. 5, p. 285.

25. John Winthrop IV to Wait Winthrop, October 24, 1717, *Winthrop Papers* microfilm, Reel 19; Wait Winthrop to Anne Winthrop, October 17, 1715, *Winthrop Papers* microfilm, Reel 18; John Winthrop IV to Wait Winthrop, October ?, 1717, *Winthrop Papers* microfilm, Reel 19.

26. John Winthrop IV to Wait Winthrop, May 3, 1716, *Winthrop Papers* microfilm, Reel 18; Wait Winthrop to John Winthrop, February 11, 1717, *Winthrop Papers* microfilm, Reel 18; Lawrence Park, "Old Boston Families: Number Three, The Savage Family," *NEHGR* 67 (1913): 198–215, 309–30, 213; Vernon N. Kisling, Jr., "Zoological Gardens of the United States," in *Zoo and Aquarium History . . .* , ed. Vernon N. Kisling, Jr. (New York: CRC Press, 2001), pp. 147–80, 147–48; John Winthrop IV to Wait Winthrop, February 18, 1717, *Winthrop Papers* microfilm, Reel 18; Postscript in Samuel Sewall to John Winthrop IV, April 8, 1717, *Winthrop Papers* microfilm, Reel 18.

27. John Winthrop IV to Wait Winthrop, April 4, 1717, *Winthrop Papers* microfilm, Reel 19; John Winthrop IV to Wait Winthrop, May 2, 1717, *Winthrop Papers* microfilm, Reel 19.

28. Lucy Lechmere to Wait Winthrop, May 24, 1716, *Winthrop Papers*, vol. 5, p. 316. See also Richard Lechmere to John Winthrop IV, July 8, 1719, *Winthrop Papers* microfilm, Reel 19; Stephen K. Roberts, "Lechmere, Sir Nicholas (bap. 1613, d. 1701)," *Oxford Dictionary of National Biography* (Oxford University Press, 2004; online ed., January 2008, http://www.oxforddnb.com/view/article/16261 [accessed September 8, 2012]).

29. John Winthrop IV to Wait Winthrop, May 2, 1717, *Winthrop Papers* microfilm, Reel 19.

30. Thomas Lechmere to John Winthrop IV, January 28, 1717, *Winthrop Papers* microfilm, Reel 18.

31. Cited in Mayo, *Winthrop Family*, p. 108; Sewall, *Diary of Samuel Sewall*, vol. 3, p. 147; [Funeral of Wait Winthrop], *Winthrop Papers*, vol. 5, p. 354.

32. Arthur M. Schlesinger, "Colonial Appeals to the Privy Council, II," *Political Science Quarterly* 28 (1913): 433–50, 440; Richard Lechmere to John Winthrop IV, July 8, 1719, *Winthrop Papers* microfilm, Reel 19; Thomas Lechmere to John Winthrop IV, August 31, 1719, *Winthrop Papers* microfilm, Reel 19.

33. Thomas Lechmere to John Winthrop, March 22, 1720, *Winthrop Papers* microfilm, Reel 19; see also Thomas Lechmere to John Winthrop, March 17, 1720, *Winthrop Papers* microfilm, Reel 19; Paul Dudley to John Winthrop IV, October 30, 1721, *Winthrop Papers* microfilm, Reel 19.

34. Thomas Lechmere to John Winthrop, July 4, 1720, *Winthrop Papers* micro-

film, Reel 19; Ann Lechmere to John Winthrop IV, May 8, 1721, *Winthrop Papers* microfilm, Reel 19; John Winthrop IV to Ann Lechmere, May 11, 1721, *Winthrop Papers* microfilm, Reel 19.

35. Thomas Lechmere to John Winthrop IV, October 26, 1719, *Winthrop Papers* microfilm, Reel 19; Thomas Lechmere to John Winthrop IV, October 30, 1721, *Winthrop Papers* microfilm, Reel 19; Joseph Talcott, *The Talcott Papers*, vol. 2, ed. Mary Kingsbury Talcott, *Collections of the Connecticut Historical Society*, vol. 5 (Hartford: Connecticut Historical Society, 1896), pp. 418n–419n.

36. Caulkins, *History of New London*, p. 477; Thomas Lechmere to John Winthrop IV, April 22, 1723, *Winthrop Papers* microfilm, Reel 19; Thomas Lechmere to John Winthrop IV, April 29, 1723, *Winthrop Papers* microfilm, Reel 19; Dexter, *Biographical Sketches of the Graduates of Yale*, p. 38; Thomas Lechmere to John Winthrop IV, April 29, 1723, *Winthrop Papers* microfilm, Reel 19.

37. John Boyle, "Boyle's Journal of Occurences in Boston, 1759–1778," *NEGHR* 84 (1930): 142–71, 248–72, 357–82, 142.

38. *Boston News-Letter*, August 15–22, 1723, p. 2.

39. *New England Courant*, August 19–26, 1723. The wording was a play on *Hudibras*, Samuel Butler's seventeenth-century satiric poem about the Cromwellian Puritan party.

40. Richard Lechmere to Thomas Lechmere, July 8, 1716, *Winthrop Papers* microfilm, Reel 19; John Winthrop IV to Anne Winthrop, August 26, 1723, *Winthrop Papers* microfilm, Reel 19; Schlesinger, "Colonial Appeals," p. 441.

41. Thomas Goddard Wright, *Literary Culture in Early New England, 1620–1730* (New Haven, CT: Yale University Press, 1920), p. 201; James H. Stark, *The Loyalists of Massachusetts* (Boston: James H. Stark, 1910), p. 413.

Chapter Ten: "A Pestilence into That Land"

1. Mager, "Zabdiel Boylston," pp. 102–3; Gurdon Saltonstall to Thomas Prince?, July 2, 1721, *Saltonstall Papers*, vol. 1, p. 342; quoted in Mager, "Zabdiel Boylston," p. 96.

2. Mager, "Zabdiel Boylston," pp. 88, 91–96, 144.

3. Ibid., pp. 103, 107.

4. John Rogers, Jr., *A Brief Account of the Late Suffering* (1726), pp. 9–10.

5. Account of Mr. Jeremiah Miller, NLCCCR, Records of Trials, vol. 13, June 18 1721; *New England Courant*, December 4–11, 1721, p. 2.

6. *DJH*, 108 (23, 30 April 1721), 113–14 (17–18 October, 6 November 1721); *New England Courant*, December 4–11, 1721, p. 2; Rogers, *James Rogers*, pp. 22, 60; Mager, "Zabdiel Boylston," p. 106.

7. Thomas Lechmere to John Winthrop, Boston to New London, October 2, 1721, *Winthrop Papers* microfilm, Reel 19; *New England Courant*, December 4–11, 1721, p. 2.

8. Gardener, *Baptists of Early America*, pp. 49–51.

9. *Samuel Beebe v. John Rogers, Jr.*, NLCCCR, Files, Box 171, File of February 1732.

10. New London Land Records, vol. 8, December 9, 1723, p. 186, NLCCO; James M. Rose and Alice Eichholz, *Black Genesis: A Resource Book for African-American Genealogy*, vol. 1 (Detroit, MI: Gale Publishing, 1978), p. 8; *Hambleton v. Jackson*, NLCCCR, Files, Box 175, File of June 1736, part 1.

11. *DJH*, 113–14 (10, 17–18 October, 6 November 1721).

12. Estates of Incompetent Persons, vol. 2, pp. 201–3, Connecticut Archives; *DJH*, 146 (2 October 1724); John Edgecombe: Division of His Estate as Widow's Thirds to Elizabeth Edgecombe, June 26, 1721, Hempstead Family Probate Records, HHA.

13. New London Town Records, vol. 8, October 25, 1721, p. 84, NLCCO; a copy of this agreement is also at NLCHS: Elizabeth Edgecombe's Deed to Joshua Hempsted of her Thirds or Dower 1721.

14. *DJH*, 146 (2 October 1724), 160 (13 October 1725), 161 (28 October 1725); Estates of Incompetent Persons, vol. 2, pp. 201–3, Connecticut Archives.

15. Joshua's use of apprenticeship runs counter to the vision suggested in Morgan, *The Puritan Family*, esp. pp. 68–79. Morgan proposes that parents might have used apprenticeship as a means to transfer authority to an unrelated adult during adolescence to ensure children's continued obedience to social norms. Vickers interprets fathers' use of child labor as exploitative: Daniel Vickers, *Farmers and Fishermen: Two Centuries of Work in Essex County, Massachusetts, 1630–1850* (Chapel Hill: University of North Carolina Press, 1994), pp. 64, 82; for apprenticing close by, as with a neighbor, see Russell, *A Long, Deep Furrow*, p. 110.

16. *DJH*, 9 (13 May 1712), 36 (12, 27 July 1714). Just what kind of schooling Joshua arranged for his children is unclear. His references to such schooling are short and elusive. See, for example, *DJH*, 2 (16 October 1711), 33 (22, 24 March 1714), or 46 (11 July 1715). During several years of Joshua junior and Nathaniel's boyhoods, there was no permanent schoolmaster in New London after Mr. Denison left in 1710, see, for example, *DJH*, 9 (24 April 1712), *DJH*, 37–38 (28, 30 August, 2, 3, 13, 21 September 1714), 43 (4 April 1715), 44 (15 April 1715).

17. For Joshua's expectation that Nathaniel would inherit the Long Island property, see DJH, 128 (13–14, 19 January 1723), 128–29 (27 March 1723), 131 (21 June 1723). *DJH*, 52 (23 January 1716); *Coit v. Edgecombe*, NLCCCR, Files, Box 159, File of November 1715, part 1; *Edgecombe v. Coit*, NLCCCR, Files, Box 161, File of March 1718; Coit is referred to as a shopkeeper in *Wheeler v. Coit*, NLCCCR, Files, Box 168, File of November 1727; for the operation of Coit taverns and the location of the Coit property, see R. B. Wall, "John Barleycorn's Days in Old Taverns of New London: Chapter III," *NLD*, May 10, 1920. Evidence of Solomon Coit's malt making appears in *Coit v. Treadway*, NLCSCR, Files, Box 10, File of September 1745; Caulkins, *History of New London*, p. 410; reference to Solomon's proposed wharf appears in ELB Transcripts, Box 2, New London Town Meetings, 1694–1741, January 13, 1724, CSL. *DJH*, 46 (22? June 1715); Marriages, Births, and Deaths in New London, pp. 298, 313, 317, 319, NLCCO.

18. *DJH*, 63 (4, 10, 12, 16–17, 21 January 1717), 66 (26 April, 1 May 1717); Caulkins, *History of New London*, pp. 358–59, 241.

19. *DJH*, 80 (4 October 1718), 103 (9 December 1720), 109 (27 May 1721), 121 (8 June 1722), 137 (16 December 1723).

20. Branch, Notebook, pp. 7 verso, 15 (Robert referred to as a lawyer based on a Southold newspaper article); see Case, ed., *Southold Town Records*, vol. 2, pp. 63, 362; ibid., vol. 1, pp. 317–18; "Daniel Osborn," Thomas Osmun Families, http://www.rootsweb.ancestry.com/~nymadiso/osman3.htm, citing Liber 28:285 Suffolk County, N.Y. VIII: 54 (accessed November 11, 2008); *DJH*, 147 (28 October 1724), 148 (17 November 1724), 152 (28 January 1725); Robert (and Stephen) worked for New London blacksmith John Richards: *DJH*, 137 (31 December 1723); *Picket v. Burrows*, NLCCCR, Files, Box 166, File of June 1726, part 1. The Youngses were near neighbors to the Bailey-Coopers: Case, ed., *Southold Town Records*, vol. 2, pp. 136–38.

21. *DJH*, 53 (2 March 1716), 76 (24 June 1718), 77 (7 July 1718), 87 (30 April 1719), 141 (9 April 1724), 149 (10 December 1724), 150 (19 December 1724), 151 (5, 15–16 January 1725); see also 148 (19 November 1724).

22. *DJH*, 154 (24 March 1725), 168 (11 May 1726), 169 (8 June 1726).

23. Caulkins, *History of New London*, pp. 240–45; John Robinson and George Francis Dow, *Sailing Ships of New England, 1607–1907*, paperback ed. (New York: Skyhorse Publishing, 2007), pp. 16, 30–31; *DJH*, 160 (12 October 1725); see *DJH*, 172 (10 August 1726), 235 (7 July 1731). Later, Jeffrey built a smaller, 570-ton great ship, the *Don Carlos*, that sailed to Lisbon: *DJH*, 264 (29 November 1733).

24. *DJH*, 128 (13–14, 19 January 1723), 128–29 (27 March 1723), 131 (21, 30 June 1723), 132 (18 July 1723).

25. *DJH*, 132 (18–19 July 1723).

26. *DJH*, 109 (30 May 1721), 110 (19 July 1721), 133 (19 August 1723).

27. *DJH*, 134 (29 September 1723), 137 (10 December 1723); Inventory of the Estate of Nathaniel Hempsted, December 22, 1732, Misc. Financial, Box 37, Photocopies: Hempstead Family Probate Documents, HHA. I am assuming that Nathaniel and Mary used the calico curtains (and not the other "blue" curtains listed) for their bedstead because of their position in the inventory.

28. *DJH*, 147 (12, 15, 27 October 1724), 149 (8, 14 December 1724), 150 (19, 21 December 1724), 157 (3, 9, 12 June 1725).

29. *DJH*, 157 (9, 12, 26 June, 2–3 July 1725), 177 (30 December 1726), see also 179 (20 February 1727); Marcus Rediker, *Between the Devil and the Deep Blue Sea: Merchant Seamen, Pirates, and the Anglo-American Maritime World, 1700–1750* (Cambridge, UK: Cambridge University Press, 1987), pp. 82, 156.

30. Joseph Coit, Personal History of New London and Norwich, January 12, 1719, p. 1, CHS; Caulkins, *History of New London*, p. 156.

31. Indian seaman George Job's contract in *Job v. Graves*, NLCCCR, Box 6, Files, File of March 1735; Rediker, *Between the Devil*, pp. 84–86, 119, 122, 126–29; Joseph Coit, Personal History of New London and Norwich, n.d., p. 3, CHS.

32. Rediker, *Between the Devil*, pp. 126–29; *DJH*, 179 (26 January, 20 February 1727).

33. Rediker, *Between the Devil*, pp. 80, 155; contrast with p. 83.

34. Schlesinger, "Appeals," p. 441; John Winthrop IV to Wait Winthrop, October 24, 1717, *Winthrop Papers* microfilm, Reel 19.

35. Schlesinger, "Appeals," p. 441.

36. Anne Winthrop to John Winthrop IV, June 1?, 1727, *Winthrop Papers* microfilm, Reel 19; Anne Winthrop to John Winthrop IV, March ?, 1728, *Winthrop Papers* microfilm, Reel 19; Privy Council Ruling, February 15, 1728, *Winthrop Papers*, vol. 5, pp. 496–509.

37. John Winthrop's Account of his Visit to Groton in Suffolk, April 1728, *Winthrop Papers* microfilm, Reel 19; Privy Council Ruling, February 15, 1728, *Winthrop Papers*, vol. 5, pp. 496–509.

Chapter Eleven: "Adam Is Come"

1. *DJH*, 187 (4–10 September 1727).

2. Ibid., (4–26 September 1727).

3. Joshua Hempsted, Account Book, 1737–1757, p. 181, NLCHS; *DJH*, 187 (4–13 September 1727).

4. *DJH*, 58 (7 September 1716), 187 (14–27 September 1727).

5. Arthur Zilversmit, *The First Emancipation: The Abolition of Slavery in the North* (Chicago: University of Chicago Press, 1967), pp. 40–44; *DJH*, 187 (21–22, 26 September 1727), 189 (4 November 1727).

6. Caulkins, *History of New London*, p. 471; Benjamin Trumbull, *History of Connecticut*, vol. 1 (New London, CT: H. D. Utley, 1898), p. 385; for colonials' engagement with news and information, see Brown, *Knowledge Is Power*.

7. Gloria L. Main, "Gender, Work, and Wages in Colonial New England," *WMQ* 51 (1994): 39–66, 53.

8. The Easthampton widow was likely Mary Gardiner Conkling (1638–1727). For a grandmother helping to wean a grandchild, see *DJH*, 224 (6 September 1730). Daughter Abigail left her child at Joshua's to wean: *DJH*, 258 (7 June 1733). *DJH*, 75 (April 21, 1718).

9. *DJH*, 97 (8 May 1720), 119 (1, 4 April 1722), 132 (22 July 1723).

10. *DJH*, 134 (1 October 1723), 135 (19 October 1723), 143 (18 June 1724), 178 (6 January 1727), 186 (31 August 1727). Thankful Smith was probably Thankful Billings Smith, wife of Daniel Smith. Alan J. C. Taylor, *Edgecombes at New London*, http://freepages.genealogy.rootsweb.com/~jvoran/edgecomb/at/edgenl_at.htm (accessed January 16, 2006).

11. *DJH*, 319 (17 August 1737); cited in William Matthews, "Early New England Words," *American Speech* 15 (1940): 225–31, 229; Russell, *A Long, Deep Furrow*, p. 87.

12. *DJH*, 188 (8 October 1727).

13. For the practice of placing the best bedstead in the hall, see the 1658 inventory of Joseph Youngs: Case, ed. *Southold Town Records*, vol. 1, p. 438. For a family of six sharing a bedroom and possibly a bed, see *John Whittley v. Joseph Dudley*, NLCCCR, Records of Trials, vol. 8, June 1712, p. 56.

14. *DJH*, 187 (27 September 1727), 188 (3 October 1727).

15. Daniel Vickers, "Competence and Competition: Economic Culture in Early America," *WMQ* 47 (1990): 3–29.

16. David A. Wells, "Glacial Action," *Records and Papers of the New London County Historical Society*, part 2, vol. 1 (1890): 31–37, see *DJH*, 107 (20 April 1721), 118 (19 February, 1 March 1722), 119–20 (10–11, 14 April 1722). Two men can build around ten feet of stone wall per day (including carting stones and laying a foundation): Susan Allport, *Sermons in Stone: The Stone Walls of New England and New York* (New York: W. W. Norton, 1990), p. 18. *DJH*, 314 (31 March 1737).

17. *DJH*, 345 (18 April 1739); John Vivian, *Building Stone Walls* (North Adams, MA: Storey Publishing, 1976), pp. 8, 51; at seventy-six Joshua put in a wall corner: *DJH*, 632 (21 May 1755); at eighty he placed foundation stones for a wall: *DJH*, 684 (13, 20 May 1758); for the technical difficulties of foundations and corners, see Vivian, *Building Stone Walls*, pp. 23–28, 36–40; *DJH*, 347 (9 June 1739).

18. *DJH*, 39 (4 November 1714), 447 (22–23 January 1746).

19. Ibid., 324 (21 November 1737), 381 (22 December 1741), 385 (15 March 1742); see also *DJH*, 326 (9 January 1738), 660 (1 December 1756).

20. Ibid., 37 (20 August 1714), 85 (11–12, 16 March 1719); see also *DJH*, 119 (11 April 1722), 208 (14 April 1729), 345 (17 April 1739); see R. B. Wall, "The Ancient Schoolhouse located by Truman's Brook: Chapter IV," *NLD*, July 20, 1909.

21. *DJH*, 427 (19 October 1744), 493 (20 July 1748); Vivian, *Building Stone Walls*, pp. 42–43.

22. *DJH*, 531 (29 January 1750).

23. Ibid., 570 (19 February 1752).

24. Ibid., 305 (13 August, 15 September 1736), 349 (5 July 1739).

25. One of these markers was the rocky hill that was probably the configuration of rocks (which included a cradle-like mass and the seeming footprints of giants) in which generations of children played: R. B. Wall, "Historical Sketches of Early Dwellers in Pearl Street," *NLD*, November 19, 1914; see *DJH*, 44 (18 April 1715); 156 (26 April 1725), 168 (2 May 1726), 195 (4 April 1728), 331 (9 May 1738), 578 (22 July 1752); Larkin, *The Reshaping of Everyday Life*, pp. 129–30.

26. Richard M. Candee, "Land Surveys of William and John Godsoe of Kittery, Maine: 1689–1769" in *New England Prospect: Maps, Place Names, and the Historical Landscape*, ed. Peter Benes, Dublin Seminar for New England Folklife (Boston: Boston University, 1980), pp. 9–46, 10, 40; W. Richeson, *English Land Measuring to 1800: Instruments and Practices* (Cambridge, MA: MIT Press, 1966), pp. 17, 25, 30–31.

27. *Acts and Laws* (1715), pp. 8–9; *DJH*, 84 (14 February, 2 March 1719), 95 (16 March 1720), 580 (27 August 1752); G. Albert Hill, "Colonial Milestones Along Connecticut Highways," *The Antiquarian* 2 (1950): 15–19; John Edgecombe used a heap of stones with a stick: *John Edgecombe v. Solomon Coit*, NLCCCR, Files, Box 161, File of March 1718; Samuel Rogers's testimony, misfiled in NLCSCR, Files, Box 10, File of March 1746; New London Land Records, vol. 4, pp. 196, 209, NLCCO.

28. *DJH*, 279 (22 November 1734), 575 (21 May 1752); that gravestones were stacked at the back of the house is an educated guess; Levine, "Colonial Long Island Grave Stones," pp. 46–57, 47, 54–55; *DJH*, 160 (2 October 1725), 187 (16 September 1727), 500 (15 December 1748); Caufield, "Connecticut Gravestones XII,"

pp. 65–79; James A. Slater and Ralph L. Tucker, "The Colonial Gravestone Carvings of John Hartshorne," in *Puritan Gravestone Art II*, Dublin Seminar for New England Folklife, ed. Peter Benes (Boston: Boston University, 1978), pp. 79–146.

29. Ludwig, *Graven Images*, pp. 233–38; Levine, "Colonial Long Island Grave Stones," p. 47.

30. Slater and Tucker, "Colonial Gravestone Carvings of John Hartshorne," pp. 79–82; James A. Slater, "John Hartshorne (1650–ca. 1737)," in James A. Slater, *The Colonial Burying Grounds of Eastern Connecticut and the Men Who Made Them . . .* (Hamden, CT: Archon Books, 1987), pp. 5–7; *DJH*, 147 (21 October 1724).

31. See *DJH*, 437 (26, 27 June 1745); Ludwig, *Graven Images*, p. 232; *DJH*, 12 (29 July 1712), 135 (16 October 1723), 147 (21 October 1724, 155 (29 March 1725), 159 (25 August 1725), 162 (30 November 1725), 172 (3 August 1726), 174 (22 September 1726), 188 (2 October 1727), 189 (4 November 1727), 198 (13 July 1728), 301 (25 June 1736), 533 (12 March 1750), 575 (21 May 1752), 595 (27 June 1753); Slater and Tucker, "Colonial Gravestone Carvings of John Hartshorne," pp. 132–33.

32. *DJH*, 169 (11 June 1726), 184 (7 July 1727), 229 (20 January 1731), 235–36 (10, 13–14 July 1731), 241 (20 December 1731), 246 (6, 12 June 1732); Joshua sometimes lettered large tombstones in situ at the burying place: *DJH*, 304 (25 August 1736).

33. Bill Ledyard, ed., *History of the Bill Family* (New York: Ledyard Bill, 1867), p. 123; *DJH*, 286 (20 December 1734), 360 (7 May 1740), 529 (27 December 1749), 588 (9 February 1753).

34. Rose, *The Village Carpenter*, pp. 121–27; *DJH*, 159 (10 August 1725), 261 (3 September 1733).

35. *DJH*, 447 (25 January 1746), 448 (8 February 1746), 476 (27 July 1747); William H. Powers, *Powers-Banks Ancestry* (Ames, IA: John Leslie Powers, 1921), p. 26.

Chapter Twelve: Bream Cove and Beyond

1. Gerald F. Moran, "Conditions of Religious Conversion in the First Society of Norwich, Connecticut, 1718–1744," *Journal of Social History* 5 (1972): 331–43; 333; only around 11 percent of men became church members after the age of forty-five in a sampling of Connecticut parishes from 1720 to 1729: Moran, "The Puritan Saint," p. 280.

2. New London, First Congregational Church, Reel 307, vol. 1, November 13, 1709, p. 10, CSL; the first years of marriage were a customary time for adults to become church members, but female communicants still dominated: Stephen R. Grossbart, "Seeking the Divine Favor: Conversion and Church Admission in Eastern Connecticut, 1711–1832," *WMQ* 46 (1989): 696–740, 706–8; Moran, "Conditions of Religious Conversion," 333–35.

3. *DJH*, 173 (2 September 1726); New London, First Congregational Church, Reel 307, vol. 1, September 2, 1726, p. 14, November 13, 1726, p. 16, CSL; the New London Congregation had always been relatively liberal in its admission policies; see, for example, its rejection of the Saybrook Platform of 1708, which attempted

to centralize and tighten church discipline: New London, First Congregational Church, Reel 307, vol. 1, p. 13, CSL; Moran, "The Puritan Saint," pp. 202–3.

4. *DJH*, 175 (13 November 1726); see New London, First Congregational Church, Reel 307, vol. 1, November 13, 1726, p. 16, CSL.

5. Nathaniel Harris Morgan, *Morgan Genealogy: A History of James Morgan of New London . . .* (Hartford, CT: Case, Lockwood and Brainard, 1869), p. 31; Caulkins, *History of New London*, p. 311; *DJH*, 175 (10 November 1726); John Morgan, NLCCCR, Trials, vol. 11, June 1718, p. 1; John Morgan, NLCCCR, Files, Box 161, File of June 1718.

6. John Morgan, NLCCCR, Trials, vol. 11, June 1718, p. 1; John Morgan, NLCCCR, Files, Box 161, File of June 1718.

7. *DJH*, 54 (22 April 1716), 55 (28 May 1716), 291 (27 September 1735), 448–49 (23, 26–27 February 1746), 544 (7 October 1750), 661 (28 December 1756); Joshua also collected fines from John Rogers and then bought his homemade shoes: *DJH*, 94 (5 February 1720), 113 (9 October 1721).

8. Johnston, "Slavery in Rhode Island," 139–40; Piersen, *Black Yankees*, pp. 117–23.

9. *DJH*, 187 (15 September 1727), 188 (7 October 1727), 190 (27 November 1727); Nathaniel had worked with a man of color before; three months before Adam's arrival, Wait Wright, the son of William and Hagar Wright, had helped Nathaniel mow Smith's lot: *DJH*, 185 (8 July 1727); Adam carted and sledded wood a great deal that first winter: *DJH*, 192 (15 January 1728), 193 (25, 29–30 January; 8, 13 February 1728), 197 (6 June 1728), 200 (4 September 1728).

10. Schaefer, *A Useful Friend*, pp. 45–52, 57; *Acts and Laws* (1715), p. 4.

11. *Acts and Laws* (1715), p. 373; see also Harrison Hewitt, "The Administration of Justice in Connecticut," in Norris Galpin Osborn, ed., *History of Connecticut in Monographic Form*, vol. 3 (New York: States History Company, 1925), pp. 1–250, 197.

12. *DJH*, 187 (21 September 1727), 219 (6 April 1730), 255 (24 February 1733), 263 (26 October 1733), 265 (24 December 1733), 276 (11 September 1734), 280 (30 December 1734).

13. John T. Hassam, "Registers of Probate for the County of Suffolk, Massachusetts, 1639–1799," Proceedings of the MHS, vol. 16, 2nd series (Boston: MHS, 1902), pp. 23–124, 25–40.

14. See Kathryn A. Clippinger, "'Dutiful 'til Death,' The life of Ann Dudley Winthrop (1684–1776)," in *Prize Essays in Early American History* (Mystic, CT: Society of the Cincinnati in the State of Connecticut and the Society of Colonial Wars, 1995); Schaefer, *A Useful Friend*, pp. 26–30; Ann Winthrop to John Still Winthrop, December 29, 1747, *Winthrop Papers* microfilm, Reel 20; for the deference with which New Londoners treated Anne Winthrop, see a letter of Martha Coit (mother to Joshua's neighors John and Capt. Joseph): Martha Coit to Anne Winthrop, Frederick L. Gay Family Papers, Box 1, February 28, 1727, MHS.

15. *DJH*, 194 (24 February 1728), 198 (1 July 1728), 201 (24 September 1728), 202–3 (7, 11, 19 November; 1, 4 December 1728), 206 (17 February 1729), 216 (12 January 1730), 224 (5 September 1730), 363 (25 July 1740).

16. Ibid., 203 (5–11 December 1728).

17. Ibid., 209 (8 May 1729).

18. Ibid. (9–10 May 1729).

19. Ibid. (25 June; 4, 8–9 July 1729).

20. Ibid. (9–10 July 1729); An Account of the Debts from the Estate of Nathaniel Hempsted, July 1729, Misc. Financial, Box 37, Photocopies: Hempstead Family Probate Documents, HHA; David Wendell Moller, *Confronting Death: Values, Institutions, and Human Mortality* (Oxford: Oxford University Press, 1996), p. 80.

21. *DJH*, 210 (30–31 July, 1–12, 18 August 1729).

22. *DJH*, 213 (6 November 1729); Nathaniel Hempstead, Probate, New London Probate Packet, Reel 983, no. 2577, CSL.

23. *DJH*, 208 (18–19 April 1729); Kisling, "Zoological Gardens of the United States," pp. 147–48.

24. Division of the estate of Joseph Truman to his sons Thomas and Joseph, April 20, 1728, Will of Joseph Truman (1696), Joseph Truman, Jr., Inventory, November 22, 1745, Misc. Financial, Box 37, Photocopies: Hempstead Family Probate Documents, HHA.

25. *DJH*, 319 (11 August 1737).

26. Ibid., 220 (24 May, 2–3 June 1730), 223 (29, 30 July 1730), 224 (6 September 1730), 225 (11 September 1730), 259 (5 July 1733), 275 (15 August 1734).

27. Ibid., 300 (18 May 1736), 301 (24 June 1736), 306 (2 October 1736), 319 (23 July 1737), 321 (19 September 1737), 345 (17 April 1739), 357 (7 February 1740).

28. Summons of William Walsworth (in Joshua's hand), *Winthrop v. Walsworth*, NLCCCR, Files, Box 163, File of February 1721.

29. *DJH*, 219 (11 April 1730), 229 (6 January 1731), 232 (24 April 1731), 240 (13 December 1731), 261 (18 August 1733), (2, 3 September 1733), 295 (1 January 1736), 296 (23, 24 January 1736), 562 (26 September 1751).

30. Ibid., 234 (16 June 1731).

31. Ibid., 301 (10 June 1736).

Chapter Thirteen: "Their Children's Children"

1. *DJH*, 337 (28 October 1738).

2. *Rex. v. Indian Kate*, NLCSCR, Files, Box 7, File of September 1737; Katherine Garret, "The Confession and Dying Warning of Katherine Garret," in *Early Native Literacies in New England: A Documentary and Critical Anthology*, ed. Kristine Bross and Hilary E. Wyss (Amherst: University of Massachuetts Press, 2008), pp. 142–47.

3. *DJH*, 330 (3 May 1738); Eliphalet Adams, *A Sermon Preached on the Occasion of the Execution of Katherine Garrett . . .* (New London, CT: Timothy Green, 1738).

4. *Rex. v. Indian Kate*, NLCSCR, Files, Box 7, File of September 1737.

5. Ibid.

6. Steenburg, *Children and the Criminal Law*, p. 151; Peter Charles Hoffer

and N. E. H. Hull, *Murdering Mothers: Infanticide in England and New England, 1558–1803* (New York: New York University Press, 1984), pp. 44–46.

7. Franklin Bowditch Dexter, ed., *Extracts of the Itinerant and Other Miscellanies of Ezra Stiles, D. D.* (New Haven, CT: Yale University Press, 1896), pp. 144–46; conversation with Paul Grant-Costa, May 5, 2012.

8. Adams, *A Sermon Preached on the Occasion*, esp. p. 26; Garret, "The Confession and Dying Warning of Katherine Garret"; *DJH*, 326 (29 January 1738), 328 (12 March 1738).

9. Adams and Pleck, *Love of Freedom*, pp. 110–12; Rogers, *James Rogers*, p. 68; *Joshua Hempsted His Book, 1727*, April 17, 1741, p. 24, March 24, 1754, p. 4, October 26, 1754, p. 5, NLCHS.

10. *DJH*, 396 (15 December 1742).

11. *Joshua Hempsted His Book, 1727*, April 4, 1756, p. 7, June 11, 1757, p. 9, NLCHS.

12. Adams and Pleck, *Love of Freedom*, p. 103.

13. William J. Brown, *The Life of William J. Brown of Providence, Rhode Island* (Providence, RI: Angell & Co., 1883), pp. 10–11; Ann Marie Plane, *Colonial Intimacies: Indian Marriage in Early New England* (Ithaca, NY: Cornell University Press, 2000), pp. 22–23; thank you to Paul Grant-Costa.

14. Mohegan Agreement Re Marrying in Other Tribes, etc., May 12, 1773, William Samuel Johnson Papers, vol. 3, pp. 72–73, CHS, Indian Papers Project Transcription; my thanks to Paul Grant-Costa.

15. Caulkins, ed., *Memoir of the . . . Rev. Eliphalet Adams*, pp. 28–31; *DJH*, 211 (19 September 1729), 233 (19 May 1731), 337 (29 October 1738), 457 (21 August 1746); Eliphalet Adams (1753), New London Probate Packet, Reel 957, p. 11; *Bill of Sale or Indenture made by Eliphalet Adams of New London, Connecticut, to Joseph and Jonathan Trumbull of Lebanon, Connecticut, whereby he sells his mulatto girl Flora, a slave for life*, May 12, 1736, CSL; see also Cotton Mather, *The Negro Christianized: An Essay to Excite and Assist that Good Work, the Instruction of Negro-Servants in Christianity* (Boston: 1706); MacSparren, *Letter Book*, pp. 4, 9, 85n.

16. Wood, *Origins of American Slavery*, p. 11; Steiner, *Slavery in Connecticut*, pp. 10–11; *Samuel Richards v. Cesar the Great*, NLCSCR, Files, Box 9, File of September 1741.

17. C. J. F. Binney, ed., *The History and Genealogy of the Prentice, or Prentiss Family*, 2nd ed. (Boston: C. J. F. Binney, 1883), pp. 273–75; New London Land Records, vol. 6, November 8, 1711, p. 247; Caulkins, *History of New London*, pp. 329–30.

18. New London Land Records, vol. 6, November 8, 1711, p. 247.

19. DJH, 75 (27 April 1718), 102 (4 December 1720), 211 (19 September 1729), 457–58 (21 August 1746), 566 (6–8 December 1751); "New London Marriages to 1800," trans. Susan G. Taylor, USGenWeb, New London, Connecticut, http://www.ctgenweb.org/town/ctnewlondon/nBailey_b.html#A (accessed April 22, 2011).

20. Justice Court, New London, Records, 1739–1779, kept by Joshua Hempsted

and John Hempsted, Box 565, June 11, 1739, p. 3, CSL; *Samuel Richards v. Cesar the Great*, NLCSR, Files, Box 9, File of September 1741; *Samuel Richards v. Jabez Hamlin*, NLCSCR, Files, Box 9, File of March 1744; New London Land Records, vol. 8, 1722, p. 107.

21. New London Land Records, vol. 8, 1722, p. 107; Caulkins, *History of New London*, pp. 78–79, 238; "Hon. Christopher Christophers and His Descendants," *New York Geneaological and Biographical Record* 50 (1919): 332–34.

22. "Hon. Christopher Christophers and His Descendants"; *Samuel Richards v. Jabez Hamlin*, NLCSCR, Files, Box 9, File of March 1744; *Samuel Richards v. Cesar the Great*, NLCSCR, Files, Box 9, File of September 1741.

23. Justice Court, New London, Records, 1739–1779, kept by Joshua Hempsted and John Hempsted, Box 565, June 11, 1739, p. 3, CSL; *Samuel Richards v. Cesar the Great*, NLCSCR, Files, Box 9, File of September 1741; *Samuel Richards v. Jabez Hamlin*, NLCSCR, Files, Box 9, File of March 1744.

24. *Samuel Richards v. Jabez Hamlin*, NLCSCR, Files, Box 9, File of March 1744; James Hammond Trumbull, ed., *The Memorial History of Hartford County, Connecticut, 1633–1884*, vol. 1 (Boston: Edward L. Osgood, 1886), pp. 120–21.

25. *Stephen Gardiner v. Cesar et al.*, NLCCCR, Files, Box 189, File of November 1743; Caroline E. Robinson, *The Gardiners of Narragansett*, ed. Daniel Goodwin (Providence, RI: Daniel Goodwin, 1919), pp. 9–12; Lillian May and Charles Morris Gardner, *Gardner History and Genealogy* (Erie, PA: Erie Printing, 1907), p. 149.

26. *Stephen Gardiner v. Cesar et al.*, NLCCCR, Files, Box 189, File of November 1743; *DJH*, 383 (30 January 1742).

27. John Demos, *The Unredeemed Captive: A Family Story from Early America* (New York: Alfred A. Knopf, 1994), pp. 142–43.

28. Benjamin W. Dwight, *The History of the Descendants of John Dwight* (New York: John F. Trow & Son, 1874), pp. 303–4; *Stephen Gardiner v. Cesar et al.*, NLCCCR, Files, Box 189, File of November 1743.

29. *Stephen Gardiner v. Cesar et al.*, NLCCCR, Files, Box 189, File of November 1743.

30. George E. Sioui, *Huron-Wendat: The Heritage of the Circle*, trans. Jane Brierley (Vancouver: University of British Columbia Press, 2000), pp. 6, 96–97; Steiner, *Slavery in Connecticut*, pp. 14–15.

31. *Stephen Gardiner v. Cesar et al.*, NLCCCR, Files, Box 189, File of November 1743; see Michael A. Gomez, *Exchanging Our Country Marks: The Transformation of African Identities in the Colonial and Antebellum South* (Chapel Hill: University of North Carolina Press, 1998), pp. 39–40, 97–98, 121–24, 140, 175; cited in Piersen, *Black Yankees*, p. 40.

32. *DJH*, 276 (9 September 1734).

33. Demos, *The Unredeemed Captive*, p. 181.

34. *DJH*, 195 (19 April 1728), 228 (31 December 1730), 439 (2–3, 6–8 August 1745), 443 (2, 5 November 1745), (26, 29–30 July 1746), 466 (28 January 1747), 476–77 (7, 10, 13, 15 August 1747), 496 (6 September 1748).

35. *DJH*, 236 (22 July 1731).

36. *Samuel Beebe, Jr., and Nathaniel Newbury v. Nathaniel Lathrop*, NLCCCR, Files, Box 168, File of June 1728, part 1.

37. *Tracy v. Hartshorn*, NLCCCR, Files, File of June 1720; *Jackson v. Tracy*, NLCCCR, Files, Files of November 1718 and November 1719; *Samuel Beebe v. John Jackson, Jr.*, NLCCCR, Trials, vol. 17, November 1731; New London Land Records, vol. 9, p. 235, NLCCO.

38. *Samuel Beebe v. John Jackson, Jr.*, NLCCCR, Trials, vol. 17, November 1731; *George Webb v. John Jackson*, General Court of Trials, 1732, in Jane Fletcher Fiske, *Gleanings from the Newport Court Files, 1659–1783* (Bedford, MA: Jane Fletcher Fiske, 1998), no. 546.

39. General Court of Trials, 1764, in Fiske, *Gleanings from the Newport Court Files*, no. 1039; Gaines and Parkhurst, "African-Americans in Newport," pp. 11–12.

40. *DJH*, 591 (14 April 1753); New London Land Records, vol. 8, December 9, 1723, p. 186; Rose and Eicholz, *Black Genesis*, p. 8.

41. *Hambleton v. Jackson*, NLCCCR, Files, Box 175, File of June 1736, part 1; the confiscated goods may or may not have been all of Peter's possessions; the attachment was for goods to the value of £30 (but the value of the actual goods attached was not indicated).

42. Rose and Eicholz, *Black Genesis*, p. 8; Rose and Brown, *Tapestry*, p. 75; *DJH*, 432 (19 March 1745).

43. *James Rogers v. Dr. Giles Goddard*, NLCCCR, Files, Box 96, Folder 17, January? 1753; Rogers, *James Rogers*, pp. 45, 47.

44. Thomas Lechmere to John Winthrop, Boston to New London, March 22, 1720, *Winthrop Papers* microfilm, Reel 19; New London Town Records, vol. 10, p. 187; *Acts and Laws* (1715), p. 164; David Menschel, "Abolition Without Deliverance: The Law of Connecticut Slavery, 1784–1848," *Yale Law Journal* 111 (2001): 183–222, 183–91, 203–4; "An Act Concerning Indian, Mulatto, and Negro Servants and Slaves," in *Acts and Laws of the State of Connecticut in America* (New London, CT: Timothy Green, 1784), pp. 233, 235; *DJH*, 273 (4 July 1734), 321 (12 September 1737).

Chapter Fourteen: "Adam Worked All Day"

1. *DJH*, 351 (10 September 1739).

2. *DJH*, 347 (30 May 1739).

3. Ibid.

4. See Jeyes, *The Russells of Birmingham*, pp. 240, 244, 249; *DJH*, 276 (11 September 1734).

5. Larkin, *The Reshaping of Everyday Life*, pp. 284–85; see *John Edgecombe His Book* [kept by Joshua], Daybooks: 1700s, September 18, 1747, HHA; *DJH*, 225 (16 September 1730), 582 (12–13, 16–17 October 1752), 602 (16 October 1753).

6. *DJH*, 343 (21, 28 February 1739).

7. Based on a tally of identifiable workers (*DJH*); see Vickers, *Farmers and*

Fishermen, p. 39; Kevin M. Sweeney, "Gentlemen Farmers and Inland Merchants: The Williams Family and Commercial Agriculture in Pre-Revolutionary Western Massachusetts," in *The Farm*, Dublin Seminar for New England Folklife, ed. Peter Benes (Boston: Boston University, 1988), pp. 60–73, 65.

8. *DJH*, 478 (26 September 1747).

9. Homage to Edward P. Jones, *The Known World* (New York: Amistad, 2003).

10. B. S. Swetland, ed., *Partial Genealogy of the Swetland Family* (Brocton, NY: Brocton Enterprise Press, 1907), pp. 1–2; ELB Transcripts, Box 2, New London Land Records, vol. 8, p. 15; "Subscribers to Prince's Chronology," *NEHGR* 6 (1852): 189–200, 198; *DJH*, 389 (22 June 1742), 390 (4 July 1742), 529 (15, 28 December 1749), 600 (19, 21 September 1753).

11. *DJH*, 349 (6 July 1739); F. W. Chapman, *The Coit Family, or the Descendants of John Coit* (Hartford, CT: Case, Lockwood and Brainard, 1874), pp. 20–26; Caulkins, *History of New London*, pp. 407–8; *DJH*, 154 (24 March 1725), 384 (26 February 1742), 386 (16 April 1742), 389 (2 July 1742), 391 (30 July 1742), 414 (20 January 1744), 416 (24, 26 February 1744), 441 (4 October 1745); see Cullon, "Colonial Shipwrights," p. 133.

12. *DJH*, 232 (24 April 1731), 233 (14 May 1731), 236 (17 July 1731), 267 (28 January 1734), 275 (24, 28 August 1734), 277 (4, 5 October 1734), 317 (4 June 1737), 389 (22 June 1742); Joshua Hempsted, Account Book, 1737–1757, pp. 23, 93.

13. Joshua Hempsted, Account Book, 1737–1757, pp. 56, 106; see Cullon, "Colonial Shipwrights," p. 93; John also provided ironwork for the New London Customs Office: Joseph Hull Papers, 1724–1761, Custom Accounts, New London, Connecticut, September 1736, American Antiquarian Society.

14. See Sweeney, "Gentlemen Farmers," pp. 64, 66; *DJH*, 376 (19 August, 19 September 1741), 378 (26 October 1741); Joshua Hempsted, Account Book, 1737–1757, p. 56.

15. Chapman, *The Coit Family*, pp. 21–26, 305, 307.

16. *DJH*, 347 (30 May 1739), 386 (10 April 1745), 393 (4 September 1742), 417 (26 March 1744), 426 (16 October 1744), 680 (19 February 1758); Chapman, *The Coit Family*, p. 306.

17. *DJH*, 409 (25 September 1743), 417 (26 March 174), 441 (3–4 October 1745), 680 (19 February 1758).

18. Baker, *History of Montville*, pp. 424–25; *DJH*, 172 (13 August 1726), 173 (25 August 1726); Rose and Brown, *Tapestry*, pp. 78–80; [Woldf], New London Vital Statistics, vol. 1, pp. 57, 59; Register 62, New London Rate Books, 1733–34, 1745–49, 1751–74, Box 21, CSL; see also an iron pot purchased from Tommy in Will of John Edgecombe, Jr., December 18, 1727, HHA.

19. *DJH*, 392 (3 September 1742).

20. Ibid., 189 (6 November 1727), 192 (5–6 January 1728), 248 (28 July 1732), 275 (9 August 1734), 341 (10 January 1739), 450 (10 April 1746).

21. Ibid., 234 (15 June 1731), 460 (11 October 1746), 492 (18 June 1748), 539 (11 July 1750), 576 (15 June 1752), 611 (5 April 1754).

22. Ibid., 188 (14 October 1727); *Acts and Laws* (1715), p. 87.

23. *DJH*, 37 (4 August 1714), 97 (13 May 1720), 98 (6 June 1720), 108 (1 May

1721), 117 (2 February 1722), 142 (22 April 1724), 156 (30 April 1725), 198 (27 June 1728), 200 (9 September 1728), 201 (14 September 1728), 236 (3, 5 August 1731), 248 (3, 7–8, 15 August 1732), 289 (18 August 1735), 371 (26, 30 April 1741), 488 (10 March 1748), 566 (18 December 1751), 606 (15 January 1754); Daboll and Crandall, "Edmund Fanning Farm."

24. *DJH*, 302 (10 July 1736), 465 (16 January 1747), 535 (2 April 1750), 658 (26 October 1756).

25. Main, *Society and Economy*, pp. 57, 77, 368–69; see Allport, *Sermons in Stone*, pp. 114–15; Rose, *The Village Carpenter*, pp. 52–53; see references to slave Cesar Hurlbut's hammer: Joshua Hempsted, Account Book, 1737–1757, p. 17; *DJH*, 196 (27 April 1728), 223 (22 July 1730), 230 (17 February 1731), 231 (2, 29 March 1731), 279 (11, 15 November 1734), 309 (16 December 1736), 495 (15 August 1748), 533 (14 March 1750), 678 (30 December 1757), 691 (30 September 1758).

26. *DJH*, 195 (4 April 1728); Simon Brown, ed., *The New England Farmer, a Monthly Journal*, vol. 12 (Boston: Nourse, Eaton & Tolman, 1860), pp. 33–34.

27. *DJH*, 195 (4 April 1728), 198 (27 June 1728), 217 (30 January 1730), 221 (21 June 1730), 271 (23 May 1734), 294 (24 December 1735), 295 (8 January 1736), 345 (16 April 1739), 436 (29 May 1745), 483 (5 December 1747), 491 (10 June 1748), 509 (15 May 1749), 554 (12 April 1751), 664 (1 March 1757), 691 (26 September 1758).

28. Ibid., 294 (12 December 1735), 296 (5 February 1736), 546 (22–23 November 1750), 673 (28 September 1757).

29. Russell, *A Long, Deep Furrow*, p. 83; *DJH*, 61 (21 November 1716), 102 (3 December 1720), 201 (14 September 1728), 212 (14 October 1729), 214 (12 December 1729), 227 (16 November 1730), 228 (12, 14 December 1730), 231 (6 March 1731), 264 (16 November 1733), 279 (23 November 1734), 280 (7 December 1734), 294 (12 December 1735), 309 (14 December 1736), 426 (10 October 1744), 528 (30 November 1749), 660 (23 November 1756).

30. *DJH*, 527 (17 November 1749); Russell, *A Long, Deep Furrow*, pp. 50–52, 83.

31. St. George, "Set Thine House in Order," p. 174; *DJH*, 2 (10, 11 October 1711), 36 (12 July 1714) , 422 (14 July 1744), 442 (11 October 1745), 561 (12 September 1751), 602 (9 October 1753), 626 (16 January 1755), 657 (21 September 1756).

32. *DJH*, 224 (26 August 1730), 456 (21 July 1746), 579 (8 August 1752).

33. Ibid., 545 (23 October 1750), 563 (19 October 1751), 613 (10 May 1754).

34. Ibid., 214 (1 December 1729), 227 (11 December 1730), 261 (25 August 1733), 264 (29 November 1733), 280 (28 December 1734), 292 (11 October 1735), 376 (24 August 1741), 402 (16 April 1743), 544 (9 October 1750), 593 (21 May 1753).

35. Ibid., 289 (13 August 1735), 324 (21 November 1737), 423 (6 August 1744).

36. Ibid., 495 (16 August 1748).

37. R. B. Wall, "Old Rogers Boat Shop Was a Famous Landmark," *NLD*, October 9, 1907; R. B. Wall, "History and Traditions of the Holt-Hempstead Tract: Chapter III," *NLD*, November 11, 1908; R. B. Wall, "How Long Bridge Section of Bank Street Was Settled: Early History of That Part of New London Told from Real Estate Records," *NLD*, August 6, 1921.

38. *DJH*, 295 (2, 3 January 1736), 307 (3 November 1736).

39. Nylander, *Our Own Snug Fireside*, pp. 95–96; Josh and Natty may have

even slept together sometimes in Joshua's trundle bed, as Natty did at eighteen: *DJH*, 307 (3 November 1736), 437 (24 June 1745).

40. *DJH*, 307 (3 November 1736).

41. Ibid.

42. Ibid.

43. Ibid.

44. Ibid., 106 (10 February 1721); *Joshua Hempsted His Book, 1695*, p. 4 verso, NLCHS.

45. *DJH*, 307 (3 November 1736).

46. Ibid.

47. [Woldf], New London Town Records, Book Second, rebound copy in custody of the Memphis Public Library, p. 22; New London Episcopal Church Records, St. James Church, vol. 1, 1725–1850, p. 1, CSL; portrait of James Tilley (1707–1765), artist John Singleton Copley, Lot 536, Sale 1618: Property from the Collection of Mrs. J. Insley Blair, January 21, 2006, New York, Rockefeller Plaza, http://www.christies.com/LotFinder/lot_details.aspx?intObjectID=4639344 (accessed November 28, 2008); *DJH*, 388 (7 June 1742), 492 (23 June 1748).

48. *DJH*, 289 (14 August 1735), 347 (12 June 1739), 388 (26 May 1742), 390 (5 July 1742), 398 (1 January 1743), 400 (21 February 1743), 406 (18, 21 July 1743), 407 (4 August 1743), 409 (20 September 1743), 412 (23 December 1743), 419 (5 May 1744), 435 (4 May 1745).

49. Wood, *Origins of American Slavery*, pp. 109–10.

Chapter Fifteen: "The Wonderfull Work of God"

1. Stout and Onuf, "James Davenport," pp. 558–59; Frank Lambert, *Inventing the Great Awakening* (Princeton, NJ: Princeton University Press, 1999), pp. 87–124; Moran, "The Puritan Saint," p. 236.

2. James Deetz, *In Small Things Forgotten: An Archaeology of Early American Life* (New York: Anchor Books, 1977); Richard L. Bushman, *The Refinement of America: Persons, Houses, Cities* (New York: Alfred A. Knopf, 1992); E. Edwards Beardsley, *The History of the Episcopal Church in Connecticut*, vol. 1, 2nd ed. (New York: Hurd & Houghton, 1869), pp. 100–101; *DJII*, 228 (25 December 1730), 315 (8 April 1737), 603 (11 November 1753), 604 (18 November 1753).

3. Lambert, *Great Awakening*, pp. 21–88.

4. Ibid., pp. 92, 97, 100; *DJH*, 364 (24 October 1740).

5. *DJH*, 371 (30–31 March 1741), 372 (24, 28, 30 May 1741), 373 (5 June 1741); Stout and Onuf, "James Davenport," pp. 563–68.

6. Moran, "The Puritan Saint," pp. 209, 217–18; *DJH*, 373 (16, 21 June 1741).

7. Stout and Onuf, "James Davenport," p. 561; Onuf, "New Lights," p. 633.

8. *DJH*, 374–75 (25 June, 5 July 1741); Stout and Onuf, "James Davenport," p. 561–67, cited on p. 563.

9. *DJH*, 375 (23, 25–26 July 1741).

10. *DJH*, 378 (1 November 1741), 380 (29 November 1741); Stout and Onuf,

"James Davenport," p. 572; the other chief Separatists were John Curtis, Peter Harris, and brothers Christopher and John Christophers. Joshua's son-in-law Daniel Starr, Betty's husband, was also a Separatist, though Betty herself was not.

11. *DJH*, 25 (3 August 1713), 674–75 (26 October, 1 November 1757); Stout and Onuf, "James Davenport," p. 570; Onuf, "New Lights," pp. 641–42; the Harris-Shepherd's Tent house still stands on Truman Street.

12. Separatists' Petition, June 2, 1742, NLCCCR, Files, Box 186, File of June 1742, part 1; dissenting Protestant sects could apply for legal recognition under the Toleration Act of May 1708. The Act was expanded to include Anglicans in 1727, Quakers in 1729, and Baptists in 1729: Onuf, "New Lights," p. 632n.

13. *DJH*, 401 (27 February, 31 March 1743).

14. Stout and Onuf, "James Davenport," pp. 576–78; Justice Court, New London, Records, 1739–1779, kept by Joshua Hempsted, Justice of the Peace, 1739–1758, and John Hempsted, Justice of the Peace, 1771–1774, Box 565, March 31, 1743, April 5, 1743, CSL.

15. Justice Court, New London, Records, 1739–1779, kept by Joshua Hempsted, Justice of the Peace, 1739–1758, and John Hempsted, Justice of the Peace, 1771–1774, Box 565, March 31, 1743, April 5, 1743, CSL; Jeremiah Miller, Jr., to John Still Winthrop, July 23, 1746, *Winthrop Papers* microfilm, Reel 20.

16. Jeremiah Miller, Jr., to John Still Winthrop, July 23, 1746, *Winthrop Papers* microfilm, Reel 20; Stout and Onuf, "James Davenport," pp. 576–78.

17. Justice Court, New London, Records, 1739–1779, kept by Joshua Hempsted, Justice of the Peace, 1739–1758, and John Hempsted, Justice of the Peace, 1771–1774, Box 565, March 31, 1743, April 5, 1743, CSL.

18. *DJH*, 401 (31 March 1743), 402 (23 April 1743), 406 (23 July 1743), 407 (12 August 1743).

19. Stout and Onuf, "James Davenport," pp. 576–78; *DJH*, 488 (6 March 1748), 498 (30 October 1748); 1757 list of brethren and sisters, New London, First Congregational Church 1670–1888, Reel 307, vol. 1, pp. 23–24, CSL; *New London Summary*, February, 2, 1759, p. 4.

20. *DJH*, 536 (5 May 1750).

21. Ibid., 300 (29 May 1736), 403 (21 May 1743), 404 (4 June 1743); Whitten, "Hempsteads of New London"; Bill Gifford, *Ledyard: In Search of the First American Explorer* (New York: Harcourt, 2007) pp. 6–9.

22. Colorful details of this story come from that family history: Branch, Notebook, pp. 15–19 (including Branch's quotes from a Southold newspaper article). Hempstead first cousins who married included John Hempstead (Joshua's son) to Hannah Salmon (his first cousin on his mother's side); Anna Hempstead (daughter of Joshua's grandson Nathaniel) to Joshua Hempstead (son of Joshua's grandson Joshua, Nathaniel's brother); Lydia Hempstead (daughter of Joshua's grandson Joshua) to William Hempstead (son of Joshua's son Stephen); and Samuel Hempstead (son of Joshua's grandson Joshua) to Lucy Hempstead (daughter of Joshua's son Stephen). *DJH*, 536 (5 May 1750).

23. *DJH*, 534 (17 March 1750), 536 (5 May 1750).

24. *DJH*, 536 (7–9 May 1750); Branch, Notebook, p. 18.

25. Branch, Notebook, p. 18.

26. *DJH*, 536 (9 May 1750), 537 (21 May 1750), 538 (6 June 1750).

27. Ibid., 539 (9 July 1750), 592 (7 May 1753), 602 (20 October 1753), 669 (19 June 1757).

28. Branch, Notebook, pp. 18–19; Hurd, *New London County*, pp. 446–47; William H. Goetzmann, *New Lands, New Men: America and the Second Great Age of Discovery* (New York: Penguin, 1986), p. 110; Gifford, *Ledyard*, pp. xii–19, 53–54, 213, 231.

29. Hempsteads like Joshua's grandson Josh were known for their large size, a fact confirmed when family graves were exhumed and moved in the nineteenth century: Branch, Notebook, pp. 26–27.

30. This characterization is based on the surviving correspondence between John and Anne Winthrop in the *Winthrop Papers*.

31. MHS, *The Generations Joined: Winthrops in America* (Boston: MHS, 1977); John Winthrop IV to John Still Winthrop, July ?, 1741, *Winthrop Papers* microfilm, Reel 20.

32. Anne Winthrop (Jr.) to John Winthrop IV, May 30, 1734, *Winthrop Papers* microfilm, Reel 19.

33. Anne Winthrop (Jr.) to John Winthrop IV, May 22, 1736, *Winthrop Papers* microfilm, Reel 19; *New London Summary,* October 10, 1760, p. 2; Gurdon Saltonstall, Jr., to John Winthrop IV, May 28, 1737, *Winthrop Papers* microfilm, Reel 19.

34. Gurdon Saltonstall, Jr., to John Winthrop IV, May 28, 1737, *Winthrop Papers* microfilm, Reel 19; Anne Winthrop to John Winthrop IV, June 16, 1737, *Winthrop Papers* microfilm, Reel 19.

35. Anne Winthrop to John Winthrop IV, June 16, 1737, *Winthrop Papers* microfilm, Reel 19; John Winthrop IV to Anne Winthrop, August 20, 1737, *Winthrop Papers* microfilm, Reel 19.

36. Gurdon Saltonstall, Jr., to John Winthrop IV, October 23, 1738, *Winthrop Papers* microfilm, Reel 19; John Winthrop IV to John Still Winthrop, July ?, 1741, *Winthrop Papers* microfilm, Reel 20; Gurdon Saltonstall, Jr., to John Winthrop IV, February 19, 1742, *Winthrop Papers* microfilm, Reel 20; Jeremiah Miller, Jr., to John Still Winthrop, August 26, 1742, *Winthrop Papers* microfilm, Reel 20.

37. Hempstead letters: Joshua Hempstead to Solomon Coit, October 17, 1732, Niantic Ferry Rights, New London Town Papers, 1674–1925, Box 5, CSL; Joshua Hempstead to Captain Daniel Coit, October 21, 1734, Groton Ferry, New London Town Records, Box 5, CSL; Joshua Hempstead to John Winthrop IV, February 8, 1742, *Winthrop Papers* microfilm, Reel 20.

38. John Winthrop IV to Wife and Children, not dated (ca. 1745), *Winthrop Papers* microfilm, Reel 20; Anne Winthrop (Jr.) to John Still Winthrop, December 8, 1743, *Winthrop Papers* microfilm, Reel 20.

39. John Winthrop IV to Anne Winthrop, August 20, 1737, *Winthrop Papers* microfilm, Reel 19.

40. Clippinger, "'Dutiful 'til death'."

41. *DJH*, 372 (17 May 1741), 432 (19 March 1745), 591 (14 April 1753).

42. Account of cheese sold at Fort Edward, Nathaniel Minor, Hoadley Col-

lection, Box 9, July and September 1757, CHS; *Rolls of Connecticut Men in the French and Indian War, 1755–1762*, vol. 2 (Hartford, CT: CHS, 1903), pp. 33, 164; *Rolls of Connecticut Men in the French and Indian War, 1755–1762*, vol. 1 (Hartford, CT: CHS, 1903), pp. 79, 90–91, 100–101, 107; Thomas L. Doughton, "Nedson, Dorus and Dixon Families: Nineteenth-Century Native Community at the Massachusetts and Connecticut Border," http://freepages.gnealogy.rootsweb.ancestry.com/~massaoit/nedson.htm (accessed November 5, 2007); William Farrand Livingston, *Israel Putnam: Pioneer, Ranger, and Major-General, 1718–1790* (New York: G. P. Putnam's Sons, 1901), pp. 17–21; *Public Records of the Colony of Connecticut*, vol. 8 (Hartford, CT: Case, Lockwood and Brainard, 1877), p. 599; *DJH*, 656 (30 August, 15 September 1756).

43. *DJH*, 596 (10 July 1753); *James Rogers v. Dr. Giles Goddard*, NLCCCR, Files Box 96, Folder 17, January? 1753.

44. *James Rogers v. Dr. Giles Goddard*, NLCCCR, Files Box 96, Folder 17, January? 1753; *DJH*, 662 (1 February 1757).

45. Rogers, *James Rogers*, pp. 65–68; Rose and Eichholz, *Black Genesis*, p. 8.

46. Johnston, "Slavery in Rhode Island, 1755–1776," p. 141; Menschel, "Abolition Without Deliverance," pp. 187–91.

47. Mary Hobbs, NLCSCR, Dockets, Box 35, September 1743; *DJH*, 312 (11 February 1737), 353 (24 October 1739), 354 (14 November 1739), 535–36 (27–28 April 1750), 546 (8 November 1750).

48. Rogers, *James Rogers*, p. 70.

Epilogue

1. The layout and distribution of the room is hypothetical, but the contents come from Joshua's diary and inventory: Joshua Hempstead (1759), New London Probate Packet, Reel 983, No. 2573, CSL; *DJH*, 505 (23 February 1749), 604 (30 November 1753); Joshua received a large number of funeral gloves during his life: *DJH*, 72 (25 January 1718), 154 (11 March 1725), 184 (1 July 1727), 185 (30 July 1727), 251 (8 November 1732), 264 (10 November 1733). Generally, black and purple gloves went to the principle mourners: Trent et al., ed., *New England Begins*, vol. 2, pp. 313–16, item 324; Joshua once received white gloves for performing a wedding: *DJH*, 617 (22 July 1754); keeping money in locked chests: *Complaint of John Rogers, son of Joseph v. Sam Wang and Sarah Indian*, NLCCCR, Files, Box 179, File of November 1738, part 1; testimonies of John Smith and Jonathan Carver in *Stark v. Clement Minor* (Joshua's son-in-law), NLCSCR, Files, Box 12, File of March 1753; Joshua's locking furniture: *DJH*, 254 (4 January 1733), 451 (3 May 1746).

2. A desk belonging to Joshua (though not necessarily the only one he owned): *DJH*, 350 (10 August 1739); this desk was an escritoire with a slanted top that lifted open: *DJH*, 348 (27 June 1739) (a late seventeenth-century New York escritoire: Neil D. Kamil, "Hidden in Plain Sight: Disappearance and Material Life in Colonial New York," in *American Furniture 1995*, ed. Luke Beckerdite and William N. Hosley [Hanover, NH: University Press of New England, 1995], p. 204); from the

countless documents of Joshua's in New London County Court Records, Joshua clearly kept his papers and documents at home in the folded "legal" style. Like many officeholders, Joshua retained some town records (or copies of records) for New London at home: *DJH*, 74 (14 March 1718); keeping records for Madam Winthrop: *DJH*, 141 (14 April 1724); Joshua's book of wills: *DJH*, 401 (25 March 1743); one occasion when Joshua's filing system failed him: *DJH*, 486 (5 February 1748). *DJH*, 131 (18 June 1723). The Adams sermons, readily available at Green's printers just up the hill, are an educated guess.

3. *DJH*, 690 (6, 13 September 1758), 692 (28 October–3 November 1758).

4. *DJH*, 692 (2–3 November 1758); Joshua Hempsted, Account Book, 1737–1757, Account of the Estate of Joshua Hempsted, Esq., p. 181.

5. *New London Summary*, December 29, 1758, p. 4; *DJH*, 692 (3 November 1758).

6. Joshua Hempstead (1759), New London Probate Packet 1675–1850, Reel 983, no. 2573, CSL.

7. Joshua left the desk to Stephen who, with his family, lived in "Nathaniel's" side of the house; Stephen stayed on at the house until 1761, when he built his own on Truman Street near his Holt in-laws: Wall, "History and Traditions of the Holt-Hempstead Tract"; Stephen's house on the corner of Truman Street and Cape Ann Lane: Branch, Notebook, p. 8; see *DJH*, 504 (17 February 1749).

BIBLIOGRAPHY

Entries from Joshua Hempstead's diary have been reproduced with his spelling and punctuation.

Spelling, punctuation, and dates in most other primary sources have been modernized. The modern spelling of Hempstead is used, although some repositories favor "Hempsted." Dates are in "new style," with the Julian calendar year adjusted to begin on January 1.

Repositories

American Antiquarian Society, Worcester, Massachusetts
Connecticut Historical Society (CHS), Hartford, Connecticut
Connecticut State Library (CSL), Hartford, Connecticut
Gilder Lehrman Collection (GLC), New York, New York
Library of Congress, Washington, D.C.
Massachusetts Historical Society (MHS), Boston, Massachusetts
New London City Clerk's Office (NLCCO), New London, Connecticut
New London County Historical Society (NLCHS), New London, Connecticut
Newport Historical Society (NHS), Newport, Rhode Island
Office of the Judge of Probate, New London, Connecticut (now housed at CSL)
Public Record Office, London, United Kingdom

Manuscript Collections

Connecticut Archives (housed at CSL)
Connecticut Justice Courts (housed at CSL)

District of New London Probate Records, Office of the Judge of Probate (formerly at New London City Hall)

Eva L. Butler Transcripts (ELB Transcripts, housed at CSL)

Frances Manwaring Caulkins Papers (FMC Papers, housed at CSL)

Frederick L. Gay Family Papers (MHS)

Hempstead Family Probate Documents (1600–1700) (HHA, now housed at NLCHS)

Hempsted House Archives (HHA, now housed at NLCHS)

Indian Papers Project (Yale University)

Livingston Papers (housed at GLC)

Massachusetts Archives

Marriages, Births, and Deaths in New London (NLCCO, housed at CSL)

Nantucket Whaling and Marine Manuscript Archives

New London County County Court Records (NLCCCR, housed at CSL)

New London County Superior Court Records (NLCSCR, housed at CSL)

New London, First Congregational Church Records (housed at CSL)

New London Land Records (housed at New London City Clerk's Office)

Probate (Public Record Office)

Records of the Connecticut Court of Assistants (CCA, housed at CSL)

Slavery Documents (1732–1861) (housed at CHS)

The Winthrop Papers (housed at MHS)

Selected Unpublished Primary Sources

May, John. Diary, 1708–1766. American Antiquarian Society.

The Winthrop Papers microfilm. Massachusetts Historical Society.

Printed and Online Primary Sources

Acts and Laws of His Majestie's Colony of Connecticut in New-England. New London, CT: Timothy Green, 1715.

Acts and Laws of the State of Connecticut in America. New London, CT: Timothy Green, 1784.

Adams, Eliphalet. *A Sermon Preached on the Occasion of the Execution of Katherine Garrett . . .* New London, CT: Timothy Green, 1738.

Barrows, C. Edwin, ed. "The Diary of John Comer." Vol. 8 of *Collections of the Rhode Island Historical Society.* Newport: Rhode Island Historical Society, 1893.

Bontemps, Arna, ed. *Five Black Lives: The Autobiographies of Venture Smith, James Mars, William Grimes, G. W. Offley, and James L. Smith.* Middletown, CT: Wesleyan University Press, 1958.

The Boston Gazette (Boston).

Boston News-Letter (Boston).

Bradstreet, Anne. "Before the Birth of One of Her Children (1678)." In *Early American Writing*, edited by Giles Gunn, 178–79. New York: Penguin, 1994.

——. "To My Dear Children." In *Early American Writing*, edited by Giles Gunn, 188–92. New York: Penguin, 1994.

Bradstreet, Simon. "Bradstreet's Journal." *New England Historical and Genealogical Register* 8 (1854): 325–33.

——. "Memoires." Manuscript reproduced in *First Impressions: Printing in Cambridge, 1639–1989*, edited by Hugh Armory, exhibition catalog, 57. Cambridge, MA: Harvard University Press, 1989.

Brown, William J. *The Life of William J. Brown of Providence, Rhode Island.* Providence, RI: Angell & Co., 1883.

Bumstead, Jeremiah. "Diary of Jeremiah Bumstead of Boston, 1722–1727." *New England Historical and Genealogical Register* 15 (1861): 193–204.

Burn, Richard. *The Justice of the Peace and the Parish Officer*, vol. 2, 2nd ed. London: Hanery Lintot for A. Millar, 1756.

Burnham, Jonathan. *A Small Tract of Arithmetick for the Use of Farmers and Country-People.* New London: Timothy Green, 1747.

Byfield, Nathaniel. "An Account of the Late Revolution in New-England." In *The Andros Tracts . . .* , edited by William Henry Whitmore, 3–8. New York: Burt Franklin, 1868.

Case, J. Wickham, ed. *Southold Town Records.* 2 vols. Southold and Riverhead, NY: Towns of Southold and Riverhead, 1882–84.

Caulkins, Frances M., ed. *Memoir of the Rev. William Adams of Dedham, Massachusetts, and of the Rev. Eliphalet Adams of New London, Connecticut.* Cambridge, MA: Metcalfe & Co., 1849.

Connecticut Courant (Hartford).

Danforth, Samuel. *A Brief Recognition of New Englands* [sic] *Errand into the Wilderness.* Cambridge, MA: Printed by S. G. and M. F., 1671.

Davis, Andrew M., ed. "Reflections upon Reflections: Or, More News from Robinson Cruso's Island . . . ," July 12, 1720. Vol. 2 in *Colonial Currency Reprints*, Prince Society Publications, 115–16, 123–24. Boston: John Wilson & Son, 1911.

Edmundson, William and John Stoddart. *A Journal of the Life, Travels, Sufferings, and Labour of Love in the Work of the Ministry.* London: Harvey and Darton, 1829.

Fiske, Jane Fletcher. *Gleanings from the Newport Court Files, 1659–1783.* Bedford, MA: Jane Fletcher Fiske, 1998.

Garret, Katherine. "The Confession and Dying Warning of Katherine Garret." In *Early Native Literacies in New England: A Documentary and Critical Anthology*, edited by Kristine Bross and Hilary E. Wyss, 142–47. Amherst: University of Massachuetts Press, 2008.

Gaustad, Edwin S. *Baptist Piety: The Last Will and Testament of Obadiah Holmes.* Grand Rapids, MI: Christian University Press, 1978.

Hamilton, Alexander. "The Itinerarium of Dr. Alexander Hamilton." In *Colonial American Travel Narratives*, edited by Wendy Martin, 173–327. New York: Penguin, 1994.

Harris, Edward Doubleday, ed. *A Copy of the Old Epitaphs in the Burial Ground of Block Island, Rhode Island*. Cambridge, MA: John Wilson & Son, 1883.

Hempstead, Joshua. *The Diary of Joshua Hempstead: A Daily Record of Life in New London, Connecticut, 1711–1758*. New London: NLCHS, 1999. (*DJH*)

Johnson, Edward. *Wonder-Working Providence of Sion's Saviour in New England*. London: 1654.

Knight, Sarah Kemble. "Journal of Madam Knight (1704)." In *Colonial American Travel Narratives*, edited by Wendy Martin, 49–75. New York: Penguin, 1994.

Lacy, Norbert B. "The Records of the Court of Assistants of Connecticut, 1665–1701." 2 vols. Unpublished M.A. thesis, Yale University, 1937. (CAC)

Livingstone, John. "The Life of Mr. John Livingstone . . ." Vol. 1 in *Select Biographies Edited for the Wodrow Society*, edited by Rev. W. K. Tweedie, 127–98. Edinburgh: Wodrow Society, 1845.

MacSparren, James. *Letter Book & Abstract of Our Services*, edited by Daniel Goodwin. Boston: Merrymount Press, 1899.

Mansfield, Helen Winslow, comp. *Old Cemetery at Block Island* . . . Salem, MA: Higginson Book Co., 1950; reprint, 1997.

Mather, Cotton. *Magnalia Christi Americana*. Vol. 2. Hartford: Silus Andrus & Son, 1853.

——. *The Negro Christianized: An Essay to Excite and Assist that Good Work, the Instruction of Negro-Servants in Christianity*. Boston: 1706.

Moody, Robert E., ed. *The Saltonstall Papers, 1607–1815*. Vol. 1. Boston: MHS, 1972.

Muskett, Joseph James, and Robert Charles Winthrop. *Evidences of the Winthrops of Groton, County Suffolk*. Privately printed, 1894–96.

New England Courant (Boston).

New England Weekly Journal (Boston).

New London Day (New London).

"New London Marriages to 1800." Transcribed by Susan G. Taylor. USGenWeb, New London, Connecticut, http://www.ctgenweb.org/town/ctnewlondon/nBailey_b.html#A (accessed April 22, 2011).

New London Summary or *The Weekly Advertiser* (New London).

Noyes, Nicholas. "An Essay against Periwigs." In *The English Literatures of America, 1500–1800*, edited by Myra Jehlen and Michael Warner (New York: Routledge, 1996).

Portrait of James Tilley (1707–1765). Artist: John Singleton Copley. Lot 536, Sale 1618: Property from the Collection of Mrs. J. Insley Blair (January 21, 2006), New York, Rockefeller Plaza, http://www.christies.com/LotFinder/lot_details.aspx?intObjectID=4639344 (accessed November 28, 2008).

"Proposal of Marriage by Daniel Hubbard for the Hand of Miss Coit." *New England Historical and Genealogical Register* 48 (1894): 465.

Rolls of Connecticut Men in the French and Indian War, 1755–1762. Vol. 2. Hartford, CT: CHS, 1903.

Rogers, John. *An Impartial Relation of an Open and Publick Dispute Agreed Between Gurdon Saltonstall, Minister of the Town of New London, and John Rogers of the Same Place.* [New York or Philadelphia?]: John Rogers, 1701.

Rogers, John, Jr. *An Answer to a Book Lately Put Forth by Peter Pratt.* New York: privately printed, 1726.

———. *A Brief Account of the Late Suffering.* 1726.

Salmon, William. *The Salmon Records: A Private Register of Marriages and Deaths of the Residents of the Town of Southold, Suffolk County, New York, 1696–1811,* edited by William A. Robbins. New York: New York Genealogical and Biographical Society, 1918.

Sewall, Samuel. *Diary of Samuel Sewall.* Vol. 3. Collections of the Massachusetts Historical Society, 5th series, vols. 5–7. Boston: MHS, 1878–1882.

———. "New England Chronology." *New England Historical and Genealogical Register* 7 (1853): 341–43.

Sigourney, L. H. *Sketch of Connecticut Forty Years Since.* Hartford, CT: Oliver D. Cooke & Sons, 1824.

"Subscribers to Prince's Chronology." *New England Historical and Genealogical Register* 6 (1852): 189–200.

"Sun and Moon Data for 29 May 1711." U.S. Naval Observatory Astronomical Applications Department. http://aa.usno.navy.mil/cgi-bin/aa_pap.pl, accessed January 11, 2007.

Talcott, Joseph. *The Talcott Papers.* Vol. 2, edited by Mary Kingsbury Talcott. *Collections of the Connecticut Historical Society,* vol. 5. Hartford, CT: Connecticut Historical Society, 1896.

Walett, Francis G., ed. *The Diary of Ebenezer Parkman, 1703–1782: First Part, Three Volumes in One, 1719–1755.* Worcester, MA: American Antiquarian Society, 1974.

Williams, Roger. *A Key to the Language of America.* London: Gregory Dexter, 1643; reprint, 1936.

The Winthrop Papers. Collections of the Massachusetts Historical Society, 5th series, vol. 8. Boston: MHS, 1882.

The Winthrop Papers. Collections of the Massachusetts Historical Society, 6th series, vol. 3. Boston: MHS, 1888.

The Winthrop Papers. Collections of the Massachusetts Historical Society, 6th series, vol. 5. Boston: MHS, 1892.

[Woldf, Grace Shaw]. New London Town Records, Book Second. (S.l.: s.n., c1900?) Rebound copy in custody of the Memphis Public Library, Memphis, TN. Transcribed by Pamela J. Taylor, online New London Town Records, Book 2. http://www.ctgenweb.org/town/ctcnewlondon/nl2.html. Part of the USGenWeb, New London, Connecticut, project. http://www.ctgenweb.org/town/ctcnewlondon/, accessed November 28, 2008.

———. New London Vital Statistics from the Collated Copy from the Original

Records. Vol 1. (S.l.: s. n., c1900?) Rebound copy in custody of the Memphis Public Library, Memphis, TN. *New London Vital Statistics Copy, Vol. 1*, transcribed by Susan G. Taylor. Part of the USGenWeb, New London, Connecticut, project. http://www.rootsweb.com/~ctcnewlo/, accessed November 16, 2006.

Unpublished Secondary Sources

Benn, Bertha Lee. "Six Generations of the Hempstead Family: Descendants of Robert the Emigrant of New London." Typescript, 1944. Housed at CSL.

Descendants of Samuel Fox of New London, Connecticut. Typescript, 1934. Housed at CSL.

Gaines, Kevin, and Beth Parkhurst. "African-Americans in Newport, 1660–1960." In *Report to the Rhode Island Black Heritage Society*. Providence, RI: NHS, 1992. Housed at NHS.

Whitten, Elizabeth P., comp. "Hempsteads of New London, CT and Vicinity." Typescript, 1984. Housed at NLCHS.

Published Secondary Sources

Adams, Katherine, and Elizabeth H. Pleck. *Love of Freedom: Black Women in Colonial and Revolutionary New England*. New York: Oxford University Press, 2010.

Adkins, Judith M. "Bodies and Boundaries: Animals in the Early American Experience." Ph.D. dissertation, Yale University, 1998.

Allen, David Grayson. *In English Ways: The Movement of Societies and the Transferal of Local Law and Custom to Massachusetts Bay in the Seventeenth Century*. Chapel Hill: University of North Carolina Press, 1981.

Armory, Hugh, and David D. Hall. *A History of the Book in America*. Vol. 1, *The Colonial Book in the Atlantic World*. Cambridge, UK: Cambridge University Press, 1999.

Axtell, James. *The School upon the Hill: Education and Society in Colonial New England*. New Haven, CT: Yale University Press, 1974.

Bailyn, Bernard. *The New England Merchants in the Seventeenth Century*. Cambridge, MA: Harvard University Press, 1955.

Baker, Henry A. *History of Montville, Connecticut, Formerly the North Parish of New London, from 1640 to 1896*. Hartford, CT: Case, Lockwood and Brainard, 1896; reprint, 2005.

Barber, John W. *Connecticut Historical Collections*. Imp. ed. New Haven, CT: privately printed, 1836.

Barbour, Lucius Barnes. "Genealogical Data from Connecticut Cemeteries." *New England Historical and Genealogical Register* 86 (1932): 372–90.

Beardsley, E. Edwards. *The History of the Episcopal Church in Connecticut*. Vol. 1, 2nd ed. New York: Hurd & Houghton, 1869.

Beebe, Clarence. *A Monograph of the Family of Beebe.* New York: Clarence Beebe, 1904.

Benes, Peter. "Another Look at Madam Knight." In *In Our Own Words: New England Diaries, 1600 to the Present,* edited by Peter Benes, 13-23. Dublin Seminar for New England Folklife. Boston: Boston University, 2006–07.

Berlin, Ira. *Many Thousands Gone: The First Two Centuries of Slavery in North America.* Cambridge, MA: Harvard University Press, 1998.

Bezís-Selfa, John. *Forging America: Ironworkers, Adventurers, and the Industrious Revolution.* Ithaca, NY: Cornell University Press, 2004.

Bill, Ledyard, ed. *History of the Bill Family.* New York: Ledyard Bill, 1867.

Binney, C. J. F., ed. *The History and Genealogy of the Prentice, or Prentiss Family.* 2nd ed. Boston: C. J. F. Binney, 1883.

Black, Robert C. *The Younger John Winthrop.* 2nd ed. New York: Columbia University Press, 1968.

Blake, S. Leroy. *The Later History of the First Church of Christ, New London, Connecticut.* New London, CT: Press of the Day Publishing, 1900.

Bolles, John A. *Genealogy of the Bolles Family in America.* Boston: Henry W. Dutton, 1865.

Bolles, John R. "A Vindication." In *The Rogerenes: Some Hitherto Unpublished Annals Belonging to the Colonial History of Connecticut,* 19-117. Boston: Stanhope Press, 1904.

Bolster, W. Jeffrey. *Black Jacks: African American Seamen in the Age of Sail.* Cambridge, MA: Harvard University Press, 1997.

Bradford, Penny, comp. "Winslow Tracy." In Bradford/Robinson Families 2002, www.gencircles.com/users/pennybradford85/1/data/1089, accessed September 12, 2007.

Branch, Mary L. B. *Misc. (1840–1922), Notebook: Family History.* Diary. Late nineteenth or early twentieth century, Box 6A, no. 29. HHA.

———. *The Old Hempstead House: The Home of Eight Generations.* New London, CT: Local History Publishing Co., 1931.

Brandt, Clare. *An American Aristocracy: The Livingstons.* New York: Doubleday, 1986.

Brinton, Ellen S. "The Rogerenes." *New England Quarterly* 16 (1943): 2–19.

Brown, Jerald E., ed. *The Years of the Life of Samuel Lane, 1718–1806: A New Hampshire Man and His World.* Hanover, NH: University Press of New England, 2000.

Brown, Richard D. *Knowledge Is Power: The Diffusion of Information in Early America, 1700–1865.* New York: Oxford University Press, 1989.

Brown, Simon, ed. *The New England Farmer, a Monthly Journal.* Vol. 12. Boston: Nourse, Eaton & Tolman, 1860.

Bushman, Richard L. *The Refinement of America: Persons, Houses, Cities.* New York: Alfred A. Knopf, 1992.

Byard, Margaret Mather. *Books in the Wilderness.* The Winthrop Collection at the New York Society Library. www.nysoclib.org/winthrop.html, accessed January 27, 2006.

Candee, Richard M. "Land Surveys of William and John Godsoe of Kittery, Maine: 1689–1769." In *New England Prospect: Maps, Place Names, and the Historical Landscape*, edited by Peter Benes, 9–46. Dublin Seminar for New England Folklife. Boston: Boston University, 1980.

Caufield, Ernest. "Connecticut Gravestones XII: John Hartshorn (1650–ca. 1738) vs. Joshua Hempstead (1678–1758)." *Connecticut Historical Society Bulletin* 32 (1967): 65–79.

Caulkins, Frances M. "Ancient Burial Ground at New London, Connecticut." *New England Genealogical and Historical Register* 11 (1857): 21–30.

———. *History of New London, Connecticut, from the First Survey of the Coast in 1612, to 1860*. New London, CT: H. D. Utley, 1895; reprint, 1985.

———. *Ye Antient Buriall Place of New London, Connecticut*. New London, CT: Day Publishing, 1899.

Chandler, George. *The Chandler Family: The Descendants of William and Annis Chandler . . .* Worcester, MA: Press of Charles Hamilton, 1883.

Channing, Edward. *The Narragansett Planters: A Study of Causes*, edited by Herbert B. Adams. Johns Hopkins University Studies in Historical and Political Science. Baltimore: Johns Hopkins University Press, 1886.

Chapman, Alison A. "'Whose Saint Crispin's Day Is It?': Shoemaking, Holiday Making, and the Politics of Memory in Early Modern England." *Renaissance Quarterly* 54 (2001): 1467–94.

Chapman, F. W. *The Coit Family; or the Descendants of John Coit*. Hartford, CT: Case, Lockwood and Brainard, 1874.

Chesebrough, Harriet C. *Glimpses of Saybrook in Colonial Days*. Saybrook, CT: Celebration 3 1/2, 1984.

Clippinger, Kathryn A. "'Dutiful 'til death,' The life of Ann Dudley Winthrop (1684–1776)." Prize Essays in Early American History. Mystic, CT: Society of the Cincinnati in the State of Connecticut and the Society of Colonial Wars, 1995.

Coe, Sophia Fidelia Hall. *Memoranda Relating to the Ancestry and Family of Sophia Fidelia Hall*. Meriden, CT: Curtiss-Way, 1902.

Cohen, Marcie. "The Journals of Joshua Whitman, Turner, Maine, 1809–1846." In *The Farm*, edited by Peter Benes, 49–59. Dublin Seminar for New England Folklife. Boston: Boston University, 1986.

Cohen, Patricia Cline. *A Calculating People: The Spread of Numeracy in Early America*. Chicago: University of Chicago Press, 1982.

The Compact Edition of the Oxford English Dictionary. Vol. 1. Oxford: Oxford University Press, 1971.

Cooke, Edward M. *The Fathers of the Towns: Leadership and Community Structure in Eighteenth-Century New England*. Baltimore: Johns Hopkins University Press, 1976.

Crane, Elaine F. *A Dependent People: Newport, Rhode Island in the Revolutionary Era*. New York: Fordham University Press, 1985.

Crosby, Alfred. *The Measure of Reality: Quantification in Western Europe, 1250–1600*. New York: Cambridge University Press, 1997.

Cullon, Joseph F. "Colonial Shipwrights and Their World: Men, Women, and

Markets in Early New England." Ph.D. dissertation, University of Wisconsin, 2003.

Daboll and Crandall. "Map of the Edmund Fanning Farm at Stonington, Connecticut 1683." Worcester, MA: Walter F. Brooks, 1902.

"Daniel Osborn." Thomas Osmun Families, http://www.rootsweb.ancestry .com/~nymadiso/osman3.htm, citing Liber 28:285 Suffolk County, N.Y. VIII: 54, accessed November 11, 2008.

Dayton, Cornelia Hughes. *Women Before the Bar: Gender, Law and Society in Connecticut, 1639–1789.* Chapel Hill: University of North Carolina Press, 1995.

Deetz, James. *In Small Things Forgotten: The Archaeology of Early American Life.* New York: Anchor Books, 1977.

Demos, John. *A Little Commonwealth: Family Life in Plymouth Colony.* New York: Oxford University Press, 1970.

———. *The Unredeemed Captive: A Family Story from Early America.* New York: Alfred A. Knopf, 1994.

De Moulin, Daniel. *A History of Surgery with Emphasis on the Netherlands.* Boston: Martinus Nijhoff Publishers, 1988.

Dexter, Franklin Bowditch. *Biographical Sketches of the Graduates of Yale College.* New York: Henry Holt, 1885.

Dexter, Franklin Bowditch, ed. *Extracts of the Itinerant and Other Miscellanies of Ezra Stiles, D. D.* New Haven, CT: Yale University Press, 1896.

Doughton, Thomas L. "Nedson, Dorus and Dixon Families: Nineteenth-Century Native Community at the Massachusetts and Connecticut Border." http://freepages.gnealogy.rootsweb.ancestry.com/~massaoit/nedson.htm, accessed November 5, 2007.

Dow, George Francis, and John Henry Edmonds. *The Pirates of the New England Coast, 1630–1730.* Salem, MA: Marine Research Society, 1923.

Dunn, Richard S. *Puritans and Yankees: The Winthrop Dynasty of New England 1630–1717.* New York: W. W. Norton, 1971.

Dwight, Benjamin W. *The History of the Descendants of John Dwight.* New York: John F. Trow & Son, 1874.

Encyclopedia of African American History, 1619–1895. Vol. 1. New York: Oxford University Press, 2006.

Encyclopædia Britannica. 1911.

Fischer, David H. *Albion's Seed: Four British Folkways in America.* Oxford: Oxford University Press, 1989.

Fitts, Robert K. *Inventing New England's Slave Paradise: Master/Slave Relations in Eighteenth-Century Narragansett, Rhode Island.* New York: Garland, 1998.

Foote, Henry W. *Annals of King's Chapel, From the Puritan Age of New England to the Present Day.* Vol. 1. Boston: Little, Brown and Co., 1882.

Forbes, Jack D. *Africans and Native Americans: The Language of Race and the Evolution of Red-Black Peoples.* Chicago: University of Illinois Press, 1993.

Fox, William Freeman. *Thomas Fox of Concord and His Descendants.* Albany: J. B. Lyon Co., 1909.

Gardener, Robert G. *Baptists of Early America: A Statistical History.* Atlanta: Georgia Baptist Historical Society, 1983.

Gifford, Bill. *Ledyard: In Search of the First American Explorer.* New York: Harcourt, 2007.

"Gleanings (No. 22)." In *New England Historical and Genealogical Register* 13 (1859): 302–3.

Goetzmann, William H. *New Lands, New Men: America and the Second Great Age of Discovery.* New York: Penguin, 1986.

Gomez, Michael A. *Exchanging Our Country Marks: The Transformation of African Identities in the Colonial and Antebellum South.* Chapel Hill: University of North Carolina Press, 1998.

Greene, Lorenzo. *The Negro in Colonial New England.* New York: Atheneum, 1971.

Grant-Costa, Paul J. "The Last Indian War in New England: The Mohegan Tribe of Indians vs. the Governour Company of Connecticut, 1703–1774." Ph.D. dissertation, Yale University, 2008.

Griffin, Augustus. *Griffin's Journal, First Settlers of Southold.* Orient, NY: Augustus Griffin, 1857; reprint, 1983.

Grossbart, Stephen R. "Seeking the Divine Favor: Conversion and Church Admission in Eastern Connecticut, 1711–1832." *William and Mary Quarterly* 46 (1989): 696–740.

Gordon-Reed, Annette. *The Hemingses of Monticello: An American Family.* New York: W. W. Norton, 2008.

Grosskopf, Denise S. "The Limits of Religious Dissent in Seventeenth-Century Connecticut." Ph.D. dissertation, University of Connecticut, 1999.

Gutstein, Morris Aaron. *To Bigotry No Sanction: A Jewish Shrine in America, 1658–1958.* New York: Bloch Publishing Company, 1958.

Hall, David D. "The Mental World of Samuel Sewall." In *Saints & Revolutionaries: Essays on Early American History,* edited by David D. Hall, John M. Murrin, and Thad W. Tate, 213–46. New York: W. W. Norton, 1984.

———. "The Uses of Literacy in New England, 1600–1850." In *Cultures of Print: Essays in the History of the Book,* 36–78. Amherst: University of Massachusetts Press, 1996.

———. *Worlds of Wonder, Days of Judgment: Popular Religious Belief in Early New England.* Cambridge, MA: Harvard University Press, 1989.

Hassam, John T. "Registers of Probate for the County of Suffolk, Massachusetts, 1639–1799." In *Proceedings of the Massachusetts Historical Society,* 2nd series, vol. 16, pp. 23–124. Boston: MHS, 1902.

Hewitt, Harrison. "The Administration of Justice in Connecticut." In *History of Connecticut in Monographic Form,* edited by Norris Galpin Osborn. Vol. 3, pp. 1–250. New York: States History Company, 1925.

Hill, G. Albert. "Colonial Milestones Along Connecticut Highways." *The Antiquarian* 2 (1950): 15–19.

Hoffer, Peter C., and N. E. H. Hull. *Murdering Mothers: Infanticide in England and New England, 1558–1803.* New York: New York University Press, 1984.

Holloway, Charles Molyneux. "Historic New London." *New England Magazine* 5 (1886): 119–40.

"Hon. Christopher Christophers and His Descendants." *New York Genealogical and Biographical Record* 50 (1919): 332–34.

Hume, Ivor N. *A Guide to Artifacts of Colonial America.* New York: Alfred A. Knopf, 1969.

Hurd, D. Hamilton. *History of New London County, Connecticut.* Philadelphia: J. W. Lewis & Co., 1882.

Ignatiev, Noel. *How the Irish Became White.* New York: Routledge, 1996.

James, Sydney V. *The Colonial Metamorphoses in Rhode Island: A Study of Institutions in Change*, edited by Bruce C. Daniels and Sheila L. Skemp. Hanover, NH: University Press of New England, 2000.

Jeyes, S. H. *The Russells of Birmingham in the French Revolution and in America, 1791–1814.* London: George Allen, 1911.

Johnston, William D. "Slavery in Rhode Island, 1755–1776." *Proceedings of the Rhode Island Historical Society* 2 (1894): 113–64.

Jordan, Winthrop. "American Chiaroscuro: The Status and Definition of Mulattoes in the British Colonies." In *Slavery in the New World*, edited by Laura Foner and Eugene D. Genovese. Englewood Cliffs, NJ: Prentice-Hall, 1969.

———. "Enslavement of Negroes in America to 1700." In *Colonial America: Essays in Politics and Social Development*, edited by Stanley N. Katz and John M. Murrin, 250–89. New York: Alfred A. Knopf, 1983.

———. "The Influence of the West Indies on the Origins of New England Slavery." *William and Mary Quarterly* 18 (1961): 243–65.

Judd, Sylvester. "The Fur Trade on Connecticut River in the Seventeenth Century." *New England Historical and Genealogical Register* 11 (1857): 217–19.

Kamil, Neil D. "Hidden in Plain Sight: Disappearance and Material Life in Colonial New York." In *American Furniture 1995*, edited by Luke Beckerdite and William N. Hosley. Hanover, NH: University Press of New England, 1995.

Karlsen, Carol F. *The Devil in the Shape of a Woman: Witchcraft in Colonial New England.* New York: Vintage, 1987.

Kerber, Linda K. *Women of the Republic: Intellect and Ideology in Revolutionary America.* Chapel Hill: University of North Carolina Press, 1980.

Kierner, Cynthia A. *Traders and Gentlefolk: The Livingstons of New York, 1675–1790.* Ithaca, NY: Cornell University Press, 1992.

Kim, Sung Bok. "Introduction: The Livingstons as Land Developers." In *A Portrait of Livingston Manor, 1686–1850*, edited by Ruth Piwonka, 11–15. Clermont, NY: Friends of Clermont, 1986.

Kim, Susan C. "Mr. Rogers's Neighborhood: Religious Dissent in New London, 1674–1721." Ph.D. dissertation, University of California, 2006.

Kimball, Everett. *The Public Life of Joseph Dudley.* New York: Longmans, Green, and Co., 1911.

Kisling, Vernon N., Jr. "Zoological Gardens of the United States." In *Zoo and Aquarium History . . .* , edited by Vernon N. Kisling, Jr., 147–80. New York: CRC Press, 2001.

Lacey, Barbara E. "Gender, Piety, and Secularization in Connecticut Religion, 1720–1775." *Journal of Social History* 24 (1991): 799–821.

Lambert, Frank. *Inventing the Great Awakening.* Princeton, NJ: Princeton University Press, 1999.

Larkin, Jack. *The Reshaping of Everyday Life, 1790–1840.* New York: Harper & Row, 1988.

Leder, Lawrence H. *Robert Livingston, 1654–1728, and the Politics of Colonial New York.* Chapel Hill: University of North Carolina Press, 1961.

Lepore, Jill. *The Name of War: King Philip's War and the Origins of American Identity.* New York: Alfred A. Knopf, 1998.

Levine, Gaynell S. "Colonial Long Island Grave Stones: Trade Network Indicators, 1670–1799." In *Puritan Gravestone Art II*, edited by Peter Benes, 46–57. Dublin Seminar for New England Folklife. Boston: Boston University, 1978.

Livingston, E. B., "Colonel John Livingston of New London . . ." *New York Genealogical and Biographical Record* 46 (1915): 230–31.

Livingston, Edwin Brockholst. *The Livingstons of Livingston Manor.* New York: Knickerbocker Press, 1910.

Livingston, William Farrand. *Israel Putnam: Pioneer, Ranger, and Major-General, 1718–1790.* New York: G. P. Putnam's Sons, 1901.

Lockridge, Kenneth A. *The Diary, and Life, of William Byrd II of Virginia, 1674–1744.* Chapel Hill: University of North Carolina Press, 1987.

———. *Literacy in Colonial New England.* New York: W. W. Norton, 1974.

———. *The New England Town: The First Hundred Years.* Expanded ed. New York: W. W. Norton, 1985.

Ludwig, Allen I. *Graven Images: New England Stonecarving and Its Symbols, 1650–1815.* Middletown, CT: Wesleyan University Press, 1966.

Lyman, Lila Parrish. *The New London Homestead of the Winthrop Family.* Stonington, CT: Pequot Press, 1957.

Macfarlane, Alan. *The Family Life of Ralph Josselin: A Seventeenth-Century Clergyman.* New York: W. W. Norton, 1977.

Mager, Gerald M. "Zabdiel Boylston: Medical Pioneers of Colonial Boston." Ph.D. dissertation, University of Illinois, 1975.

Main, Gloria L. "Gender, Work, and Wages in Colonial New England." *William and Mary Quarterly* 51 (1994): 39–66.

Main, Jackson Turner. *Society and Economy in Colonial Connecticut.* Princeton, NJ: Princeton University Press, 1985.

Manegold, C. S. *Ten Hills Farm: The Forgotten History of Slavery in the North.* Princeton, NJ: Princeton University Press, 2010.

Matson, Cathy. *Merchants and Empire: Trading in Colonial New York.* Baltimore: Johns Hopkins University Press, 1998.

Matthews, William. "Early New England Words." *American Speech* 15 (1940): 225–31.

May, Lillian, and Charles Morris Gardner. *Gardener History and Genealogy.* Erie, PA: Erie Printing, 1907.

Mayo, Lawrence Shaw. *The Winthrop Family in America.* Boston: MHS, 1948.

McBride, Kevin A. "'Ancient and Crazie': Pequot Lifeways during the Historic

Period." In *Algonkians of New England: Past and Present*, edited by Peter Benes, 63–75. Dublin Seminar for New England Folklife. Boston: Boston University, 1991.

McBurney, Christian M. "The Rise and Decline of the South Kingston Planters, 1660–1783." B.A. thesis, Brown University, 1981. On file at NHS.

McDermott, William P. "The Livingstons' Colonial Land Policy: Personal Gain over Public Need." In *The Livingston Legacy: Three Generations of American History*, edited by Richard T. Wiles, 10–37. Annandale-on-Hudson, NY: Bard College, 1987.

McGlynn, Margaret. "Idiots, Lunatics and the Royal Prerogative in Early Tudor England." *Journal of Legal History* 26 (2005): 1–20.

McLoughlin, William. *Soul Liberty: The Baptists' Struggle in New England, 1630–1833*. Hanover, NH: University Press of New England, 1991.

Melish, Joanne P. *Disowning Slavery: Gradual Emancipation and "Race" in New England, 1780–1860*. Ithaca, NY: Cornell University Press, 1998.

Menschel, David. "Abolition Without Deliverance: The Law of Connecticut Slavery, 1784–1848." *Yale Law Journal* 111 (2001): 183–222.

Moller, David Wendell. *Confronting Death Values, Institutions and Human Mortality*. Oxford: Oxford University Press, 1996.

Moran, Gerald F. "Conditions of Religious Conversion in the First Society of Norwich, Connecticut, 1718–1744." *Journal of Social History* 5 (1972): 331–43.

——. "The Puritan Saint: Religious Experience, Church Membership, and Piety in Connecticut, 1636–1776." Ph.D. dissertation, Rutgers University, 1974.

Moriarty, G. Andrew. "Early Block Island Families." *New England Historical and Genealogical Register* 82 (1928): 457–59.

Morgan, Edmund S. *American Slavery, American Freedom*. New York: W. W. Norton, 2003.

——. *The Puritan Family: Religion and Domestic Relations in Seventeenth-Century New England*. New ed. New York: Harper & Row, 1966.

——. *Visible Saints: The History of a Puritan Idea*. New York: Cornell University Press, 1963.

Morgan, Nathaniel Harris. *Morgan Genealogy: A History of James Morgan of New London . . .* Hartford, CT: Case, Lockwood and Brainard, 1869.

Mumford, James Gregory. *Mumford Memoirs, Being the Story of the New England Mumfords from the Year 1655 to the Present Time*. Boston: B. D. Updike, 1900.

Murrin, John M. "Anglicizing an American Colony: The Transformation of Provincial Massachusetts." Ph.D. dissertation, Yale University, 1966.

——. "The Bench and Bar of Eighteenth-Century Massachusetts." In *Colonial America: Essays in Politics and Social Development*, edited by Stanley N. Katz, 415–49. Boston: Little, Brown, 1976.

——. "East Hampton in the 17th Century." Lecture delivered May 30, 1998. http://www.easthamptonlibrary.org/lic/lectures/murrinlecture.htm, accessed January 18, 2006.

Naramore, Bruce E. "Introduction." In *The Livingston Legacy: Three Centuries of American History*, edited by Richard T. Wiles. Annadale-on-Hudson, NY: Bard College, 1987.

Nash, Gary B. *The Urban Crucible: The Northern Seaports and the Origins of the American Revolution.* Cambridge, MA: Harvard University Press, 1979.

Nylander, Jane C. *Our Own Snug Fireside: Images of the New England Home, 1760–1860.* New Haven, CT: Yale University Press, 1994.

O'Brien, Jean M. *Dispossession by Degrees: Indian Land and Identity in Natick, Massachusetts, 1650–1790.* New York: Cambridge University Press, 1997.

Onuf, Peter S. "New Lights in New London: A Group Portrait of the Separatists." *William and Mary Quarterly* 37 (1980): 627–43.

Pagan, John Rushton. *Anne Orthwood's Bastard: Sex and Law in Early Virginia.* New York: Oxford University Press, 2003.

Park, Lawrence. "Old Boston Families: Number Three, The Savage Family." *New England Historical and Genealogical Register* 67 (1913): 198–215, 309–30.

Parkhurst, Charles D. "Comments on, and Corrections of, Some Curious Errors, Which Are to be Found Recorded in the Introduction to Hempstead's Diary." *New York Genealogical and Biographical Record* 51 (1920): 259–65.

Pestana, Carla Gardina. *Liberty of Conscience and the Growth of Religious Diversity in Early America, 1636–1786.* Exhibition catalog. Providence: John Carter Brown Library, 1986.

"Phases of the Moon and Percent of the Illuminated." U.S. Naval Observatory Astronomical Applications Department. http://aa.usno.navy.mil/faq/docs/moon_phases.html, p. 2, accessed January 11, 2007.

Piersen, William. *Black Yankees: The Development of an Afro-American Subculture.* Amherst: University of Massachusetts Press, 1988.

Piwonka, Ruth. *A Portrait of Livingston Manor, 1686–1850.* Clermont, NY: Friends of Clermont, 1986.

Plane, Ann Marie. *Colonial Intimacies: Indian Marriage in Early New England.* Ithaca, NY: Cornell University Press, 2000.

Plank, Geoffrey. *An Unsettled Conquest: The British Campaign Against the Peoples of Acadia.* Philadelphia: University of Pennsylvania Press, 2001.

Poteet, J. M. "The Lordly Prelate: Gurdon Saltonstall against His Times." *New England Quarterly* 53 (1980): 483–507.

Powers, William H. *Powers-Banks Ancestry.* Ames, IA: John Leslie Powers, 1921.

Public Records of the Colony of Connecticut, 1636–1776. 15 vols. Hartford, CT: Case, Lockwood and Brainard, 1850–1890.

Puckett, Newbell Niles. *Black Names in America: Origins and Usage,* edited by Murray Heller. Boston: G. K. Hall, 1975.

Purvis, Thomas L., ed. *Colonial America to 1763, Almanacs of American Life.* New York: Facts on File, 1999.

Rediker, Marcus. *Between the Devil and the Deep Blue Sea: Merchant Seamen, Pirates, and the Anglo-American Maritime World, 1700–1750.* Cambridge, UK: Cambridge University Press, 1987.

Reid, John G. "The 'Conquest' of Acadia: Narratives." In John G. Reid et al., *The "Conquest" of Acadia, 1710: Imperial, Colonial, and Aboriginal Constructions,* 3–24. Toronto: University of Toronto Press, 2004.

Reiss, Oscar. *Blacks in Colonial America*. Jefferson, NC: McFarland & Co., 1997.

Richeson, W. *English Land Measuring to 1800: Instruments and Practices*. Cambridge, MA: MIT Press, 1966.

Richter, Daniel K. *Facing East from Indian Country: A Native History of Early America*. Cambridge, MA: Harvard University Press, 2001.

Roberts, Stephen K. "Lechmere, Sir Nicholas (bap. 1613, d. 1701)." *Oxford Dictionary of National Biography*. Oxford University Press, 2004. Online ed., January 2008, http://www.oxforddnb.com/view/article/16261, accessed September 8, 2012.

Robinson, Caroline E. *The Gardiners of Narragansett*, edited by Daniel Goodwin. Providence, RI: Daniel Goodwin, 1919.

Robinson, John, and George Francis Dow. *Sailing Ships of New England, 1607–1907*. Paperback ed. New York: Skyhorse Publishing, 2007.

Rogers, James Swift. *James Rogers of New London, Ct.: And His Descendants*. Boston: James Swift Rogers, 1902.

Rose, James M., and Barbara W. Brown. *Tapestry: A Living History of the Black Family in Southeastern Connecticut*. New London, CT: NLCHS, 1979.

———, and Alice Eichholz. *Black Genesis: A Resource Book for African-American Genealogy*. Vol. 1. Detroit, MI: Gale Publishing, 1978.

Rose, Walter. *The Village Carpenter*. Hertford, UK: Stobart Davies, Ltd., 1995.

Ross, Richard Shannon. "Slavery on Long Island: Its Rise and Decline during the Seventeenth through Nineteenth Centuries." Ph.D. dissertation, St. John's University, 1985.

Russell, Howard S. *A Long, Deep Furrow: Three Centuries of Farming in New England*. Hanover, NH: University Press of New England, 1982.

Sainsbury, John A. "Indian Labor in Early Rhode Island." *New England Quarterly* 48 (1975): 378–93.

Sanford, Don A. *A Choosing People: The History of the Seventh Day Baptists*. Nashville, TN: Boardman Press, 1992.

Sanford, Ilou M., and Don A. Sanford. *Newport Seventh Day Baptist Trilogy*. Bowie, MD: Heritage, 1998.

Schaefer, Patricia M. *A Useful Friend: A Companion to the Joshua Hempstead Diary, 1711–1758*. New London, CT: NLCHS, 2008.

Schlesinger, Arthur M. "Colonial Appeals to the Privy Council, II." *Political Science Quarterly* 28 (1913): 433–50.

Schultz, Eric B., and Michael J. Tougias. *King Philip's War: The History and Legacy of America's Forgotten Conflict*. New York: W. W. Norton, 2000.

Shepard, Alexandra. *Meanings of Manhood in Early Modern England*. Oxford: Oxford University Press, 2003.

Shields, David. "A History of Personal Diary Writing in New England, 1620–1745." Ph.D. dissertation, University of Chicago, 1982.

Singer, Roberta. "The Livingstons as Slave Owners: The 'Peculiar Institution' of Livingston Manor and Clermont." In *The Livingston Legacy: Three Centuries of American History*, edited by Richard T. Wiles. Annandale-on-Hudson, NY: Bard College, 1987.

Sioui, George E. *Huron-Wendat: The Heritage of the Circle*, translated by Jane Brierley. Vancouver: University of British Columbia Press, 2000.

Slater, James A. "John Hartshorne (1650–ca. 1737)." In James A. Slater, *The Colonial Burying Grounds of Eastern Connecticut and the Men Who Made Them . . .* , 5–7. Hamden, CT: Archon Books, 1987.

———, and Ralph L. Tucker. "The Colonial Gravestone Carvings of John Hartshorne." In *Puritan Gravestone Art II*, edited by Peter Benes, 79–146. Dublin Seminar for New England Folklife. Boston: Museum of Fine Arts, 1978.

Stark, James H. *The Loyalists of Massachusetts*. Boston: James H. Stark, 1910.

Steenburg, Nancy H. *Children and the Criminal Law in Connecticut, 1635–1855*. New York: Routledge, 2005.

Steiner, Bernard. *History of Slavery in Connecticut*, edited by Herbert B. Adams. Johns Hopkins University Studies in Historical and Political Science. Baltimore: Johns Hopkins University Press, 1893.

St. George, Robert Blair. *Conversing by Signs: Poetics of Implication in Colonial New England Culture*. Chapel Hill: University of North Carolina Press, 1998.

———. "Set Thine House in Order: The Domestication of the Yeomanry in Seventeenth-Century New England." In *New England Begins: The Seventeenth Century*, edited by Robert F. Trent et al. Vol. 2, 159–86. Boston: Museum of Fine Arts, 1982.

Stilgoe, John R. *Common Landscape of America, 1580–1845*. New Haven, CT: Yale University Press, 1982.

Stone, George E. *The Oxford Descendants of Gregory Stone of Cambridge, Massachusetts*. Amherst, MA: Carpenter & Morehouse, 1904.

Stout, Harry S., and Peter Onuf. "James Davenport and the Great Awakening in New London." *Journal of American History* 71 (1983): 556–78.

Sturt, George. *The Wheelwright's Shop*. Cambridge, UK: Cambridge University Press, 1923; reprint, 1993.

Sweeney, Kevin M. "Gentlemen Farmers and Inland Merchants: The Williams Family and Commercial Agriculture in Pre-Revolutionary Western Massachusetts." In *The Farm*, edited by Peter Benes, 60–73. Dublin Seminar for New England Folklife. Boston: Boston University, 1988.

Swetland, B. S., ed. *Partial Genealogy of the Swetland Family*. Brocton, NY: Brocton Enterprise Press, 1907.

Tarule, Robert. *The Artisan of Ipswich: Craftsmanship and Community in Colonial New England*. Baltimore: Johns Hopkins University Press, 2004.

Tannenbaum, Rebecca J. *The Healer's Calling: Women and Medicine in Early New England*. Ithaca, NY: Cornell University Press, 2002.

———. *Health and Wellness in Colonial America*. Denver, CO: Greenwood, 2012.

Tappan, Daniel Langdon, comp. *Tappan-Toppan Genealogy . . .* Arlington, MA: Daniel Langdon Tappan, 1915.

Taylor, Alan J. C. *Edgecombes at New London*. http://freepages.genealogy.roots web.com/~jvoran/edgecomb/at/edgenl_at.htm, accessed January 16, 2006.

Totten, John R. *Christophers Genealogy: Jeffreys and Christophers, Christophers of New London, Connecticut*. New York: New York Genealogical and Biographical Society, 1921.

Trumbull, Benjamin. *History of Connecticut.* Vol. 1. New London, CT: H. D. Utley, 1898.

Trumbull, James Hammond, ed. *The Memorial History of Hartford County, Connecticut, 1633–1884.* Vol. 1. Boston: Edward L. Osgood, 1886.

Ulrich, Laurel Thatcher. *Goodwives: Image and Reality in the Lives of Women in Northern New England, 1650–1750.* New York: Alfred A. Knopf, 1982.

——. *A Midwife's Tale: The Life of Martha Ballard, Based on Her Diary, 1785–1812.* New York: Vintage Books, 1990.

Utter, George B. *Old "Westerie," Rhode Island.* Westerly, RI: Westerly Chamber of Commerce, 1936.

Vickers, Daniel. "Competence and Competition: Economic Culture in Early America." *William and Mary Quarterly* 47 (1990): 3–29.

——. *Farmers and Fishermen: Two Centuries of Work in Essex County, Massachusetts, 1630–1850.* Chapel Hill: University of North Carolina Press, 1994.

Vivian, John. *Building Stone Walls.* North Adams, MA: Storey Publishing, 1976.

Wall, R. B. "The Ancient Schoolhouse located by Truman's Brook: Chapter IV." *New London Day,* July 20, 1909.

——. "Historical Sketches of Early Dwellers in Pearl Street." *New London Day,* November 19, 1914.

——. "History of the St. James Church Since Foundation in 1725: In Step with Progress of Age." *New London Day,* September 21, 1925.

——. "History and Traditions of the Holt-Hempstead Tract: Chapter III." *New London Day,* November 11, 1908.

——. "How Long Bridge Section of Bank Street Was Settled: Early History of That Part of New London Told from Real Estate Records." *New London Day,* August 6, 1921.

——. "John Barleycorn's Days in Old Taverns of New London: Chapter III." *New London Day,* May 10, 1920.

——. "Old Rogers Boat Shop Was a Famous Landmark," *New London Day,* October 9, 1907.

——. "Old Waterford Fishermen Worked Hard for a Living: Constant Facing of Perils of Deep Was a Hazardous Task and Many Were Buried in Watery Graves." *New London Day,* March 14, 1923.

——. "Stories of Waterford: Echoes of Stormy Days." *New London Day,* June 9, 1915.

Waller, G. M. *Samuel Vetch: Colonial Enterpriser.* Chapel Hill: University of North Carolina Press, 1960.

Waller, Maureen. *1700: Scenes from London Life.* New ed. London: Sceptre, 2001.

Waller-Frye, George. *Adam and Katherine Rogers of New London, Connecticut, James and Katherine Merritt of Killingworth, Connecticut.* Storrs, CT: Spring Hill Press, 1977.

Warren, Wendy. "Enslaved Africans in New England, 1638–1700." Ph.D. dissertation, Yale University, 2008.

Waters, Thomas Franklin, and Robert Charles Winthrop, Jr. *A Sketch of the Life of John Winthrop the Younger . . .* Publications of the Ipswich Historical Society. Vol. 7. Cambridge, MA: University Press, 1899.

Watson, Aldren A. *The Blacksmith: Ironworker and Farrier.* Paperback ed. New York: W. W. Norton, 2000.

Watson, John L. "Passages in the Life of Priscilla (Thomas) Hobart." *New England Historical and Genealogical Register* 27 (1873): 24–26.

Weeden, William B. *Early Rhode Island: A Social History of Its People.* New York: Grafton Press, 1910.

Wheeler, Richard Anson. *History of the Town of Stonington . . .* New London, CT: Press of the Day, 1900.

Wells, David A. "Glacial Action." In *Records and Papers of the New London County Historical Society,* part 2, vol. 1, 31–37. 1890.

Wight, D. P. "Graduates of Harvard College Born in Dedham." *New England Historical and Genealogical Register* 4 (1850): 354.

"William Keeney from England to New London." *Keeney Update* 17 (March 2000). http://www.keeneyklan.com/Roscoe/KeeneyUpdate/v17n1March2000/image4.html, accessed January 6, 2007.

Williams, Anna B. "A History of the Rogerenes." In *The Rogerenes: Some Hitherto Unpublished Annals Belonging to the Colonial History of Connecticut,* 121–341. Boston: Stanhope Press, 1904.

Wilson, Lisa. *Ye Heart of a Man: The Domestic Life of Men in Colonial New England.* New Haven, CT: Yale University Press, 1999.

Wood, Betty. *The Origins of American Slavery: Freedom and Bondage in the English Colonies.* New York: Hill & Wang, 1997.

Woodward, Walter. *Prospero's America: John Winthrop, Jr., Alchemy, and the Creation of New England Culture, 1606–1676.* Chapel Hill: University of North Carolina Press, 2010.

Wootton, Charles W., and Mary Virginia Moore. "The Legal Status of Account Books in Colonial America." *Accounting History* 5 (2000): 33–58.

Wright, Thomas G. *Literary Culture in Early New England, 1620–1730.* New Haven, CT: Yale University Press, 1920.

Yirush, Craig. *Settlers, Liberty, and Empire: The Roots of Early American Political Theory, 1675–1775.* New York: Cambridge University Press, 2011.

Zilversmit, Arthur. *The First Emancipation: The Abolition of Slavery in the North.* Chicago: University of Chicago Press, 1967.

PHOTOGRAPH CREDITS

1. Harvard Art Museums / Fogg Museum, Harvard University Portrait Collection, Gift of Robert Winthrop, representing the Winthrop family, to Harvard University, 1964, H609 Photograph: Imaging Department © President and Fellows of Harvard College

2. Harvard Art Museums / Fogg Museum, Harvard University Portrait Collection, Gift of Robert Winthrop, representing the Winthrop family, to Harvard University, 1964, H602 Photograph: Imaging Department © President and Fellows of Harvard College

3. Livingston Family Papers, General Collection, Beinecke Rare Book and Manuscript Library, Yale University

4. Yale University Art Gallery, Gift of Roswell Saltonstall, B.A. 1751, M.A. 1754

5. Harvard Art Museums / Fogg Museum, Harvard University Portrait Collection, Gift of Robert Winthrop, representing the Winthrop family, to Harvard University, 1964, H603 Photograph: Imaging Department © President and Fellows of Harvard College

6. Harvard Art Museums / Fogg Museum, Harvard University Portrait Collection, Gift of Robert Winthrop, representing the Winthrop family, to Harvard University, 1964, H604 Photograph: Imaging Department © President and Fellows of Harvard College

7. Courtesy of The Hempsted Houses, New London, owned and operated by Connecticut Landmarks. Photograph: Andrew Hogan

8. Courtesy of The Hempsted Houses, New London, owned and operated by Connecticut Landmarks. Photograph: Andrew Hogan

9. Connecticut State Library

10. Collection of the New London County Historical Society, New London, Connecticut. Photograph: Andrew Hogan

11. Courtesy of The Hempsted Houses, New London, owned and operated by Connecticut Landmarks. Photograph: Andrew Hogan

12. Collection of the New London County Historical Society, New London, Connecticut. Photograph: Andrew Hogan

13. Courtesy of the Massachusetts Historical Society

14. Courtesy of The Hempsted Houses, New London, owned and operated by Connecticut Landmarks. Photograph: Andrew Hogan

INDEX

Page numbers beginning with 343 refer to notes.

ABOUT THE AUTHOR

Allegra di Bonaventura holds a Ph.D. in history from Yale University and a J.D. from Yale Law School. She is currently an assistant dean at the Yale Graduate School of Arts and Sciences.